I0154916

Songs From The Summit

Songs From The Summit

Lucia Alexis Gainer

Perennial House

Songs From the Summit

Original and revised material
Copyright © 2011 by Lucia Alexis Gainer

All rights reserved, including the right to reproduce
this book or portions thereof in any form whatsoever
except as provided by U. S. Copyright Law.

Perennial House
P. O. Box 4750
Fresno, CA 93744-4750

Library of Congress Control Number: 2011922390

ISBN: 978-0-9833496-0-0

Unless otherwise noted, Scripture quotations are from the
Authorized King James Version.

Visit our website at Perennialhouse.org

Printed in the United States of America

As we make our way, day by day, toward the higher elevations of faith, we may discover our journey begins to lead us into territory that is fraught with upheaval and unexpected challenges. We still encounter the occasional green pasture and placid stream, but now there are also deserts to cross, swift rivers to ford and mountains to climb. The higher we go, the narrower the road becomes. Sometimes we fear we may get lost; we even lose our footing from time to time. Eventually, we recognize our own strength is not going to be sufficient. We will have to have the strength of Another if we are ever to reach the top.

It is just at this point we can take heart, for it is when our own strength fails us that God promises to provide all we need. If we will call upon Him, He promises to hear. If we will just ask, He assures us He will give. It is His delight to give to His children, good measure, pressed down and running over, if they will turn from self and respond to His call of Love.

Though our journey may be full of the unforeseen and unexpected, we need not fear, for God's Word tells us that nothing, absolutely nothing – neither "death, nor life, nor angels, nor principalities, nor powers, nor things present, nor things to come, nor height, nor depth, nor any other creature – shall be able to separate us from the love of God which is in Christ Jesus our Lord" (Ro 8:38-39). And so, at each and every turn, we can know that God will be our Defender, our Comforter and our Guide, Who shall each day provide us with fresh songs of deliverance to surround and strengthen us, until we reach the Summit, which is the safety of His loving embrace.

This edition of *Songs From the Summit* contains study guides for both individuals and groups. These guides may be found beginning on Page 317.

The summit of love, its crowning summit, is the life of abandonment to God.

– Msgr. Charles Gay

Oh earth, earth, earth, hear the Word of the Lord.

– (Je 22:29)

"Commit thy way unto the LORD; trust also in him; and he shall bring it to pass." (Ps 37:5)

Many years ago a young girl went away to boarding school. She had a deep love for the Lord and those who knew her were struck by her gentle ways and kind heart. During her first term she wrote a letter to one of her former teachers back home. In the letter she described in detail what her room was like. On her desk she kept something quite unusual: "...those who come into my room cannot understand it," she wrote. "It is a blank sheet of paper, with my signature at the bottom. God has permission to put on it whatever He wills; it is signed in advance." This devout girl was not destined to live a long life – she died at the age of twenty – but long after she went home to be with the Lord her faith and spirit of love continued to inspire the family and friends she left behind.

As we begin this New Year, we might ask ourselves if we possess this same attitude of surrender. Can we face the days ahead with the same willingness to have God accomplish in our lives all that He wishes? Such an attitude is a tall order. Self so often wants to get in the way. And yet, isn't this our deepest desire? To give everything to God? To have only His will performed in our lives? We need have no fear about what lies ahead this year. If we put our hand in God's hand and trust Him to guide our every step, He will show us the way. He knows the path that is best for us. He is faithful. He provides whatever His children need, whether it be power or provision, strength or comfort, deliverance or grace.

Today, on this first day of the New Year, we can choose to erase our own plans from the pages of our lives and, instead, leave them blank, with our signatures at the bottom, to show God that He has our permission to do whatever seems best in His sight.

"Write deep in your heart this New Year's Day this word of sublime confidence, 'Jehovah-Jireh.' It tells you that you can trust God always; that no promise of his ever fails; that he does all things well; that out of all seeming loss and destruction of human hopes he brings blessing. You have not passed this way before. There will be sorrows and joys, failures and successes this year, just as there were last year. You cannot forecast individual experiences. You cannot see a step before your feet. Yet Jehovah-Jireh calls you to enter the New Year with calm trust. He bids you put away all anxieties and forebodings — 'The Lord will provide.' "

– J. R. Miller

Thanksgiving and the voice of melody,
This New Year's morning, call me from my sleep;
A new, sweet song is in my heart for Thee,
Thou faithful, tender Shepherd of the sheep;
Thou knowest where to find, and how to keep
The feeble feet that tremble where they stray,
O'er the dark mountains, 'through the whelming deep,'
Thy everlasting mercy makes its way.

                                    –Anna Waring

"Because thou hast made the Lord, which is my refuge, even the most High, thy habitation; There shall no evil befall thee..." (Ps 91:9-10)

JANUARY 2 ---

"I will instruct thee and teach thee in the way which thou shalt go: I will guide thee with mine eye." (Ps 32:8)

Many of us used to handle our problems by either running away from them or trying to bulldoze our way through them. Though we weren't aware of it at the time, we had fallen into the "fight or flight syndrome." Neither one of these methods work very well, as many of us discovered. Whether we were dealing with a relationship problem, an emotional problem, a financial problem or even an addiction problem, we found out that trying to duck it or bombard it with our self-will usually didn't solve anything.

There is another way we can handle our problems. It neither causes us to run away from them or attack them with our self will. This way is called acceptance.

Some of us had a very rough time with this word at first. "Acceptance!" we cried. "Are you kidding? How on earth can we deal with our problems by simply accepting them? Christians aren't supposed to accept problems. We're supposed to solve them. Our job is to get victory over our struggles, not allow them to get the victory over us. Aren't you really suggesting we just give in to evil?"

Not at all. That is not what is meant here by the word "acceptance." Acceptance, in this instance, means recognizing that we do indeed have a problem and will be better able to respond to it if we first accept the fact that God, for some reason, has permitted us to have it, at least for today.

When we accept that we really do have a problem, we've taken the first step in dealing with it. Acceptance means we've stopped trying to pretend it doesn't exist. It also means we recognize that we can't just throw our self-will against it in hopes it will disappear. It means we're willing to enter the process of resolving our problem in a mature way, and it puts us in the right position to hear from God about how He wants us to respond to it. The fact is, we can trust God to help us deal with any problem we may have if we will not fall into the "fight or flight" syndrome, but will instead become willing to accept it for what it is.

> God's love is more than able
> To see to all our needs,
> He knows we must be strengthened,
> We are but fragile reeds.
> His guiding hand will lead us,
> His grace will light the way,
> His mercy will provide for us
> Today and every day.

God, please help me to accept life on life's terms today, and show me how to respond to the challenges You are allowing to come my way.

JANUARY 3 --

"...to set at liberty them that are bruised..." (Luke 4:18)

Jesus was in the synagogue in Nazareth on the Sabbath and began to teach. The attendant handed Him the scroll containing the Book of Isaiah and He read the following words from its first chapter:

"The Spirit of the Lord God is upon me; because the Lord hath anointed me to preach good tidings unto the meek; he hath sent me to bind up the brokenhearted, to proclaim liberty to the captives, and the opening of the prison to them that are bound" (v. 1). All eyes were upon Him as He rolled up the scroll, handed it back to the attendant and sat down.

"This day," He said, "is this scripture fulfilled in your ears" (Lu 4:21).

At this, many became enraged. Was this not Jesus, a mere carpenter's son? Who did He think He was to make such a proclamation? They did not understand Who He really was, or what He was really saying.

The same is true today. Many still do not realize Who Jesus is; that when He speaks, His words are words of life; and that what we need, only He can give.

He knows we are sinners and therefore need to have the good news of salvation given to us. He knows that many of us suffer from broken hearts and need Someone who will come and mend them. He knows we are captives - captives to our weaknesses and sin natures - that we need Someone with the power to set us free. Most of all, He knows we are bound. Bound by failures, hurts, heartaches, bitterness, sadness, depression, disappointments, griefs, or attitude problems that hound us and over which

3

we cannot get the victory without His healing touch. How well Jesus knew His listeners back then. How well He knows us today. We need His Presence, His power, His life, His love.

JANUARY 4 ---

"I will help thee, saith the LORD..." (Is 41:14)

"'It is but a small thing for Me, your God, to help you. Consider what I have done already. What? Not help you? Why, I bought you with My blood. What? Not help you? I have died for you, and if I have done the greater, will I not do the lesser? Help you? It is the least thing I will ever do for you; I have done more, and will do more. Before the world began, I chose you. I made a covenant for you. I laid aside My glory and became a man for you; I gave My life for you; and if I did all this, I will surely help you now. In helping you, I am giving you what I have bought for you already. If you had need of a thousand times as much help, I would give it to you. You require little compared with what I am ready to give. It may be much for you to need, but it is nothing for me to bestow....'

Do you want more wisdom than exists in the Father, more love than displays itself in the Son, or more power than is manifest in the influence of the Spirit? Bring your empty pitcher. Surely this well will fill it. Hurry, gather up your wants, and bring them here – your emptiness, your woes, your needs. Behold, this river of God is full for your supply; what can you desire beside? Go forth, my soul, in this which is your might. The Eternal God is your helper."   – Charles Spurgeon

JANUARY 5 ---

"...weeping may endure for a night, but joy cometh in the morning." (Ps 30:5)

It is difficult when you are weeping to believe that joy will come again. When you hurt so bad that there is nothing that can comfort you, it is hard to be told to cheer up. When a broken heart is bleeding, words do little to bandage the wound, and yet we all yearn at just those times for a word of comfort or understanding. We ache to hear something that will lessen the pain. There is something that can help us. That is to remember that though the night is dark at this moment -- perhaps there is no light anywhere in sight -- the morning is going to come. The Lord promises that it shall be so.

Our suffering here on earth, deep as it may be, is only temporary. This, too, shall pass. We will emerge from our tunnel of pain, or, if it is a very great loss, we shall at least come to the place where the pain will lessen and God will help us bear what we have to bear. In the meantime, we need to remember that God's ultimate plan for us is for our good. Even if we feel He is doing nothing to help us, even if we feel He has abandoned us, we must choose to trust what is true: that God is a good God and He will, in the long run, bring good out of our situation. He will lead us to the other side of our suffering. We will find our way through the night and into the morning light and all the joy that is awaiting us there.

One final thought: Many a faithful child has been chosen by God, for His own secret purposes, to endure a time of great suffering. Why this is, we do not know. It seems that it is often the son or daughter who is closest to the Lord who is asked to endure an episode of great loss, great grief, great sadness. If you doubt the truth of this, study your Lord. Look at the burdens of trial and sorrow He had to bear. Take heart. He will bring you through.

The purest gold is that which has endured the hottest flames of the crucible. The choicest wines must age in the darkness and depths of the cellar. But the flames only last until the impurities within the gold are removed; the wine only remains in the darkness until it is fully aged, and then it is brought into the light so that its goodness may be poured forth.

JANUARY 6 --

"And there were in the same country shepherds abiding in the field, keeping watch over their flock by night. And, lo, the angel of the Lord came upon them, and the glory of the Lord shone round about them..." (Lu 2:8-9)

God's way of looking at things is very different than the way the world looks at things. People sometimes spend the better part of their lives trying to become successful or famous, but God tends to give honor, not to the rich or the proud, but to the humble.

On a night over 2,000 years ago, when God decided to announce that the Savior of the world was about to be born, He sought out a group of shepherds keeping watch over their flocks. These men did not occupy a position of great prestige in their culture. They didn't receive high honors, wield great power or have large bank accounts. They were not members of the "in crowd." Instead, they lived humbly, mostly out of doors. And yet it was to these men that the Angel of the Lord was sent to announce the birth of the Savior of the world.

The Magi, on the other hand, also received a sign. These men were of the elite class, distinguished foreigners from the East. They did indeed receive a sign from God, but instead of being visited by the Angel of God, they were simply shown a star. How like God. To honor the poor and humble with the greater manifestation of His glorious workmanship.

In the same manner, when God sent His Son into the world, it was not to be born into noble surroundings. Instead, His mother gave birth to him in a stable, surrounded by beasts of burden. He was wrapped, not in sumptuous silks, but in simple woven cloth. This is the economy of God -- to send His Presence into the lowly place, where worldly finery and honors do not intrude.

Our hearts are to become lowly places, places that are humble enough to receive the Lord. If we will allow Him to come and sweep them clean of pride and worldly preoccupations, He will settle into them and make them His home. If we will let Him show us each day how to live in humility, patience and love, they will become habitations that are fit for a King.

Lord, I pray that I may have a humble shepherd's heart, that it might be a place where You will want to come and live.

JANUARY 7 --

"For she said within herself, If I may but touch his garment, I shall be whole." (Ma 9:21)

"Feeble faith is better than none. If God made no response except to perfect faith, who could hope for help? But God has regard for beginnings, and his eye perceives greatness in the germ. The hand of the woman in the crowd trembled as it was stretched toward Jesus, and the faith back of it was superstitiously reverent, trusting in the virtue of the robe, rather than in the One who wore it; yet the genuineness of that faith, feeble though it was, triumphed in God's loving sight. Real trust is real power, though the heart and hand both tremble.

> Rest in the Lord, my soul,
> Commit to Him thy way,
> What to thy sight seems dark as night,
> To Him is bright as day.
>
> Rest in the Lord, my soul,
> He planned for thee thy life,
> Brings fruit from rain, brings good from pain,
> And peace and joy from strife.
>
> Rest in the Lord, my soul,
> This fretting weakens thee,
> Why not be still? Accept His will,
> Thou shalt His glory see."
> — Maltbie Davenport Babcock

"But Jesus turned him about, and when he saw her, he said, Daughter, be of good comfort; thy faith hath made thee whole. And the woman was made whole from that hour." (Ma 9:22)

JANUARY 8 ---

"And do not forget to do good, and to impart [to others]; for by such sacrifices God's favour is obtained." (He 13:16)

"Christian men and women have it in their power, by a very little sacrifice, to add millions to the treasury of the Lord. Have you found the joy of sacrifice for Jesus? Have you given up something that you might give it to Him? Are you giving your substance to Jesus? He will take it, and will return to you a thousandfold more.

I should rather be associated with a work founded on great sacrifice than on enormous endowments. The reason God loved the place where His ancient temple rose in majesty was because there Abraham offered his son and David his treasure. The reason redemption is so dear to the Father and the heavenly world is because its foundation stone is the cross of Calvary. And the Christian life that is dearest to the heart of God, that will rise to the highest glory and usefulness, is the one whose foundation principle is sacrifice and self-renunciation. This is why the Master teaches us to give, because giving means loving, and love is but another name for life."

– A. B. Simpson

JANUARY 9 ---

"Likewise the Spirit also helpeth our infirmities: for we know not what we should pray for as we ought: but the Spirit itself maketh intercession for us with groanings which cannot be uttered." (Ro 8:26)

Victory often comes to us in a far different manner than that which we had imagined. This is why it is important to remember that after we have prayed, God's response may not immediately match up with what we have asked Him to do. During these times of delay we must believe the Father has heard us and strive to practice our faith, even when what He sends looks like the very opposite of what we have asked for. In between the time of our prayer and the time of its fulfillment, there is often a time of trial, of preparation and of testing that must first take place before the door to our blessing can be opened to us.

Have you asked the Lord to be your Provider? Then don't be surprised if there is upheaval in your job or unexpected expenses come pouring in like a flood. This may be the time God has chosen to help you recognize that it is not the world that is your source -- not a job or a trust fund or a business venture -- but God alone Who is your supply.

Have you sought the Lord to make you unselfish? Then don't be surprised if your own plans are destroyed, if you are placed in a position where you must give and not receive, if you are called on to serve and sacrifice instead of reap a return. How else shall you learn to say, "Not my will, but Thine?" How else will you come to the place where the flesh shall at last be overcome?

Did you ask the Lord to make you gentle? Then don't be surprised if you are plunged into a storm of humiliations or attacks on your character. These are sometimes the very tools God permits to be used upon us when He knows we are ready to have the rough edges of our personalities removed.

Have you asked the Lord to take you into the deeper realms of holiness? Then don't be surprised that you have entered a desert place, where there is no water of refreshing, where you wonder if He may not have abandoned you after all. The traits of holy tenderness and humility are not developed in the lush expanses of green pastures but on the harsh sands of trials and tribulations, where faith alone gives us the courage to follow the path that God asks us to walk.

This life in which I find myself is still a total mystery,
The more I try to rise above, the more I fall continuously.
And though I use my cane of faith, it is so brittle and so dry,
It often breaks beneath the weight of self I frequently apply.
I must be shaped and molded, this I heartily desire,
Yet I find I often flinch at the chisel and the fire.
God seeks my liberation from the sin imprisoning me,
I must trust and then implore Him not to rest until I'm free.

JANUARY 10 --

"When cometh Jesus from Galilee to Jordan unto John, to be baptised of him." (Ma 3:13)

"One of the most wonderful events ever transacted on this earth is recorded in this passage. We behold the Son of God in great humility coming to be baptized by John, as though he had been a sinner, and we behold the Everlasting Father and the Spirit, honoring him with unspeakable honor....

After he had humbled himself by being baptized, his Father exalted him by sending the Holy Spirit down upon him, and by declaring, 'This is my beloved Son, in whom I am well pleased.'

What must John the Baptist have felt when he beheld this scene? Here were no terrors like those on Mount Sinai; here were no thunders nor lightnings; no blackness, and darkness, and tempest – all was light and peace and love. It is wonderful to think that a mortal man would have been permitted to witness such a display of the divine glory. But as John was appointed to direct men to the Savior, it was right that he should receive the strongest proof of his being the Son of God. And could he have received stronger proof than he did receive on the banks of the Jordan? Impossible.

What exceeding love is expressed in the words, 'This is my beloved Son, in whom I am well pleased.' This declaration must have comforted the heart of the Man of Sorrows – though the world hated him He knew the Father loved him. Would it comfort us to think the Father loved us, and was well pleased with us? If we believe in Jesus, He does love us, and is well pleased with us for His sake. All believers are 'accepted in the beloved.' What sweet words are those. They have sustained the people of God in a dying hour. How could any man bear the thought of entering God's presence, were it not for the assurance that the Father will receive him in the name of His own beloved Son."   – F. L. Mortimer

JANUARY 11 --

"The LORD is their strength, and he is the saving strength of his anointed." (Ps. 28:8)

Believers are often taken with the idea of strength. Because we sense how powerless we are in so many situations, we pray for strength and power to overcome the obstacles in our lives.

It is undoubtedly true that God does give His children strength and power to accomplish His will, but we sometimes fail to understand that true spiritual strength must first be grounded on the firm foundation of humility. God seldom gives great power to those who have not learned to walk before Him in genuine humility of heart. He may require His people to undergo extensive training in the School of Humility before He empowers them to act as vessels of His strength and power.

We must get over the idea that humility is a passive virtue. To the contrary, it requires tremendous strength of character to walk before God in humility. It requires the ability to act with maturity, behave appropriately and respond obediently to the things God asks us to do. Humble servants of God are usually men and women who have endured many trials and testings. They have learned how to put aside the flesh and face the truth, not only about the challenges they are facing, but about their own flaws and limitations.

"The reason God is so great a lover of humility," said St. Vincent de Paul, "is that he is the great lover of truth. Now humility is nothing but truth, while pride is nothing but lying."

Therese of Lisieux also attested to the fact that truth and humility go hand in hand. One day near the end of her life, a visitor came to her bedside and the two talked at length about the virtue of humility. "It has always seemed to me," said Therese, "that humility is simply truth. I do not know whether I am humble, but I do know my soul has ever sought the truth."

Open my eyes, that I may see
Glimpses of truth thou hast for me;
Place in my hands the wonderful key
That shall unclasp and set me free.
Silently now I wait for thee,
Ready, my God, thy will to see.
Open my eyes, illumine me -- Spirit divine.
                                        –Clara Scott

JANUARY 12 --

"And the Lord said, Simon, Simon, behold, Satan hath desired to have you, that he may sift you as wheat: But I have prayed for thee, that thy faith fail not: and when thou art converted, strengthen thy brethren." (Lu 22:31-32)

"What a scene does this unfold. Satan tempting, Jesus praying. Satan sifting, Jesus pleading. The 'strong man' assailing, the 'stronger than the strong' beating him back. Believer, here is the past history and present secret of your safety in the midst of temptation. An interceding Savior was at your side, saying to every threatening wave, 'Thus far shall you go, and no farther.' God often permits His people to be on the very verge of the precipice, to remind them of their own weakness; but never farther than the brink. The restraining hand and grace of Omnipotence is ready to rescue them: 'Although he stumbles, yet he shall not be utterly cast down.' And why? 'For the Lord upholds him with His right hand.'
The wolf may be prowling for his prey, but what can he do when the Shepherd is always there, tending with the watchful eye that 'neither slumbers nor sleeps?' Who cannot subscribe to the testimony, 'When my foot slipped, Your mercy, O Lord, held me up?' Who can look back on his past pilgrimage and fail to see it crowded with monuments of help containing this inscription: 'You have delivered my soul from death, my eyes from tears, and my feet from falling?' My soul, where would you have been this day, had you not been kept by the power of God?"   – John MacDuff

JANUARY 13 ---

"For we are his workmanship." (Eph 2:10)

"Consider what is here declared of those who are saved by grace through faith – that they are God's 'workmanship,' the fruit and product of his creative hand. All, then, that we are, and all that we have that is spiritual, and as such acceptable to God, we owe to the special operation of his power. There is not a thought of our heart, word of our lips, or work of our hands which is truly holy and heavenly, simple and sincere, glorifying to God or profitable to man, of which he is not by his Spirit and grace the divine and immediate Author. How beautifully is this expressed by the Church of old, and what an echo do her accents find in every gracious heart: 'But now, O Lord, you are our Father; we are the clay, and you our potter; and we all are the work of your hand.' (Is 64:8)

How suitable, how expressive is the figure of the clay and the potter. Look at the moist clay under the potter's hand. How soft, how tender, how passive is the clay; how strong, how skillful are the hands which mold it into shape. As the wheel revolves, how every motion of the potter's fingers shapes the yielding clay, and with what exquisite skill does every gentle pressure, every imperceptible movement impress upon it the exact form which it was in his mind to make it assume. How sovereign was the hand which first took the clay, and as divine sovereignty first took it, so divine sovereignty shapes it when taken into form."   – Joseph Philpot

JANUARY 14 ---

"For the weapons of our warfare are not carnal, but mighty through God to the pulling down of strong holds;" (II Co 10:4)

One of the enemy's primary goals is to discourage the disciple. He will go to any lengths to steal his hope or convince the follower of Christ that his case is a sad one and probably doomed to failure. Many times we fall simply because we are afraid we're going to fall, or because we remember we have fallen in the past, and before we even get into the test we've convinced ourselves that we are simply destined to fall.

When we enter into the deeper places in Christ we would do well to remember we are entering into a constant state of warfare. Though our battlefield is here on earth, the source of our strategies and victory is not here at all. It is located in those heavenly places where we are seated with our Lord, and it is there that we are to wage war against our spiritual enemies. Rather than discourage us, our temptations and battles ought to encourage us, for these are often signs that we are making progress in the inner life.

11

"As a fact, temptations generally increase in strength tenfold after we have entered into the interior life, rather than decrease; and no amount or sort of them must ever for a moment lead us to suppose we have not really found the true abiding place. Strong temptations are generally a sign of great grace, rather than of little grace. When the children of Israel had first left Egypt, the Lord did not lead them through the country of the Philistines, although that was the nearest way; for God said, 'lest peradventure the people repent when they see war, and they return to Egypt.' But afterwards, when they learned better how to trust Him, He permitted their enemies to attack them. Then also in their wilderness journey they met with but few enemies and fought but few battles, compared to those in the land, where they found seven great nations and thirty-one kings to be conquered, besides walled cities to be taken, and giants to be overcome... The very power of your temptations, dear Christian, therefore, may perhaps be one of the strongest proofs that you really are in the land you have been seeking to enter, because they are temptations peculiar to that land."

--Hannah Whitall Smith

JANUARY 15 --

"As ye have therefore received Christ Jesus the Lord, so walk ye in him: Rooted and built up in him, and stablished in the faith, as ye have been taught, abounding therein with thanksgiving." (Co 2:6-7)

"It is of inconceivable importance that we should have right thoughts of what Christ is, of what really constitutes him the Christ, and especially of what may be counted his chief characteristic, the root and essence of all his character as our Redeemer. There can be but one answer: it is his humility. What is the incarnation but his heavenly humility, his emptying himself and becoming man? What is his life on earth but humility; his taking the form of a servant? And what is his atonement but humility? 'He humbled himself and became obedient unto death.' And what is his ascension and his glory, but humility exalted to the throne and crowned with glory? 'He humbled himself, therefore God highly exalted him.'

In Heaven, where he was with the Father, in his birth, in his life, in his death, in his sitting on the throne, it is all, it is nothing but, humility. Christ is the humility of God embodied in human nature; the Eternal Love humbling itself, clothing itself in the garb of meekness and gentleness, to win and serve and save us. As the love and condescension of God makes him the benefactor and helper and servant of all, so Jesus of necessity was the Incarnate Humility. And so he is still in the midst of the throne, the meek and lowly Lamb of God."

– Andrew Murray

"Love worketh no ill to his neighbor: therefore love is the fulfilling of the law." (Ro 13:10)

"'Love,' says St. Augustine, 'is the only worship God exacts, and which alone is pleasing to Him.' Faith alone does not honor God -- the devils believe and tremble. Hope without love is not enough, because it stops short at God's promises without going on to Himself. Charity alone reaches Him, is united to Him, and rests in Him as in the supreme Good. What avails the practice of exterior works, if they are not animated and quickened by the heart? Men only pay attention to outward demonstrations, and they judge the heart by them, for they cannot see any deeper. But God looks upon the heart. According to the state of the heart, He appraises all else."

-- Jean Nicolas Grou

"Our Lord does not say that the objects of worldly ambition are bad; He says they are fleeting. What He denies is not their legitimacy, but their permanence. He says the man who drinks of the earthly fountain will thirst again; the man who drinks of the heavenly fountain will never thirst. What is this magic fountain of abiding waters? It is Love.

Love is the only thing which I need never outgrow. I am bound to outgrow everything else. How many gifts to my youth would be gifts to my old age? Wealth, fame, power, physical beauty, are all for the morning and the midday; they are little coveted at evening. But love in its old age can keep the dew of its youth. I have seen a virtuous attachment, which was formed by the girl and the boy, retain amid the shadows its morning glow. The heart never grows old with time. It may grow old with grief, or bitterness, or care -- but not with time. Time has no empire over the heart. It has an empire over the eye, over the ear, over the cheek, over the hand -- but not over the heart. The heart may be swept by storms, but not corroded by decay. It keeps no record of the flying years; it is untouched by the winter snow. The inscription upon its gates is always: 'There shall be no night here.'"   -- George Matheson

"I waited patiently for the LORD; and he inclined unto me, and heard my cry." (Ps. 40:1)

Our English word "patience" is derived from a Latin word meaning "suffering." The deeper implication of this word suggests the state of being under some form of constraint or pressure from which we would desire to be set free. Our natural response to evil is, understandably, resistance. All of us possess the instinct to resist evil. We recoil from it by nature. This is a healthy instinct. If we didn't have it, there would be something wrong with us. Life, however, has a way of bringing pain and suffering into our lives on a regular basis, and try as we might, we often find we can't escape from it. This is where patience comes in. We must learn how to practice patient endurance in the face of suffering.

Patient endurance is something few of us are born with. God must work it within our hearts. When life hands us something painful and we discover that no amount of personal effort is able to push it away, we have to develop patient endurance. Those of us who are not patient by nature can attest to the fact that it often takes years of work to begin to grow in the area of patient endurance.

There is, however, an even deeper form of patience than patient endurance. It is the stage of actively surrendering to God. It is choosing to align our wills with God's will and surrender our own preferences where our circumstances are concerned. Once again, only God can bring us to the stage of active surrender. Only He can teach us how to align our wills to His will, even in the midst of suffering. Only He can change us from people who always seek our own will into those who instead seek only His.

Why does my path lead through struggle and pain
While another receives his desires?
Because, dear child, a surrendered heart
Can only be formed in life's fires.
Why is my way often laden with tears
When the faces of many wear smiles?
Because, dear child, humility comes
After walking adversity's miles.

Why do some gather flowers and ferns
While so much of my harvest is thorns?
Because, dear child, the Way of the Cross
Must take you through countless storms.
God's ways, to be sure, will perplex our hearts
If we view them through worldly eyes,
But if we'll gaze through the lens of trust
We'll discover God's ways are wise.

One day we'll see His grace alone
Gave us power to endure,
Transformed our sinful natures,
Made them loving, kind and pure.

"Doth not behave itself unseemly, seeketh not her own, is not easily provoked, thinketh no evil;" (I Co 13:5)

"Guilelessness is the grace for suspicious people. And the possession of it is the great secret of personal influence. You will find, if you think for a moment, that the people who have influenced you in a positive way are the ones who believe in you. In an atmosphere of suspicion men shrivel up; but in a believing atmosphere they expand and find encouragement. It is a wonderful thing that here and there in this hard, uncharitable world there should still be left a few rare souls who think no evil. This is the great unworldliness. Love 'thinketh no evil,' imputes no motive, sees the bright side, puts the best construction on every action. What a delightful state of mind to live in. What a stimulus and benediction even to meet with it for a day. To be trusted is to be saved. And if we try to influence or elevate others, we shall soon see that success is in proportion to their belief of our belief in them. For the respect of another is the first restoration of the self-respect a man has lost; our ideal of what he is becomes to him the hope and pattern of what he may become." -- Henry Drummond

"The habit of judging is so nearly incurable, and its cure is such an almost interminable process, that we must concentrate ourselves for a long while on keeping it in check, and this check is to be found in kind interpretations. We must come to esteem very lightly our sharp eye for evil, on which perhaps we once prided ourselves as cleverness. We must look at our talent for analysis of character as a dreadful possibility of huge uncharitableness. We are sure to continue to say clever things, so long as we continue to indulge in this analysis; and clever things are equally sure to be sharp and acid. We must grow to something higher, and something truer, than a quickness in detecting evil." -- Frederick William Faber

"And when he came to himself, he said, How many hired servants of my father's have bread enough and to spare, and I perish with hunger? I will arise and go to my father, and will say unto him, Father, I have sinned against heaven, and before thee." (Lu 15:17-18)

Many of us can identify with the plight of the prodigal son. We know what it's like to fool ourselves. We've been through the wringer of trying to win at life, only to find that our way didn't work. And, like the prodigal, we worked hard to avoid that awful state called "surrender."

A recovering alcoholic once spoke about his struggle with addiction and with surrender by putting it this way:

"I never once surrendered to anything in my life before I finally surrendered to God. It wasn't in my nature to surrender. I had been taught by my upbringing that surrender was only for cowards. In fact, my genetic makeup wouldn't have allowed me to surrender. Fortunately, God kept at me. He knew if I didn't somehow learn to do life His way instead of my own way I was destined to die."

This man came to understand what the prodigal son went through because he went through the same experience himself. He went his own way, tried to make life work out according to his own plan, and found in the end that he couldn't do it. He had to admit he couldn't find the kind of life he really wanted on his own. He had to have help. When he was at his lowest ebb, he realized the only source of help available to him was God. In other words, "he came to himself." At that point, he surrendered his life to God, and that was the point at which everything turned around. After decades of addictive drinking, he was healed of the obsession to drink. He made the decision to do things God's way. He let go and allowed God to be in control of his life. Since that moment of surrender – at this writing over thirty years ago – he has never had to take another drink.

Many of us can nod in heartfelt agreement. Yes, there have been mistakes. Yes, there have been blunders. Yes, there have been failures and sin. All of these were somehow necessary for us to come to the realization that we could not do it without God. How blessed we are that God has infinite patience and tenderness. Instead of seeing only our arrogance and denial and failures, Christ sees what we can become, in Him, and invites us to give Him the chance to transform our lives.

JANUARY 20 ---

"Howbeit for this cause I obtained mercy, that in me first Jesus Christ might shew forth all longsuffering, for a pattern to them which should hereafter believe on him to life everlasting." (I Ti 1:16)

The longer we walk with Jesus, the greater becomes our understanding of the extent and depth of our own sinfulness, and of the mercy God has extended to us through His gift of redemption. As an example, just look at how the Apostle Paul's attitude toward himself changed over the years.

Before coming to Christ, Paul had been a proud man. His father, a Pharisee and Roman citizen, had raised him in strict accordance with Jewish tradition and law. Paul was the kind of man who thought he had all the answers. He believed the people who followed Christ were heretics and felt justified in going to any lengths to stop them. Then God touched Paul, and, in an instant, he was changed. His life would never be the same. He came to understand that only by the grace of God had he been saved out of a life of sin.

In the early stage of his Christian walk, around 55 A.D., Paul wrote to believers in Corinth . He told them he was "the least of the apostles...not meet to be called an apostle, because I persecuted the church of God" (I Cor. 15:9). His self image had gone from arrogant keeper of the Law to least of the apostles, but this was just the beginning.

Over the next six years Paul passed through many trials and persecutions that drew him even closer to his Lord. When he wrote to fellow believers in A.D. 61, he noted that the grace of God had been "given unto me by the effectual working of his power. Unto me, who am less than the least of all saints, is this grace given, that I should preach among the Gentiles the unsearchable riches of Christ;" (Ep 3:7-8). Now Paul had gone from "least of the apostles" to "least of all saints," but there was still more change ahead for this disciple of God.

More trials awaited him over the next three years, more experiences that revealed to him the incredible grace and love of God. Sometime between 64 A. D. and 67 A.D., he wrote his first letter to Timothy. In it he noted that God had called him, even though he "was before a blasphemer, and a persecutor, and injurious: but I obtained mercy, because I did it ignorantly in unbelief. And the grace of our Lord was exceeding abundant with faith and love which is in Christ Jesus. This is a faithful saying, and worthy of all acceptation, that Christ Jesus came into the world to save sinners; of whom I am chief." (I Ti 1:13-15)

From keeper of the law, to least of apostles, to least of saints, to chief of sinners; Paul's estimation of himself continually decreased as his knowledge of God continually increased. It is a process that naturally occurs in the life of every growing believer. In the walk of faith, we are bound to see our failings with greater clarity as we mature, but, praise God, we will at the same time grow to understand with increasing appreciation the incredible mercy of God.

> The Man of Sorrows came to glory
> By a painful, crooked road,
> And upon His holy shoulders
> Carried every sinful load;
> Bore the weight of every failing,
> Every brokenness and need,
> So that freedom everlasting
> Would be won for you and me.

"Blessed are the poor in spirit: for theirs is the kingdom of heaven." (Matt 5:3)

A theologian once noted that all the food in the world was divine love made edible. The same kind of logic might be applied to every other blessing we possess. The food we eat, the air we breathe, the water we drink, all come to us because of the goodness of God, not because of any worthiness on our part.

The same is true of the positive traits we may possess. If we are able to show any mercy, any kindness, any love to others, or if we receive these things from those around us, it is only because God has placed them within us, not because we have any innate goodness within ourselves.

And what about our salvation? Could any of us obtain conviction of sin or forgiveness on our own? Never. These were made possible for us only because the Holy Spirit came to lead us to repent of our sins and because Jesus Christ chose to die in our place so we could be reconciled to God. If we will examine each and every blessing we possess, we are bound to recognize that every one of them has come to us only because we have a kind and loving God.

Like it or not, we possess nothing. We are completely, hopelessly poor. We only exist because God has willed us into existence and we only continue to exist because God keeps operating upon us with His Breath of Life. An accident or twist of fate could end our lives in a moment. So could a malfunction in an organ or an injury to a tiny vessel in the brain. Our life continually hangs by a thread and that thread is continuously attached to God's will. To those who are still under the illusion that they can control their own lives, this may seem an unpleasant truth, but to the children of God it is a cause for endless rejoicing. It reminds us that all we have is pure gift. We can never qualify for God's loving kindness but He gives it to us anyway, simply because He is a loving God. Because we are joint heirs with His Son, Jesus Christ, God the Father delights in giving us the Kingdom. Here on earth we are endowed with wonderful blessings and gifts, and in the life to come we will share a love with Him that will never end. This is prosperity beyond description. This is joy beyond measure. This is the ultimate blessing for those that are poor.

"But the hour cometh, and now is, when the true worshippers shall worship the Father in spirit and in truth: for the Father seeketh such to worship him." (Jo 4:23)

How to Adore God in Spirit and in Truth:
"There are three points to consider here: First, to adore God in Spirit and

in truth means to adore Him as we should. Because God is a Spirit, He must be adored in spirit. That is, we must worship Him with a humble, sincere love that comes from the depth and center of our soul. Only God can see this adoration, which we must repeat until it becomes part of our nature, as if God were one with our soul and our soul were one with God. Practice will demonstrate this.

Secondly, to adore God in truth is to recognize Him for what He is, and ourselves for what we are. Adoring God in truth means that our heart actually sees God as infinitely perfect and worthy of our praise. What man, regardless of how little sense he may have, would not exert all his strength to show his respect and love of this great God?

Thirdly, to adore God in truth is to admit that our nature is just the opposite of His. Yet, He is willing to make us like Him, if we desire it. Who would be so rash as to neglect, even for a moment, the respect, the love, the service, and the continual adoration that we owe Him?"

– Brother Lawrence

JANUARY 23 --

"Being confident of this very thing, that he which hath begun a good work in you will perform it until the day of Jesus Christ:" (Ph 1:6)

At the start of our Christian life we may feel we know exactly where we are going and what God's plan for us will be. We may say to ourselves, "Surely, I am called to do this;" or, "Certainly, He is guiding me over here." At times, God will indeed give us clear direction, but there may also be times when He calls us to take paths that are not so well defined. After we have walked with Him a while, we may find ourselves facing circumstances where God's will is less and less obvious. Twists and turns in the road may appear that we never expected. His ways may baffle us. The road ahead may become increasingly obscure.

At some point, our journey may take us to places where the way is dark or laden with shadows. Our former certainty as to what God is driving at may diminish. We may recognize that we aren't nearly as insightful about God's will as we once thought. He increasingly allows us to be taken where we do not wish to go. He calls on us to endure things we never dreamed would happen. Our prayers do not get answered with the delightful frequency we used to experience. His answers to them arrive in ways we would not wish. Our plans go awry and we become perplexed. We wonder if we may have lost our way, or, worse still, whether God may even have forgotten us.

Dear one, remember that God's own do not lose their way. God knows exactly where they are on the road to His Kingdom. He always keeps watch over them, but He does eventually lead them out of the Valley of

Self-Sufficiency so He can teach them to walk by faith rather than sight. He guides them along many paths where they will encounter situations they cannot handle in their own strength. This is the only way they can discover that God alone can do the work; they cannot do it themselves.

Our peace and joy ultimately lie in recognizing this great truth. Yes, God must do it. He must do it all. And He will do it all, on our behalf. The work of transformation in us will not happen because of our dedication or our talents or our ability to figure everything out. It will happen because God will do the work. He alone knows how to bring about the changes He wants to make in us. He alone has the power and grace to accomplish them.

JANUARY 24 ---

"Take therefore no thought for the morrow: for the morrow shall take thought for the things of itself. Sufficient unto the day is the evil thereof." (Matt 6:34)

"God gives us life by days, little single days. Each day has its own duties, its own needs, its own trials and temptations, its own griefs and sorrows. God always gives us strength enough for the day as He gives it, with all that He puts into it. But if we insist on dragging back tomorrow's cares and piling them on top of today's, the strength will not be enough for the load. God will not add strength just to humor our whims of anxiety and distrust. So the lesson is that we should keep each day distinct and attend strictly to what it brings us. [The noted English clergyman] Charles Kingsley said: 'Do today's duty, fight today's temptation, and do not weaken and distract yourself by looking forward to things which you cannot see and could not understand if you saw them.' We really have nothing at all to do with the future, save to prepare for it by doing with fidelity the duties of to-day.

No one was ever crushed by the burdens of one day. We can always get along with our heaviest load until the sun goes down; that is all we ever have to do. Tomorrow? Oh, you may have no tomorrow; you may be in heaven. If you are here, God will be here too, and you will receive new strength sufficient for the new day.

> One day at a time. A burden too great
> To be borne for two can be borne for one;
> Who knows what will enter tomorrow's gate,
> While yet we are speaking all may be done.
> One day at a time, but a single day,
> Whatever its load, whatever its length;
> And there's a bit of precious Scripture to say,
> That according to each shall be our strength."
> – J. R. Miller

"But lift thou up thy rod, and stretch out thine hand over the sea, and divide it: and the children of Israel shall go on dry ground through the midst of the sea." (Ex 14:16)

The children of Israel were trapped in an impossible situation. On one side was the Red Sea. On the other, Pharaoh and his Egyptian army were fast approaching, bent on destroying God's people.

Certainly, in the natural way of looking at things, the Israelites had no way of escape. But Moses commanded them to stand their ground: "Fear not," he told them, "stand still, and see the salvation of the Lord, which he will show to you to day..." (v. 13)

No doubt the children of Israel hoped at this point that God would swoop down and destroy the Egyptian army, but He didn't. Instead, He spoke to Moses: "Wherefore criest thou unto me?" He said; "speak unto the children of Israel, that they go forward. But lift thou up thy rod, and stretch out thine hand over the sea, and divide it: and the children of Israel shall go on dry ground through the midst of the sea" (Ex 14:15-16). At that moment, the angel of the Lord, who had gone before the camp as a pillar of cloud, moved to the rear of the throng and stationed himself between the children of God and their pursuers. Then Moses stretched out his hand, just as God had instructed him. And the Lord began to move.

God often acts in this manner with His people. Though He always hears our cries for help and deliverance, He sometimes requires us to take a step of faith before He will visibly work in our behalf.

As Moses stretched out his hand, the Lord brought a great wind out of the east. It forced the sea to roll back all through the night, thus opening a way of escape for the children of God. Not only did they make their way through the midst of the sea, but the ground upon which they walked was dry. Though Pharaoh's men pursued them, God protected the Israelites. He unhinged the wheels of the Egyptian chariots and caused the waters to come together again. Pharaoh's entire army was destroyed.

Sometimes God seems to go to great lengths to engineer us into circumstances where our faith is tested to the limit; where we must step out in faith without having any idea of what He is going to do to help us. But if we will trust Him and do all He tells us to do, we can be sure God will do everything necessary to bring us safely through our sea of trouble. He will part the waters for us. He will guide us to the other side.

"Keep back thy servant also from presumptuous [sins]; let them not have dominion over me: then shall I be upright, and I shall be innocent from the great transgression." (Ps 19:13)

The more we read God's Word and seek His presence, the more we will discover which aspects of our personalities are valuable and in accordance with His will, and which are hangovers from our old lives and need to be cast away. It may be frightening to contemplate getting rid of behaviors and beliefs that no longer work for us, but we can do it if we take life a day at a time and ask God to help us identify what it is in us He wants to change.

At first, we may feel it's easier to stay the way we are than go through all the pain of change. But as we progress in the spiritual life we will come to recognize that our defects and sinful behaviors no longer work for us. Whether the challenge we're facing is the eradication of a minor fault or the removal of a major flaw in our characters, at some point, if we are truly walking with God, the time will come when we'll discover we want to be free of it. We will no longer want to stay the same. The closer we get to God, the more we will desire to become like Him and leave our old selves behind.

When we are ready and willing to allow God to remove our defects, He will come in and show us what part we must play in releasing them. They may not be immediately removed as we would wish. The process of getting rid of them usually takes time – sometimes, a very long time, indeed. But God will help us as we turn our lives and our wills over to Him on a daily basis. Have I become willing to let God deal with my defects of character? Am I prepared to take action if that is what He asks me to do?

Lord, what defects of character do You want me to work on today? What do you want me to do; to release; to change; so that I may have a closer walk with You?

JANUARY 27 --

"If ye endure chastening, God dealeth with you as with sons; for what son is he whom the father chasteneth not?" (He 12:7)

God knows all about the challenges you are facing, about each and every detail of your life. There is nothing that escapes His notice. There isn't a single problem you have that He is not aware of and deeply interested in seeing turned, at some point along the way, into something that will help conform you to the image of His Son. You may not feel that He knows and cares, but He does. He knows about your struggles, your fears, your wounds, your failings.

He knows each worry that has ever lodged in your mind. He knows the number of the hairs on your head at this very moment. He knows you inside and out, and because of this He also knows how to deal with you. He understands what it will take to get you to focus on a certain matter, what tool to use to shape your character and mold you into the person He intends you to become.

Sometimes, in the process of transformation, God uses blessings to reveal His goodness and mercy: "And I will make them and the places round about my hill a blessing; and I will cause the shower to come down in his season; there shall be showers of blessing" (Ez 34:26). At other times, however, He may use chastenings: "For whom the Lord loveth he chasteneth, and scourgeth every son whom he receiveth" (He 12:6). Sometimes He inserts a thorn in our flesh: "And lest I should be exalted above measure through the abundance of the revelations, there was given to me a thorn in the flesh, the messenger of Satan to buffet me, lest I should be exalted above measure" (II Cor 12:7). The word "flesh," in this instance, is derived from the Greek word "sarx," which can mean either the physical flesh or the flesh of our fallen human nature. None of us like having a thorn in the flesh. Thorns are sharp and painful; after a while they can become so irritating we want to scream. But thorns also prod us to examine our reactions under stress and suffering, and force us to recognize how imperfect our natures are when we are faced with adversity. Adversity doesn't cause us to become sinful. It just forces our sinfulness to the surface so it can be seen for what it is.

Because God loves us, He knows what we need, and He knows what must be done to establish our characters upon a solid foundation of faith and trust. That takes some doing -- and sometimes a great deal of pain -- but we can be comforted by reminding ourselves that the work He is performing in us isn't just for a lifetime, but for all eternity.

JANUARY 28 --

"Evening, and morning, and at noon will I pray, and cry aloud: and he shall hear my voice." (Ps 55:17)

"The more praying there is in the world, the better the world will be, the mightier the forces against evil everywhere. Prayer, in one phase of its operation, is a disinfectant and a preventive. It purifies the air; it destroys the contagion of evil. Prayer is no fitful, short-lived thing. It is no voice crying unheard and unheeded in the silence. It is a voice which goes into God's ear, and it lives as long as God's ear is open to holy pleas, as long as God's heart is alive to holy things. God shapes the world by prayer. Prayers are deathless. The lips that uttered them may be closed to death, the heart that felt them may have ceased to beat, but the prayers live before God, and God's heart is set on them and prayers outlive the lives of those who uttered them; they outlive a generation, outlive an age, outlive a world. That man is the most immortal who has done the most and the best praying. He is God's hero, God's saint, God's servant. A man can pray better because of the prayers of the past; a man can live holier because of the prayers of the past;

the man of many and acceptable prayers has done the truest and greatest service to the incoming generation. The prayers of God's saints strengthen the unborn generation against the desolating waves of sin and evil."

– E. M. Bounds

"Prayer is not overcoming God's reluctance, but laying hold of His willingness."

– Martin Luther

The best prayer is the practical prayer: Two children were afraid they would be late for school. One said, "Let's pray that God will get us to school on time so we don't get into trouble." "No," said the other child, who had a better idea; "let's run as fast as we can and while we run we'll pray that He'll get us there on time."

JANUARY 29 --

"This is my commandment, That ye love one another, as I have loved you." (Jo 15:12)

"All extreme sensitiveness, fastidiousness, suspicion, readiness to take offence and tenacity of what we think our due, come from self-love, as does the unworthy secret gratification we sometimes feel when another is humbled or mortified. [So does our] cold indifference, the harshness of our criticism, the unfairness and hastiness of our judgments, our bitterness towards those we dislike and many other faults which must more or less rise up before most men's consciences when they question them sincerely as to how far they do indeed love their neighbors as Christ has loved them. [God] will root out all dislikes and aversions, all readiness to take offence, all resentments, all bitterness, from the heart which is given up to His guidance. He will infuse His own tender love for man into His servant's mind, and teach him to 'love his brother as Christ has loved him.'"

– Jean Nicolas Grou

"But love ye your enemies, and do good, and lend, hoping for nothing again; and your reward shall be great, and ye shall be the children of the Highest: for he is kind unto the unthankful and to the evil." (Lu 6:35)

JANUARY 30 --

"...that ye, being rooted and grounded in love,..." (Eph 3:17)

Roots, by nature, are designed to reach down into the soil and draw up the moisture and nutrients they need. Some of us, however, have damaged roots.

There are many reasons why our roots may become damaged. In some cases it can be a result of having grown up in an environment of abuse, addiction or some other form of dysfunction. Sometimes it can be due to bad choices we have made or hurts inflicted by people we love. These situations can make our roots dry and brittle. Yet the life force within us keeps looking for what our roots need. Sometimes we go in search of what we need in all the wrong places. The only lasting help for damaged roots lies in a relationship with Jesus Christ.

Many years ago, in Hampton Court, London, there was a grapevine that bore thousands of bunches of grapes. Visitors were astounded at its prolific harvest. Sometime later it was found that several of the vine's roots had traveled over one hundred yards in order to reach the moisture of a river that flowed nearby.

Our roots are like those of the grapevine at Hampton Court. They are equipped to find what they need. When we come to know Christ, our roots can stop trying to draw what they require from the old life and start drawing from Christ, Who has everything we need to live healthy and productive lives. We are to draw our life from Christ, not just in a figurative way, but literally.

"Giving thanks unto the Father, which hath made us meet to be partakers of the inheritance of the saints in light: Who hath delivered us from the power of darkness, and hath translated us into the kingdom of his dear Son:" (Col 1:12-13). In this case, the word "translate" means "to bear or carry from one place to another; to transfer." This is exactly what Christ has done for us through His sacrifice at the Cross. He has rescued us from the power of darkness and transferred us into His kingdom. Just think of this. Our supply of healing, of love, of transformation, need never again be in short supply. Our supply of Spirit Life will never run out because we now live in the Kingdom of God.

Let us reach out to Christ, Who is the Source of everything we need. Let us send our roots deep into the rich medium of His Life, which He will gladly bestow upon anyone who will call upon His name.

"...that ye, being rooted and grounded in love, May be able to comprehend with all saints what is the breadth, and length, and depth, and height; And to know the love of Christ, which passeth knowledge, that ye may be filled with all the fulness of God." (Ep 3:17-19)

My roots are still so bound, Lord,
They need to be set free,
I pray You will untangle them
That they might nourish me.
Some are damaged, some are dry,

They need Your gentle touch
To make them able to receive
The Life they need so much.
Feed them Lord, with heavenly food,
So they will heal and grow,
And pass along to others
The Love they've come to know.

JANUARY 31 --

"And when they wanted wine, the mother of Jesus saith unto him, They have no wine…Jesus saith unto them, Fill the waterpots with water. And they filled them up to the brim. And he saith unto them, Draw out now, and bear unto the governor of the feast. And they bare it." (Jo 2:3, 7-8)

The miracles performed by Jesus Christ during His public ministry gave men the opportunity to see, in clear focus, what the Father is always doing in a manner so grand that His work is often taken for granted. Water had been turned into wine for centuries before the miracle at Cana, but it had been accomplished through the lengthy process of natural growth, beginning with soil and root, continuing through the fertile vine and ending with the production of fruit and juice and, finally, the fermentation process. When Christ created wine for the wedding guests, He accelerated this process so that we might see and better appreciate the love of the Father and His determination to provide for us in every area of our lives.

"…His miracles in bread and in wine were far less grand and less beautiful than the works of the Father they represented, in making the corn to grow in the valleys, and the grapes to drink the sunlight on the hillsides of the world, with all their infinitudes of tender gradation and delicate mystery of birth. But the Son of the Father be praised, who, as it were, condensed these mysteries before us, and let us see the precious gifts coming at once from gracious hands – hands that love could kiss and nails could wound…"   -- George MacDonald

FEBRUARY 1 --

"And when he had called the people unto him with his disciples also, he said unto them, Whosoever will come after me, let him deny himself, and take up his cross, and follow me." (Mark 8:34)

"Here lies the great difference between the world's gospel and the Lord's Gospel. The world says, 'Take care of yourself.' The Lord says, 'Let yourself go, and take care of others and the glory of your God.' The world says,

'Have a good time, look out for Number One.' But the world gets left in the end, and the last comes in first. The man that lets go gets all, and the man who holds fast loses what he has, and the Lord's words come true: Whosoever will save his life shall lose it: and whosoever will lose his life for my sake shall find it.'

So the law of sacrifice is the greatest law in earth and heaven. The law of sacrifice is God's great law. It is written in earth and every department of nature. We tread on the skeletons of [countless] generations that have lived and died that we might live. The very heart of the earth itself is the wreck of ages and the buried life of former generations. All nature dies and lives again, and each new development is a higher and larger life built on the wrecks of the former. A corn of wheat must fall into the ground and die, or else be a shriveled-up seed, but as it dies it lives and multiplies, and grows into the beautiful spring, the golden autumn and the multiplied sheaves. And so it is in the deeper life of the higher world, as you rise from the natural to the spiritual. Everything that is selfish is limited by its selfishness. The river that ceases to run becomes a stagnant pool, but as it flows it grows fresher, richer, fuller.

If you turn your natural eye upon yourself, you cannot see anything. It is as you look out that the vision of the world bursts upon you. The very law of the natural life is love for others, caring for others by giving away and letting go. It is death and self-destruction to be selfish."

– A.B. Simpson

FEBRUARY 2 --

"Pray without ceasing." (I Th 5:17)

"First. The holiest, most universal and most necessary practice in the spiritual life is the presence of God. To practice the presence of God is to take pleasure in and become accustomed to His Divine company, speaking humbly and lovingly to Him at all times, and at every moment, especially in times of temptation, pain, spiritual dryness, revulsion to spiritual things and even unfaithfulness and sin.

Second. We must apply ourselves continually to the end that all our actions may be little spontaneous conversations with God, coming from an inner purity and simplicity of heart.

Third. We must weigh all our actions without the impetuosity or impulsiveness that mark a distraught spirit. As we carry out our duties, we must work gently, tranquilly and lovingly with God, asking Him to accept our labor. Through our continual attention to God, we will crush the head of the devil and make his weapons fall from his hands.

Fourth. During our work and other activities, and even during our times of reading or writing, even though they may be spiritually oriented, and, yes, even more during our outward devotions and prayers, we ought to stop for a moment, as often as we can, to adore God deep within our hearts and take pleasure in Him, even though we might have to do this briefly and in secret. Since you are not unmindful of the fact that God is present before you as you carry out your duties, and you know that He is at the depth and center of your soul, why not stop from time to time, whatever you are doing -- even if you are praying aloud -- to adore Him inwardly, to give praise to Him, to beseech Him, to offer Him your heart, and to thank Him for His goodness?"

-- Brother Lawrence

FEBRUARY 3 --

"Be strong and of a good courage, fear not, nor be afraid of them: for the Lord thy God, he it is that doth go with thee; he will not fail thee, nor forsake thee." (De 31:6)

One evening a woman had to travel by car to another city where she had been asked to speak to a group of believers. When she arrived the sun was just setting and it cast a beautiful crimson glow across the sky. Her hosts welcomed her and they spent a pleasant evening together in the church hall.

When the gathering ended, however, she emerged to discover a dense fog had enveloped the countryside. She had experienced several close calls driving under such conditions in the past so it was with a sense of dread that she got behind the wheel and began her long journey home.

As she made her way through the night, things went from bad to worse. She had at least been able to see a short distance ahead of the car when she started out, but before long the visibility dropped nearly to zero. A blanket of fear enveloped her. She worried that she might be struck from behind by another car or stray off the road completely. She drove at a snail's pace, and prayed for help. Then she saw a welcome sight.

Just ahead was a large truck, also going at a snail's pace, with both cab and trailer covered with bright red lights. She pulled up behind it and decided to stay close to it and allow it to guide the way. She clung to that truck as if it were a life raft. When its driver slowed down, she did, too; when he accelerated, she did the same. She did not dare allow herself to lose sight of it; the sheer size of that truck moving through the shroud of mist helped clear a tunnel through the fog and allowed her to see a bit more clearly. Even though she was afraid, she felt comforted by those bright red lights in the night and was grateful for the protection the truck provided as the two vehicles made their way through the night.

By the time she reached her home town the fog had abated a little. When it came time to take her turnoff she blinked her headlights as a 'thank you' to the truck driver. He blinked back and honked in response. He had known she was there all the time. As she drove the last leg of her journey she prayed that he, too, would reach his destination safely.

God is like that brightly lit truck. He goes before us into the future we cannot see to light the way. If our way seems dark or shrouded in mist, we can trust Him to guide us. He knows the way that we should take. He is able to see, not just part of the road, but all the way to its end. He will never leave us to make our way alone, and, if we will stay close to Him, He will never allow evil to overtake us. He will always go before us, to lead us safely home.

FEBRUARY 4 --

"And being found in fashion as a man, he humbled himself, and became obedient unto death, even the death of the cross. Wherefore God also hath highly exalted him, and given him a name which is above every name:" (Ph 2:8-9)

"Listen to the words in which our Lord speaks of his relation to the Father, and see how unceasingly he uses the words 'not' and 'nothing' of himself. The 'not I' in which Paul expresses his relation to Christ, is the very spirit of what Christ says of his relation to the Father:

> The Son can do nothing of himself. (Jo 5:19)
> I can of my own self do nothing; my judgment is just, because
>   I seek not mine own will. (Jo 5:30)
> I receive not glory from men. (Jo 5:41)
> I am come not to do mine own will. (Jo 5:38)
> My teaching is not mine. (Jo 7:16)
> I am not come of myself. (Jo 7:28)
> I do nothing of myself. (Jo 8:28)
> Neither came I of myself, but He sent me. (Jo 8:42)
> I seek not mine own glory. (Jo 8:50)
> The words that I say, I speak not from myself. (Jo 14:10)
> The word which ye hear is not mine. (Jo 14:24)

...[Christ] resigned himself with his will and his powers entirely for the Father to work in him. Of his own power, his own will, and his own glory, of his whole mission with all his works and his teaching, of all this he said, 'It is not I; I am nothing; I have given myself to the Father to work; I am nothing, the Father is all.'

This life of entire self-abnegation, of absolute submission and dependence upon the Father's will, Christ found to be one of perfect peace and joy. He lost nothing by giving all to God. God honored his trust, and did all for him, and then exalted him to his own right hand in glory. And because Christ had thus humbled himself before God, and God was ever before him, he found it possible to humble himself before men, too, and to be the Servant of all. His humility was simply the surrender of himself to God, to allow Him to do in him what he pleased, whatever men around might say of him, or do to him." — Andrew Murray

FEBRUARY 5 --

"For he is our God; and we are the people of his pasture, and the sheep of his hand. To day if ye will hear his voice." (Ps 95:7)

One of the best ways to prevent our minds from falling into worry is to keep our thinking in Today.

Behind us is the past. There is nothing we can do to change it. Vain regrets can do nothing but deplete our effectiveness. If we've made mistakes we cannot undo them, but we can take them to the Lord and do business with Him about anything that needs to be corrected: Do we need to make amends to someone? Then let us do it. Is something still troubling us that needs to be discussed with someone who is trustworthy and can keep our confidence? Then let us do it. Have we held back from extending forgiveness to someone whose sins or character flaws caused us pain? If so, then let us do now what needs to be done.

Before us stretches the future. We can't possibly know what tomorrow will bring, but we do know God will be in every one of our tomorrows, to guide us, direct us, and give us His grace. Let us release everything to Him, including the fears we have about what tomorrow may bring. The most effective way to do this is usually to focus on today, and what we can do with it. Today is the day where our choices count. Today is the day we can take action. What choices do we need to make and act upon today?

> I do not ask to see the way
> My feet will have to tread,
> But only that my soul may feed
> Upon the Living Bread.
>
> 'Tis better far that I should walk
> By faith close to His side;
> I may not know the way I go,
> But oh, I know my Guide.
> — E. S. Hall

FEBRUARY 6 --

"And we desire that every one of you do shew the same diligence to the full assurance of hope unto the end: That ye be not slothful, but followers of them who through faith and patience inherit the promises." (He 6:11-12)

God has made many promises to His children and, because He is faithful, He can always be trusted to keep them. He will fulfill His word to us – at the appropriate time. Sometimes, however – because most of us are impatient -- we have the tendency to grasp at God's promises. We want them now. We don't want to wait. We don't trust that He will provide what we need at the proper time. There are times when taking hold of a promise and claiming it as our own is a show of faith, but at other times, insisting a promise be kept Right Now can be an impertinence. Only God knows the perfect way to fulfill His promises.

The world's way of handling difficulties is to attempt to eradicate them immediately. It wants its answers now. It doesn't want to wait. As believers, we can fall into this same kind of thinking. When we have a problem we may read about a promise of God, decide it is just the one we need, and start claiming it or demanding that it come to us, even before asking God if it is really His will for us at this particular time.

God often allows His children to go through a growth process where His promises are concerned. He may delay the full impartation of a promise while we go through a process of maturation and transformation. We may need to continue in prayer or undergo a period where our faith is tested. We may have to surrender our will in a certain situation and instead wait upon God to show us if there is something within us that needs to be changed.

How does God want us to respond when we find ourselves having to wait for His promises to be fulfilled? He wants us to persevere – to keep on keeping on. It is essential we learn to do this if we are ever to become mature Christians. We need to persevere, not with resentment or impatience, but with a spirit of worship, prayer and an attitude of surrender, trusting that His timing in all things is perfect. If we stumble into times of discouragement or fear, we need not condemn ourselves; instead, we can decide to persevere again, as soon as we are able. We can dust ourselves off, intensify our prayer, and simply keep going, no matter what. If the doors in your life seem shut against one of God's promises right now, keep walking. Persevere. God will open the doors at the appropriate time. You can trust Him. Let Him do it, in His way and in His time.

FEBRUARY 7 ---

"Thou knowest my downsitting and mine uprising, thou understandest my thought afar off. Thou compassest my path and my lying down, and art acquainted with all my ways." (Ps 139:2-3)

"Our God knows us and understands us, and is acquainted with all our ways. No one else in all the world understands us. Our actions are misinterpreted, it may be, and our motives misjudged. Our natural characteristics are not taken into account, nor our inherited tendencies considered. No one makes allowances for our ill health; no one realizes how much we have to contend with. But our Father knows it all. He understands us, and His judgment of us takes into account every element, conscious or unconscious, that goes to make up our character and to control our actions. Only an all-comprehending love can be just, and our God is just. No wonder Faber can say:

> There is no place where earth's sorrows
> Are more felt than up in Heaven;
> There is no place where earth's failings
> Have such kindly judgment given.

Some of you have been afraid of His justice, perhaps because you thought it would be against you. But do you not see now that it is all on your side... because 'He knoweth our frame and remembereth that we are dust?' No human judge can ever do this; and to me this comprehension of God is one of my most blessed comforts. Often I do not understand myself; all within looks confused and hopelessly tangled. But then I remember that He has searched me, and that He knows me and understands the thoughts which so perplex me, and that, therefore, I may just leave the whole miserable tangle to Him to unravel. And my soul sinks down at once, as on downy pillows, into a place of the most blissful rest."

– Hannah Whitall Smith

FEBRUARY 8 --

"...But where sin abounded, grace did much more abound: That as sin hath reigned unto death, even so might grace reign through righteousness unto eternal life by Jesus Christ our Lord." (Ro 5:20-21)

On May 10, 1748, a ship crossing the Atlantic encountered a sudden, violent storm. The captain of the ship, a jaded cynic named John Newton, was seldom affected by even the fiercest storms. But this time it was different. Waves of terrifying size rose above the bow of his ship and he found himself overtaken by feelings he had never encountered before.

There were many men on Newton's ship. His cargo, in fact, was men, for Newton's business was the transport of slaves. Newton's conscience had been dulled by his repeated participation in such a sinful business; in fact, his rebelliousness was legendary. His crew referred to him as "The Great Blasphemer." Now, as the storm raged, Newton found himself seized by an unspeakable fear. Sensing his death was imminent and overtaken with a relentless dread, Newton realized the depth of his sin and his desperate need to be cleansed and forgiven. He cried out for help in a desperate prayer to God.

Miraculously, God spared the ship and brought it through the storm. Newton, his crew and his cargo of slaves survived. From that moment on, Newton gave himself without reservation to God. He sensed that somehow, in the midst of the storm, God had remade him. Appalled by his moral corruption and the misery he had caused innocent people, he set himself to right in any way possible the wrongs he had perpetrated on humanity by his slave trafficking.

Newton left the sea and entered the Christian ministry. He spoke out whenever he could about his past sins and the evils of slavery. A man by the name of William Wilberforce was greatly moved by Newton's ministry. Wilberforce went on to play a major role in helping to abolish slavery throughout England.

Newton became well known for his work to put an end to slavery, but he is also remembered for another work. He wrote a song that has inspired generations of believers. The name of the song is "Amazing Grace."

Amazing grace! how sweet the sound,
That saved a wretch like me!
I once was lost, but now am found,
Was blind, but now I see.
Through many dangers, toils and snares,
I have already come;
'Tis grace hath brought me safe thus far,
And grace will lead me home.

Jesus only spoke the word grace once in the New Testament, but what He said summed it all up. "My grace," He said, "is sufficient for thee…" (II Co 12:9).

FEBRUARY 9 --

"And he turned to the woman, and said unto Simon, Seest thou this woman? I entered into thine house, thou gavest me no water for my feet: but she hath washed my feet with tears, and wiped them with the hairs of her head." (Lu 7:44)

The woman who washed Christ's feet with her tears was a notorious sinner. She was so notorious that Simon wondered how the Lord could even allow her to touch him. But Jesus was not concerned with her sins. He was concerned with her heart.

The way Jesus treated this woman says much about how he receives sinners. He could have shaken his finger at her and condemned her for her wrongdoing, but He didn't. He could have told her all the things that were wrong with her or how important it was to live a holy life. But He didn't. Instead, He remained silent and allowed her to come and weep at His feet.

Her tears indicated that she knew she knelt before the one Man Who was able to provide the mercy and the love she so desperately needed. She knew He had the power to wipe away the sins and the sinfulness that had devastated her life, just as she wiped with her hair the dust from His feet.

Christ's attitude toward us is the same as it was toward this woman. His wish is not to condemn us. He doesn't seek to find fault with us or accuse us. He wants to offer us pardon and carry in our behalf the burden of sin we've been carrying, so that we might no longer be bowed down by the weight of it. He wants to see us set free. He has no reproach for those who come to him with an open heart and a sincere wish to confess their sins and be made whole: "and him that cometh to me I will in no wise cast out." (Jo 6:37)

FEBRUARY 10 ---

"But we will give ourselves continually to prayer, and to the ministry of the word."
(Ac 6:4)

There is a great deal more to prayer than folding the hands, bending the knee or bowing the head. Prayer can be expressed in an almost infinite number of ways.

It can take the form of an understanding smile when we know someone has had a difficult day. It can extend the hand of friendship when we sense someone is suffering from loneliness. It can speak a few words of encouragement into a world that is all too often inundated with words of rejection and criticism.

We can also express prayer by having the willingness to talk through a problem with another person rather than becoming argumentative or entering into an angry silence. We can pray by having the strength of character to listen when someone points out a personal shortcoming we need to correct, or by extending forgiveness when someone hurts us. We can pray by speaking out for what is right, even if it means we will suffer negative consequences, or by reaching out to help another who has a need. There are many different forms our prayers may take, but we can be confident that God is aware of them all. He knows we are praying to Him when we try to live as He would wish.

Yes, prayer can wear a hundred different faces and can be practiced in almost any situation. We needn't think that prayer has to be relegated to certain times or certain locations. Almost any place can become a place of prayer. And God will hear our prayers, even if no one else does.

Lord, help me make today a day that is filled with the kind of words and behavior that You can look upon as effective prayer.

"Be careful for nothing; but in every thing by prayer and supplication with thanksgiving let your requests be made known unto God." (Ph 4:6)

Paul gives us a prescription in the above passage for what to do when we fall into worry and fear. The question is, will we do what He says?

Most of us would probably have to admit that when we find ourselves beset by worry, we are more prone to do what the world says to do than what God says to do. The world has any number of ways it uses to respond to stress and anxiety. Most of them fall into one of three categories.

The first of these is self-will. "Just be strong," it tells us. "Go out and make something happen. Get tough. Get moving. Don't let anybody shove you around."

The second way the world has of responding to worry or trouble is the way of self-pity: "You poor thing," it whispers, "it's all so unfair. What a pity you are being treated this way. What a sad situation. You'll be better off if you just hang your head and learn to live with defeat."

Then there is the third way, which is the way of escape. There are any number of ways this method can be manifested. Perhaps by the use of drugs or alcohol, gambling or pornography. Or maybe by overeating, over-spending, overworking or the obsessive pursuit of money, power or prestige. Almost any behavior can serve as a means of escape as long as it serves to divert us from the pain we feel deep inside – anything to sidetrack us from dealing with the reality of life. Yes, the world has many remedies for anxiety. The problem is, none of them work for very long.

God, on the other hand, understands our tendency to worry. He knows that because of our sinful and untrusting natures we are prone to fret. In fact, the more sensitive we become to the needs of others, and the closer we draw to God, the more we may be tempted to fret because we become more aware of life's many dangers and more sensitive to the suffering that others experience. But God has the remedy for worry. His way is completely different than the ways of the world. His way enables us to rise above our circumstances. His way is to help us reach that place where the problems of life no longer have the power to keep us in perpetual worry and fear.

"Be careful for nothing," writes Paul. He means, in this case, that we should not become full of anxiety over things. He then gives us three things we should do. He is very specific, and though many of us may think we do these things, chances are that if we lack peace we have not really done all three things in the order given. If we will do them, we will see that God is faithful. He will deliver us from worry if we will do what He says.

First, Paul tells us to worship God. Now, isn't it true that most of the time when we are fearful we are likely to rush to God with our problem and keep the focus on ourselves rather than on Him? But here, Paul tells us to do just the opposite. We are to shift our focus onto God and to force ourselves, if need be, to worship Him for all the glorious qualities of goodness and power that He possesses. Next, we are to make our requests known to Him. There is profound psychology here. Many times we keep our worries inside our heads where they rush round and round, yielding only negativity and confusion. But God tells us to come out with them. To tell him openly of our desires. Sometimes amazing things will happen when we do this. Sometimes, as we talk to God, the situation we are up against will become more clear. Sometimes He will give us a new thought, a new attitude or a new action that had not occurred to us before. He may give us greater revelation about the problem we are facing, or a deeper understanding of the issue at hand. Sometimes we may hear nothing at all from Him directly. At these times, we must trust that He has heard us, and, because we have done as He said, trust that He will be faithful to do what is best in response to our prayer.

The third and final thing Paul tells us to do is to give God thanks. Yes, even before we see the answer, we are to thank Him for it. We should also thank Him for the many other blessings and favors He has extended to us in the past, especially for our salvation. If God was willing to sacrifice Himself for us even before we knew Him, we can certainly trust that He will never leave us or forsake us now that we are His children. If we will do these three things, and continue to do them while we work through the challenges that confront us, we can be assured that we will receive the promise contained in the very next verse:

"And the peace of God, which passeth all understanding, shall keep your hearts and minds through Christ Jesus." (Ph 4:7)

FEBRUARY 12 ---

"...for I have created him for my glory, I have formed him; yea, I have made him." (Is 43:7)

God's work upon the soul is performed in much the same way as a beautiful tapestry is prepared by a workman who labors according to the Master Designer's perfect plan. The workman applies stitch after stitch into the canvas, according to the daily instructions of the master artist, who is the only one who knows how the finished work is to appear. It isn't for the workman to question why certain threads are ordered, or where the stitches will be placed. His job is to work them into the fabric, step by step.

We are like the workman, and the threads we're given to work with are the circumstances of our lives. We may wonder how in the world God can make something beautiful from our lives when so many of the threads seem to be damaged, frayed or made up of colors we would never choose. Why doesn't He repair all our imperfections? Why does He use so many dark threads when it appears to us that the lighter ones would produce something much more pleasing? We cannot know the answers to these questions now, but God knows the answers, and we can trust that His finished work in us will be perfection. Our job is to continue to work, day by day, according to the plan God sets before us.

"We have been compared to the weavers of the Gobelin tapestry, who may have to work a number of apparently drab and somber, uninteresting and common things into the pattern on the wrong side of the woof. It is only when the work is completed that they can see and admire the design that is worthy of the palace of the king! So it is with your life and mine: We work, we suffer, and see neither the end nor the fruit. But God sees it, and when He releases us from our task, He will disclose to our wondering gaze what He, the great Artist, has woven out of those toils that now seem so sterile."
-- F. B. Meyer

"It is by these stitches that God accomplishes those marvels of which we sometimes catch a glimpse now, but which will not be truly known until the great day of eternity. How good and wise are the ways of God! All that is sublime and exalted, great and admirable in the task of achieving holiness and perfection, he has kept for his own power; but everything that is small, simple and easy he leaves us to tackle with the help of grace."
-- Jean-Pierre de Caussade

There's a weaving in eternity
Upon a blessed tapestry,
From where you stand you cannot see
The beauty of its artistry,
But you can know with certainty
God's plan is forming you and me;

Someday you'll see the pattern
Of the One whose hand is sure,
And discover He has made you
Holy, joyful, lovely, pure.

FEBRUARY 13 ---

"For God sent not his Son into the world to condemn the world; but that the world through him might be saved. He that believeth on him is not condemned:..." (Jo 3:17-18)

An elderly woman who had often wrestled with doubts about God's love for her was in a state of great discouragement. She looked back at all the failures in her life, the many physical problems she had endured, the pain she had experienced as a result of growing up in an emotionally troubled family, and wondered, "Does God really care?" She had asked God for forgiveness and invited Him to be Lord of her life, but she was troubled by the fact that she could not feel His presence. Because of this lack of feeling, she seldom prayed.

One day she wondered aloud to a visitor, "Why don't I have a greater sense of God's presence? I never seem to get through to Him. How do I know He really cares about me at all?"

So many people struggle with these same questions. They rely on their feelings rather than on the fact that God hears and welcomes into His family all who call upon Him in faith. Her visitor saw the struggle and pain behind the old woman's words. She sensed a barrier existed, not on God's part – certainly not -- but on the part of her friend, who seemed to be mired in the quicksand of doubt.

"You've asked Christ into your heart, have you not?" asked her friend.

"Yes, I have. I have done so over and over."

"Oh, my dear," said her visitor, "that is a surrender God only asks you to make once. Please try to understand. He isn't holding out on you. He doesn't require you to come again and again. If you have called upon Him once and applied the faith you have, then you are His."

"But I can't feel His presence," the elderly woman objected.

Suddenly the visitor caught sight of the real problem. It was the pall of shame and unworthiness that hung over the old woman's spirit. At some point in her life she had come to believe that acceptance and love had to be earned. At some level she still believed she needed to do something more to earn entry into the kingdom of God. She was blinded on the issue of faith, believing that peace with God comes from some effort on our part, rather than as His free gift to us.

"Don't you see?" asked the friend. "What you feel is of no importance whatsoever. The truth is you are IN His family. There is nothing more you need do – nothing more you or anyone else CAN do – but accept the truth of it. Stop refusing to accept it because some particular feeling is missing. Entering into God's Kingdom has nothing to do with feelings. It has only to do with taking Him at His word. That is what faith is. That is all He asks you to do."

Suddenly the old woman's face softened. Her visitor could tell that at last the truth had gotten through. A look of peace and relief flooded into the old woman's eyes, then spread across her face. She finally recognized that the work of salvation was all God's doing, not partly His and partly hers. The only effort required of her was to accept His free gift by faith.

Over the next several weeks the old woman's entire demeanor changed. She began to speak lovingly about Christ and about her decision to leave in

His hands all the things that had previously troubled her. A greater gentleness came over her. A look of love could be seen in her eyes. A few months later, God called her to come home to Him. Her family was able to rejoice, knowing she had acquired in the last days of her life the peace she had so earnestly sought.

Dear one, if you struggle over whether you are accepted of God, remember, the work is not yours to do. It is His. If you have sincerely asked Jesus to be your Savior, then rest assured you are His. Leave your feelings and your circumstances in His hands. Leave everything to Him and rest in His unlimited Love.

FEBRUARY 14 --

"There was in the days of Herod, the king of Judaea, a certain priest named Zacharias, of the course of Abia: and his wife was of the daughters of Aaron, and her name was Elisabeth. And they were both righteous before God, walking in all the commandments and ordinances of the Lord blameless." (Lu 1:5-6)

"Of course, this does not mean that they [Zacharias and Elisabeth] were absolutely faultless, but that their lives were so beautiful, so sincere and faithful, that God saw nothing in them to blame or rebuke. This is very beautifully illustrated in one of Mrs. Herrick Johnson's tender little poems [see below]. A mother is sitting at her work, her mind perplexed as she thinks of her poor, faulty life. She had longed to serve the Master, and had tried to do so; but it seemed to her that she had utterly failed. Just then she turned the garment she was mending, and her eye rested on an odd little bundle of mending and patchwork done by some other hand. Her heart grew tender as the truth flashed over her. Her little daughter had wanted to help her. To be sure, she had made a botch of it; but the mother knew it was the best she could do, and she felt a strange yearning for her child. Then a voice whispered, 'Art thou tenderer for the little child than I am tender for thee?' She understood it all in a flash, and her perplexed faith brightened into peace."   --J. R. Miller

> For I thought, when the Master Builder
> Comes down his temple to view,
> To see what rents must be mended,
> And what must be built anew,
>
> Perhaps, as he looks o'er the building,
> He will bring my poor work to the light,
> And seeing the marring and bungling,
> And how far it all is from right,

He will feel as I felt for my darling,
And say as I said about her:
Dear child! she wanted to help me,
Her love for me was the spur;

And for the true love that is in it,
The work shall seem perfect as mine;
And because it was willing service,
I will crown it with plaudits divine.
                              -- Mrs. Herrick Johnson

FEBRUARY 15 --

"My times are in thy hand;" (Ps 31:15)

"We live in a world of mysteries. They meet our eye, awaken our inquiry, and baffle our investigation at every step. Nature is a vast arcade of mysteries. Science is a mystery, truth is a mystery, religion is a mystery, our existence is a mystery, the future of our being is a mystery. And God, who alone can explain all mysteries, is the greatest mystery of all. . . .

Remembering the past, you are, perhaps, ready to say: 'Could I but have foreseen, I would have arranged things better. Had I anticipated the result of such a step, or have known the outcome of such a movement, or have safely calculated the consequences of such a measure, I might have pursued an opposite course, and have averted the evil I now deplore, and have spared myself the misery I now feel.' But hush this vain reasoning! God, your God, dear believer, had in wisdom, faithfulness, and love, hidden all the future from your view. 'You shall remember all the way which the Lord your God has led you these forty years.' How has he guided, counseled, and upheld you? He has led you by a right way. In perplexity he has directed you. In sorrow he has comforted you. In slippery paths his mercy has held you up, and when fallen he has raised you again. From seeming evil he has produced good. The mistakes you have made and the follies you have committed in the blindness of your path, and in the sinfulness of your heart, have led you to a closer acquaintance with and to a stronger confidence in God. They have opened up to you new and more glorious views of his character, led you closer to the feet of Jesus in self-knowledge and self abhorrence, and have unlocked to you springs of spiritual blessings -- fresh, sanctifying, and, unspeakable.

Beloved, God has placed us in a school in which he is teaching us to lay our blind reason at his feet, to cease from our own wisdom and guidance and lean upon and confide in him, as children with a parent. The goodness of God to us, combined with a jealous regard to his own glory, constrains him to conceal the path along which he conducts us. His promise is, 'I will bring the blind by a way that they knew not; I will lead them in paths that they have not known. I will make darkness light before them, and crooked things straight. These things will I do unto them, and not forsake them.'"

-- Octavius Winslow

FEBRUARY 16 --

"In thy name shall they rejoice all the day: and in thy righteousness shall they be exalted." (Ps 89:16)

If there is one thing in life you can depend on it is that the unexpected is going to happen. We can all testify to this fact. We get ourselves all set to have things go a certain way, and then, without warning, everything gets undone.

We want our lives to be successful and productive, and they are plagued with failures and setbacks. We want to see our loved ones happy, and discover their lives, like ours, are fraught with challenges. We want to experience joy and peace, and instead find trouble and upheaval at every turn.

Saint Teresa once wrote that she asked God why He brought so many trials into her life. His response was to tell her: "I give my heaviest crosses to my best friends."

"No wonder," she replied, "that You have so few friends."

Times of upheaval and trial are often the means God uses to reveal to us how much we need Him. It is often in the midst of our difficulties that God imparts His most significant graces into our lives. When we are hurting, we frequently become more willing to reach out to Him and thereby discover His power and wisdom. When we have to walk through trials we learn to trust in Him instead of ourselves. When suffering comes we learn how to resist our initial tendency to pull away from God or dispute with Him, and discover how to humble ourselves enough to lean on Him. As we grow through these times, we learn to stop asking, "Why me, Lord?" and begin to ask, "Lord, what do You wish to reveal to me in the midst of this challenge?"

FEBRUARY 17 --

"And Moses made a serpent of brass, and put it upon a pole, and it came to pass, that if a serpent had bitten any man, when he beheld the serpent of brass, he lived." (Nu 21:9)

We sometimes hear that real faith is "believing" for something to happen, as though we are undergoing a test which requires us to try to get some blessing out of God by focusing on that blessing as hard as we can. But faith, as defined by some of the great saints, is not so much looking for the blessing as looking to the One Who blesses. God wants to impart blessings into our lives, but He wants us to learn to pursue Him, not the blessings He has to offer.

A beautiful picture of faith is given in the book of Numbers. The children of Israel, under the leadership of Moses, journeyed from Mount Hor by way of the Red Sea, and because the way was hard they became discouraged and began to murmur against God. Fiery serpents appeared in the camp and bit many of the people; a significant number died. The people cried out to Moses, acknowledged their sin and asked Him to go to God in their behalf. Moses prayed for them and God instructed him to construct a serpent and place it upon a pole so that all who had been bitten would be able to see it. He told Moses that all who would gaze upon the serpent and believe would receive healing. Moses did as he was told. He had a serpent made out of brass, placed it upon a pole and circulated it throughout the camp. Those who were ill didn't even have to rise up to touch the serpent as it was circulated; all they had to do was look upon it and they were healed.

Over 400 years ago Nicholas of Cusa wrote about the unspeakable comfort of knowing that God's care for him was constant and all-enveloping:

"When all my endeavor is turned toward You, because all Your endeavor is turned toward me; when I look unto You alone with all my attention, and do not turn aside the eyes of my mind because You enfold me with Your constant regard; when I direct my love toward You alone because You, who art Love's very self, have turned Yourself toward me alone. And what, Lord, is my life, save that embrace wherein Your delightful sweetness so lovingly enfolds me?"

As with the serpent of brass, it is when we turn our gaze upon the Lord, and recognize that this act alone is enough to reach Him, that we become able to enter into a deeper understanding of faith.

FEBRUARY 18 --

"He shall choose our inheritance for us, the excellency of Jacob whom he loved. Selah." (Ps 47:4)

"A ship of large tonnage is to be brought up the river. Now, in one part of the stream there is a sand-bank. Should someone ask, 'Why does the captain steer through the deep part of the channel, and deviate so much from a straight line?' his answer would be, 'Because I should not get my vessel into harbor at all if I did not keep to the deep channel.' So, it may be, you would run aground and suffer shipwreck if your divine Captain did not steer you into the depths of affliction, where waves of trouble follow each other in quick succession.

Some plants die if they have too much sunshine. It may be that you are planted where you get but little; you are put there by the loving Husbandman, because only in that situation will you bring forth fruit unto perfection.

Remember this: had any other condition been better for you than the one in which you are, divine love would have put you there. You are placed by God in the most suitable circumstances, and if you had the choosing of your lot, you would soon cry, 'Lord, choose my inheritance for me, for by my self-will I am pierced through with many sorrows.' Be content with such things as you have, since the Lord has ordered all things for your good. Take up your own daily cross; it is the burden best suited for your shoulder, and will prove most effective to make you perfect in every good word and work to the glory of God. It is not for your busy self and proud impatience to choose, but for the Lord of Love!

> Trials must and will befall —
> But with humble faith to see
> Love inscribed upon them all,
> This is happiness to me."
> – Charles Spurgeon

FEBRUARY 19 --

"And was transfigured before them: and his face did shine as the sun, and his raiment was white as the light." (Ma 17:2)

If we take the time to study the cycle of nature – first life, then death, then the passage through death to life again, it reveals to us the mystery of metamorphosis as a way of passage into a higher form of life.

When we were in school we probably learned about metamorphosis. It was the process whereby an insect became a pupa, and a tadpole changed into a frog. Even though it is a great mystery, this process goes on all around us every day. It is the process whereby life seemingly comes to an end, but, after an appointed time, something miraculous happens. What apparently was life's end becomes the starting point for a new life, a higher life, a life with greater possibilities than anyone could have imagined.

Peter, James and John had the chance to see this transformation process for themselves. When they went with Jesus one day to a high mountain they saw Him transfigured before their eyes; the actual Greek word for what happened is "metamorphose," which means "to be transformed or changed." For those few moments they saw through the veil and observed the form Christ's body would have in eternity. As believers we will also go through this metamorphosis process. We will enter into what looks from the outside like death -- like a caterpillar entering into its cocoon -- but we will emerge, on the other side, into new life. Like Christ, we will be changed into something more wonderful than words can tell.

> He may lead us to the depths,
> And plant our spirits there,
> But He will raise us to Himself,
> Set free from sorrow, death, despair.

FEBRUARY 20 --

"Thou shalt guide me with thy counsel, and afterward receive me to glory." (Ps 73:24)

"The whole question of vocation is intimately connected with prayer; and many an aspiring soul finds prayer a weariness, if not a torture, simply because he lacks the courage to face the question as to whether his daily work is in a line with his true vocation. 'The trivial round, the common task,' will not in itself 'furnish all we ought to ask.' If mending shoes runs counter to God's will for us, it will prove as inimical to our spiritual life as the most ambitious self-chosen career. Self-will, or sheer spineless drifting with the tide, is every bit as wrong in the cottage as it is in the palace, and to remain in the kitchen from sheer laziness and cowardice is as reprehensible as to usurp the throne out of motives of greed and ambition.

It all runs back to the question that lies at the root of the spiritual life: Is the central element in our communion with God an act of self-surrender, or is it, on the contrary, a demand of self-love? Is the symbol of our prayer the open hand, or the open heart? Are we using God as a means of self-realization, or are we offering ourselves as a means of glorifying him? And if we mean self-surrender, has our offering been made in an honest, generous spirit, unconditionally and without reservations? Have we interpreted it emotionally, or are we seeking to work it out in the affairs of daily life?" – Brigid Herman

"The mark of a saint is not perfection, but consecration. A saint is not a man without faults, but a man who has given himself without reserve to God." – Bishop Westcott

"I have very often said unto you, and now again I say the same: Forsake yourself, resign yourself, and you shall enjoy great inward peace. Give all for all; ask for nothing; require back nothing; abide purely and unhesitatingly in me, and you shall possess me; you shall be free in heart, and darkness shall not tread you down. Let this be your endeavor, your prayer, your desire: that you may be stripped of selfishness, and follow Jesus; may die to yourself, and live eternally to Me." – Thomas a' Kempis

Though Christ a thousand times
In Bethlehem be born,
If he's not born in thee
Thy soul is still forlorn
                        – Angelus Silesius

FEBRUARY 21 --

"Put on therefore, as the elect of God, holy and beloved, bowels of mercies, kindness, humbleness of mind, meekness, longsuffering;" (Col. 3:12)

"Someone has said that the most spiritual people are the easiest to get along with. When one has a little of the Holy Spirit it is like 'a little learning, a dangerous thing.' But a full baptism of the Holy Spirit and a really disciplined, established and tested spiritual life makes one simple, tender, tolerant, considerate and childlike.

James and John, in their early zeal, wanted to call down fire from heaven on the Samaritans. But John, when elderly, allowed Demetrius to exclude him from the church, and, with the patience of Jesus, suffered on Patmos for the kingdom. And the aging Paul was willing to take back even Mark, whom he had refused as a companion in his early ministry, and to acknowledge that he was profitable to him for the ministry." – A. B. Simpson

FEBRUARY 22 --

"The fool hath said in his heart, There is no God. They are corrupt, they have done abominable works, there is none that doeth good." (Ps 14:1)

The renowned scientist and mathematician Blaise Pascal was a keen observer of man's penchant for escaping reality. He once observed:

"Since men are unable to cure death, misery or ignorance, they imagine they can find happiness by not thinking about such things."

Pascal, however, was determined to try to get men to think about reality, especially about the reality of their need for God, and how pride keeps them from facing it. In his famous work, *Pensees*, he wrote:

"It is the nature of self-esteem and of the human self to love only oneself and to consider oneself alone. But what can a man do? He wants to be great and finds that he is small; he wants to be happy and finds that he is unhappy; he wants to be perfect and finds that he is riddled with imperfections; he wants to be the object of men's affection and esteem and sees that his faults deserve only their dislike and contempt. The embarrassing position in which he finds himself produces in him the most unjust and criminal passion that can possibly be imagined; he conceives a mortal hatred of the truth which brings him down to earth and convinces him of his faults. He would like to

45

be able to annihilate it, and, not being able to destroy it in himself, he destroys it in the minds of other people. That is to say, he concentrates all his efforts on concealing his faults both from others and from himself, and cannot stand being made to see them or their being seen by other people.... Jesus Christ did nothing but teach men that they only loved themselves, that they were slaves, blind, sick, unhappy and sinful; that he had come to deliver them, bring them light, sanctify and heal them."

FEBRUARY 23 --

"Cast thy burden upon the Lord, and he shall sustain thee: he shall never suffer the righteous to be moved." (Ps 55:22)

"The greatest burden we have to carry in life is self. The most difficult thing we have to manage is self. Our own daily living, our...feelings, our special weaknesses and temptations, and our peculiar temperaments, our inward affairs of every kind, these are the things that perplex and worry us more than anything else, and that bring us most often into bondage and darkness. In laying off your burdens, therefore, the first one you must get rid of is yourself. You must hand yourself and all your inward experiences, your temptations, your temperament, your feelings, all over into the care and keeping of your God, and leave them there. He made you, and therefore He understands you and knows how to manage you, and you must trust Him to do it.

Say to him, 'Here, Lord, I abandon myself to You. I have tried in every way I could think of to manage myself, and to make myself what I know I ought to be, but have always failed. Now I give it up to You. Take entire possession of me. Work in me all the good pleasure of Thy will. Mold and fashion me into such a vessel as seems good to You. I leave myself in Your hands, and I believe You will, according to Your promise, make me into a vessel unto Your honor, sanctified, and meet for the Master's use, and prepared unto every good work.' And here you must rest, trusting yourself to Him continually and absolutely."   – Hannah Whitall Smith

FEBRUARY 24 --

"I will say of the LORD, He is my refuge and my fortress: my God; in him will I trust." (Ps. 91:2)

Are you facing a storm today? Have circumstances brought dark clouds into your life? Are difficulties washing over you like the waves of an angry sea, so that you fear you may not be able to stay afloat?

Dear One, hold onto God's promise: "The righteous cry, and the Lord heareth, and delivereth them out of all their troubles" (Ps. 34:17). It is a promise that supersedes every difficulty. No matter what is happening in the natural realm, this promise guarantees that God will see you through. Do not listen to your circumstances. Listen instead to the promises of God.

Is the enemy whispering that God has forgotten you? Do you feel you are all alone, that you will have to handle that difficult situation all by yourself? Then hold onto this promise: "Thou art my hiding place; thou shalt preserve me from trouble; thou shalt compass me about with songs of deliverance..." (Ps. 32:7) Don't listen to what your fear has to say. Listen, instead, to the promises of God.

Whatever storm clouds have gathered over your life today, there is a Place of Refuge. Whether the winds and rain be comprised of trials, of fears, of regrets or temptations, of doubts or brokenness, the storm need not enter into your soul. You can instead invite the promises of God to come inside of you. You may rest in them until the storm is past. And while the storm rages, you can recall what God has already done for you in the past, what miracles He has already performed when you needed His help.

Your deliverance will come again. Until then, hang on to the promise: "He shall cover thee with his feathers, and under his wings shalt thou trust: his truth shall be thy shield and buckler." (Ps. 91:4)

FEBRUARY 25 --

"Therefore the redeemed of the LORD shall return, and come with singing unto Zion; and everlasting joy shall be upon their head: they shall obtain gladness and joy; and sorrow and mourning shall flee away." (Is 51:11)

In heaven the angels, cherubim and seraphim will sing of God's glory, but only those songs sung by man will have the unique tones characteristic of those who have experienced the redeeming grace of God.

Only man will be able to express what it was like to come to the precipice of hopelessness and despair and almost miss the unutterable blessing of eternal life. Only man will be able to tell about the sacred privilege of being saved by Christ from the ravages of sin and rebellion. His songs alone will be able to describe the grace that transformed him from a lost sinner into a redeemed and eternal child of God.

Think of how glorious the songs of the redeemed will be. They will express the joy of how wonderful it feels to have every sadness, fear and grief removed; of finally having shame and mourning taken away, of realizing we shall ever be with our loving Lord. We cannot sing these songs as yet. We have not been fitted with our heavenly, eternal voices, but one day we will. And then, what a glorious day it will be. We will sing of all the blessings God has bestowed upon us, and we shall have no less than all of eternity in which to give full expression to our joy.

The Lord lives and I'm redeemed
From all the adversary's schemes,
Redeemed from darkness, given Light,
Given power, given might,
Able to endure each trial,
In His presence all the while,
Taking all as from His hand,
Though I may not understand;

I know Christ will meet my need,
In His wisdom I'll succeed,
At His feet I'll place my fears,
In His shadow cry my tears;
Knowing soon the door will open,
Every dream will rise unbroken,
Every winter storm will end,
So that spring may come again;

Christ, my Spring, will soon be here,
Even now my heart is cheered,
Lord, I place my trust in You,
I know You will see me through.

FEBRUARY 26 --

"And the servant of the Lord must not strive; but be gentle unto all men, apt to teach, patient," (II Ti 2:24)

There is a great misconception in the world today about gentleness Many people believe that to be gentle is to be weak. They couldn't be more wrong. Few things take more strength and maturity than the character trait of gentleness.

Jesus had the greatest spiritual strength of any man who ever lived, but he exhibited great gentleness, especially toward those who were weak. He also exhibited gentleness toward those who sought to destroy Him. He wasn't gentle because He was intimidated or overwhelmed by His enemies. He was gentle because He was obedient to His Father's will, and this was the way His Father wanted Him to respond. It was His Father's will that Christ turn the other cheek rather than strike out against those who opposed Him. It was His Father's will that He exercise self-restraint and meekness in the midst of persecution.

Many men and women who have had great strength of character have also been gentle.

Abraham Lincoln was known for his gentleness toward people, even toward those who sought to undermine him during the treacherous days of the Civil War, yet he was a strong and powerful leader during the conflict and made many decisions that were unpopular. He stayed calm in the midst of opposition and criticism in order to be able to keep firm control as President and do what he thought was right.

Mother Teresa was famous throughout the world for her kindness, but she was also a woman with great strength of character. She would gladly speak to anyone who wished to talk to her, but as soon as she was finished she quickly returned to her duties and her prayers. She was not afraid to turn down invitations when she felt they did not further her work. Instead, she kept her focus on how she could help those entrusted to her care, no matter how many times she encountered difficulties and roadblocks along the way.

God's Word teaches us that we are to crucify the flesh and seek to become people who exhibit gentleness. We need to fight the tendency within us to lash out, respond with harshness or become rebellious when we face opposition. We need to pursue the trait of gentleness. As we do, we can trust that God will respond by giving us more of this precious fruit of the Spirit. The fruit of gentleness in our lives will be proof, not of our weakness, but of our increasing strength in the Lord.

FEBRUARY 27 ---

"When Jesus had lifted up himself, and saw none but the woman, he said unto her, Woman, where are those thine accusers? hath no man condemned thee? She said, No man, Lord. And Jesus said unto her, Neither do I condemn thee: go, and sin no more." (Jo 8:10-11)

"It is one thing that can be said of Christ, though it cannot be said of all His disciples: He was not censorious. How He kept silence is remarkable. How often His disciples did inconsistent, stupid things through ignorance, and the worst that Christ said to them was, 'O ye of little faith.' Sometimes He did not speak at all, but only by a sigh showed that He was vexed.

We don't do much good by speaking too much about the faults of others. If we could learn Christ's solemn way of speaking a little, we would be much more likely to reach our end. He never talked to others about the faults of His disciples, and, when others tried to find fault with them, He was very quick to defend them. When they were blamed for plucking the ears of corn, He interposed and gave a defense for them. When they were blamed for not fasting, He gave good reasons why they should not. When 'they all forsook Him and fled,' He was not offended in them. We never read of His upbraiding them. When Peter denied Him did He utter a word of reproach? He only gave Him a look that was silent, but how it touched Peter's soul!

When He said to Him by the Sea of Galilee three times, 'Lovest thou Me?' there was evidently an allusion to his thrice-repeated denial. Doubtless Peter longed to have Him speak of it, that he might have the opportunity of confessing his sin and being forgiven. But Christ never said more about it than that. When He speaks about His disciples in the seventeenth of John, you would think these men were faultless! He says they have kept His word, they have believed on Him, they are not of the world, even as He is not. He never speaks of their failures, He just speaks of their faith.

Oh believer, what a Savior you have! How He will hide all your sins, and speak only of your faith to the Father. It is not that He does not see wherein you fail, but it is just His exceeding loving-kindness. The very height of this is seen in His dealings with the beloved John. Never man had a sorer heart than John when he came back and stood at the Cross for some hours before his Master died. John, who used to lay his head on Christ's bosom, had forsaken Him and fled! But Christ has not a word of rebuke for him. He looks upon him, and before the end comes He says to him, 'There is My mother; she is your mother now. Take her home with you. I forgive you; I can trust you, John.' Such is grace. If it were not that we know all this, I don't know how we could take our places in glory before the throne. Our worst sin will be completely gone, and no holy angel will be more welcome than we will be!"   -- Andrew Bonar

FEBRUARY 28 --

"But many that are first shall be last; and the last first." (Mk 10-31)

The Parable of the Trees

Once there were three trees. Each one wanted more than anything to be put to some meaningful use in life.

The first was a cedar tree. His dream was to be selected by some skilled craftsman who would appreciate the beautiful grain of his wood and fashion him into a treasure chest. Then, he reasoned, he could become the repository of some important person's most precious possessions.

The second tree was an oak. He wanted to grow so straight and strong that he would be selected for use in a fine sailing vessel. He could see himself upon the high seas, mounting the crests of powerful waves and transporting precious cargo to ports all over the world.

The third tree was a pine. Though his wood was too soft to endure great stress, he hoped his branches would be fragrant and pleasing enough to reflect, in some small way, the glory of God.

All of the trees' hopes, however, were dashed.

The cedar tree was purchased by a farmer, not a craftsman. He had the tree cut up and fashioned into a simple trough that he placed in his barn, where it held nothing but feed for his livestock.

The oak fared little better. He was felled and sold to a fisherman who made him into a little boat. Day after day, gliding over the waters of an inland lake, he mourned that he had become something so ordinary.

The pine tree had the worst experience of all. His life was cut short by a bolt of lightning that felled him during a terrible storm. He was hauled away and dumped in a scrap heap where he lay, forgotten, for many years. Why, he wondered, couldn't he have served his God in some meaningful way?

Then things began to change.

One night the cedar-trough was dragged out of the stall he normally occupied, placed in a quiet corner of the stable and filled with clean straw. A stranger came and laid a newborn baby upon it. Others came soon after, dressed in fine robes. They knelt before the little trough and worshiped the tiny child.

Some years later, several men came to where the little oak-boat was moored. They untied him from his moorings and rowed him a little ways off shore. One of the men rose and spoke to a large crowd of people that had gathered at the water's edge. "There," cried someone in the crowd, pointing toward the little boat, "that man there, on the boat, that's Jesus."

Not long after this, at the scrap heap, several men searched through the pieces of wood until they came across the discarded pine. They hauled him out, cut off a piece near one end and lashed the two pieces together to form a cross. They took him into the city, shoved him into the arms of a blood-stained man and made the man carry the cross to a hill. There, they nailed the man to a cross and crucified him. The pine tree held Him as he suffered, saw the agony upon His face, felt the man's blood as it flowed to the ground and watched as He gave up His Spirit to God.

In this manner, the trees did indeed receive the desires of their hearts. The cedar tree, in the form of a manger, was fashioned to hold the greatest treasure the earth has ever known. The boat made of oak was chosen to transport the most holy and important passenger of all time. The pine tree, once discarded, became the symbol that will stand forever as a sacred monument to the love of God. All three saw their initial hopes dashed. And all three had to suffer through times of disappointment, obscurity and trial before they became fit for use by their Lord. But eventually, they all received their hearts' desires – in ways more glorious than anything they could have ever imagined.

FEBRUARY 29 --

"Behold, God is my salvation; I will trust, and not be afraid: for the LORD JEHOVAH is my strength and my song; he also is become my salvation." (Is 12:2)

"It is by an act of simple, prayerful faith that we transfer our cares and anxieties, our sorrows and needs, to the Lord. Jesus invites you come and lean upon Him, to lean with all your might upon that arm that balances the universe, upon the One that was pierced by the soldier's spear. But you doubt, and ask, 'Is the Lord able to do this thing for me?' And so, while you are debating a matter about which there is not the shadow of a doubt, the burden is crushing your gentle spirit to the dust. And all the while Jesus stands at your side and lovingly says, 'Cast your burden upon Me and I will sustain you. I am God Almighty. I bore the load of your sin and condemnation up the Mount of Calvary, and the same power of omnipotence, and the same strength of love that bore it all for you then, is prepared to bear your need and sorrow now. Roll it all upon Me. Lean hard. Let Me feel the pressure of your care. I know your burden, child. I shaped it. I formed it in My own hand and made no proportion of its weight to your unaided strength. For even as I laid it on, I said I shall be near, and while she leans on Me, this burden shall be Mine, not hers. So shall I keep My child within the encircling arms of My own love. Here, lay it down. Do not fear to impose it on a shoulder which upholds the government of worlds. Come closer. You are not near enough. I would embrace your burden. You love Me. I know it. Don't doubt, but, loving Me, lean hard!'"

-- Octavius Winslow

MARCH 1 --

"...for every one that exalteth himself shall be abased; and he that humbleth himself shall be exalted." (Lu 18:14)

"[The disciples had a] fervent attachment to Jesus. They had forsaken all for him. The Father had revealed to them that he was the Christ of God. They believed in him, they loved him, they obeyed his commandments. They had forsaken all to follow him. When others went back, they clung to him. They were ready to die with him. But deeper down than all this there was a dark power, of the existence and the hideousness of which they were hardly conscious, which had to be slain and cast out before they could be the witnesses of the power of Jesus to save. It is even so still. We may find professors and ministers, evangelists and workers, missionaries and teachers, in whom the gifts of the Spirit are many and manifest, and who are the channels of blessing to multitudes, but of whom, when the testing time comes, or closer contact gives fuller knowledge, it is only too painfully clear that the grace of humility as an abiding characteristic is scarce to be seen. All experience tends to confirm the lesson that humility is one of the chief and highest graces and one of the most difficult to attain; it is one to which our foremost efforts ought to be directed and one that only comes in power when the fullness of the Spirit makes us partakers of the indwelling Christ, and He lives with us.... Let us consider deeply how far the disciples were advanced while this grace was still so terribly lacking, and let us pray to God that other gifts may not so satisfy us, that we never grasp the fact that the absence of this grace is the secret cause of why the power of God cannot do its mighty work. It is only where we, like the Son, truly know and show that we can do nothing of ourselves, that God will do all."   -- Andrew Murray

MARCH 2 ---

"But I keep under my body, and bring it into subjection: lest that by any means, when I have preached to others, I myself should be a castaway." (I Cor 9:27)

Saint Francis of Assisi was fond of addressing others, including the animals he so loved, as "brother" or "sister." He often referred to his body as "Brother Ass," and insisted upon the necessity of buffeting it so that its appetites would not be allowed to assume a position of control over his life. Today, "Brother Ass" causes a lot of trouble for many of us. In some cases, his appetites are so out of control that we try to medicate him with over-eating, over-drinking or over-working, all of which may result in drastic consequences for our health. On the other hand, we may try to control him so rigidly that we succumb to negative behaviors like anorexia or compulsive exercising. Either way, it never works very well when we try to heal our emotional wounds with behaviors that harm our bodies. The Bible teaches us that we need to keep our appetites under subjection. If our appetite problems are minor, we can often bring things into better alignment by making minor adjustments in how we treat our bodies. If they are severe, we may need to ask for help from a person or a group that has been able to gain victory over that same problem. There is no shame in admitting we need help in bringing our behaviors under control. The only shame is in not doing something to get the help we need.

"Brother Ass is entirely in the ascendant just now. Everyone is considering the body and how it ought to be dieted and how exercised, and the doctor is a far greater autocrat than the priest ever was; so that to seek for pleasures and rewards that are not physical is not popular. The modern man diets to get uric acid out of his system, the monk of old dieted in order to get strength into his soul; the modern woman gets up early, not in order to seek the Holy Spirit by prayer, but to do breathing exercises to give capacity to her lungs. And the quaintest thing to the looker-on at these ridiculous rites is that their devotees are so weak and so miserable; whereas, when Brother Ass is treated to a little wholesome neglect, he generally becomes a contented and obedient animal."   – Honnor Morten

"I am the door: by me if any man enter in, he shall be saved, and shall go in and out, and find pasture." (Jo 10:9)

"Christ is both the way and the door. Christ is the staircase and the vehicle, like the throne of mercy over the Ark of the Covenant, and the mystery hidden from the ages. A man should turn his full attention to this throne of mercy, and should gaze at him hanging on the cross, full of faith, hope and charity, devoted, full of wonder and joy, marked by gratitude, and open to praise and jubilation. Then such a man will make with Christ a 'pasch,' that is, a 'passing-over.' Through the branches of the cross he will pass over the Red Sea, leave Egypt and enter the desert. There he will taste the hidden manna, and rest with Christ in the sepulcher, as if he were dead to things outside. He will experience, as much as is possible for one who is still living, what was promised to the thief who hung beside Christ: Today you will be with me in paradise." – Saint Bonaventure

"Many who hear the word of Christ do not understand it, because they will not. But we shall find one scripture expounding another, and the blessed Spirit making known the blessed Jesus. Christ is the Door. And what greater security has the church of God than that the Lord Jesus is between it and all its enemies? He is a door open for passage and communication. Here are plain directions how to come into the fold; we must come in by Jesus Christ as the Door. By faith in him as the great Mediator between God and man. Also, we have precious promises to those that observe this direction. Christ exhibits all the care for his church, and every believer, which a good shepherd has for his flock; and he expects the church, and every believer, to wait upon him, and to stay in his pasture." --Matthew Henry

"Now He that raised Him from the dead will raise us also; if we do His will and walk in His commandments and love the things which He loved, abstaining from all unrighteousness, covetousness, love of money, evil speaking, false witness; not rendering evil for evil or railing for railing or blow for blow or cursing for cursing; but remembering the words which the Lord spake, as He taught; Judge not that ye be not judged. Forgive, and it shall be forgiven to you. Have mercy that ye may receive mercy. With what measure ye mete, it shall be measured to you again; and again, Blessed are the poor and they that are persecuted for righteousness' sake, for theirs is the kingdom of God." -- Polycarp

"Finally, brethren, whatsoever things are true, whatsoever things are honest, whatsoever things are just, whatsoever things are pure, whatsoever things are lovely, whatsoever things are of good report; if there be any virtue, and if there be any praise, think on these things." (Ph 4:8)

Some mornings, upon awakening, we may find we have company. There, on the bedpost, we may discover an Old Crow by the name of "Worry." There he sits, waiting for us to open our eyes so that he can start chattering away in the hopes of getting us to feel upset before our feet even hit the floor. He is a patient old bird. His fondest wish is to get us to think about all the things in our lives that aren't going right.

The Old Crow has any number of tricks tucked up his feathers. He is always ready to whisper doubting words in our ear, or ask us why we should have faith when God doesn't seem to be helping us very much. He also likes to interrupt our prayers, delay our praise and diminish our worship. He is always conniving to rob us of our hope and our joy.

The only effective way to shoo off the Old Crow is to confront him with action.

For instance, we can pray first thing in the morning, before he starts chattering away. We can stay in the now as much as possible, refusing to fret about the things of the past or look with fear into the future. God's grace, after all, is not for yesterday or tomorrow. It is for today. If there is something in the past that requires some kind of action, such as making amends or resolving a problem that still bothers us, we can take care of it. Otherwise, we need to trust the past to God's care and get on with our lives. If there are problems on the horizon of tomorrow, we can remember God's grace will be there to help us handle them when we get there. And we can remember an old adage: "Eighty percent of whatever you worry about isn't going to happen anyway."

One more thing: we can count our blessings. God has been faithful to us in the past. Surely He will be so again. He will provide all we need, and more.

These are a few of the ways we can prevent the Old Crow from getting the upper hand today.

Wherever He may guide me, no want shall turn me back.
My Shepherd is beside me, and nothing can I lack.
His wisdom ever waking, His sight is never dim.
He knows the way He's taking, and I will walk with Him
                       -- Anna Waring

"For to me to live is Christ, and to die is gain." (Ph 1:21)

"I had always known that Christ was my Saviour, but I had looked upon Him as an external Saviour, one who did a saving work for me from outside, as it were; one who was ready to come close alongside and stay by me, helping me in all that I needed, giving me power and strength and salvation. But now I know something better than that. At last I realized that Jesus Christ was actually and literally within me; and even more than that, He had constituted Himself my very life, taking me into union with Himself – my body, mind, and spirit – while I still had my own identity and free will and full moral responsibility.

Wasn't this better than having Him as a helper, or even than having Him as an external Saviour; to have Him, Jesus Christ, the Son of God, as my very own life? It meant that I need never again ask Him to help me as though He were one and I another, but rather, simply to do His work, His will, in me, and with me, and through me. My body was His, my mind His, my will His, my spirit His; and not merely His, but literally part of His. What He asked me to recognize was: 'I have been crucified with Christ and it is no longer I that live, but Christ that liveth in me.' Jesus Christ had constituted Himself my life; not as a figure of speech, remember, but as a literal, actual fact, as literal as the fact that a certain tree has been made into this desk on which my hand rests. For 'your bodies are members of Christ,' and 'ye are the body of Christ.'

Do you wonder that Paul could say with tingling joy and exultation, 'to me to live is Christ?' He did not say, as I had mistakenly been supposing, 'To me to live is to be Christ-like,' nor, 'to me to live is to have Christ's help,' nor, 'To me to live is to serve Christ.' No, he plunged through and beyond all that in the bold, glorious, mysterious claim: 'To me to live is Christ!'"

--Charles G. Trumbull

"But God hath chosen the foolish things of the world to confound the wise; and God hath chosen the weak things of the world to confound the things which are mighty;" (I Cor 1:27)

"Of ourselves we may have but little weight, no particular talents or position, or anything else to put onto the scale; but let us remember that again and again God has shown that the influence of a very average life, when once really consecrated to Him, may outweigh that of almost any number of merely professing Christians. Such lives are like Gideon's three hundred, carrying not even the ordinary weapons of war but only trumpets and lamps and empty pitchers, by whom the Lord wrought great deliverance, while He did not use the others at all. For He has chosen the weak things of the world to confound the things which are mighty.

Should not all this be an additional motive for desiring that our whole selves should be taken and kept?

I know that whatsoever God does, it shall be forever. The Lord is our Keeper, and He is the almighty and the everlasting God, with whom is no variableness, neither shadow of turning. He will never change His mind about keeping us, and no man is able to pluck us out of His hand, for He says, 'You shall stay with me for many days.' And He that keeps us will not slumber. Once having undertaken His vineyard, He will keep it night and day till all the days and nights are over and we know the full meaning of the salvation ready to be revealed in the last time, unto which we are kept by His power.

And then, forever for Him! Passing from the gracious keeping by faith for this little while to the glorious keeping in His presence for all eternity. Forever fulfilling the object for which He formed us and chose us, we showing forth His praise, and He showing the exceeding riches of His grace in His kindness toward us in the ages to come. He for us, and we for Him, forever. Oh, how little we can grasp this. Yet this is the fruition of being 'kept for Jesus.'"   – Frances Ridley Havergal

MARCH 7 --

"For even Christ pleased not himself..." (Ro 15:3)

"Let this be a day of self-forgetting ministry for Christ and others. Let us not once think of being ministered unto, but rather say with Him: 'I am among you as he that serveth' (Lu 22:27). Let us not drag our burdens through the day but drop all our loads of care and be free to carry His yoke and His burden. Let us make the happy exchange, relinquishing ours and taking His. Let the covenant be: 'Thou shalt abide for me ... so will I also be for thee' (Ho 3:3).

In such abiding we lose our heaviest load -- ourselves -- and find our highest joy, divine love, 'more blessed to give than to receive' (Ac 20:35). Let us do good to all men as we have opportunity. Let us lose no occasion of blessing, and let us look for ingenious ways of service and usefulness. Especially let us seek to win others to Christ."   – A. B. Simpson

"How easily and contentedly we speak of Jesus Christ as our example. Do we realize what it means? If we did, it would revolutionize our life. Do we begin to know our Bible as He did? Do we begin to pray as He did? How thoughtful He was for others, how patient toward dullness, how quiet under insult! Think of what it meant for Him to take a basin and towel like a slave and wash the disciples' feet. Do we stoop to serve? Can any one say of us, as was said of Him, that we go about 'doing good?' Think of his words, servants of his: 'I have given you an example, that ye should do as I have done to you.'

'Christlike' is a word often on our lips. Do not speak it too lightly. It is the heart of God's predestination. It is our high calling."

– Maltbie Davenport Babcock

MARCH 8 --

"Behold, the LORD thy God hath set the land before thee: go up and possess it, as the LORD God of thy fathers hath said unto thee; fear not, neither be discouraged." (De 1:21)

It's easy to fall into discouragement when we realize how unable we are to live a holy life. Sometimes this is simply due to our having to encounter the normal ups and downs of the Christian life. It's never pleasant to find out how prone we are to fall; having to face our failings is part of the process of becoming more humble. But there are times when excessive discouragement may be an indication of spiritual pride. If we're too disturbed over our shortcomings it may be because we have fallen into the trap of believing we're rather special, and we don't like seeing ourselves knocked off the pedestal. Otherwise, why would we be so disturbed?

Humility isn't attaining near-perfection. It's recognizing that even though we are going to try each day to be the best we can be, we will still fail on a regular basis, and not being too disturbed about it. It's seeing and accepting ourselves as we really are: flawed, frail and prone to fall, just like everybody else.

"We have expected something from ourselves, and have been sorely disappointed not to find that something there, and are discouraged in consequence. This mortification and discouragement are really a far worse condition than the temptation itself, though they present an appearance of true humility, for they are nothing but the results of wounded self-love. True humility can bear to see its own utter weakness and foolishness revealed, because it never expected anything from itself, and knows that its only hope and expectation must be in God. Therefore, instead of discouraging the soul from trusting, it drives it to a deeper and more utter trust. But the counterfeit humility which springs from self, plunges the soul into the depths of a faithless discouragement, and drives it into the very sin at which it is so distressed."   -- Hannah Whitall Smith

"After this manner therefore pray ye: Our Father which art in heaven, hallowed be Thy Name." (Ma 6:9)

"The Lord's Prayer is a temple reared by Christ Himself, the embodiment of His ideal, and as we repeat these simple and wonderful sentences we cannot but think of the multitudes who have been molded by them and have poured into these petitions their hearts' desires.

Our Lord was not always insisting on prayer, but He was constantly praying to His Father Himself. His disciples knew His habit of getting away for secret prayer, and they had on more than one occasion seen the transfiguring glory reflected on His face. Happy we would be if the glory of fellowship and communion with God were so apparent that men would come to us saying, 'Teach us to pray' (Ex 34:35).

Prayer must be simple. The Jewish proverb said, 'Everyone who multiplies prayer is heard,' but our Lord forbade senseless repetition by His teaching of the simple, direct, and intelligible petitions of this prayer.

Prayer must be reverent. The tenderest words, the simplest confidences, the closest intimacy will be welcomed and reciprocated by our Father in Heaven. But we must remember that He is the great King, and His Name is Holy. Angels veil their faces in His Presence. Let us remember that 'God is in Heaven, and thou upon earth; be not rash with thy mouth, and let not thine heart be hasty to utter anything before God' (Ec 5:2).

Prayer must be unselfish. Our Lord so wove intercession into the structure of this prayer that none can use it without pleading for others. Sorrow or sin may isolate us and make us feel our loneliness and solitude, but in prayer we realize that we are members of the one Body of Christ, units in that great multitude which no man can number.

Prayer must deal with real needs. Daily bread stands for every kind of need, and the fact that Jesus taught us to pray for it, suggests that we may be sure that it is God's will to give. Prayer must be in faith. We need to believe that we are as certain to prevail with God as the goodman of the house with his friend; and if, among men, to ask is to get, how much more with Him who loves us with greater love than a father's love (Lu 11:9-13)."

-- F. B. Meyer

"Who delivered us from so great a death, and doth deliver: in whom we trust that he will yet deliver us." (2 Co 1:10)

"Paul is a master at arithmetic – his faith was always a ready reckoner. Here we find him computing by the Believer's Rule of Three; he argues from the past to the present, and from the present to things yet to come. [This text] is a brilliant example of arriving at a comforting conclusion by the Rule of Three: 'Who delivered us from so great a death, and does deliver; in whom we trust that he will yet deliver us.' Because our God is 'the same yesterday, today, and for ever,' his love in time past is an infallible assurance of his kindness today, and an equally certain pledge of his faithfulness tomorrow. Whatever our circumstances may be, however perplexed may be our pathway, and however dark our horizon, yet, if we argue by the rule of 'He has, He does, He will,' our comfort can never be destroyed. Take courage then. If you had a changeable God to deal with, your souls might be full of bitterness, but because he is 'the same yesterday, today, and for ever,' every repeated display of his grace should make it easier for you to rest upon him; every renewed experience of his fidelity should confirm your confidence in his grace. May the most blessed Spirit teach us to grow in holy confidence in our ever faithful Lord." – Charles Spurgeon

MARCH 11 --

"Casting all your care upon him; for he careth for you." (I Pe 5:7)

Some of us are almost driven in the way we work to resolve every problem that comes into our lives. We fret about this dilemma, we worry about that challenge. We may resolve ninety-nine out of one-hundred problems during our day, but the one that's left is the one we focus on, and we can't rest until we've figured how it, too, is going to be resolved. Someone once called this trait of needing to solve everything as being "addicted to resolution." This kind of thinking can make us tired and short-tempered. And if we do it repeatedly, it can also make us miserable. What is the remedy?

First, we can recognize that constantly acting like we have to be responsible for solving everything says much more about us than it does about our circumstances. Life is full of problems, certainly, but when we get to the point where we feel we must fix everything in our lives, or the lives of those around us, we're probably out of balance. Yes, we need to act responsibly. Yes, we need to face our challenges. But our job is not to climb into the driver's seat of life and control everything. That seat is reserved for God.

Something is not right in us when we begin to micro-manage the world. More than likely, when this symptom rises to the surface, it's time to take a reading of our Pride-Index. Do we really think others can't get along without our constant help? Do we honestly believe God wants us to live in a state of 'drivenness?' Can we legitimately claim that our impatient striving to manage everything improves our lives or the lives of those we love? In many cases we will be forced to admit it does just the opposite.

It may be hard to let go and let God, but it's usually the only way to get our problems back where they belong: into God's hands. We need to do the footwork. Then we need to leave the results up to Him. In many cases, it isn't until we really do let go of certain problems that God can get hold of them and resolve them in the way He knows is best.

Lord, just for today, just for this hour, perhaps even just for this moment, help me to let go of the things I feel driven to resolve. I give them to You to handle in the way that is best. Please give me the wisdom to know what I need to do, and what I should not do. Show me how to cast my cares upon You and allow You to lead the way.

MARCH 12 ---

"Take my yoke upon you, and learn of me; for I am meek and lowly in heart..." (Ma 11:29)

"To believe in [Christ] is to do as He does, to follow Him where he goes. We must believe in Him practically -- altogether practically -- as He believed in His Father.... It is not to take Him in any way theoretically, to hold this or that theory about why He died, or wherein lay His atonement: such things can be revealed only to those who follow Him in His active being and the principle of His life, who do as He did, live as He lived. There is no other following. He is all for the Father; we must be all for the Father, too, otherwise we are not following Him. To follow Him is to be learning of Him, to think His thoughts, to use His judgments, to see things as He saw them, to feel things as He felt them, to be hearted, souled, minded, as He was, that we may also be of the same mind with His Father. This is what it is like to deny self and go after Him; nothing less, even if it be the working of miracles and casting out of devils.

[If we were to stay] busy from morning till night doing great things for Him on any other grounds, we should but earn the reception, 'I never knew you.' When He says, 'Take my yoke upon you,' He does not mean a yoke which He would lay upon our shoulders; it is His own yoke He tells us to take, and to learn of Him. It is the yoke He is Himself carrying, the yoke His perfect Father had given Him to carry." – George MacDonald

"...entire surrender to Jesus is the secret of perfect rest. Giving up one's whole life to Him, for Him alone to rule and order, taking up His yoke and submitting to be led and taught, to learn of Him, abiding in Him, to be and do only what He wills -- these are the conditions of discipleship without which there can be no thought of maintaining the rest that was bestowed upon our first coming to Christ. The rest is in Christ, and not something He gives apart from Himself, and so it is only in having Him that the rest can really be kept and enjoyed." – Andrew Murray

MARCH 13 --

"Fret not thyself because of evil men, neither be thou envious at the wicked: For there shall be no reward to the evil man; the candle of the wicked shall be put out." (Pr 24:19-20)

When God is silent toward those who choose to mock Him, his people often yearn to see Him rise up to defend Himself and to make Himself known in the evil time. They know that only the light of the Lord's presence can dispel the darkness of an unbelieving age. The enemy is persistent in his attacks on the Lord's children, and in his attempts to deface God's work, but God knows His time of response and deliverance. He always brings an end to the evildoer's works. He always arises to overthrow the ungodly. He will save His honor. He will provide for his people. He will be faithful to reward the righteous.

"Say ye to the righteous, that it shall be well with him: for they shall eat the fruit of their doings. Woe unto the wicked! It shall be ill with him: for the reward of his hands shall be given him." (Is 3:10-11)

"For in the time of trouble he shall hide me in his pavilion: in the secret of his tabernacle shall he hide me; he shall set me up upon a rock. And now shall mine head be lifted up above mine enemies round about me: therefore will I offer in his tabernacle sacrifices of joy; I will sing, yea, I will sing praises unto the Lord." (Ps 27:5-6)

Though the time is evil, the Lord is not unmindful of His work, but has a purpose in waiting to defend His name. In the meantime, the Lord will give strength and protection to his people.

MARCH 14 --

"Let this mind be in you, which was also in Christ Jesus." (Ph 2:5)

"When did Jesus bear the cross? Not that moment alone, surely, when the bitter tree was placed on His shoulders on the way to Golgotha. Its vision may be said to have risen before Him in His infant dreams in Bethlehem's cradle. It is there its reality began and He didn't cease carrying it until his work was finished and the victory won. A cloud of old hovered over the mercy seat in the tabernacle and temple. So it was with the Great Antitype:

the living Mercy Seat. He had a cloud of woe hanging over Him: 'He carried our sorrows.'

We ought often to ponder under the shadow of our Lord's cross. It would help us think more lightly of our own... 'If we were deeper students of His bitter tempest we would think less of our own ripplings' (Evans).

The saint's cross assumes many and diverse shapes. Sometimes it is a bitter trial, the crushing pang of bereavement, the desolate household, the aching heart. Sometimes it is the crucifixion of sin, the determined battling with 'lusts that war against the soul.' Sometimes it is the resistance against the evils and practices of a lying world and vindicating the honor of Christ, causing us to bear the taunt and ridicule and shame. And as there are different crosses, so there are different ways of bearing them. To some, God says, 'Put your shoulder to the burden, lift it up and bear it.' To others, He says, 'Be still, bear it, and suffer!'

Your cross may be hard to endure, it may involve deep struggles — tears by day, watchings by night – but you can rejoice in the assurance that He gives not one atom more of earthly trial than He sees to be really needful; not one unnecessary thorn pierces your feet.

In the very bearing of the cross for His sake there are mighty compensations. What new views of your Savior's love, His truth, His promises, His sustaining grace, His sufferings, His glory. What an increase in nearness to Him, in delight in prayer, in inner sunshine when it is darkest without. The waves cover you, but underneath them all, are 'the everlasting arms.'" – John MacDuff

MARCH 15 ---

"Ye shall observe to do therefore as the LORD your God hath commanded you: ye shall not turn aside to the right hand or to the left. Ye shall walk in all the ways which the LORD your God hath commanded you, that ye may live, and that it may be well with you, and that ye may prolong your days in the land which ye shall possess." (De 5:32-33)

"All our movements should be under the direction of God. In olden times, God guided his people by a pillar of fire and cloud, which lifted and moved when they were to move, showing them the way, and which rested and settled down when they were to halt. In these days of so much fuller revelation, there is no need for any such visible token of guidance, yet the guidance is no less real and no less unmistakable.

It was an angel that bid Joseph to flee into Egypt. Angels [may not] now appear to our eyes, but who will say that they do not whisper in our ears many a suggestion which we suppose to come from our own hearts? At least we know that in some way God will always tell us what to do; and if only we have ears to hear we shall never fail of guidance. We should always wait for

God's bidding before taking any step. Especially in times of danger, we should wait and not move until he brings us his word.

It ought to give us great comfort and a wonderful sense of safety to know that God is caring for us so faithfully. Some people laugh at the simple child-like faith of believers and say it is all fancy, that there is no one in heaven taking care of us. But we need not be worried by such skeptics. There is a God in heaven, and he is our Father. He never sleeps. He has charge of all the affairs of this universe, and is always 'at the helm.'

This should give us all confidence. Our whole duty is to be always ready to obey. Whenever the voice bids us to arise and depart, there is some reason for it, and we should not hesitate to obey. Wherever we are sent we should quietly stay until once again God calls us away. The place of duty is always the place of safety, and we should never move until God brings us word."   -- J. R. Miller

MARCH 16 ---

"The LORD hath appeared of old unto me, saying, Yea, I have loved thee with an everlasting love: therefore with lovingkindness have I drawn thee." (Je 31:3)

"A woman with child makes ready for the babe she expects; prepares its cradle, its linens, the child's clothes and even a nurse; even so, our Lord, while hanging on His Cross, prepared all that you would need for your happiness, all the means, the graces, the leadings by which He would lead your soul onwards towards perfection.

Surely we ought to always remember this, and ask fervently, 'Is it possible that I was loved, and loved so tenderly by my Saviour, that He should have thought of me individually, and in all these details by which He has drawn me to Himself?' With what love and gratitude ought I to use all He has given me! The Loving Heart of my God thought about my soul, loved it and prepared endless means to promote its salvation, even as though there were no other soul on earth, just as the sun shines on each spot of earth as brightly as though it shone nowhere else, but reserved all its brightness for that alone. So Our Dear Lord thought and cared for every one of His children as though none other existed. 'Who loved me, and gave Himself for me,' St. Paul says, as though he meant, 'for me alone, as if there were none but me He cared for.' Let this be engraved on your soul, my child, in order to cherish and nourish your good resolutions, which are so precious to the Heart of our Saviour."   – St. Francis de Sales

MARCH 17 ---

"For thou hast delivered my soul from death, mine eyes from tears, and my feet from falling." (Ps 116:8)

Many individuals who today are living examples of God's redeeming power were once considered hopeless by society. The world tends to give up on people who are flawed or wounded, but God never gives up. He knows that no one is beyond His ability to transform and heal.

Society is prone to put labels on those that it looks upon as outcasts. It sees people who are damaged and calls them "losers." It sees those whose sins have gotten the best of them and calls them "bums, degenerates, castaways, hopeless." God does not look at them that way, and thank God that He does not.

There is the successful surgeon who is respected as a man of integrity by all his peers and associates. What many don't know about him is that he was once so overwhelmed by his drinking problem that he had to stop practicing medicine and ended up living on the streets. Finally, after years of trying to overcome his problem on his own, he turned to God, and from that moment on his life began to turn around. He sought help, attained sobriety and after a period of time was able to resume his practice. Today he assists others who need a helping hand.

There is the attractive young mother of two who works at a women's shelter and regularly helps out at her children's school. What most do not know is that she was once on the streets, having been abused and turned out by parents who were addicted to drugs. She reached out to the Lord, got into a half-way house and went back to school. Now she is gainfully employed and also volunteers each week to pray for others who need help to change their lives.

We cannot know what really goes on in people's hearts. But God knows. He knows the truth about each and every one of us and looks at each of us as a precious child, worth more than all the riches the world has to offer. We are worth the world to Christ. He died for each of us, that we might be redeemed. He paid the ultimate price. Since He was willing to do that, we can certainly trust Him to also come up with a plan to help us when we need to change. No matter how far down we have gone, God can always pull us back up. He numbers the hairs of our heads. He cares about the sparrows. He treasures each person on this earth, and so should we.

We may not understand what has caused a person to fall but we can always pray for that person. We can ask God to show him or her how to turn to Christ for the help that is needed. We can offer a helping hand when that would be appropriate. And we can remember that God often fashions His greatest saints out of people that the world said were great failures.

Lord, please show me who to pray for today. Help me to intercede for them in a way that will reflect Your desire to see their lives healed and transformed.

"It is good that a man should both hope and quietly wait for the salvation of the LORD." (La 3:26)

"The Lord does not bring his poor and needy children to a throne of grace and send them away as soon as they get there. His purpose is to show them who they are, to make them value his favors, to cause them to sink lower and lower in themselves, that they may rise higher and higher in Christ.... The work of the Spirit in the hearts of the redeemed is radical work, work that goes to the very bottom of things; nothing flimsy, nothing superficial, nothing which can be effaced and obliterated springs from Him, but that which shall have an abiding effect, that which shall last for eternity. The Lord is fitting His people for eternity, and therefore His work in them is thorough work; it goes right through them; it leaves nothing covered up and masked over, but turns all up from the very bottom, 'discovering the foundation unto the neck' (Hab. 3:13), and doing in a man spiritually what He said He would do in Jerusalem: 'I will wipe Jerusalem as a man wipes a dish, wiping it, and turning it upside down' (II Kings 21:13).

Therefore, He does not answer the prayers of His children immediately when they come to His throne of mercy and grace, but rather He deepens those convictions that He has implanted; He makes the burdens heavier that He has put upon their backs; He hides Himself instead of discovering Himself, and draws back further instead of coming nearer. Now this is intended to make them wait with greater earnestness, with more unreserved simplicity, with more absolute dependence upon Him and Him alone to communicate the blessing, with greater separation of heart from all the strength of the creature, with a firmer resolution in the soul to cast away all its own righteousness, and to hang solely and wholly upon the Spirit's teachings, and Jesus' sweet revelation of himself."   – Joseph Philpot

"There failed not ought of any good thing which the LORD had spoken to the house of Israel; all came to pass." (Joshua 21:45)

"Some day even you, trembling, faltering one, shall stand upon those heights that Joshua knew. As you look back upon all you have passed through, all you have narrowly escaped, all the perils through which He guided you, the stumblings through which He guarded you and the sins from which He saved you; you will shout, 'Salvation to our God, which sitteth upon the throne, and unto the Lamb' (Rev 7:10).

Some day He will sit down with us in that glorious home, and we shall have all the ages in which to understand the story of our lives. He will read over again this marked old Bible with us. He will show us how He kept all these promises, He will explain to us the mysteries that we could not understand, He will recall all the finished story. Then I am sure we will cry: 'Blessed Christ! You have been so true, you have been so good. Was there ever love like this?' And then the great chorus will be repeated once more: 'There failed not ought of any good thing which the Lord had spoken... all came to pass.'"   -- A. B. Simpson

MARCH 20 ---

"To hear the groaning of the prisoner; to loose those that are appointed to death;" (Ps 102:20)

"There is a grace of kind listening as well as a grace of kind speaking. Some men listen with an abstracted air, which shows that their thoughts are elsewhere. Or they seem to listen, but by distracted answers and irrelevant questions show that they have been occupied with their own thoughts, as being more interesting, at least in their own estimation, than what you have been saying. Some listen with a kind of importunate ferocity which makes you feel that you are being put upon your trial, and that your auditor expects beforehand that you are going to tell him a lie, or be inaccurate, or say something of which he will disapprove, and that you must mind your expressions. Some interrupt, and will not hear you to the end. Some hear you to the end, and then talk to you about a similar experience which has befallen them, making your case only an illustration of their own. Some, meaning to be kind, listen with such a determined, lively, violent attention, that you are at once made uncomfortable, and the charm of conversation is at an end. Many persons, whose manners will stand the test of speaking, break down under the trial of listening... Kind listening is often an act of the most delicate interior mortification and is a great assistance towards kind speaking. Those who govern others must take care to be kind listeners, or else they will soon offend God."   – F. W. Faber

The believer whose heart is ripe with love doesn't need to look for the shortcomings in others. He doesn't compare himself with them; instead, his desire is to be supportive, caring and quick to overlook their personal flaws and failings.

Those people who help us the most are generally the ones who are gentle. Gentle people are approachable. We are able to sense that they wish us well. Instead of being critical, they encourage us. Instead of focusing on our faults, they want to hear about our successes. They don't care much about their own achievements; they care about the achievements of others. Their love shines through because they are humble. They have usually spent years in God's School of Suffering and so they are not overwhelmed when times of trial and suffering come. This school has taught them how to empathize with the trials of others and how to love without conditions.

MARCH 21 ---

"In the beginning was the Word, and the Word was with God, and the Word was God. The same was in the beginning with God. All things were made by him; and without him was not any thing made that was made. In him was life; and the life was the light of men. And the light shineth in darkness; and the darkness comprehended it not." (Jo 1:1-5)

"Who is the Word spoken of in these verses? He is the Son of God. He is called the Word because he makes God, his Father, known to us. How is it that our thoughts are made known to our fellow creatures? By our words. Thus, the unseen Father is made known to men by his Son Jesus Christ. No man can know the Father but by the Son. The Son and the Father are distinct persons, for it is written in the first verse, 'The Word was with God;' that is, the Son was with the Father. Yet the Son and the Father are one God, for it is added, 'The Word was God.'

But even if we had not found this sentence, 'The Word was God,' we would have known that he was God, by the things that are said of him in the following verses.

First, it is declared that he was from the beginning with God. Now God is the First, and if the Son of God is from everlasting, then he is First, and he must be God.

Again, it is declared that all things were made by him. Thus we know the Son is the Creator of the world. He cannot then be a creature, for no creature can 'create.' God alone can create.

Then again, it is said, He is the 'Life.' He gives life. All the angels in heaven cannot give life to the smallest insect, or even to the lowest flower, but the Son can give life to the creatures he has made; not only natural life, but spiritual and eternal life.

Lastly, it is declared that he is the Light of men, a brighter light than the sun, a light which shines into the heart and enlightens the dark mind.

And what is Man called? Observe the name that is given to him. He is called 'Darkness.' In the fifth verse it is written, 'The light shines in darkness, and the darkness comprehends it not.' Ever since Satan, the prince of darkness, tempted Adam and Eve to eat the forbidden fruit, the minds of men have been dark; they have neither known what is right, nor loved what is good. Christ came into the world to bring light to the dark minds of men. But alas, how few receive him. Most people are so pleased with the trifles of time or so much taken up with the cares of the world, that they turn away from the Son of God. This blessed book, this Bible, which we hold in our hands, tells us about Him. Does not each of us wish to be happy forever?

Then let us listen attentively, and let us entreat God to give us faith that we may believe and be saved."   -- F. L. Mortimer

"And be not conformed to this world: but be ye transformed by the renewing of your mind, that ye may prove what is that good, and acceptable, and perfect will of God."
(Ro 12:2)

Many of us who have come through tough times know what it's like to have a sense of impending doom. That hopeless feeling is a terrible way to live. Today, as children of God, one of our greatest joys is knowing that we never again have to live with the cloud of impending doom hanging over our heads. Does this mean, however, that once we become born again all our negative thinking patterns just disappear? Probably not. Many of us may continue to struggle with feelings of fear or anxiety, and, once in a while, we may even experience that old sense of impending doom. We may worry that such a feeling indicates there is something wrong with our commitment to God, but it does not. Once we have given our lives to God we can trust that He will always be there for us, even in the midst of our occasional struggles with negative thinking patterns. Once we have turned to Him, we can be certain He will never fail or forsake us.

Negative thought patterns are a distorted way of looking at life. Being negative is believing things that aren't true. Before we came to know God, many of us tended to believe a lot of things that simply were not accurate. Today, as believers, we don't have to believe the things we used to believe. We can change our thinking patterns so they become more positive. If we want to know what is true, about ourselves, about others and about life in general, we can go to God's Word. That is where the truth is. That is where we can go to find strength to press on and to learn more about God and the wonderful things He has in store for us. When we take in His Word, its power begins to drive out the negative, destructive thinking patterns we may have acquired in the past.

In addition to reading God's Word, we need to make prayer a daily practice. It's important that we not merely think about prayer, or read about it, but we must actually do it. Direct contact with God through daily prayer opens the way for Him to minister into our lives the healing we need. When we hit a rough spot during our day we can take our feelings of fear, anxiety, worry, depression or anger to God, and ask Him to help us return to a place of peace. If we are in upheaval, we can ask Him to help us settle down and decide what it is we should do next. We can ask Him to help us deal with one thing at a time rather than trying to tackle all our problems at once.

A third action we can take, especially if our turmoil is great, is to get our focus off of ourselves and concentrate instead on seeing what we can do to help someone else, especially someone who may have a need that is greater than our own. When we help someone else, we often find our own thinking becomes more balanced. We see our difficulties with greater clarity and recognize that challenges are a part of nearly everyone's life. This can help us to remember that no matter what we are facing, God will indeed help us to face our challenges, and will help us to work through them, in His way and in His time.

MARCH 23 --

"The leaves thereof were fair, and the fruit thereof much, and in it was meat for all: the beast of the field had shadow under it, and the fowls of the heaven dwelt in the boughs thereof, and all flesh was fed of it." (Da 4:12)

God works by the Rule of the Seasons. We can see this rule at work in almost everything He does.

Study, for instance, the peach tree. In early spring it stands bare in the garden, looking to the untrained eye no different than it did in the depths of winter. Its branches are leafless. It shows no signs of life. But something is happening, deep inside this tree. The Life Force that God put within it is beginning to flow, even though its work is not yet apparent. It is sending energy out into the tree's branches. Before long these branches will be adorned with tiny leaf tips and by April they will bear hundreds of fluffy pink blossoms. The bees will come. Fertilization will occur. The fruit will form and begin to grow.

Over the next few months the tree will experience spring showers, warm, sunny days, long summer nights – all necessary to the maturation process. By late summer, the sweet scent of ripening fruit will fill the air.

By the time autumn arrives, the tree's leaves will have completed their annual task of processing sunlight into the energy the tree required. Fruit, and the seed necessary for reproduction, will have been produced. The time of harvest will be at hand. At last, the tree's work for the season will be completed. The supple green leaves will begin to change. Their color will fade and a few will drift to the ground. More and more will fall until, by the time the harsh November winds begin to blow, all the leaves will lie at the base of the tree like a pool of molten gold.

At first glance it would seem the glorious season of fruit-bearing has come to an end, never to return, but it is not so. Autumn does signal the end of one season, but it also whispers of springs that are yet to come. The energy once expended on fruit-bearing now withdraws itself into the tree where it will be utilized to help the tree grow and become capable of bearing even more fruit during the year ahead. The life force will be hidden for a time, but it will still be there, deep inside the tree, waiting for the time to emerge once more.

Dear one, if the green leaves in your life have grown brittle and fallen away, if the precious fruit you had hoped to see has not yet appeared, remember, there is another season ahead. God is already at work upon it, and you can trust Him to prepare you for the coming harvest. God's ways of growth and fruit-bearing never change. He works by the Rule of the Seasons. This is true in nature, and it is true in us, as well.

MARCH 24 --

"God, who commanded the light to shine out of darkness, hath shined in our hearts, to give the light of the knowledge of the glory of God in the face of Jesus Christ." (I Co 4:6)

"The way to think of God so as to know Him is to think of Christ. Then we see Him, and can understand how tender and merciful and good He is. We see that if He sends us sorrows and difficulties, He only sends them because they are the true blessings, the things that are truly good. He would have us like Himself, with a happiness like His own, and nothing below it; and so, as His own happiness is in taking sorrow and infirmity, and ever assisting and giving and sacrificing Himself, He gives us sorrows too, and weaknesses, which are not the evils that we think them, but are what we should be most happy in, if we were perfect and had knowledge like Him. So there is a use and a service in all we bear, in all we do, which we do not know, but which He knows, and which, in Christ, He shows to us. It is a use for others, a hidden use, but one which makes all our life rich, and that richest which is most like Christ's."   -- James Hinton

"The God who revealed Jesus in the flesh and perfected Him, will reveal Him in you and perfect you in Him. The Father loves the Son, and delights to work out His image and likeness in you. Count upon it, that this blessed work will be done in you as you wait on your God and hold fellowship with Him.

The likeness to Christ consists chiefly in two things: the likeness of His death and of His resurrection (Ro 6:5). The death of Christ was the consummation of His humility and obedience, the entire giving up of His life to God. In Him we are dead to sin. As we sink down in humility and dependence and entire surrender to God, the power of His death works in us and we are made conformable to His death. And so we know Him in the power of His resurrection, in the victory over sin, and all the joy and power of the risen life. Therefore, every morning present yourselves unto God as those that are alive from the dead. He will maintain the life He gave, and bestow the grace to live as risen ones."   -- Andrew Murray

Christ, our Dayspring, Great I Am,
King of Kings and Spotless Lamb,
Shares with man His holiness,
Bequeathes forgiveness, bends to bless.
In His people He abides,
Offering the Sacrifice;

Mercy through His blood is shed,
Souls from evil's grasp are led,
Call Him Savior, Lord on High,
All His virtues glorify,
Let Him rise Who for us died,
Christ, be ever magnified.

MARCH 25 --

"...Who giveth songs in the night." (Job 35:10)

"There are times in which the heart has to fill the place of the eye. We see nothing; the sky is dark; yet we are not dismayed. There is no ray of light upon our path that we can discern, no opening in the cloud, no break in the gloom. Yet, somehow, the heart sings -- sings in the shadow, sings in the silence. And at these times we are to take the song as the substitute for the sun. We are to impute to the heart's singing all that is wanting to the eye's vision. The song is itself to be our revelation. 'If it were not so I would have told you' ...

If my soul says 'Yes,' and God does not say 'No,' the 'Yes' is to prevail. The silence of God is vocal. If hope cries, and He answers not, hope's cry is to be itself the answer, for He has sent me a wing instead of a star; He has given me a song in the night.

My soul, be not so anxious about the reason for your peace. Is it not written that there is a peace which passeth understanding? What is that but a song in the night? It is one of the songs without words. It gives no explanation of its music. Clouds and darkness may be around you, yet you may still be able to sing. Do not distress yourself by trying to find a cause for your joy. Remember the bush that was all in flame and yet was not consumed? The facts were all against its permanence; it was unreasonable that it should live. But it did live; and why? Because there was a voice speaking within it, singing within it, against facts, in spite of reason, in defiance of circumstances. It was a song without words, a comfort without cause, a strength without the legions of angels. So, often times, it shall be with you.

There shall be moments in your life in which your Gethsemane may reveal no flower, in which the cup shall not pass from you, in which the legions of angels shall not come; and yet, strange to say, you will be strong. You will fly without pinions; you will walk without feet; you will breathe without air; you will praise without words; you will laugh without sunshine; you will bless without knowing why, for the song of your heart will itself be your light, and your joy shall be only from God."   – George Matheson

MARCH 26 --

"The meek will he guide in judgment; and the meek will he teach his way." (Ps 25:9)

"The first and the worst cause of error that prevails in this day and age is spiritual pride. This is the main door by which the devil comes into the hearts of those who are zealous for the advancement of the Faith. It is the chief inlet of smoke from the bottomless pit, to darken the mind and mislead the judgment. This is the main handle by which the devil has hold of religious persons, and the chief source of all the mischief that he introduces, to clog and hinder the work of God. This cause of error is the mainspring, or at least the main support, of all the rest. Until this disease is cured, medicines that are meant to heal other spiritual diseases are applied in vain.

It is by this that the mind defends itself in other errors and guards itself against light, by which it might be corrected and reclaimed. The spiritually proud man is full of light already; he does not need instruction, and is ready to despise the offer of it. But, if this disease is healed, other things are easily rectified. The humble person is like a little child; he easily receives instruction; he is jealous over himself, sensible of how liable he is to go astray, and therefore, if it be suggested to him that he does so, he is ready to be impartial and inquire to see if it is true. Nothing sets a person so much out of the devil's reach as humility, and so prepares the mind for true divine light without darkness, and so clears the eye to look on things as they truly are."
                                                          -- Jonathan Edwards

MARCH 27 --

"Yea, though I walk through the valley of the shadow of death, I will fear no evil: for thou art with me; thy rod and thy staff they comfort me." (Ps 23:4)

A man who was an expert hunter rose early one morning to the sound of the baying of a score or more of hounds in the distance. It was obvious to his trained ears that they were in hot pursuit of their quarry. Looking across a broad field, he spotted a young fawn making its way through the tall grass and surmised from the way it ran that its strength was nearly expended. Reaching the rails of a nearby fence, it leaped across them and, completely exhausted, crouched not ten feet from where the man stood. Only moments later, two of the hounds made their way over the fence. The fawn ran toward the man and, cowering, pushed its head between his legs. In an instant, he scooped the fawn into his arms, and, swinging round and round as the dogs came upon him, managed to fight them off. "I felt," he said, "that all the dogs in the world could not, would not, be able to capture that fawn after its weakness had appealed to my strength."

And so it is with God. When we approach Him in our human helplessness, he is faithful to scoop us up into His everlasting arms and protect us from the assaults of the enemy. We should do well to remember that when the hounds of sin or misfortune or the strategies of the evil one rise up against us, we can always run into the protective arms of our loving and almighty God.

> When all my strength and faith have been expended,
> And all my hopes of victory have ended,
> When every step becomes a painful strain,
> And all my life is marred with failure's stain,
> I look to find my Refuge and I climb,
> Into Christ's arms so loving and divine,
> I lay upon His heart my dying soul,
> And find not only am I safe, but whole.

MARCH 28 ---

"Now faith is the substance of things hoped for, the evidence of things not seen. For by it the elders obtained a good report." (He 11:1-2)

"God delights to increase the faith of His children. Our faith, which is feeble at first, is developed and strengthened day by day. We ought, instead of wanting no trials before victory, no exercise for patience, to be willing to take them from God's hand as a means. I say, and I say it deliberately, trials, obstacles, difficulties, and sometimes defeats, are the very food of Faith. I get letters from so many of God's dear children who say: 'I'm writing this because I am so weak in faith.' Just so, surely as we ask to have our faith strengthened, we must feel a willingness to take from God's hand the means for strengthening it. We must allow Him to educate us through trials and bereavements and troubles. It is through trials that faith is exercised and developed more and more. God affectionately permits difficulties, that He may develop unceasingly that which He is willing to do for us, and to this end we should not shrink, but if He gives us sorrow and hindrances and losses and afflictions, we should take them out of His hands as evidences of His love and care for us in developing more and more of that faith which He is seeking to strengthen in us.

The Church of God does not recognize God as the beautiful and lovable One that He is; this is the reason why we are so little blessed. Beloved brothers and sisters in Christ, seek to learn about God's blessedness for yourselves; I cannot give you this understanding. In my darkest moments I am able to confide in Him, for I know what a beautiful and kind and lovable Being He is, and, if it be the will of God to put us in the furnace, let Him do it, that we may come to know Him in the ways He would reveal Himself, so that we may know Him better. Then we would see that God is a lovable Being, and will be satisfied with Him, and we can say: 'It is my Father, let Him do as He pleases.'" – George Mueller

MARCH 29 --

"For what shall it profit a man, if he shall gain the whole world, and lose his own soul?" (Ma 8:36)

What is our purpose in life? Is it to become prosperous? To attain a position of influence or power? To gain preeminence in our chosen profession? Some people think so. And they spend their lives pursuing such things. They strive for money or prestige or success because they believe these are the things that will give life meaning. They are under the impression that fulfillment comes as a result of personal achievement rather than having a relationship with God.

Some years ago eight of the most successful businessmen in the United States met in the hotel of a large city to discuss financial strategies and future plans for their respective industries. These men possessed between them what appeared to be the greatest financial security of any eight people in the country. They included the president of a steel company, the head of a giant utility, the president of a gas company, a speculator in the agricultural industry, the president of the New York Stock Exchange, a high-ranking member of the President's Cabinet, who also happened to be a multi-millionaire, a Wall Street financier and a bank president.

Thirty years later a researcher sought to find out what had happened to these men. What he discovered surprised him:

The president of the steel company had died bankrupt.
The president of the utility had died penniless in a foreign country.
The president of the gas company had died after a debilitating mental illness.
The agricultural speculator had died overseas, penniless.
The President of the Stock Exchange had been sentenced to prison.
The Cabinet member had been sentenced to prison; he was pardoned when it was discovered he had a terminal illness.

The Wall Street financier had committed suicide.

The bank president had committed suicide.

If wealth and success brought satisfaction to the human spirit, wouldn't these individuals have been the most contented and peaceful of men? Instead, they discovered that temporal success and wealth could not satisfy the yearning for meaning that exists deep in the heart of every man and woman. The only thing that will satisfy that yearning is having a personal relationship with the living God.

"The rich man shall lie down, but he shall not be gathered: he openeth his eyes, and he is not" (Job 27:19); "He that trusteth in his riches shall fall: but the righteous shall flourish as a branch." (Pr 11:28)

MARCH 30 --

"Suffer it to be so now: for thus it becometh us to fulfil all righteousness..." (Ma 3:15)

"One meaning of Christ's words here is that, as Man taking the place of sinful men, He had to take upon Him all the conditions of humanity. He had no sins of His own to confess and yet He came to John as other men came. He did this because He was in the place of sinners. A little later John pointed to Christ and said, 'Behold, the Lamb of God, which taketh away the sin of the world.' So we see Jesus coming to be baptized, because 'all we like sheep have gone astray, and the Lord hath laid on Him the iniquity of us all.' This baptism with water, however, was but the merest shadow of what the bearing of our sins cost Him.

In William Holman Hunt's painting, 'The Shadow of the Cross,' Jesus is represented at thirteen standing in the carpenter's shop at the close of the day. He stretches out His arms, and the setting sun casts a shadow in the form of a cross on the opposite wall. The thought is that early in life the shadow of the cross fell over Jesus' soul. No doubt the thought is true. But it was here, especially, as Jesus entered His public ministry, that the shadow of the Cross fell upon Him. It was only a baptism of water, but it was symbolic of another baptism -- the baptism of sorrow, of death, of curse, for He 'redeemed us from the curse of the law by being made a curse for us.' Here we see Him beginning to enter the baptism from which He finally emerged on the morning of His resurrection. We ought never forget, as we enjoy the blessings of redemption, what it cost our Lord to procure them for us. He endured the baptism of sorrow, pain, and death, that we might receive the blessings of peace and joy. He tasted death for us that we might attain unto a deathless life."   – J. R. Miller

Jesus, when I turn to You
My heart discovers grace,
It longs beyond the veil to see
Into Your loving face.
One day I'll stand before You,
And with the angels tell,
Of how you chose at Calvary
To save the saints from hell.

Who can know the cost you bore
To set us free that day?
When men your flesh and heartstrings tore
As Your Father turned away.
My Savior, like a holy seed,
Was laid within the tomb,
He took with Him my every need
And with my sin was doomed.

But God reached down with love divine
Into that hopeless hole,
And Christ emerged, the Living Vine
Abloom with risen souls.

MARCH 31 --

"They that trust in the Lord shall be as mount Zion, which cannot be removed, but abideth forever." (Ps 125:1)

"There is no peace more wonderful than the peace we enjoy when faith shows us God in all created things. All that is dark becomes light, and what is bitter, sweet. Faith transforms ugliness into beauty, and malice into kindness. Faith is the mother of tenderness, trust and joy. It cannot feel anything but love and pity for its enemies, by whom it is so greatly enriched, for the more harsh the actions of creatures against us, the more beneficial God makes them for our souls. The human instrument tries to injure us, but the divine craftsman, in whose hands it is, ensures that it takes from our souls all that would harm them. The will of God has only delights, favors and riches for all souls who are obedient to it. We cannot trust it too much or abandon ourselves to it too completely. If we leave everything to God, he will do all that is necessary for our holiness. Faith cannot doubt this. The more unreliable, disgusted, despairing and unsure of themselves our senses are, the more emphatically does faith exclaim: 'God is here! All goes well!'

There is nothing that faith cannot overcome. It pierces through the darkest shadows and the thickest clouds to reach the truth, embraces it and can never be torn from it." – Jean-Pierre de Caussade

> Whose eye foresaw this way? Not mine.
> Whose hand marked out this day? Not mine.
> A clearer eye than mine, 'Twas Thine.
> A wiser hand than mine, 'Twas Thine!
> Then let my hand be still, In Thine,
> And Let me find my will, In Thine!
> --Maltbie Davenport Babcock

Sometimes the spirit must soak a while in suffering, in order that its most stubborn stains may be removed.

APRIL 1 --

"But the fruit of the Spirit is love, joy, peace, longsuffering, gentleness, goodness..." (Ga 5:22)

"Goodness is a fruit of the Spirit. Goodness is just 'Godness.' It is being like God. And godlike goodness has special reference to the active benevolence of God. The apostle Paul gave us the difference between goodness and righteousness in Romans 5:7: 'Scarcely for a righteous man will one die: yet peradventure for a good man some would even dare to die.' The righteous man is the man of stiff, inflexible uprightness, but he may be as hard as a granite mountainside. The good man is that mountainside covered with velvet moss and flowers and flowing with cascades and springs. Goodness respects 'whatsoever things are lovely.' It is kindness, affection, benevolence, sympathy, rejoicing with those who rejoice, and weeping with those who weep.

Lord, fill us with Thyself, and let us be God-persons and good persons and so represent Thy goodness.

> There are lonely hearts to cherish,
> While the days are going by;
> There are weary souls who perish,
> While the days are going by."
> -- A. B. Simpson

APRIL 2 --

"Hungry and thirsty, their soul fainted in them. Then they cried unto the Lord in their trouble, and he delivered them out of their distresses." (Ps 107:5-6)

George Matheson was no stranger to suffering. By the time he was eighteen he had lost the sight in both his eyes, yet his deepest desire in life was to know God. Matheson was a gifted poet. The wealth of inspiration he left behind testifies to the close relationship with God he enjoyed and makes it clear that his blindness was not able to deter him from being used by the Lord to encourage and strengthen thousands of his fellow believers.

On June 6, 1882, Matheson was staying with his family in an old parsonage where they had gathered to celebrate the marriage of his sister. Though he was never to reveal the source of it, Matheson was almost overcome that night with a sense of deep anguish. Alone, almost overwhelmed by the darkness of his blindness and of his own hurting heart, he cried out to Christ. As he struggled, words began to well up inside him. They were words, not of pain, but of comfort, and they began to tumble out onto the paper before him. The poem seemed to come from someplace far beyond the room in which he sat. Later he was to say: "I had the impression of having it dictated to me by some inward voice rather than of working it out myself." These are the lines he wrote:

O Love that wilt not let me go,
I rest my weary soul in thee;
I give thee back the life I owe,
That in thine ocean depths its flow
May richer, fuller be.
O light that followest all my way,
I yield my flickering torch to thee;
My heart restores its borrowed ray,
That in thy sunshine's blaze its day
May brighter, fairer be.
O Joy that seekest me through pain,
I cannot close my heart to thee;
I climb the rainbow through the rain,
And feel the promise is not vain,
That morn shall tearless be.
O Cross that liftest up my head,
I dare not ask to fly from thee;
I lay in dust, life's glory dead,
And from the ground, there blossoms red,
Life that shall endless be.

Matheson recalled the poem took him less than five minutes to write. He made only one small revision, changing the phrase "I climb" to "I trace." The ease with which the words came surprised him because he usually had to spend long hours creating his poems and had to make many revisions before he was satisfied with them. "O Love That Wilt Not Let Me Go" went on to become one of the most beloved poems in both Britain and America.

APRIL 3 --

"Confess your faults one to another, and pray one for another, that ye may be healed. The effectual fervent prayer of a righteous man availeth much." (Ja 5:16)

"Always guard yourself from being too anxious because of your faults. First of all, such distress only stirs up the soul and distracts you to outward things. Secondly, your distress may actually spring from a secret root of pride. What you are experiencing is, in fact, a love of your own worth.

To put it in other words, you are simply hurt and upset at seeing what you really are. If the Lord should be so merciful as to give you a true spirit of His humility, you will not be surprised at your faults, your failures, or even your own basic nature. The more clearly you see your true self, the clearer you also see how miserable your self nature really is, and the more you will abandon your whole being to God. Seeing that you have such a desperate need of Him, you will press toward a more intimate relationship with Him.

This is the way you should walk, just as the Lord Himself has said: 'I will instruct thee and teach thee in the way which thou shalt go: I will guide thee with mine eye.'" -- Madame Guyon

"Be not amazed at finding yourself sensitive, impatient, haughty, self-willed; you must be made to perceive that such is your natural disposition. 'We must bear the yoke of the daily confusion of our sins,' said St. Augustine. We must be made to feel our weakness, our wretchedness, our inability to correct ourselves. We must despair of our own heart, and have no hope but in God. We must bear with ourselves, without flattering, and without neglecting a single effort for our correction. We must be instructed as to our true character, while waiting for God's time to take it away. Let us become lowly under his all-powerful hand; yielding and manageable as often as we perceive any resistance in our will. Be silent as much as you can. Be in no haste to judge; suspend your decisions, your likes and dislikes. Stop at once when you become aware that your activity is hurried, and do not be too eager even for good things." -- Francois Fenelon

APRIL 4 --

"But God forbid that I should glory, save in the cross of our Lord Jesus Christ, by whom the world is crucified unto me, and I unto the world." (Ga 6:14)

"There is no doubt of what God means in the Cross. He means love. It is the measure of the meaning of man's existence. Measure all by the Cross. Do you want success? The cross is failure. Do you seek a good reputation? The cross is infamy. Do you live for happiness? The cross is pain and sharpness. Do you live that the will of God may be done, in you and by you, in both life and death? Then, and only then, is the Spirit of the Cross within you. When once a man has learned that, the power of the world over him is gone, and it is not necessary, through criticism or invitation, to urge him to cease loving the world. He cannot love the world, for he has got an ambition that is above the world. He has planted his foot upon the Rock, and when all else is gone, he will still abide forever."   – Robertson of Brighton

"This is the best possible world for one who is called according to God's purpose, or to purposes according to God's calling... If we believe 'God is wisdom, God is love,' then we should act as though we believe it, and face our tasks with fidelity and our tests with fortitude.

God knows why we are here, and has told us: to learn and to do, for the sake of discipline and duty. Can we imagine a world better fitted for those ends than this world? How long we are to suffer or serve is for God to say. Let us not look too much out of the school-room windows or too impatiently at the clock. When God's time for us comes, well and good. Until then, this world is the best for us, and we must make the most of it, and do our best for it."   – Maltbie Davenport Babcock

APRIL 5 ---

"And he called unto him the twelve, and began to send them forth by two and two, and gave them power over unclean spirits;" (Mark 6:7)

"Jesus draws and drives. He draws us irresistibly to himself. His peace sings its soft music within. His love kindles fires on the hearthstone of the heart. So he drives us out; not *from* him, but *for* him, out to others, nearest and farthest. For love serves. It gives freely. It goes gladly. It sacrifices without thinking of the cost. It must serve; this is its life. It can serve, for only love-service is real service."   -- S. D. Gordon

"The religion of Christ teaches the most beautiful courtesy. We are not to seek to be ministered unto, but to minister; not to get distinction and praise, but to live quietly. Kossuth said that of all natural emblems he would choose for his life the dew. It makes no noise, seeks no praise, writes no record, but is content to sink away and be lost in the flowers and grass blades, to be remembered only in the new beauty and sweetness it imparts to nature. Those who always demand that they shall be recognized, and their name attached to everything they do, have not learned the mind of

Christ so well as those who are content to have Christ honoured, to do good to others, and to be remembered only in the new blessing and good which they leave in other lives."   -- J. R. Miller

APRIL 6 --

"O Israel, thou hast destroyed thyself; but in me is thine help." (Ho 13:9)

"God is all-wise, and therefore takes no rash, precipitate steps. As the original plan of salvation was devised by infinite wisdom, so all the successive steps of the execution of that plan are also directed by the same boundless wisdom... In his dealings with his people, God does not put them all at once into possession of all the blessings which he has laid up for them. He has pardoned their sins; but he does not immediately, after he calls them through grace, put into them a complete understanding of this blessing. He has first to teach them their need of it. He has to prepare their heart for the right reception of it. It is no common gift, and he has to teach them how to value it. They are saved from wrath and eternal misery, from his dreadful displeasure and ever-burning indignation against sin, but they need to be shown, and made deeply to feel, from what they are saved, as well as to what they are saved. Just as the oak does not grow to its full stature in a day, but needs years of sunshine and storms in order that it may grow strong and tall and put down strong roots, so do God's children need months and years of trial and temptation, that they may push a deep root downwards, and shoot healthy and vigorous growth upwards.

Therefore, before the soul can know anything about salvation, it must learn deeply and experimentally the nature of sin, and of self, as stained and polluted by it. It is proud, and needs to be humbled; careless, and needs to be awakened; alive, and needs to be killed; full, and requires to be emptied; whole, and needs to be wounded; clothed, and requires to be stripped. It is, by nature, self-righteous and self-seeking; is buried deep in worldliness and carnality; is utterly blind and ignorant; is filled with presumption, arrogance, conceit, and enmity, and hates all that is heavenly and spiritual. Sin, in all its various forms, is its natural element... To make man the direct opposite of what he originally was; to make him love God instead of hating him; to fear, instead of mocking him; to obey, instead of rebelling against him, requires the implantation of a new nature by the immediate hand of God himself."
                                                                                             -- Joseph Philpot

APRIL 7 --

"These things have I spoken unto you, that My joy might remain in you, and that your joy might be full." (Jo 15:11)

"[Our Lord spoke the above words] on the eve of Gethsemane and the night before His crucifixion. How could He have even a thought of joy? Note how confidently He speaks of it: abiding, remaining, persistent joy. Like a hot geyser-spring, rising from unknown depths on an ice-bound world. How could He think of joy at such a moment? One answer alone seems possible. He knew that by His supreme sacrifice He was creating a well-spring of joy for all future generations. The spring of His joy was perennial because of the joy He was about to create for myriads. This joy was characteristic of His whole ministry. It seems to have been an unfailing fountain. How could it be otherwise when He was always ministering to others, when He was forever fulfilling His Father's loving will for men? It is in harmony with His often-repeated 'Be of good courage,' whether He was about to heal pain and disease, or proclaim the forgiveness of sin. The New Testament rings with this call to rejoice, and to rejoice greatly!

Our joy, like Christ's, consists in self-giving. We pass on to others the joy and love with which He fills our hearts, and in doing so, we are made infinitely happy. Let us today fix these thoughts in our mind. God is Love, and that Love cannot be self-contained.

Day by day let us abide in Him, with our heart-gate open to the incoming of His love, that He may be able to speak a word to those that are weary, to proclaim liberty to the captives, and the opening of the prison to them that are bound. We are not to create, but to pass on. Not to inaugurate, but to transmit. The love and grace of Christ were always expressed in acts of ministry. He was not content with speaking the word of cheer, but ministered in such a way that joy and gladness were the immediate result. We must not be well-wishers only, but well-doers, if it be only to help to lift a burden, or to guide the perplexed, or to give a caress to some lonely despairing soul. In all such acts of ministry we are giving our Saviour the opportunity of expressing Himself through us, and of fulfilling our joy."

-- F.B. Meyer

APRIL 8 --

"Here is a boy with five small barley loaves and two small fish, but how far will they go among so many?" (Jo 6:9)

In the sixth chapter of the Gospel of John we read about the great crowd of people who followed Jesus to the far shore of the Sea of Galilee because of the healings He had performed on many who were sick. As evening approached, it became clear they had not brought food with them and would soon grow hungry. Jesus asked His disciples how the people should be fed. Philip was perplexed. He answered that it would take eight months' wages to even begin to feed such a large crowd. Then Andrew approached and reported that a boy had brought forward five small loaves of barley bread, plus a couple of little fish. The prospect of feeding such a crowd with so few resources seemed absurd, but Jesus took the loaves and the fishes and had the disciples go among the people to tell them to sit down in a grassy area nearby. Jesus thanked His Father for the food and began to hand it out. Miraculously, as the food was given out, it multiplied so that everyone present was given all he needed to be satisfied. By the time all the food was distributed there were enough fragments of bread left over to fill twelve baskets.

This story itself is food for us. It is filled with symbols of the love and generosity of our Lord. It also teaches us that Jesus desires to be our Bread of Life and to see Himself multiplied through us.

Like the barley loaves that were handed out that day by the Sea of Galilee, Christ will put Himself into the lives of others if we will only give Him to them. How do we give Jesus away to others? By sharing about how God has helped us in the past. By giving help and encouragement to those in need. By praying for others and speaking the truth in love. There are an infinite number of ways we can give away our little loaves of Christ to others. Even one small act, if performed out of love for Jesus, will be multiplied by the Lord, whose delight it is to feed those who are hungry and strengthen those who are weak and in need of a Shepherd's love.

Another thing we might remember is that after the people were filled, Christ made it clear that even the fragments of bread should be gathered. "Let nothing be wasted," He said. When we receive the Bread of Life for ourselves, it is important that once we are fed we take what is left over and share it with others, that the Lord might multiply His Body yet again, and again and again. As the Bread of Life, He continues to multiply Himself every day, wherever He is offered, to everyone who will eat of the eternal life He wishes to share.

Lord, help me remember to take what You offer to me -- to feed each day upon Christ, who is the Bread of Life. And once I have been filled, help me not to lose one fragment of You, but to offer it to others who also need to be filled and satisfied with Your Life.

APRIL 9 --

"...and he calleth his own sheep by name, and leadeth them out. And when he putteth forth his own sheep, he goeth before them, and the sheep follow him: for they know his voice." (Jo 10:3-4)

"He only asks you to yield yourself to Him, that He may work in you to will and to do by His own mighty power. Your part is to yield yourself, His part is to work; and never, never will He give you any command which is not accompanied by ample power to obey it. Take no thought for the morrow in this matter; but abandon yourself with a generous trust to your loving Lord, who has promised never to call His own sheep out into any path without Himself going before them to make the way easy and safe. Take each onward step as He makes it plain to you. Bring all your life in each of its details to Him to regulate and guide. Follow gladly and quickly the sweet suggestions of His Spirit in your soul. And day by day you will find Him bringing you more and more into conformity with His will in all things; molding you and fashioning you, as you are able to bear it, into a vessel unto His honor, sanctified and meet for His use, and fitted to every good work."

-- Hannah Whitall Smith

"Let us do what we know He requires of us, and, as soon as we know His will, let us not spare ourselves, but be very faithful to Him. Such faithfulness ought not merely to lead us to do great things for His service, but whatever our hand finds to do, and which belongs to our state of life. The smallest things become great when God requires them of us; they are small only in themselves; they are always great when they are done for God, and when they serve to unite us with Him eternally."

– Francois Fenelon

APRIL 10 ---

"For the law of the Spirit of life in Christ Jesus hath made me free from the law of sin and death." (Ro 8:2)

"Be content to go on quietly. When you discover something in yourself which is earthly and imperfect, be patient while you strive to cast it out. Your perceptions will grow; at first God will show you very obvious stumbling-blocks. Be diligent in clearing these away, and do not aim at heights to which you are not yet equal. Leave all to God, and while you earnestly desire that He purify you, and seek to work with Him to that end, try to be satisfied with the gradual progress He sets before you; and remember that He often works in ways unseen by us."

-- Jean Nicolas Grou

Not yet thou knowest what I do
Within thine own weak breast,
To mould thee to My image true,
And fit thee for My rest.
But yield thee to My loving skill,
The veiled work of grace,
From day to day progressing still,
It is not thine to trace.

– Frances Ridley Havergal

"For God sent not his Son into the world to condemn the world; but that the world through him might be saved." (Jo 3:17)

"We need devise no elaborate theory or method of God-centered prayer. There is only one rubric: the lifting up to God of our honest desire to know him and to be made one with him. God-conscious prayer at its highest involves honest thinking, and a firm resolution to bring all our problems to the searchlight of his truth and to submit all our work to the touchstone of his interests and intentions. A lifelong discipline -- intellectual, spiritual and moral -- is needed before we can call ourselves adept in creative prayer. Yet the least gifted and most poorly equipped soul can attain mastery in it; for, from first to last, simple, honest desire for the love and fellowship of God is the key to all its mysteries.

God-centered prayer, then, means to enter the world of reality. It may be defined as a progressive revaluation of the whole of life in accordance with a revolutionary experience we might call a shifting of centers; but it is far better to approach it more simply, and conceive of it as a living way -- the way of Love. For that world of reality of which God is the center is the world of enduring and victorious Love, and its highway -- the great orienting path that gives it coherence -- is Christ. 'Your life is our way,' said Thomas a'Kempis; and the life of Christ in its eternal significance is indeed at once the way that each individual disciple has to tread, and the way of God in human history."   -- Brigid Herman

"What boundless gratitude is Your due, for revealing to me and to all faithful people the true and holy way to Your eternal Kingdom. Your life is our Way, and by holy patience we will journey onwards to You, who are our crown and consummation. If You, Lord, had not gone before us and showed the way, who could follow? How many would have stayed behind and far distant, had they not Your glorious example for their guide? Even now we are cold and careless, although we have heard of Your teaching and mighty acts. What would happen to us had we not Your light as our guide?"

                                                            – Thomas a'Kempis

"And the Lord turned, and looked upon Peter. And Peter remembered the word of the Lord." (Lu 22: 61)

"Peter, before he denied Christ, had cast out devils and healed the sick; and yet the flesh had power, and the flesh had room in him. Oh, beloved, we want to realize that it is just because there is so much of that self-life in us that the power of God cannot work in us as mightily as God is willing that it should work. Do you realize that the great God is longing to double his blessing, to give tenfold blessing through us? But there is something hindering him, and that something is a proof of nothing but the self-life. We talk about the pride of Peter, and the impetuosity of Peter, and the self-confidence of Peter. It all rooted in that one word, self. Christ had said, 'Deny self,' and Peter had never understood, and never obeyed; and every failing came out of that.

What a solemn thought, and what an urgent plea for us to cry: 'O God, do discover this to us, that none of us may be living the self-life.' It has happened to many a one who had been a Christian for years, who had perhaps occupied a prominent position, that God found him out and taught him to find himself out, and he became utterly ashamed, falling down broken before God. Oh, the bitter shame and sorrow and pain and agony that came to him, until at last he found that there was deliverance. Peter went out and wept bitterly, and there may be many a godly one in whom the power of the flesh still rules.

Another lesson: it is the work of our blessed Lord Jesus to discover the power of self.

How was it that Peter, the carnal Peter, self-willed Peter, Peter with the strong self-love, ever became a man of Pentecost and the writer of his epistle? It was because Christ had charge over him, and Christ watched over him, and Christ taught and blessed him. The warnings that Christ had given him were part of the training; and last of all there came that look of love. In his suffering, Christ did not forget him, but turned round and looked upon him -- and 'Peter went out and wept bitterly.' And the Christ who led Peter to Pentecost is waiting today to take charge of every heart that is willing to surrender itself to him."   – Andrew Murray

APRIL 13 ---

"He is not here: for he is risen, as he said. Come, see the place where the Lord lay."
(Ma 28:6)

"And so all the disciples were in a mood of deepest and darkest depression. The light had been cut off from their minds. They were in the dark. The taste had gone out of their lives. Everything had become stale and profitless. Simon Peter was gloomy with despondency and haggard with remorse. Two disciples were walking in the twilight to Emmaus, 'looking sad,' communing about the awful and sudden eclipse in which their hopes had been so miserably quenched....

And then came the cry, 'He is risen!' The Lord is alive! His tomb is empty. He has shaken off death and its grave clothes. He has marched out of the grave!

Think of that trumpet note pealing through the late night. Think of that great burning light streaming through the darkness, kindling life after life into blazing hope again. First the Magdalene, now Peter, now John, now the two journeying to Emmaus, now Thomas, until the entire disciple band was a circle of light again. It was an almost unspeakable revolution. 'The people that sat in darkness have seen a great light.' 'The Lord is risen indeed.'

Before the Easter morning the trumpet had seemed to the apostles to give an uncertain sound; there was either a trembling in its notes or a trembling in their ears; but now, with the resurrection, all uncertainty had gone, and the trumpet rang out its glorious blast, firm and rich and clear...

In the power of the resurrection the apostles saw a vast reservoir of spiritual energy for the quickening and emancipation of the race. This was their reasoning and their faith, that the Lord, who had emerged from the grave, and had thereby vanquished death, had the power to vanquish all death, whether it enthroned itself in body, mind, or soul. This was their faith, as this was their evangel, that in Christ we, too, can rise out of death into newness of life, that, just as He walked out of that tomb, we, too, can walk out of the grave and graveyard of our own corrupt past, and, in vigor and sweetness of being, become alive unto God." – J. H. Jowett

APRIL 14 --

"And the angel answered and said unto the women, Fear not ye: for I know that ye seek Jesus, which was crucified." (Ma 28:5)

"It must have been a glad errand to the angels who were sent to minister at the grave of the Redeemer, to roll the stone away, to keep watch at the empty sepulcher, and to tell the good tidings to the disciples who came with such heavy hearts. Their message was one of great joy. Jesus, whom His friends sought dead, was alive again for evermore. He had been in the grave, but He was not there now.

The empty tomb has many glorious voices. It tells us first that Jesus actually died. He was buried here, just in this place. His head lay there, His feet here. Here are the grave-clothes, the piece of fine linen which gentle hands wound around Him. Here is the napkin that covered His face. He lay just here. Look at the place and mark it well, and never forget that He actually was dead. This is important, for upon His death your acceptance with God depends.

But look again. The grave is empty now. He *was* here, but He is not here now, for He is risen. The grave is empty. Here are the grave-clothes, but there is no body. He is gone. The empty tomb tells, then, of resurrection. Death could not hold the Christ. He burst its bands and conquered the grave's power. This is important, for a dead Christ could not have saved us. Had He never risen, how could He have stood for us before God? How could He be our help in weakness, our support in trial, our Comforter, our Friend, if His dust lay yet in the grave? Therefore He is alive to intercede for us, to help us, to save us.

Still another truth which the empty tomb teaches us is that all who sleep in Jesus shall rise, too. One precious word of Scripture says: 'For if we believe that Jesus died and rose again, even so them also which sleep in Jesus will God bring with Him.' So let us learn to see through the grave to the life beyond." – J. R. Miller

APRIL 15 --

"What is man, that thou art mindful of him? And the son of man, that thou visitest him?" (Ps 8:4)

A Meditation

– Humble yourself utterly before God, saying with the Psalmist: "Oh Lord, I am nothing in respect of You. What am I, that You should remember me?" Reflect upon the fact that you would be lost in an abyss of nothingness, if God had not called you forth. And you would be eternally lost if He had not shed His blood for the remission of your sins; and what would have become of you in such a case?

– Ponder His goodness. Think upon what you owe your Great and Good Creator. It is He that has taken you out of your nothingness and made you what you are. Let Him be praised for every blessing and benefit you possess.

– Praise God for His patience with you over the years. Think of how He has loved you, despite your rebellions, your unruly affections, the many times you have departed from Him and given yourself to sin, the occasions when you have ignored His goodness, as though He had not even created you.

– Offer Him thanksgiving. Oh God, truly I am the work of Your Hands; help me to remember this. What have I to glory in? How is it that I can often exalt myself, when it is You alone Who are worthy of being exalted above all things. O my God, I offer You with all my heart the being You have given me. I dedicate and consecrate it to You.

--Adapted from a Meditation by St. Francis de Sales

APRIL 16 --

"Henceforth I call you not servants; for the servant knoweth not what his lord doeth: but I have called you friends; for all things that I have heard of my Father I have made known unto you." (Jo 15:15)

"The precious Lord Jesus Christ is our friend. Oh, let us seek to realize this. It is not merely a religious phrase or statement, but truly, He is our friend. He is the Brother 'born for adversity,' the one who 'sticks closer than a brother,' who will never leave and never forsake us.

When we cannot sleep at night, we can say to Christ, 'My precious Friend, will You give me a little sleep?' When in pain, we can say, 'My dear Friend, if it may please You, will You take away this pain? But if not, if You see that it's better that it should continue, sustain, help, and strengthen me.' When we feel lonely and tired, we can turn to Jesus; He is willing to be our friend in our loneliness. For sixty-two years and five months I had a beloved wife, and now in my ninety-second year I am left alone. But I turn to my precious Lord as I walk up and down in my room, and say, 'Jesus, I am alone, and yet not alone. You are with me; You are my friend; now Lord, comfort me and strengthen me, give to Your poor servant everything You see he needs.'

This is a reality, not a fable, that the Lord Jesus Christ is our friend. We should not be satisfied until we are brought to this, that we know the Lord Jesus Christ experientially and habitually to be our friend. Just ponder this. Habitually, never leaving, never forsaking us, at all times and under all circumstances ready to prove Himself to be our friend.

He is willing not merely to grant this for a few months, or a year or two, but to the very end of our earthly pilgrimage. David, in Psalm 23 says: 'Yea, though I walk through the valley of the shadow of death, I will fear no evil, for Thou art with me.' Oh, how precious this is. For this 'Lovely One' is coming again, and soon. Soon He will come again; and then He will take us home and there we shall be forever with Him. Oh, how precious is that bright and glorious prospect. Here again the practical point is to appropriate this to ourselves. 'He is coming to take me: poor, guilty, worthless, hell-deserving me. He is coming to take me to Himself.' And to the degree in which we enter into these glorious things, the joys of heaven have already commenced." – George Mueller

APRIL 17 ---

"For whosoever will save his life shall lose it; but whosoever shall lose his life for my sake and the gospel's, the same shall save it." (Mark 8:35)

"The law of sacrifice is the law of God. God, who lived in supreme self-sufficiency as the Father, Son and Holy Ghost, gave Himself. God's glory was in giving Himself, and so He gave Himself in the creation, in the beauty of the universe, so formed that every possible sort of happiness could come according to its natural law. And then God gave Himself in Jesus Christ. 'God so loved the world that he gave.' He gave His best, His all; gave His only begotten Son. The law of God is sacrifice. He loved until he gave all.

Then it is the law of Christ Himself. He came through God's sacrifice, and He came to sacrifice. He laid His honors down, left the society of heaven for a generation, and lived with creatures farther beneath Him than the groveling earth worm is beneath man. He made Himself one of them, and became a brother of this fallen race. He was always yielding and letting go, always holding back His power and not using it. He was always being subject to the will of the men beneath Him, until at last they nailed Him to the cross. His whole life was a continual refusing of Himself, carrying their burdens and sharing their sorrows. And so love and sacrifice is the law of Christ. 'Bear ye one another's burdens, and so fulfill the law of Christ.' The law of Christ is the bearing of others' burdens, the sharing of others' griefs, sacrificing yourself for another." — A. B. Simpson

I would not have the restless will
That hurries to and fro,
Seeking for some great thing to do,
Or secret thing to know;
I would be treated as a child,
And guided where I go.

Wherever in the world I am,
In whatsoever state,
I have a fellowship with hearts
To keep and cultivate;
And a work of lowly love to do
For the Lord on whom I wait.

So I ask Thee for the daily strength,
To none that ask denied,
And a mind to blend with outward life
While keeping at Thy side;
Content to fill a little space,
If Thou be glorified.
               --Anna Waring

APRIL 18 ---

"For whom the LORD loveth he correcteth; even as a father the son in whom he delighteth." (Pr 3:12)

From a letter to one of his pupils:
"I am rejoiced to find that God has reduced you to a state of weakness. Your self-love can neither be overcome nor vanquished by any other means ... it was hidden from your eyes while it fed upon the subtle poison of an

apparent generosity by which you constantly sacrificed yourself for others. God has forced it to cry aloud, to come forth into open day, and display its excessive jealousy. Oh how painful, but how useful, are these seasons of weakness. While any self-love remains, we are afraid of its being revealed, but so long as the least symptom of it lurks in the most secret recesses of the heart, God pursues it, and by some infinitely merciful blow, forces it into the light. The poison then becomes the remedy; self-love, pushed to extremity, discovers itself in all its deformity, plunges into despair ... and the flattering illusions of a whole lifetime are dissipated. God sets before your eyes your idol, self. You behold it, and cannot turn your eyes away; and as you have no longer any power over yourself, you cannot keep the sight from others.

Thus to exhibit self-love without its mask is the most mortifying punishment that can be inflicted. We no longer behold it wise, discreet, polite, self-possessed and courageous in sacrificing itself for others; it is no longer the self-love whose nourishment consisted in the belief that it had need of nothing, and the persuasion that its greatness and generosity deserved a different name. It is the selfishness of a silly child, screaming at the loss of an apple; but it is far more tormenting, for it also weeps from rage that it has wept; it cannot be still, and refuses all comfort, because its venomous character has been detected. It beholds itself foolish, rude, and impertinent, and is forced to look its own frightful countenance in the face.... You ask for a remedy, that you may get well. You do not need to be cured, but to be slain; seek not impatiently for a remedy, but let death come."

--Francois Fenelon

Often at the mercy-seat, while calling on Thy name,
Swarms of evil thoughts I meet, which fill my soul with shame.
Agitated in my mind, like a feather in the air,
Can I thus a blessing find? My soul, can this be prayer?

But when Christ my Lord and Friend, is pleased to show His power,
All at once my troubles end, and I've a golden hour;
Then I see His smiling face, feel the pledge of joys to come,
Often, Lord, repeat this grace, 'till thou shalt call me home.
--John Newton

APRIL 19 --

"Rest in the LORD, and wait patiently for him...those that wait upon the LORD, they shall inherit the earth." (Ps 37:7, 9)

Somehow, in some way, God will eventually engineer us into a place where all our self effort and praying will cease to accomplish what we are after and we will have to wait upon God and God alone for deliverance from our struggle. This is the Lesson of Waiting. Why must we learn this lesson? Because it is only when we have exhausted all of our own strength and found all other means of help has come to no avail that we can understand at heart-depth how utterly dependent we are upon the Lord – not for most things, but for every thing.

Are you in God's waiting room today? It is not by accident, Dear One. God places His children in His waiting room when He knows they are ready to go to a higher place with Him. If you are having to learn the Lesson of Waiting, do not fear that He has forgotten you. He has not. He will not forsake you. He has brought you to this place to accomplish His next important work within you.

"Give God His glory by resting in Him, by trusting Him fully, by waiting patiently for Him. This patience honors Him greatly. It leaves Him, as God on the throne, to do His work. It yields self wholly into His hands. It lets God be God. If your waiting is for some special request, wait patiently. If your waiting is more an exercise of the spiritual life seeking to know and have more of God, wait patiently. Whether it is in the shorter specific periods of waiting, or as the continuous habit of the soul, rest in the Lord, be still before the Lord, and wait patiently. 'They that wait on the Lord shall inherit the land.' " — Andrew Murray

APRIL 20 ---

"Arise, shine; for thy light is come, and the glory of the LORD is risen upon thee." (Is 60:1)

"It is a great thing to be a Christian. The very name is a noble one, beyond all the noble names of earth. The thing itself is inconceivably blessed and glorious. To say, 'I am a Christian' is to say, 'I belong to God's nobility; I am of the peerage of heaven.'

Much, then, is expected of you. Do not disgrace the old family name. Do nothing unworthy of Him who represents you in heaven, and whom you represent on earth. He is faithful to you; be faithful to Him. Let men know what a Lord and Master you serve. Be His witnesses; be His mirrors; be His living epistles. Let Him speak through you to the world; and do speak of Him. Let your life tell your fellow men what He is, and what He is to you. Speak well of Him to men, as He speaks well of you to God. He has honored you by giving you His name; He has blessed you by conferring on you sonship, and royalty, and an eternal heritage: see that you do justice to His love and magnify His greatness.

Let your light shine. Do not obstruct it, or hide it, or mingle darkness with it. 'Arise, shine; for thy light is come, and the glory of the Lord is risen upon thee.'

It is the light of love that you have received; let it shine. It is the light of holiness; let it shine. And if you ask, 'How am I to get the light and to maintain it in fulness?, my answer is 'Christ shall give you light' (Ep 5:14). There is light enough in Him who is the light of the world. 'The Lamb is the light thereof' (Re 21:23). There is no light for man but from the Lamb. It is the Cross, the Cross alone, that lights up a dark soul and keeps it shining, so that we walk in light as He is in the light; for 'God is light, and in Him is no darkness at all.'

Be true to Him who loved you, and washed you from your sins in His own blood... Follow Him. His first words to you were, 'Come to me.' You came and found rest. But He adds these two other messages: 'Abide in me,' and 'Follow me.' You take up your cross as He took up His; and you follow Him. You go forth without the camp, bearing His reproach (Lu 9:23; He 13:13). Through good report and through bad report you follow Him. He draws you, leads you, keeps you; and so you follow Him. Your whole life is to be one continuous following of the Lord."   – Horatius Bonar

APRIL 21 --

"And he laid it upon my mouth, and said, Lo, this hath touched thy lips; and thine iniquity is taken away, and thy sin purged." (Is 6:7)

God knew all along we would need a Savior. He saw what sin had done to us, how it had distorted and perverted human nature, recognized we could never achieve on our own the perfection required to come into His holy presence. And so He sent His Son.

One of the words for sin in the Bible is "khaw-taw," a Hebrew word that is derived from an archery term which means "to miss the mark." We know from experience, as flawed human beings, that we are bound to miss the mark much of the time. We'd like to behave perfectly toward everyone, but we don't. We'd like to say things in the right way and with a pure heart, but we don't. We'd like to have good motives for everything we do, but we don't. We're sinners. We can't get the arrow to land in the center of the target, no matter how hard we try. God knew what flawed marksmen we would be. And He knew that even if we worked all day long, every day, for the rest of our lives, we could never become perfect shots. It just isn't in us.

There is another Hebrew word for sin. It is "khat-taw-aw," which can have two meanings. It can mean either the offense of sin itself, or the sacrifice offering necessary to remit the sin. This word is a perfect description of Christ. He not only became the offense of sin for us, but He also became the sacrifice for sin that we needed so that we would not have to pay the price ourselves.

When it comes to achieving a perfect score with God, Jesus has already hit the mark in our behalf. His marksmanship is always perfect. In essence, whenever we shoot and miss, our Father doesn't record our score. Instead, He lets us put down Jesus' perfect score on our scorecards. With rules like that, we are destined to win. The perfection we wish we could obtain, but cannot obtain in our own strength, is already ours, through Christ, Who has already achieved a perfect score. Our sin – our failure to hit the mark – is never going to be counted against us.

> No strength of our own and no goodness we claim;
> Yet, since we have known of the Savior's great Name,
> In this our strong tower for safety we hide:
> The Lord is our power, 'The Lord will provide.'
> --John Newton

APRIL 22 --

"For whom the Lord loveth he chasteneth, and scourgeth every son whom he receiveth." He 12:6)

The purpose of our lives in this world is not to be high achievers or materially secure -- it is to be prepared for our eternal life with Christ.

If we try to make life a place of comfort and ease, we'll probably end up being disappointed. But if we view it instead as a spiritual "work-out," we'll end up much happier. A spiritual work-out is where we exercise our spiritual muscles, build up our moral strength and do all the various exercises God prescribes into order to transform us into the likeness of Jesus Christ.

Oddly enough, those who insist upon trying to make happiness the goal of their lives often end up being unhappy. They often experience disappointment because life seldom measures up to their expectations. If we believe life should be like a comfortable cocoon we're going to be disturbed most of the time. Conversely, if we recognize we are here to be trained up in the ways of God, we will struggle, certainly, but we will also receive many unexpected and delightful blessings along the way because the Lord will sustain us as we seek to do His will and learn from the circumstances and problems He allows us to encounter.

Those who do not know Christ may pursue the pleasures of this world in the pointless quest for fame or affluence, but those who have set their hearts to follow Christ know that trials are part of the process God uses to train us. How can we expect to be free from trials when Scripture teaches us that "we must through much tribulation enter into the kingdom of God" (Acts 14:22)? Even Christ, who was sinless, learned "obedience by the things which he suffered" (He 5:8). This same pattern of perfecting will also be applied to those who call Him "Lord." As we walk through our challenges, however, we will also have God's assurance that they are being used to "make you perfect, stablish, strengthen, settle you" (I Pet 5:10).

"What man of you, having an hundred sheep, if he lose one of them, doth not leave the ninety and nine in the wilderness, and go after that which is lost, until he find it?" (Lu 15:4)

"A wild young fellow, who was brought to the Lord at a mission meeting, and who became a rejoicing Christian and lived an exemplary life afterward, was asked by someone what he did to get converted. 'Oh,' he said, 'I did my part, and the Lord did His.'

'But what was your part,' asked the inquirer, 'and what was the Lord's part?' 'My part, he said, 'was to run away, and the Lord's part was to run after me until He caught me.'

God's part is always to run after us. Christ came to seek and to save that which is lost. This is always the divine part; but in our foolishness we do not understand it, but think that the Lord is the one who is lost, and that our part is to seek and find Him. The very expressions we use show this. We urge people to 'seek the Lord,' and we talk about having 'found' Him... Because we do not know Him, we naturally get all sorts of wrong ideas about Him. We think He is an angry Judge who is on the watch for our slightest faults, or a harsh Task-master determined to exact from us the uttermost service...

But I can assert boldly, and without fear of contradiction, that it is impossible for anyone who really knows God to have such uncomfortable thoughts about Him. Plenty of outward discomforts there may be, and many earthly sorrows and trials, but through them all, the soul that knows God realizes that everything that tender love and divine wisdom can do for us will be unfailingly done. Not a single loophole for worry or fear is left to the soul that knows God.

'Ah, yes,' you say, 'but how am I to get to know Him. Other people seem to have some kind of inward revelation that makes them know Him, but I never do; and no matter how much I pray, everything seems dark to me. I want to know God, but I do not see how to manage it.'

Your trouble is that you have got a wrong idea of what knowing God is, or at least the kind of knowing I mean. For I do not mean any mystical interior revelations of any kind. Such revelations are delightful when you can have them, but they are not always at your command, and they are often variable and uncertain. The kind of knowing I mean is just the plain matter-of-fact knowledge of God's nature and character that comes to us by believing what is revealed to us in the Bible concerning Him. The Apostle John at the close of his gospel says, regarding the things he had been recording, 'and many other signs truly did Jesus in the presence of His disciples which are not written in this book: but these are written that ye might believe that Jesus is the Christ, the Son of God; and that, believing, ye might have life through His name.' It is believing the thing that is written, not the thing that is inwardly revealed, that is to give life; and the kind of knowing I mean is the knowing that comes from believing the things that are written."   --Hannah Whitall Smith

APRIL 24 ---

"...behold, now is the accepted time; behold, now is the day of salvation." (II Co 6:2)

"No loving word was ever spoken, no good deed ever done, 'tomorrow.' We cannot act in the unborn future, nor in the dead past; only in the living present. That is why [today is so crucial]. Today holds life and death, character and destiny, in its hands. Opportunity says with Jesus, 'Me ye have not always.' We say: 'I will take my chances. There is plenty of time.' Ah, how often do we say, 'some other time,' to find that there is no other time. Some things we can do 'not always.' How shall we find out what things can be done any time, and what things now or never? Only by living in the faith that today is the only day we have and challenging every opportunity for its meaning. Esau filled his life with regret for trifling one day; Esther's was full of glory for one day's courage. Peter slept one hour, and lost a matchless opportunity. Mary's name is fragrant forever for the loving deed of a day. Do your best now."   – Maltbie Davenport Babcock

"If I did not simply live from one moment to the next, it would be impossible for me to keep my patience. I can see only the present, I forget the past and I take good care not to think about the future. We get discouraged and feel despair because we brood about the past and the future. It is such folly to pass one's time fretting, instead of resting quietly on the heart of Jesus."   –Saint Therese

Today I can make the decision to take some time to appreciate the things I'm so prone to take for granted. I can watch a child at play, give God thanks for my blessings, appreciate a kindness done to me or reach out to help someone who needs encouragement or understanding. I can slow down a little, give my full attention to whatever I'm doing and make the choice to really listen when someone wants to talk to me. These are all ways I can be more receptive to the Lord's presence in my life today.

APRIL 25 ---

"And let us not be weary in well doing: for in due season we shall reap, if we faint not." (Ga 6:9)

One day, near dusk, a woman took a walk down an unfamiliar lane and came upon a most charming garden. Its owner obviously had put much time and thought into its planting for it was full of fragrant flowers and shrubs. Everywhere she looked she saw lavender, Dianthus, lobelia, daisies and many other charming plants lining its winding paths; upon its walls climbed roses, honeysuckle, jessamine and other vines. The little garden was a sweet oasis that appeared, on that spring evening, to be as perfect as it could be.

Some time later she again passed by the little plot, anxious to see what was in bloom, but this time her heart sank. The owner had torn out almost all of the annual and perennial plants, and the roses and vines had been cut back so severely they looked like lifeless sticks. She felt almost overcome with grief: how could someone spoil such a lovely place, for it had so clearly whispered of the love and beauty of God?

Time passed. Months went by. The woman had stopped passing by the garden because she knew the sight of it would break her heart, but one day business required her to travel down the lane. She steeled herself for a look as she came upon the place; once again she was shocked at what she saw.

There, shining under the rays of a glorious noonday sun, was a garden so lovely that it quite outdid the one she had first discovered. The owner had again planted many of the same shrubs and flowers as before -- lavender and daisies and Dianthus and honeysuckle again lined the paths, but now they were joined by a lush array of other plants: lamb's ears, snapdragons, violets, forget-me-nots, columbine, lilies and many other flowers had been added to garden. But this was not all. Along the fences she again saw the roses and honeysuckle and jessamine, just as before, but now their blossoms were more lush and vigorous than ever; they were literally covered with masses of blooms. Other vines had been added: trumpet vines, clematis, wisteria and many more. The splendor of this second garden was beyond anything she could have imagined when she first set eyes upon the place.

Dear Reader, if your garden has been drastically pruned and you fear that all your work has been in vain, take heart. The True Husbandman knows how precious it was to you. If He has chosen to cut back parts of it and remove plants you thought would always be in bloom, remember it is only to make way for a more beautiful garden in the future. Give Him the time He needs; have faith in His good and loving plans for you; allow Him to work in His own way, and one day you will see a harvest that will be greater than anything you have yet imagined.

APRIL 26 ---

"And he said to me, My grace suffices thee; for my power is perfected in weakness. Most gladly therefore will I rather boast in my weaknesses, that the power of the Christ may dwell upon me." (II Cor 12:9 - Darby Translation)

One of the hardest things to do is admit we are powerless over something. After all, our entire culture seems to be based on the belief that the more power you have, the better your life will be. It is constantly urging us to succeed, achieve, be strong, overcome, make it happen. Nevertheless, walking with the Lord will at some point require us to recognize that we are powerless over much of life and even over many things within ourselves. If we fail to recognize our powerlessness, it is impossible for us to come into right relation with God, for He alone is the One Who truly has all power.

It often takes a crisis of some kind to teach us how powerless we are. The person who works too hard may become ill or overwhelmed and realize he is a workaholic. The person who has escaped into drugs or alcohol discovers she is addicted. We may engage in immoral activities, cling to relationships that are destructive, abuse ourselves or others, or try so hard to make things right for the people we love that we end up trying to control them and discover they don't want to be around us anymore. All kinds of difficulties may develop to show us we've slipped into an unhealthy way of living, even though that was never our intention. Such things may have to happen to us before we can admit we are powerless.

Fortunately, admitting we are powerless isn't the end – even though it may sometimes feel like it. It can actually be a new beginning. Admitting we are powerless over something can open the door to a better relationship with God. It can become the foundation for a healthier lifestyle and our first step toward victory. When we admit we are powerless over something, we are then free to recognize it is God who has the power to help us make any necessary changes and transform our lives. He is the One who knows how to make us into healthier, more balanced and more productive people.

Lord, please show me the areas where I need to admit my powerlessness. Help me to surrender these areas to You, and to trust that You will show me what You want me to do.

APRIL 27 --

"Verily, verily, I say unto you, He that entereth not by the door into the sheepfold, but climbeth up some other way, the same is a thief and a robber." (Jo 10:1)

"The only way into the Church of God, either for ministers or members, is by Christ, and through faith in Him.

Many enter in by learning; learning is not to be despised. But it is not the door. There are many that enter into the ministry by having eminent gifts, but these are not the door. And those that enter in by such a way are thieves and robbers for they enter not in by the door... Remember then, and never forget it, that the right way into the ministry is through Jesus Christ.

None can tell of sin but those who have felt its burden. None can tell of pardon, but those who have tasted of it. None can tell of Christ's power to sanctify, but those who have holiness in their hearts. Brothers and sisters, hold such in reverence, flee from all others; they may have learning, they may have gifts, they may have the flattery of the common people, but they are thieves and robbers.

But, further, there are many members who enter into the fold another way; they also are thieves and robbers. There are many who enter in by the door of knowledge — they have got acquainted with Bible knowledge, they can tell about a sinner's acceptance with God; but if you have not come into the fold by being washed in the blood of Christ, you are a thief and a robber.

Some enter into the fold by a good life. As touching the law they are like Paul, blameless. They say they are not thieves, not swearers, not drunkards, they think they have a right to enter in — a right to sit at the Lord's table; but Christ says it over and over again, such as these are thieves and robbers. Remember, if you are admitted into the fold on account of your morality, your outward decency, your good life, you are a thief and a robber. There is a day coming when those who have entered into the sheepfold, not by the door, but some other way, will look back and see their guilt when they shall enter an undone eternity.

Observe that Christ is a present entrance. There is a time in each of your lives — or rather I should say, history — that the door of the sheepfold is open to you. 'I am the door; by me if any man enter in, he shall be saved;' but time will pass away. It is but a moment compared with eternity. This is a solemn truth. If I could promise you that the door will stand open for a hundred years, yet it would still be wisdom on your part to enter in now; but I cannot answer for a year, I cannot answer for a month, I cannot answer for a day, I cannot answer for an hour; all that I can answer for is, it is open now. Tomorrow it may be shut forever."   – Robert Murray McCheyne

APRIL 28 ---

"He that findeth his life shall lose it; and he that loseth his life for my sake shall find it." (Matthew 10:39)

"I am amazed at the almost audacious candor of the program [laid out by Jesus]. There is no hiding of the sharp flint, no softening of the shadow, no gilding of the cross. The hostilities bristle in naked obtrusiveness. Every garden is a prospective battlefield: 'I am not come to send peace, but a sword.' The choice of the Christ involves a perpetual challenge to war.

Now, if this be the program of the kingdom, what shall we do? What are we tempted to do? We are tempted to frame for ourselves a very perverted conception of the characteristics of a reasonable life. If our surrounding can be so hostile, if our difficulties can be so stupendous, if the hatred we may awake can be so intense, if we can call into being a mighty army of aliens, surely the policy dictated by a sane and healthy judgment will be this: Take the line of least resistance; keep your lips closed; go with the stream; look after yourself!

This is the method of reasonableness. This is the policy which assures self-preservation. This is the secret of a successful and progressive life. Keep your lips closed is the 'policy of silence;' 'go with the stream' is the policy of opportunism; 'look after yourself' is the policy of self-aggrandizement. Such is the counsel of Mr. Worldly Wiseman, who strenuously urges upon me this threefold policy of silence, drifting, and suction, if amid all these sleeping hostilities I would attain to a roomy and successful life.

But the Master absolutely reverses this counsel. Not by the policy of the world shall we ever attain to self-preservation and enrichment; it is a policy which speedily and inevitably leads to impoverishment and self-destruction. The policy of the world supposedly leads to an apparent 'finding.' In reality it is a terrible 'losing.' Along these roads the apparent finder is the loser; the loser is the winner.

Let us proclaim the methods of the Lord. It is not by silence but by expression that we win: 'Whoever shall confess Me before men.' It is not by drifting but by endurance that we win: 'He that endureth to the end shall be saved.' It is not by self-aggrandizement but by self-sacrifice that we win: 'He that loseth his life for My sake shall find it.' This is the secret of Jesus: life is sustained and enriched by expression, by endurance, and by sacrifice."

– J. H. Jowett

APRIL 29 --

"Herein is love, not that we loved God, but that He loved us, and sent His Son to be the propitiation for our sins." (I Jo 4:10)

"If I felt my heart as hard as a stone; if I did not love God or man or woman or little child, I would yet say to God in my heart, 'O God, see how I trust You, because You are perfect, and not changeable like me. I do not love You. I love nobody. I am not even sorry for it. You see how much I need You to come close to me, to put Your arm around me, to say to me, 'My child;' for the worse my state, the greater is my need of my Father who loves me. Come to me and my day will dawn; my love will come back, and, oh, how I shall love You, my God, and know that my love is Your love, my blessedness Your being.'"   – George MacDonald

"All creatures that have wings can escape from every snare that is set for them, if only they will fly high enough; and the soul that uses its wings can always find a sure 'way to escape' from all that can hurt or trouble it. What then are these wings? Their secret is contained in the words, 'They that wait upon the Lord.' The soul that waits upon the Lord is the soul that is entirely surrendered to Him, and that trusts Him perfectly. Therefore, we might name our wings the wings of Surrender and of Trust. If we will only surrender ourselves utterly to the Lord, and will trust Him perfectly, we shall find our souls 'mounting up with wings as eagles' to the heavenly places in Christ Jesus, where earthly annoyances or sorrows have no power to disturb us."   -- Hannah Whitall Smith

APRIL 30 --

"And in the morning, It will be foul weather to day: for the sky is red and lowring. O ye hypocrites, ye can discern the face of the sky; but can ye not discern the signs of the times?" (Ma 16:3)

"Dear reader, do not think that the study of prophecy consists merely in the setting of dates or forecasting future events. For wise reasons the Master has withheld from us 'the day and the hour' when He will come, but He called the Pharisees hypocrites because they could not discern the signs of the times, and He has commanded us to 'Watch,' and he has pronounced a blessing upon the study of prophecy.

Peter exhorts us to give heed unto the sure word of prophecy. 'All Scripture is given by inspiration of God, and is profitable for doctrine, for reproof, for correction, for instruction in righteousness.' (II Ti 3:16)

The greater part of this Scripture consists of prophecy, and if Christians would give more attention to it, they would not find themselves distracted from present service, but they would find much light thrown on their present path, much practical encouragement given to their ministry. Their faith would rest upon a deeper comprehension of God's character and ways, and their spiritual horizon would stand out in clearer outline than before.

But to perceive and understand all this requires much more than a surface study of Scripture, or the mere forecasting of future events. It must be read in its profounder teachings, in those wonderful depths of meaning that underlie its illustrations, its metaphors, its history... Such a study of God's word will be found of paramount importance to meet the skepticism of the day, for it furnishes us out of God's own armory, and trains us in His school of warfare. See how God uses prophetic truth to confound the philosophers and skeptics. And He points to the prophecies fulfilled as an assurance of the accomplishment of the new things declared by Him... 'Despise not prophesyings' (I Th 5:20)."   – William Blackstone

"Being justified freely by his grace through the redemption that is in Christ Jesus:"
(Ro 3:24)

"You know in daily life what absolute surrender is. You know that everything has to be given up to its special, definite object and service. I have a pen in my pocket, and that pen is absolutely surrendered to the one work of writing, and that pen must be absolutely surrendered to my hand if I am to write properly with it. If another holds it partly, I cannot write properly. This coat is absolutely given up to me to cover my body. This building is entirely given up to religious services. And now, do you expect that in your immortal being, in the divine nature that you have received by regeneration, God can work His work, every day and every hour, unless you are entirely given up to Him? God cannot. The Temple of Solomon was absolutely surrendered to God when it was dedicated to Him. And every one of us is a temple of God, in which God will dwell and work mightily on one condition -- absolute surrender to Him. God claims it, God is worthy of it, and without it God cannot work His blessed work in us.

God not only claims it, but God will work it Himself. I am sure there is many a heart that says: 'Yes, but absolute surrender implies so much.' Someone says: 'Oh, I have passed through so much trial and suffering, and there is so much of the self-life still remaining, and I dare not face the entire giving of it up, because I know it will cause so much trouble and agony for me.'

Imagine, that God's children have such thoughts of Him, such cruel thoughts. I come to you with a message, fearful and anxious one. God does not ask you to give the perfect surrender in your strength, or by the power of your will; God is willing to work it in you. Do we not read: 'It is God that worketh in us, both to will and to do of his good pleasure?' And that is what we should seek for -- to go on our faces before God, until our hearts learn to believe that the everlasting God Himself will come in to turn out what is wrong, to conquer what is evil, and to work what is well-pleasing in His blessed sight. God Himself will work it in you."   – Andrew Murray

"Being justified freely by his grace through the redemption that is in Christ Jesus:"
(Ro 3:24)

"...Be it always remembered, that we cannot be saved by the merit of our own works, because holy works are themselves a gift, the work of the grace of God. If you have faith, and joy, and hope, who gave them to you? These did not spring up spontaneously in your heart. They were sown there by the hand of love. If you have lived a godly life for years, if you have been a diligent servant of the church and of your God, in whose strength have you done it? Is there not One who works all our works in us? Could you work out your own salvation with fear and trembling if God did not first work in you both to will and to do of his good pleasure? How can that, then, claim a reward, which is, in itself, the gift of God? I think the ground is cut right away from those who would put confidence in human merit, when we show, first of all, that, in Scripture, salvation is clearly said to be 'not of works, lest any man should boast;' and, secondly, that even the good works of believers are the fruit of a renewed life; for 'we are his workmanship, created in Christ Jesus unto good works, which God hath before ordained that we should walk in them.'

Further, if salvation were not a free gift, how else could a sinner get it? I will pass over some of you, who fancy that you are the best people in the world. It is sheer fancy, mark you, without any truth in it. But I will say nothing about you. There are, however, some of us, who know that we were not the best people in the world; we who sinned against God, and knew it, and who were broken in pieces under a sense of our guilt. I know, for one, that there would have been no hope of heaven for me, if salvation had not been the free gift of God to those who deserved it not.

> All that I was, my sin, my guilt,
> My death, was all mine own;
> All that I am, I owe to thee,
> My gracious God, alone."
> ----Charles Spurgeon

MAY 3 --

"Watch and pray, that ye enter not into temptation: the spirit indeed is willing, but the flesh is weak." (Ma 26:41)

"We need to watch our prayers as well as watch for the answers to our prayers. It requires as much wisdom to pray rightly as it does faith to receive the answers to our prayers.

A Christian confided that he had been in years of darkness because God had failed to answer certain of his prayers. As a result, he had been in a state bordering on infidelity. A very few moments were sufficient to convince this friend that his prayers had been entirely unauthorized and that God had never promised to answer such prayers. They were for things which, in the exercise of ordinary wisdom, he should have accomplished himself. The result was deliverance from the cloud of unbelief which was almost wrecking his Christian life. There are some things about which we do not need to pray as much as to take the light which God has already given. Many people are asking God to give them peculiar signs, tokens and supernatural intimations of His will. Our business is to use the light He has given, and then He will give whatever more we need." – A. B. Simpson

MAY 4 ---

"How God anointed Jesus of Nazareth with the Holy Ghost and with power: who went about doing good, and healing all that were oppressed of the devil; for God was with him." (Ac 10:38)

"Jesus fitted his help in just where it was needed. He never used his power to show that he could, but to help somebody. The people were hungry, and he fed them. The widow was broken-hearted over her boy, and Jesus brought him back to life. The tax-collector called, and he helped Peter pay the bill. The wedding supplies ran out, and he renewed them. His power is at hand today to help in the common things of our daily lives....

Jesus couldn't help working. He had a tender heart. He felt the need of the crowds. He couldn't withstand the plea of their need. His heart responded. His hand reached out quickly to help. No criticism or scorn or opposition could hold back the thing so sorely needed. The work grew out of a heart in touch with his Father and with the needy crowds. This is the secret of working, now as then." – S. D. Gordon

MAY 5 ---

"Glory ye in his holy name: let the heart of them rejoice that seek the Lord. Seek the Lord, and his strength: seek his face evermore." (Ps 105:3-4)

"Imitate a little child, whom one sees holding tight with one hand to its father, while with the other it gathers strawberries or blackberries from the wayside hedge.

Even so, while you gather and use this world's goods with one hand, always let the other be fast in your Heavenly Father's hand, and look round from time to time to make sure that He is satisfied with what you are doing, at home or abroad. Beware of letting go, under the idea of making or receiving more; if He forsakes you, you will fall to the ground at the first step. When your ordinary work or business is not specially engrossing, let your heart be fixed more on God than on it; and if the work be such as to require your undivided attention, then pause from time to time and look to God, even as navigators who make their way to port by continually looking toward the stars in the heavens rather than down upon the deeps on which they sail. If you do this, God will work with you, in you, and for you, and your work will be blessed." – St. Francis de Sales

"Neither by the blood of goats and calves, but by his own blood he entered in once into the holy place, having obtained eternal redemption for us." (He 9:12)

"The Epistle to the Hebrews was written by the eternal Spirit for the whole Church of God in all ages. It shows us on what footing we are to stand before God as sinners; and in what way we are to draw near as worshippers.

There is no day nor hour in which evil is not coming forth from us, and in which the great blood shedding is not needed to wash it away. This epistle is manifestly meant for the whole life of the saint, and for the whole history of the Church. God's purpose is that we should never, while here, get beyond the need of expiation and purging; and though vain man may think that he would better glorify God by sinlessness, yet the Holy Spirit in this epistle shows us that we are called to glorify God by our perpetual need of the precious blood shedding upon the cross. No need of washing may be the watchword of some; they are beyond all that! But they who, whether conscious or unconscious of sin, will take this epistle as the declaration of God's mind as to the imperfection of the believing man on earth, will be constrained to acknowledge that the blood shedding must be in constant requisition, not (as some say) to keep the believer in a sinless state, but to cleanse him from his hourly sinfulness.

Boldness to enter into the holiest is a condition of the soul which can only be maintained by continual recourse to the blood of sprinkling, alike for conscious and for unconscious sin: the latter of these being by far the most subtle and the most terrible, that for which the sin-offering had to be brought.

'If we say that we have no sin, we deceive ourselves, and the truth is not in us.' The presence of sin in us is the only thing which makes such epistles as that to the Hebrews at all intelligible. When, by some instantaneous act of faith, we soar above sin (as some think they do), we also bid farewell to the no longer needed blood, and to the no longer needed Epistle to the Hebrews.

'Through the veil, which is His flesh,' is our one access to God; not merely at first when we believed, but day by day, to the last. The blood-stained pavement is that one which we tread, and the blood-stained mercy-seat is that before which we bow. In letters of blood there is written on that veil, and that mercy-seat, 'I am the way, the truth, and the life; no man cometh to the Father but by me:' and, again, 'Through Him we have access, by one Spirit, unto the Father.'" – Horatius Bonar

"But as many as received him, to them gave he power to become the sons of God, even to them that believe on his name:" (Jo 1:12)

"It is a fact that God loves each of us with the tenderest and most particular love. You may not believe or feel it; the warm summer sun may be shining against your shuttered and curtained window without making itself seen or felt within; but your failure to realize and appreciate the fact of God's love toward you cannot alter its being so.

It is a fact that in Jesus every obstacle has been removed out of the way of your immediate forgiveness and acceptance. God was in the dying Savior, putting away sin, bearing our sins in His own body on the tree, reconciling the world to Himself. You may not believe this, or feel the joy of it, but that does not alter the fact that it is so.

After the peace was signed between the North and the South in the great American war, there were soldiers hiding in the woods, starving on berries, who might have returned to their homes. They either did not know, or did not credit, the good news, and they went on starving long after their comrades had been welcomed by their wives and children. Theirs was the loss, but their failure in knowledge or belief did not alter the fact that peace was proclaimed and that the door was wide open for their return.

A friend may have paid all my debts in my native village, from which I have fled, fearing arrest and disgrace. He may have done it so speedily that my credit has never been impaired, or my good name forfeited. There may be all the old love and honor waiting to greet me. He may have told me; but if I still absent myself and refuse to return, my folly in this respect cannot undo those beneficent acts, though it perpetuates my misery.

It is a fact that as soon as a soul trusts Christ, it is born into Christ's family, and becomes a child of God. There is no doubt about this. You may not feel good; you may be conscious of recent failure; you may even spend your days under a pall of somber depression; but if you have received Christ, and truly trusted in Him, you have been born again, not of man, or the will of the flesh, but of God (John 1:12). You may be a prodigal or inconsistent child, but you are a child. If you were wise you would take the child's place at the Father's table and enjoy His smile. But if you still remain out in the cold, as the elder brother in the parable, you do not alter the fact that your place is ready for you to occupy whenever you will."   --F.B. Meyer

"Ask, and it shall be given you; seek, and ye shall find; knock, and it shall be opened unto you:" (Ma 7:7)

"The tenor of Christ's teachings is to declare that men are to pray earnestly -- to pray with an earnestness that cannot be denied. Heaven has harkening ears only for the whole-hearted, and the deeply-earnest. Energy, courage, and persistent perseverance must back the prayers which heaven respects, and God hears. All these qualities of soul, so essential to effectual praying, are brought out in the parable of the man who went to his friend for bread at midnight.

This man entered on his errand with confidence. Friendship promised him success. His plea was the pressing of a truth; he could not go back empty-handed. The flat refusal chagrined and surprised him. Here even friendship failed! But there was something to be tried yet -- stern resolution, set, fixed determination. He would stay and press his demand until the door was opened and the request granted. This he proceeded to do, and by dint of importunity secured what ordinary solicitation had failed to obtain...

Importunate praying never faints nor grows weary; it is never discouraged; it never yields to cowardice, but is buoyed up and sustained by a hope that knows no despair, and a faith which will not let go. Importunate praying has patience to wait and strength to continue. It never prepares itself to quit praying, and declines to rise from its knees until an answer is received."
                                                                    --E.M. Bounds

"I was never deeply interested in any object, never prayed sincerely and earnestly for it, but that it came at some time, no matter how distant the day. Somehow, in some shape, probably the last I would have devised, it came."
                                                                    – Adoniram Judson

MAY 9 --

"For we are unto God a sweet savour of Christ..." (II Co 2:15)

As we inch our way forward in the Christian life we begin to sense within ourselves an increasing desire to leave behind the heavy weight of self and move forward into the higher regions where God's presence is to be found. We find ourselves becoming less and less interested in accomplishing those things which are of our own wills, and more and more attracted to those mysteries and activities that grace reveals to us as the will of God. We yearn to find a way to devote ourselves to God's service, to seek His interests and to adapt ourselves to His movements so that there should be an ever-diminishing disparity between His will and our own. Thus, the great precept that sums up the supernatural life -- "Thou shalt love the Lord thy God with all thy heart, and with all thy soul, and with all thy mind, and with all thy strength" (Mark 12:30) -- ceases being merely a lofty ideal and begins to come into focus for us on a deeply personal level.

The Apostle Paul tells us that in order to fulfill this precept, we are to seek to please God "in all things" (Co 1:10), and to "grow up in all things" (Ep 4:15), and thus, when we begin to digest his meaning in these phrases we discover that each and every action we perform is capable of being endued by God with His grace and bringing glory to His Name: "Whether therefore ye eat, or drink, or whatsoever ye do, do all to the glory of God" (I Co 10:31).

This opens up to us an amazing prospect, for we begin to recognize that through God's grace and love, our every action -- not only our so-called spiritual exercises, such as praying or obeying the Commandments or the taking of Communion, but even the most ordinary and mundane activities, such as conducting our business affairs, talking with a friend, raking the leaves, playing with a child or enduring a time of suffering, may become an offering of ourselves to God. In essence, these actions, if offered "in Christ," can become threads which will make up the fabric of our lives. When touched by God's grace and love, this fabric becomes something divine.

"When grace and love seize hold of everything in our life," writes Dom Columba Marmion, "then every bit of our existence is like a perpetual hymn to the glory of the Heavenly Father. Through our union with Christ, our life becomes for the Father a censer from which rise perfumes that cause Him to rejoice." Paul alluded to this sweet smell exuded by the faithful believer when he wrote, "We are the fragrance of Christ for God" (II Co 2:15).

Let us recognize, then, the almost unlimited opportunities each day presents to us of glorifying God by the attitudes we assume and the actions we perform, and remember that God is ready and willing to give us all we need to live in a manner that is pleasing to Him, for, as Paul reminds us, "I can do all things through Christ which strengtheneth me." (Ph 4:13).

MAY 10 --

"...I will have mercy, and not sacrifice: for I am not come to call the righteous, but sinners to repentance." (Ma 9:13)

"You need not fear the greatness or number of your sins. For are you a sinner? So am I. Are you the chief of sinners? So am I. Are you a backsliding sinner? So am I. And yet the Lord (forever adored be His rich, free and sovereign grace) is my righteousness.

Come, then, young men, who (as I acted once myself) are playing the prodigal and wandering away... Your heavenly Father calls you. Young women, I see many of you adorned as to your bodies; but are not your souls naked? Which of you was ever dressed in this robe of invaluable price? Seek for the Lord to be your righteousness.

To you who are in business, what profit will there be of all your labor under the sun if you do not secure this pearl of invaluable price? Labor therefore no longer so anxiously for the meat which perishes, but seek for the Lord to be your righteousness that will entitle you to life everlasting.

Gray-headed sinners, I could weep over you who do not know that the Lord is your righteousness. Your sun will set and leave you in an eternal darkness. But don't be afraid. All things are possible with God. If you come, though it be at the eleventh hour, Christ Jesus will not cast you out. Seek the Lord and ask Him to let you know how it is that a man may be born again when he is old.

I must not forget the lambs of the flock. Come then, you little children, come to Christ; the Lord Christ shall be your righteousness. Do not think that you are too young to be converted. If your fathers and mothers will not come to Christ, you come without them. Lead them and show them how the Lord may be their righteousness. Our Lord Jesus loved little children. You are His lambs. He bids me feed you. Ask the Lord to be your righteousness. Even so, come Lord Jesus, come quickly, into all our souls."

--George Whitefield

MAY 11 --

"Hitherto have ye asked nothing in my name: ask, and ye shall receive, that your joy may be full." (Jo 16:24)

"It is not every believer who has yet learned to pray in Christ's name. To ask not only for His sake, but in His name, as authorized by Him, is a high order of prayer. We would not dare to ask for some things in that blessed name, for it would be a wretched profaning of His name; but when the petition is so clearly right that we dare set the name of Jesus to it, then it must be granted. Prayer is all the more sure to succeed because it is for the Father's glory through the Son. It glorifies His truth, His faithfulness, His power, His grace. The granting of prayer, when offered in the name of Jesus, reveals the Father's love to Him, and the honor which He has put upon Him. The glory of Jesus and of the Father are so wrapped up together that the grace which magnifies the one magnifies the other. The channel is made famous through the fullness of the fountain, and the fountain is honored through the channel by which it flows. If the answering of our prayers would dishonor our Lord, we would not pray; but since in this thing He is glorified, we will pray without ceasing in that dear name in which God and His people have a fellowship of delight."   – Charles Spurgeon

"Lord, teach me what it is to pray in Your Name. Teach me so to live and act, to walk and speak, so to do all in the Name of Jesus, that my prayer cannot be anything else but in that blessed Name, too.

And teach me, Lord, to hold fast the precious promise that whatsoever we ask in Your Name, You will do, the Father will give. Though I do not yet fully understand, and still less have fully attained, the wondrous union You mean when You say, 'In My Name,' I would yet hold fast the promise until it fills my heart with undoubting assurance: Anything in the Name of Jesus."

– Andrew Murray

MAY 12 ---

"But rejoice, inasmuch as ye are partakers of Christ's sufferings: that, when his glory shall be revealed, ye may be glad also with exceeding joy." (I Pe 4:13)

"It is possible to evade a multitude of sorrows by the cultivation of an insignificant life. Indeed, if it be a man's ambition to avoid the troubles of life, the recipe is perfectly simple: let him shed his ambitions in every direction, let him cut the wings of every soaring purpose, and let him assiduously cultivate a little life, with the fewest correspondences and relations.

By this means a whole continent of afflictions will be escaped and will remain unknown. For instance, cultivate deafness, and you are saved from the horrors of discords. Cultivate blindness, and you are saved from the assault of the ugly. Stupefy a sense, and you shut out a world... And, indeed, that is why so many people, and even so many professedly Christian people, get through life so easily, and with a minimum acquaintance with tribulation. It is because they have reduced their souls to a minimum, that their course through the years is not so much the transit of a man as the passage of an amoeba. They have no finely organized nervous system or they have deadened and arrested the growth of one nerve after another. They have cut the sensitive wires which bind the individual to the race, and they are cosily self-contained, and the shuddering sorrow of the world never disturbs their seclusion. Tiny souls can dodge through life; bigger souls are blocked on every side.

As soon, therefore, as a man begins to enlarge his life, his resistances are multiplied. Let a man tear out of his soul the petty selfish purpose and enthrone a world purpose, the Christ purpose, and his sufferings will be increased on every side. Every addition to spiritual ambition widens the exposure of the soul, and sharpens its perception of the world's infirmity and the sense of its own restraints. How then was it with that vast spiritual ambition of the Savior? That all-absorbing redemptive purpose was bound to introduce Him to ceaseless suffering."

--J. H. Jowett

MAY 13 --

"And as they were eating, Jesus took bread, and blessed it, and brake it, and gave it to the disciples, and said, Take, eat; this is my body." (Ma 26:26)

"There was a meaning in every act. The bread was an appropriate emblem of Christ's body. Bread is food; Christ is food for our spirits.

Something may be learned from the manner in which bread is prepared. The wheat is crushed and broken, and then the bread is baked in the fire before it is ready for use. So Christ died, His body was bruised and broken, and He was exposed to the fire of great suffering before He could become the food and life of our souls.

The breaking of the bread is also significant, denoting the breaking of the body of Christ on the cross. We ought never to forget, as we enjoy the blessings of grace, what it cost our Lord to provide them for us. Whenever we sit at our Lord's table and see the bread broken, we should remember the anguish and suffering endured by our Redeemer in saving us.

The giving of the bread to the disciples also had a deep meaning. It signified how freely Christ offered Himself to men. He is always standing, reaching out His hands with the bread of life, imploring men to take freely all the blessings of salvation.

The taking of the bread by the communicant is significant of the act of faith by which Christ Himself is received. He offers; we receive. It is not enough that Christ gave Himself on the cross for sinners, and now holds out to us with pierced hands the blessings of redemption. These stupendous acts of love and grace alone will not save us. There is a needed link which we must supply: we must reach out our hands and accept and take what Christ so graciously and lovingly offers to us. Then, since bread to nourish us must be eaten, we must receive Christ into our life as our soul's sustenance and feed upon Him."   --J. R. Miller

MAY 14 --

"Better it is to be of an humble spirit with the lowly, than to divide the spoil with the proud." (Pr 16:19)

Scripture teaches us that Moses "was very meek, above all the men which were upon the face of the earth" (Nu 12:3). Yet Moses was also a man of tremendous inner strength. He confronted Pharaoh, led the children of Israel out of captivity and obeyed God even when it looked like such obedience might lead to certain disaster. Just how did Moses acquire this unique mixture of meekness and strength? It was as a result of God's constant chastening and training over a period of many years.

In the beginning of Moses' life, his idea of delivering his people from captivity was to kill their enemies. At the age of 40, after watching a cruel Egyptian taskmaster beat an Israelite, Moses murdered the offender. His action resulted in his becoming a fugitive and having to flee to the hot desert of Midian. There he became a shepherd, a way of life despised by many. For the next forty years he did not lead his people. He led only sheep. But during those years of seeming abandonment, loneliness, sorrow and perplexity, something momentous was taking place in Moses. God was transforming him from a self-willed man into a stable man of God.

God was able to speak to Moses in the Midian desert. Why the desert? Because when you come to the desert you find it is empty of everything else. God can speak to us when we come to the place where everything else is absent. In many cases it is only in the desert places that we consent to listen to God's voice and His voice alone.

At the end of those desert years, Moses knew who he was before God. He had learned to listen to God. He had become a man God could use to accomplish His will. Moses had also learned how much God loved him. He trusted in this infinite love, and in the fact that God knew exactly how to deliver his people from their oppressors.

For most of us, humility comes through pain. It comes when our egos are deflated, our selfishness uncovered, our vanities exposed. But when it does arrive, even in small doses, it opens the door to the rejuvenating breath of the Holy Spirit and His work in our lives. How freeing to realize that even though we cannot accomplish the miracles we need, God can and will do them for us, if we will humbly take our place before Him.

We may trust Him solely
All for us to do;
They who trust Him wholly,
Find Him wholly true.

Stayed upon Jehovah,
Hearts are fully blest,
Finding, as He promised,
Perfect peace and rest.
                    --Frances Ridley Havergal

MAY 15 --

"For I came down from heaven, not to do mine own will, but the will of him that sent me." (Jo 6:38)

"The greatest glory we can give to God is to do his will in everything. Our Redeemer came to earth to glorify his heavenly Father and to teach us by his example how to do the same.

[Jesus] frequently declared that he had come to earth not to do his own will, but solely that of his Father: 'I came down from heaven, not to do my own will, but the will of him that sent me.' He spoke in the same strain in the garden when he went forth to meet his enemies who had come to seize him and to lead him to death: 'But that the world may know that I love the Father; and as the Father gave me commandment, even so I do. Arise, let us go hence.' (Jo 14:31)

Because David fulfilled all his wishes, God called him a man after his own heart... David was always ready to embrace the divine will, as he frequently stated: 'My heart is fixed, O God, my heart is fixed' (Ps 57:7). He asked God for one thing alone: to teach him to do his will (Ps 143:10).

He who gives his will to God, gives him everything. He who gives his goods in alms, his blood in scourgings, his food in fasting, gives God what he has. But he who gives God his will, gives himself, gives everything he is...

If we would completely rejoice the heart of God, let us strive in all things to conform ourselves to his divine will. Let us not only strive to conform ourselves, but also to unite ourselves to whatever dispositions God makes of us. Conformity signifies that we join our wills to the will of God. Uniformity means more; it means that we make one will of God's will and ours, so that we will only what God wills; that God's will alone, is our will.

This is the summit of perfection and to it we should always aspire; this should be the goal of all our works, desires, meditations and prayers."

– St. Alphonsus de Ligouri

MAY 16 ---

"...Behold the Lamb of God, which taketh away the sin of the world." (Jo 1:29)

"Perhaps the greatest portion of the energy in this world goes toward the endeavor to rid itself of discomfort. Some, in order to escape it, leave their natural surroundings behind them and with a continuous effort attempt to keep rising in the social scale, only to discover that at every new ascent fresh trouble awaits them, since the truth is they have simply brought the trouble with them.

Others make haste to be rich, and are slow to find out that the poverty of their souls, despite the fact that their purses are filling, still keeps them unhappy. Some court endless change, not realizing that it is upon themselves that the change must take place if they are to be set free. Others expand their souls with knowledge, only to find that contentment will not dwell in the great house they have built...

However absurd the statement may appear to the one who has not yet discovered this fact for himself, the cause of every man's discomfort is evil -- moral evil; first of all, evil in himself, in his own sin, his own wrongness, his own un-rightness; and then, evil in [others]. Foolish is the man, and there are many such men, who would rid himself or his fellows of discomfort by waging war on the evils around him while he neglects that integral part of the world wherein lies his true business, namely, his own character and conduct.

The one cure for any organism is to be set right -- to have all its parts brought into harmony with each other. The one comfort is to know this cure is in process. Rightness alone is the cure. The return of the organism to its true self is its only possible ease. To free a man from suffering, he must be set right, put in health; and the health at the root of man's being is to be set free from wrongness, that is, from sin... I do not mean set free from the sins he has done -- that will follow; I mean the sins he is doing, or is capable of doing; the sins in his being which spoil his nature, the wrongness in him, the evil he consents to, the sin he is, which makes him do the sin he does.

To save a man from his sins is to say to him, in a perfect and eternal manner, 'Rise up and walk. Be at liberty in your essential being. Be free as the son of God is free.' To do this for us, Jesus was born, and remains born to all the ages."   – George MacDonald

MAY 17 --

"That the trial of your faith, being much more precious than of gold that perishes, though it be tried with fire, might be found unto praise and honor and glory at the appearing of Jesus Christ." (I Peter 1:7)

"The trial of faith is a test of its character; it is the furnace that tries the ore to discover what kind it is. It may be brass, or iron, or clay, or perhaps precious gold; but the crucible will test it. There is much that passes for real faith which is no faith; there is much spurious, counterfeit metal; it is the trial that brings out its real character. The true character of Judas was not known until his covetousness was tempted; Simon Magus was not discovered to possess a spurious faith until he thought to purchase the gift of God with money; Demas did not forsake the apostle until the world drew him away. But true faith stands the trial. Where there is a real work of grace in the heart, no tribulation, or persecution, or power of this world will ever be able to expel it. But if all is chaff, the wind will scatter it; if all is but dross and tinsel, the fire will consume it. Let the humble and tried believer, then, thank God for every test that brings out the real character of his faith and proves it to be 'the faith of God's elect.' God will test His own work in the soul; every grace of His own Spirit he will at one time or another place in the crucible;

but never will He remove His eye from it; He will 'sit as a refiner,' and watch that not a grain of the precious metal is consumed; He will be with His child in all and every affliction; not for one moment will He leave him. Let there be gratitude rather than murmuring, joy rather than sorrow, when we encounter the tests which a loving and faithful Father brings, 'that the trial of your faith might be found unto praise and honor and glory at the appearing of Jesus Christ.'"   --Octavius Winslow

MAY 18 ---

"I am crucified with Christ: nevertheless I live; yet not I, but Christ liveth in me: and the life which I now live in the flesh I live by the faith of the Son of God, who loved me, and gave himself for me." (Ga 2:20)

"The world says, 'Look out for yourself;' but Jesus says, 'Not I, but Christ.' Not only your old self, but the new man, with all his strength and self-confidence, must die. Not only Ishmael must go out and be an outcast, but Isaac must be yielded and not hold up his head again.

It is so easy to talk about this. The longer I live -- the longer I know myself and friends -- the more thoroughly I am satisfied that this is the great secret of failure in our Christian life. We come a little way with Jesus but we stop at Gethsemane and Calvary. They followed Him in His ministry in Galilee. The Sermon on the Mount was splendid morality. They loved the feeding of the thousands, and said, 'What a blessed King He would make!' They would not have to work as they used to. But when He stands and talks about Calvary and speaks of the cross for them as well as for Him, and how they must go with Him and go with Him all the way, they say, 'This is a hard saying; who can bear it?'

And a few days after, you could count them on your fingers. They said, 'We do not understand Him; we thought He would be a king.' They were not willing to go to the cross.

I am sure this is where multitudes have stopped short. They have said yes to self and no to God, instead of saying no to self and yes to God. Oh, it is so much easier to talk than to live! There is no use in talking about it unless the Holy Ghost shall bring it home to us.

A writer has recently said that there are three baptisms to be baptized with. First, the baptism of repentance -- we turned from sin to God. Second, the baptism of the Holy Ghost, when we receive the Holy Spirit to live in us. Third, the baptism into death, after the Holy Spirit comes in. While he, perhaps, has no Scriptural authority for this precise distinction, there is no doubt that there are these three steps to take. After you receive the baptism of the Holy Ghost, after God comes to live in you, after the Holy Spirit makes your heart His home, then it is that you have to go with Christ into His own dying, and so He says, 'If any man will come after me, let him deny himself, and take up his cross daily, and follow me.' And so He said about Himself, 'I have a baptism to be baptized with; and how am I straitened till it be accomplished!' I have a burial to be buried with. He was going out into deeper dying every day, and His heart was all pent up with it, until He went down into Gethsemane, down to Joseph's tomb, and down into Hades, and He passed through the regions of the dead and opened first the gates of heaven. That is what Jesus saw before Him after He was baptized on the banks of the Jordan.

Oh beloved, who have received the baptism of the Holy Ghost, it is you who have to go down into His death. Now, I know that in a sense we take all that by faith when we consecrate ourselves to Christ, and we count it all real and God counts it all real; but, my dear friends, you have to go through it step by step. I know God treats us as though it was accomplished, as though we were sitting on the throne. But we must go through the narrow passage and the secret places of the stairs. There must be no fooling here. You may count it all done; but step by step it must be written on the records of your heart."   --A.B. Simpson

"Take courage. Offer your sufferings unceasingly to Him. Ask for strength to endure them. Above all, make it a habit to converse often with Him and forget Him as little as you are able. Worship Him in your infirmities and present them to Him from time to time as an offering of sacrifice. In the worst of your pains ask Him humbly and lovingly, as a child would ask his loving father, for conformity to His holy will and for the help of His grace... God has many ways to draw us to Himself. He sometimes hides from us, but faith alone, which will not fail us in need, must be our only support. We must make our faith in God the sole foundation of our trust and confidence."   --Brother Lawrence

MAY 19 --

"For the Lord God is a sun and shield: the Lord will give grace and glory: no good thing will he withhold from them that walk uprightly." (Ps 84:11)

Many people find it a pleasant pastime to talk about religion, to evaluate different doctrines, to comment on the failings of those who are walking down the pathway of faith. It can be enjoyable to discuss the spiritual life, if we can hold it at arm's length. But it is quite a different thing to personally enter into the spiritual life and attempt to live by its principles.

C. S. Lewis likened living the spiritual life to encountering a strong wind. There is, he noted, little about a wind to vex us if we simply lie on the ground and allow it to sweep over us, but it is quite another thing to stand up and attempt to walk against it.

So it is with living according to God's Word. If we lie down and never attempt to live out what it teaches, life may not oppose us to any great extent. We may wonder why people of faith make so much of life's trials and tribulations. But let us stand up and do our best to live according to God's precepts and we will soon come to understand how great the forces are that will line up against us, and how insufficient our unaided strength is to combat them. Only then will we understand how great are the powers of the enemy, the unbelieving world and our own weaknesses and sin, for they will all come against us as a strong, opposing wind. Yet, once we make this effort to live entirely as God would have us live, we will discover how great is His strength to supply what we need. We will discover that God, if need be, will move heaven and earth in order to help us do His will.

> The kingdom that I seek is Thine; so let the way
> That leads to it be Thine, else I must surely stray.
> Take Thou my cup and it, with joy or sorrow fill,
> As best to Thee may seem, choose Thou my good and ill;
> Not mine, not mine the choice, in things though great or small;
> Be Thou my guide, my strength, my wisdom, and my all
> --Horatius Bonar

MAY 20 --

"Then came she and worshipped him, saying, Lord, help me." (Ma 15:25)

"There are many cases in which we have no express promise to plead, and yet faith has room for work.

The Syro-Phoenician woman had no such promise, neither had the centurion. They were both Gentiles and their requests were for temporal blessings, yet in both cases Christ was delighted with their confidence in Him. These were the only cases in which He said He had found great faith, and He gave them all they wanted.

The Syro-Phoenician woman had heard about Christ and His ways, the kindness and compassion He showed to multitudes. What He did for others He could do for her daughter, and she determined to apply to Him. All apparent repulse could not shake her out of faith in Him. 'Truth, Lord, yet...'

The centurion felt utterly unworthy, and had very low thoughts of himself, but he had most lofty thoughts of Christ, and true thoughts of His heart. 'Speak the word only.' Faith believes no ill of God, but all good of Him. It leans on His graciousness, even when it cannot point to His faithfulness, and says, 'Do as Thou hast said.'

The Lord is delighted with faith manifested in this form. 'Do this for me, for Thou art gracious,' rather than 'because Thou art faithful.' David showed this faith in God when he preferred to fall into the hands of God rather than into those of men. Such confidence in Him gives Christ joy. Shall we not gratify Him by confiding in Him, whether we have a promise or not?

Perhaps you look at the verse, 'Whatsoever ye shall ask in faith, believing, ye shall receive,' and yet you can't put your foot on a promise for the blessing asked, and so you feel you cannot ask with faith. But yet faith has its sphere here. It looks at God's graciousness; this is what Abraham did on Mount Moriah. He offered up Isaac, believing that the Lord who had given him would raise him up again, though he knew not how. God has not bound Himself to give you what you ask, but your prayer will be heard, and He will have respect to your faith in Him. So it is with prayer for the conversion of friends -- either for an individual, a family, or a community. He does in hundreds of cases what we ask because He has respect to our faith in Him."   --Andrew Bonar

MAY 21 --

"And I heard a loud voice saying in heaven, Now is come salvation, and strength, and the kingdom of our God, and the power of his Christ: for the accuser of our brethren is cast down, which accused them before our God day and night." (Re 12:10)

"In ancient courts of justice the accuser stood at the right hand of the judge, and brought against the accused all his crimes. So is it with Satan. You will observe that from the first moment a spark of grace is put into your heart, Satan stands at the bar of God to accuse you. And what does he accuse you of? First, he accuses you of sin. He says, 'That soul is vile. Yes, there is none like it.' Or sometimes he accuses you of unbelief: 'That soul has denied thee.' Or sometimes he accuses you of going back after you had been awakened: 'That soul was awakened and has gone back; even after you visited that soul, it went back.'

He says to the sinner, 'How can you come? You are too vile.' Or sometimes he says, 'It is too late; you might have been saved had you come sooner. You might have been saved had you come in youth. Or you might have been saved had you come when you were first awakened, but now it is of no use, it is too late.' Or sometimes he takes another plan. When you are awakened to come, he stirs up corruption within you; even when you are upon your knees he stirs up corruption in order to shut your eyes from seeing the mercy seat. He stirs up the sin that is in your heart. He makes you concentrate on it in order to keep you away from Christ. Learn two lessons from this.

1. Learn that it is a solemn thing to be under conviction of sin. It is true, you are seeking Christ, but it is also true that Satan is ready to resist you. Do not think you are safe because you are under conviction. Remember you are not saved because you have got a sight of your sins. It is not every awakened sinner that is a saved man. And if it is a solemn thing to be awakened, what must be the danger of those of you who are not awakened, who are not seeking Christ, who are asleep over hell?...

2. A second lesson for those who are under real conviction. Remember it is only Satan that resists you. God does not resist you. Christ does not resist you. The Holy Ghost does not resist you. Remember, whoever says your sins are too many to be forgiven, it is not God, it is not Christ. It is Satan. Christ invites you to come to him. The Holy Spirit invites you, and all the friends of Christ invite you. Do not be driven back."

-Robert Murray McCheyne

MAY 22 ---

"I will therefore that men pray every where..." (I Ti 2:8)

"You will recall that Paul encourages us to 'pray without ceasing' (I Th 5:17). The Lord also invites us to 'watch and pray' (Mark 13:33, 37). It is apparent from these verses, as well as many more, that we should all live by this kind of experience, this prayer, just as we live by love.

Once the Lord spoke and said, 'I counsel you to buy from me gold tried in the fire that you may be rich.' (Re 3:18) Dear reader, there is gold available to you. This gold is much more easily obtained than you could ever imagine....

I give you an invitation: If you are thirsty, come to the living waters. Do not waste your precious time digging wells that have no water in them (Jo 7:37; Je 2:13).

If you are starving and can find nothing to satisfy your hunger, then come. Come, and you will be filled. You who are poor, come. You who are afflicted, come. You who are weighed down with your load of wretchedness and your load of pain, come. You will be comforted.

You who are sick and need a physician, come. Don't hesitate because you have diseases. Come to your Lord and show Him all your diseases, and they will be healed. Come.

Dear child of God, your Father has His arms of love open wide to you. Throw yourself into His arms. You who have strayed and wandered away as sheep, return to your Shepherd. You who are sinners, come to your Savior."

–Madame Guyon

"Lord, teach us to pray. None can teach like Jesus, none but Jesus; therefore we call on Him, 'Lord, teach us to pray.' A pupil needs a teacher who knows his work, who has the gift of teaching, who in patience and love will descend to the pupil's needs. Blessed be God. Jesus is all this and much more. He knows what prayer is. It is Jesus, praying Himself, who teaches to pray. He knows what prayer is. He learned it amid the trials and tears of His earthly life. In heaven it is still His beloved work: His life there is prayer. Nothing delights Him more than to find those whom He can take with Him into the Father's presence..."   – Andrew Murray

"The spirit of prayer is the fruit and token of the Spirit of adoption."
                                                                    – John Newton

MAY 23 --

"And he said, So is the kingdom of God, as if a man should cast seed into the ground; And should sleep, and rise night and day, and the seed should spring and grow up, he knoweth not how." (Mk 4:26-27)

"The doctrine of the kingdom, received in a good and honest heart, is like seed sown by a man in his ground, properly prepared to receive it; for when he has sown it, he sleeps and wakes day after day, and, looking on it, he sees it spring and grow up through the virtue of the earth in which it is sown, though he knows not how it does so; and when he finds it ripe, he reaps it, and so receives the benefit of the sown seed. So is it here: the seed sown in the good and honest heart brings forth fruit with patience; and this fruit increases daily, though we do not know how the Word and Spirit work that increase; and then Christ the husbandman, at the time of the harvest, gathers this good seed into the kingdom of heaven."   – Daniel Whitby

"The kingdom of God, which is generated in the soul by the word of life, under the influence of the Holy Spirit, is at first very small; there is only a blade, but this is full of promise, for a good blade shows there is a good seed at the bottom, and that the soil in which it is sown is also good. Then the strong stalk grows up, and the ear is formed; the faith and love of the believing soul increase abundantly; it is justified freely through the redemption that is in Christ; it has the ear which is shortly to be filled with the ripe grain, the outlines of the whole image of God. Then the full corn. The soul is purified from all unrighteousness; and, having escaped the corruption that is in the world, it is made a partaker of the Divine nature, and is filled with all the fullness of God."   --Adam Clarke

Jesus, Lord of Heaven above,
Earth beneath is all Thy own,
In the depths of Heavenly love,
Let my human heart be sown.

Sown in weakness, raised in power,
Sown in suffering, raised in peace,
It shall brave the blighting hour,
In the year of drought increase.

Never hurt by sun or storm,
Blest its every stage shall be,
Dying in its mortal form,
Living evermore in Thee.
                    --Anna Waring

MAY 24 ---

"For I am the Lord, I change not;" (Mal 3:6)

"I pray that you may be enabled more and more to honour the Lord by believing His promises, for He is not like a man that should fail or change, or be prevented by anything unforeseen from doing what He has said. And yet we find it easier to trust to worms than to the God of truth. Is it not so with you? And I can assure you it is often so with me. But here is the mercy, that His ways are above ours, as the heavens are higher than the earth. Though we are foolish and unbelieving, He remains faithful; He will not deny Himself.

I recommend to you especially that promise of God, which is so comprehensive that it takes in all our concerns; I mean, that all things shall work together for good. How hard it is to believe, that not only those things which are grievous to the flesh, but even those things which draw out our corruptions and discover to us what is in our hearts, and fill us with guilt and shame, should in the end work for our good. Yet the Lord has said it. All your pains and trials, all that befalls you in your own person, or that affects you upon the account of others, shall in the end prove to your advantage. And your peace does not depend upon any change of circumstance which may appear desirable, but in having your will surrendered to the Lord's will, and made willing to submit all to His disposal and management. Pray for this, and wait patiently for Him, and He will do it. Be not surprised to find yourself poor and helpless; all whom He favors and teaches will find themselves so. The more grace increases, the more we shall see to abase us in our own eyes; and this will make the Saviour and His salvation more precious to us. He takes His own wise methods to humble you, and to prove you, and I am sure He will do you good in the end." --John Newton

Descend, O Heavenly Dove,
Abide with us alway;
And in the fulness of Thy love,
Cleanse us, we pray.
– John Brownlie

MAY 25 --

"And it came to pass in those days, that he went out into a mountain to pray, and continued all night in prayer to God." (Lu 6:12)

Sometimes life gets to be too much for us. We may feel so frustrated or overwhelmed by events that we simply cannot pray. Perhaps we don't even want to pray.

When we find ourselves in this situation we ought not be too hard on ourselves. We shouldn't beat ourselves up and tell ourselves we're being "unspiritual." Instead, we might take a closer look at what is really going on. Are we experiencing fear, disappointment, grief, loneliness, loss, upheaval or sadness? Any of these things can rob us of the desire to pray. During such times, it's good to have a prayer or two available that we can use to help us get back on track. Sometimes just praying a well-loved prayer can shed light into the shadows in which we find ourselves.

If you already have a favorite prayer or two, you might get copies of them and tuck them away for use on those days when you find it hard to pray. If you like, you might pray the prayer which appears below; it focuses on thanking God for what He has done for us in the past and on how we can trust Him to take care of any concerns that may be weighing on us today. Better yet, you might want to write your own prayer for use on those days when spontaneous prayer just seems too difficult. The best prayer we can pray is, of course, the Lord's Prayer, the one Jesus taught to His disciples when they came to Him and asked Him to teach them how to pray (Matthew 6:9-13).

Dear Lord, I want to thank You today, for loving me and redeeming me. I thank You because I know You are there for me, even during times like this, when I can't seem to feel Your presence. Sometimes, when I'm hurting, I don't want to pray, Lord. Part of me wants to throw myself into Your arms but the other part of me wants to run away. So here I am, Lord, reaching out, even though I don't really feel like it and I don't know what to say.

I thank You, Lord, for all those things I so often take for granted, like being able to breathe, to see, to hear, to know that I am not alone because You are always with me. I thank you for those countless things You have done for me in the past. For finding me when I was lost. For helping me get up when I was down. For guiding me when I couldn't see the way. For moving me forward when I wanted to stop dead in my tracks.

Forgive me, Lord, for the things I have done that have grieved You. Renew a right spirit within me. Cleanse me. Help me. Please set right in me the things that need to be made straight. Ignite in me the fire of Your Presence. Show me how to accomplish Your will.

I lift up these dear ones to You, Lord (mention by name). Bless them, Lord. Meet their needs. Give them the power they need to overcome their difficulties, to serve You, and to accomplish Your will. I also pray for these who do not know You (mention by name). They need You so much. Draw them to You. Open their eyes, their ears, their hearts, that they may recognize who You really are and call upon You to be their Savior.

Please give me Your strength, Lord, in those areas where I have been weak. Give me Your gentleness where I have been harsh. Give me Your warmth and kindness where I have been cold. Give me the courage to do Your will. And then give me the willingness to leave all my concerns in Your loving arms, where they belong. Amen.

MAY 26 ---

"I will heal their backsliding, I will love them freely: for mine anger is turned away from him." (Ho 14:4)

"If [God] willed to stop at this moment the most bloody persecutor, the most filthy and licentious man, if He willed to turn the blackest-hearted atheist into one of the most brilliant of saints, there is nothing in His way to stop Him; in a moment omnipotent love can do it; the means are provided, both in the blood of Christ for cleansing, and in the power of the Spirit for renewing the inner man. Therefore, I say it is established beyond doubt, that there is nothing in man which can conquer divine love.

'What is the practical use of this?' one might ask. The practical use of this is to set the gate of mercy wide open. I always like to preach sermons which leave the door of mercy open for the worst of sinners, but today I set it wide open. A man has dropped in here who has been thinking for years, 'I gave myself up to sin in my youth, and I have gone astray ever since; there is no hope for me.' I tell you, dear soul, all that you have ever done is no bar to God's love to you, for he does not love you because of anything good in you, and that which is black in you cannot prevent his loving you if he so wills it. I tell you what I would have you do... If you in your soul can now trust the love of God in Christ, you are saved; no matter who you may be, you are saved this morning, and you shall go out of this house a regenerate soul, for you have believed in Jesus; therefore, the love of God is come to you, all your past life is forgotten and forgiven; all your past ingratitude, and blasphemy and sin are cast into the depths of the sea; and, as far as the east is from the west, so far hath he removed your transgressions from you.

I have known the time when, if I had heard the sermon of this morning, faint and feeble though it be, I should have danced for joy. I feel an intense inward satisfaction and delight while preaching it, for I believe it is the opening of the prison to them that are bound. Christ died not for the righteous but for sinners. He gave himself for our sins and not for our righteousness; ... I know that many will see nothing in this doctrine. Of course, none but the sick see any value in the healing medicine. I know there are some who will think this sermon is not for them. Oh! may the Spirit of God make some accept of this comfort; but they will not unless the Spirit of God makes them. Too many of us are like foolish patients who will not take the physician's medicine, and he has need to hold us, and thrust it down before we will take it. This is how the Lord deals with many, not against their will, but yet against their will as it used to be, he gives them the medicine of his grace, and makes them whole.

To sum up all in one, what I mean is this: there have straggled in here this morning the poor working man, the struggling mechanic, the man who leads a fast life, the fellow who leads a coarse life, the woman, perhaps, who has gone far astray; I mean to say to such, you are lost, but the Son of man is come to seek and to save you. I mean to say to you, sons and daughters of moral parents, who are not converted, but perhaps feel yourselves even worse than the immoral, I mean to say to you that you are not past hope yet. God will love you freely, and this is how his love is preached to you; Whosoever believeth on the Lord Jesus Christ shall be saved. Come as you are; God will accept you as you are. Come as you are, without any preparation or fitness; come as you are, and where the cross is lifted high with the bleeding Son of God upon it, fall flat on your face, accepting the love manifested there, willingly receiving this day the grace which God willingly and freely gives.

> Just as I am, and waiting not
> To rid my soul of one dark blot,
> To thee whose blood can cleanse each spot,
> O Lamb of God, I come."
>   – Charles Spurgeon

"...Let the Lord be magnified, which hath pleasure in the prosperity of His servant." *(Ps 35:27)*

"What is 'prosperity?' Is it a full cup? Ample riches? Worldly applause? An unbroken circle? No, these are often a snare, received without gratitude, dimming the soul from seeing its nobler destiny. In a spiritual sense, it often means God taking us by the hand into the Valley of Humiliation; leading us as He did his servant Job of old, out of his sheep, oxen, camels, health, wealth, children; in order that we may be brought before Him in the dust, and say, 'Blessed be His holy name!'

Yes, the very reverse of what is known in the world as Prosperity often forms the background on which the Rainbow of Promise is seen. God smiles on us through these rainbows and teardrops of sorrow! He loves us too well. He has too great an interest in our spiritual welfare to permit us to live in what is misnamed 'Prosperity.' He may instead put a thorn in our nest so that we will fly and cease living on the ground.

I may not be able now to understand the mystery of these dealings. I may be asking through the tears, 'Why this unkind attack on my earthly happiness? Why have my branches been so severely pruned? Why has my fruit withered away?' The answer is plain. It is your soul's prosperity He has in view. The afflictions you are enduring are no arbitrary appointments. There is righteous necessity in all God does. As He lays His hand upon you and leads you by ways you know not, and which you never would have chosen, He whispers, 'Beloved, I wish above all things that you would prosper, and be in health.'

Rest in the quiet consciousness that all is well. Murmur at nothing which brings you nearer His own loving Presence. Be thankful for your very cares, because you can confidently cast them all upon Him. He has your temporal and eternal 'prosperity' too much at heart to appoint one superfluous pang, one needless stroke. Commit all that concerns you to His keeping, and leave it there."   – John MacDuff

"And the child grew, and waxed strong in spirit, filled with wisdom: and the grace of God was upon him." (Lu 2:40)

"One of the chief influences in molding Christ's life was His mother. When God wants to prepare a man for a great mission, He first prepares a noble mother, and puts the child into her bosom to be trained. The Jews had a saying: 'God could not be everywhere, and therefore he made mothers.'

Nearly all the truly great men of the world have received the inspiration and stamp of their lives from their mothers. When Moses was to be trained for his work, the Lord put the little babe back in the hands of its mother as his first teacher. There is no doubt that in preparing Mary to be the mother of the Saviour, the rarest and loveliest graces of womanhood were wrought by God into her nature....surely we may believe that no more perfect woman ever lived.

'And Mary said, My soul doth magnify the Lord,
And my spirit hath rejoiced in God my Saviour.
For he hath regarded the low estate of his handmaiden:
For, behold, from henceforth all generations shall call me blessed.
For he that is mighty hath done to me great things;
And holy is his name.' -- (Luke 1:46-49)

Such a mother would exert a wonderful influence over the child Jesus. She was His first teacher. Her love wrapped Him around in its warm folds in His earliest infancy and through all His youth and young manhood. Her sweet life was the atmosphere that hung over His tenderest years. Her prayers kept heaven lying ever close about Him. Her hands guided His feet and shaped His character. What a blessed mission is that of a mother, any mother! What woman in whose arms God has laid an immortal life will despise her glorious calling? What woman so honored will not die rather than prove unfaithful to her holy trust?"   – J. R. Miller

MAY 29 ---

"A merry heart doeth good like a medicine; but a broken spirit drieth the bones." (Pr 17:22)

Most of us know how discouraging it can be to look at our flaws, but God doesn't show us the truth about ourselves to dishearten us. To the contrary, He wants us to be cheerful. If you ever feel discouraged about all your shortcomings or past failures you will find the Bible is full of imperfect human beings that God chose to use and bless, despite their defects.

Take Abraham. Yes, He became a man who walked with God and had great strength of character, but early in life he lacked courage; yet God chose Him to be the father of nations. David was also flawed. His tumultuous life contained grievous personal failures. Yet he was called "the apple of God's eye." Peter denied the Lord, not once but three times, yet the Lord raised him up to become a mighty man of faith. Paul was once a vicious persecutor of Christians, yet look how God redeemed him and used him to reach the world with the Gospel message. God knows we have all failed, but He still wants to use us as part of His wonderful plan of redemption. On days when we're tempted to be critical of ourselves, we can remember that God wants us to concentrate on the good things. He wants us to have a merry heart and to be about His business.

Here are a few suggestions as to what we can do whenever we're tempted to get down on ourselves because of our shortcomings:

1. We can remind ourselves that we are to wear our imperfections like a loose garment, not a straight jacket. God knows we are flawed, but He still loves us. He has a plan as to how to straighten us out. We need to do our best; then we should trust Him to remove our defects in His way and in His time.

2. We can do something during the day just for the fun of it. Yes, believe it or not, serious, committed, caring Christians can do something just for the fun of it. If you refuse to consider trying this, someone might get the idea you take yourself too seriously.

3. We can make the decision to laugh at least twice today: once at ourselves, and then once more, just for good measure.

4. We can allow ourselves to fail at something today without beating ourselves up for it.

5. We can make a point of encouraging someone else. Helping another person usually helps us take the focus off of ourselves.

MAY 30 --

"...God resisteth the proud, but giveth grace to the humble. Submit yourselves therefore to God..." (Ja 4:6-7)

"I am going to reveal to you a secret of happiness. If, every day, for five minutes, you will silence your imagination, close your eyes to things of sense and your ears to earthly sounds in order to enter into yourself, and there, in the sanctuary of your soul which is the Temple of the Holy Ghost, speak to the Divine Spirit, saying:

'Oh, Holy Spirit, Soul of my soul, I adore You. Enlighten, guide, strengthen and console me; tell me what I should do; give me Your orders. I promise to be submissive in all that You desire of me and to accept all that You allow to happen to me. Grant only to me to know Your will.'

If you do this, your life will flow along happily, serenely, and full of consolation, even in the midst of ordeals, because grace will be given to you in proportion to your trials, giving you strength to bear them. Thus you will arrive at the Gate of Paradise filled with merit. This submission to the Holy Spirit is the secret of sanctity."   – Cardinal Mercier

Like a river glorious,
Is God's perfect peace,
Over all victorious,
In its bright increase.
Perfect, yet it floweth,
Fuller every day,
Perfect, yet it groweth,
Deeper all the way.
                    --Frances Ridley Havergal

MAY 31 --

"Then called I upon the name of the Lord; O Lord, I beseech thee, deliver my soul. Gracious is the Lord, and righteous; yea, our God is merciful." Ps 116:4-5).

Sometimes well-meaning believers try to encourage their fellow Christians by suggesting that if they pray in the right way they can expect all their problems to be removed. Trials can be difficult enough to handle without being told that if your problems don't go away you must not be praying properly, or that since you have a problem there must be something wrong with your attitude. Such "encouragement" can make people feel like spiritual failures. What should our attitude be where our problems are concerned?

A British pastor once said: "Life is not a garden; it's a gymnasium." Life, for most of us, is an ongoing series of exercises in which our spiritual "muscles" are constantly being strengthened by all the challenges, dilemmas, disappointments, frustrations, heartaches and all those other problems that come our way.

Does this mean we can't expect God to ever remove our problems? Of course not. He often removes them. Sometimes, after we pray, He removes them quickly. Sometimes He removes them over time. Sometimes they are only removed after what seems like a very long time. But God is always faithful to give us His guidance, direction and help as we work our way through our challenges. Sometimes He may allow our challenges to stay for a time so that He may train us up in the ways of trust and faith. Sometimes, in the midst of our trials, He may reveal to us areas in which we need to grow. Sometimes, if we have prayed diligently and still find our challenges are not being removed, we may need to recognize that in all likelihood we are probably meant to deal with them as they are, at least for the time being. This probably means, for at least a while longer, that we are to remain in the gymnasium.

It's tempting to believe that, with prayer, our problems should all go away. It would certainly make life easier if they did. If God has miraculously delivered us from one problem, it's easy to think He should miraculously deliver us from any similar problems that come along. But He doesn't always work in the same way, even though the situations may be similar. We can't always understand why God does not remove certain forms of suffering. His reasons are beyond our human understanding. His eternal purposes are greater than what we can comprehend. What "worked" in one situation may not work the next time. What happens to you may not happen to me. We can't put God in a box and say that there is some formula to which He must adhere. Life is not that predictable and neither is God.

What is predictable is that God will be faithful as we deal with our problems. Some of them will baffle and perplex us; some may even drive us to exasperation, but God will see us through every one of them. One day, joyfully, we'll arrive at the place where problems will be a thing of the past. We will no longer be in the gymnasium. We will be with God, problem-free, perfected and pure.

JUNE 1 --

"And he said to them all, If any man will come after me, let him deny himself, and take up his cross daily, and follow me." (Lu 9:23)

"Christ is the way out, and the way in; the way from slavery, conscious or unconscious, into liberty; the way from the hostile environment we live in to the home we desire but do not know... He is not only the way, but the leader in the way and the captain of our salvation. We must become as little children, and Christ must be born in us. We must learn of Him, and the one lesson He has to give is Himself. He does first everything that He wants us to do; He is Himself all He wants us to be. We must not merely do as He did; we must see things as He saw them, regard them as He regards them. We must take the will of God as the very life of our being. We must not try to get our own way, nor trouble ourselves as to what may be thought or said of us.

The world must be to us as nothing...do not misunderstand me ...when I say the world, I do not mean the world God made, and even less the human hearts that live in it; but the world man makes by choosing the perversions of his own nature – a world apart from and opposed to God's world. By the world, I mean all those ways of judging, regarding, and thinking -- whether political, economical, ecclesiastical, social, or individual -- which are not divine. They are not God's ways of thinking or judging. They do not take God into account or set His will as supreme, as the one and only law of life...

From everything that is against the teaching and thinking of Jesus, from the world in the heart of the best man in it, specially from the world in his own heart, the disciple must turn to follow Him. The first thing in all progress is to leave something behind; to follow Him is to leave one's self behind. 'If any man would come after me, let him deny himself.'"

– George MacDonald

"As thou hast sent me into the world, even so have I also sent them into the world. And for their sakes I sanctify myself, that they also might be sanctified through the truth." (Jo 17:18-19).

"The standard of practical holy living has been so low among Christians that any good degree of real devotedness of life and walk is looked upon with surprise, and even often with disapproval by a large portion of the Church. And, for the most part, the professed followers of the Lord Jesus Christ are so little like Him in character or in action that to an outside observer there would not seem to be much harmony between them.

But we who have heard the call of our God to a life of entire consecration and perfect trust must do differently from all this. We must come out from the world and be separate, and must not be conformed to it in our characters nor in our purposes. We must no longer share in its spirit or its ways. Our conversation must be in Heaven, and we must seek those things that are above, where Christ sits on the right hand of God. We must walk through the world as Christ walked. We must have the mind that was in Him."

--Hannah Whitall Smith

It isn't doing things for Christ that is the most essential thing – it is becoming more and more like Him that is the goal we must constantly pursue. All our working for Him, writing about Him and talking of Him is good in itself, but if we are not continually becoming more Christ-like in our natures we are still falling short of the core purpose of our lives.

If the people who know us best were asked whether we have become more like Christ over the last few years, what would they say? If we have held back in allowing God to change us, we can deepen our surrender to Him starting today. Are there changes God has wanted to make that I have been resisting? Have I been trying to change myself in my own strength, rather than allowing God to change me in His way? Today, I can make the effort to allow Him to make whatever changes He knows to be best.

Have Thine own way, Lord, have Thine own way.
Wounded and weary, help me, I pray.
Power, all power, surely is Thine,
Touch me and heal me, Savior divine.
Have Thine own way, Lord, have Thine own way.
Hold o'er my being absolute sway,
Fill with Thy Spirit, till all shall see
Christ only, always, living in me.
-- Adelaide A. Pollard

"In whom we have redemption through his blood, the forgiveness of sins, according to the riches of his grace;" (Ep 1:7)

How much grace does Jesus have for those who come to Him? The answer is, more than enough.

Just ask the Apostle Paul. Christ's grace was more than enough to transform this once angry persecutor of believers into a man who was so submitted to Christ that his only desire in life was to serve Him. Just ask the Apostle Peter. Christ's grace was more than enough to turn this once profane and cowardly disciple into a courageous and faithful defender of the faith.

Just ask David, a man overcome by the sins of the flesh, but who found enough grace in his Lord's loving-kindness that he was described as a "man after God's own heart" and was able to repent of the wrongs he committed.

Just ask anyone who has personally sought out Christ for mercy and see what answer you receive. You will hear from every one a marvelous testimony of how large was the supply of grace that Christ made available. Every story of Christ's grace is a story of abundance. With Him, there is no supply that is not full to overflowing, with more besides.

God's grace is more than enough for me, for you, and for all those for whom you are praying. No matter how dark our past has been or how bleak our future may look at this moment, Christ's grace is more than enough. No matter how frail we may feel or how narrow the road to victory may appear, Christ's grace is more than enough. The darker our road, the more light will Christ's grace provide. The greater our sinfulness, the farther His grace will be able to reach. The higher the mountain we have to climb, the greater will be the strength He shall provide. We have only to come. We need never fear that Jesus will not have enough grace for us, for His supply is as limitless as His love.

Jesus, full of every grace,
Let us come before Thy face,
Grant the joy of sin forgiven,
Foretaste of the bliss of Heaven.

Vine of Heaven, Thy blood supplies
This blest cup of sacrifice;
Lord, Thy wounds our healing give,
To Thy cross we look and live.
                              – Anonymous

"I say unto you, Though he will not rise and give him, because he is his friend, yet because of his importunity he will rise and give him as many as he needeth." (Lu 11:8)

"Importunity has various elements. The chief ones are perseverance, determination, and intensity. Importunity begins with the refusal to readily accept a denial. This refusal develops into a determination to persevere, to spare no time or trouble, until an answer comes. Then this determination grows into an intensity in which the whole being is given to God in supplication. Boldness comes to lay hold of God's strength. At one time it is quiet and restful; at another, passionate and bold. At one point it waits in patience, but at another, it claims at once what it desires. In whatever different shape, importunity always means and knows [that] God hears prayer -- 'I must be heard...'

Why is it that so many of God's children have no desire for this honor of being princes of God, strivers with God, and prevailing? The phrase our Lord taught us, 'What things soever ye desire...believe that ye receive them,' is nothing but His expression of Jacob's words: 'I will not let thee go except thou bless me.' This is the importunity He teaches. We must learn to claim and take the blessing.

Remember the marks of the true intercessor as taught in the parable: a sense of the need of souls, a Christ-like love in the heart, a consciousness of personal impotence, faith in the answer of prayer, courage to persevere in spite of refusal, and the assurance of an abundant reward. These are the qualities that change a Christian into an intercessor and call forth the power of prevailing prayer."   – Andrew Murray

"Comfort ye, comfort ye my people, saith your God." (Is 40:1)

"Beloved, there is a Shelter for us from the sense of past guilt. We have broken our Maker's law, and therefore we are afraid. But our Maker came from heaven to earth. Jesus, the Christ of God, was made man and bore – that we might never bear – His Father's righteous wrath. Because Christ suffered for me, my guilt is gone. My punishment was endured by my Substitute. Therefore, I hear His voice, 'Comfort ye, comfort ye my people.' He who trusts Christ says: 'Now I have no fear about the present, nor about the future. Let catastrophe follow catastrophe. Let the world crash and all the universe go to ruin; beneath the wings of the Eternal God I am safe. All things must work together for my good, for I love God and have been called according to His purpose (Ro 8:28).' What a blessed Shelter! When we enter fully into the truth of our adoption by God, we are filled with unutterable peace. The Holy Ghost, the Comforter, abides in us, and we fly to Him and receive consolations so rich and powerful that this day we feel at peace in the midst of discomforts; and if perplexed, we are not in despair. There is a shelter in the atonement of Christ, in the Fatherhood of God, in the abiding presence of the Comforter."   – C. H. Spurgeon

> Come, and He will give you rest,
> Trust Him, for His word is plain,
> He will take the sinful-est,
> Christ receiveth sinful men.
>
> Now my heart condemns me not,
> Pure before the law I stand,
> He who cleansed me from all spot,
> Satisfied its last demand.
> – Erdmann Neumeister

JUNE 6 --

"Behold, I stand at the door, and knock: if any man hear my voice, and open the door, I will come in to him..." (Re 3:20)

"Ah, how rare it is to find a soul still enough to hear God speak! The slightest murmur of our vain desires or of a love fixed upon self, confounds all the words of the Spirit of God. We hear well enough that he is speaking, and that he is asking for something, but we cannot distinguish what is said, and are often glad enough that we cannot... Need we be astonished, then, if so many people, pious indeed, but full of amusements, vain desires, false wisdom and confidence in their own virtues, cannot hear it, and consider its existence as a dream of fanatics? Let us recognize, then, the fact that God is incessantly speaking in us. He speaks in the impenitent also, but, stunned by the noise of the world and their passions, they cannot hear Him; the interior voice is to them a fable...

God speaks, too, in wise and enlightened persons, whose life, outwardly correct, seems adorned with many virtues; but such are often too full of themselves and their lights, to listen to God. Everything is turned into reasoning; they substitute the principles of natural wisdom and the plans of human prudence, for what would come infinitely better through the channel of simplicity and docility to the word of God. They seem good, sometimes better than others; they are so, perhaps, up to a certain point, but it is a mixed goodness. They are still in possession of themselves, and desire always to be so, according to the measure of their reason; they love to be in the hands of their own counsel, and to be strong and great in their own eyes.

God, whose sole desire is to communicate Himself, cannot, so to speak, find where to set his foot in souls so full of themselves, who have grown fat upon their own wisdom and virtues; but, as says the Scripture, 'his secret is with the righteous' (Pr 3:32).   – Francois Fenelon

JUNE 7 ---

"Thou gavest also thy good Spirit to instruct them, and withheldest not Thy manna from their mouth, and gavest them water for their thirst." (Ne 9:20)

"When we are thoroughly emptied of ourselves – when our knowledge is shown to be ignorance, our wisdom folly, our righteousness filthy rags, and our strength weakness – then we begin to long after the teachings of the blessed Spirit. We must be purged and tried before we can value and receive the treasures of grace. When we are well exercised and tried in our souls, then we begin to long after the teachings of the Holy Spirit, that he would shed abroad the love of God in our soul, visit and guide us, overshadow us with his holy presence, and drop into our hearts his secret unction.

Before we are brought here, we do not know the personality of the Holy Spirit. We have no evidence in our conscience that he is God; we cannot worship and adore him as the Third Person in the blessed Godhead. But when we are brought to this spot – that we know nothing without his teaching, feel nothing without his giving, and are nothing without his making – this makes us pant and sigh after his teachings and leadings; and we are brought to wait in the posture of holy adoration and still quietness for the dew and unction of the Spirit to fall upon our conscience."

                                                                                              -- Joseph Philpot

JUNE 8 ---

"And he spake a parable unto them to this end, that men ought always to pray, and not to faint;" (Luke 18:1)

"How lightly we are often prone to treat the privilege of prayer. We encounter a problem or a need, pray once or twice, perhaps a week or so, and if we do not see the work accomplished we decide the battle is over; we might as well give up. We shake our heads and say, 'Oh, He must not wish to do this thing for me,' and then we feel depressed and defeated. It doesn't dawn on us that God, the Master of the Universe, does indeed hear and respond to prayer, but that His ways, and His timing, are beyond our poor abilities to understand. Sometimes He must do this thing first, or sometimes that, before our prayer can receive its full answer. Some needs require a month of concerted prayer. Some a year. Some a decade. Some a lifetime. And between our first prayer about the matter and God's answer to it there must be continuing, believing, heartfelt prayer. How much must we pray? Until we learn to 'pray fervently' (Ja 5:17); to 'pray, and not faint' (Lu 18:1); to 'pray without ceasing' (I Th 5:17). We must pray that much, and not a syllable less.

Nothing distinguishes the children of God so clearly and strongly as prayer. It is the one infallible mark and test of being a Christian. Christian people are prayerful, the worldly-minded, prayerless. Christians call on God; worldlings ignore God, and do not call on His Name. But even the Christian has need to cultivate continual prayer. Prayer must be habitual, but much more than a habit. It is duty, yet one which rises far above, and goes beyond, the ordinary implications of the term. It is the expression of a relation to God, a yearning for Divine communion. It is the outward and upward flow of the inward life toward its original fountain. It is an assertion of the soul's paternity, a claiming of the sonship, which links man to the Eternal."   --E.M. Bounds

JUNE 9 --

"... The Lord looseth the prisoners: The Lord openeth the eyes of the blind..." (Ps 146:7-8)

Denial can be a problem for almost any of us. Even if we have been Christians for many years, have worked hard to be good people and tried to do all that we believe God would have us do, we can still suffer from denial. Denial is a particularly debilitating character defect. It can damage our ability to grow closer to the Lord or hear His directions for our lives.

Someone once said denial is the only defect of character that fools us into thinking there is nothing wrong with us. It has the ability to keep us in the dark about the very things we need to change. The letters of the word "denial" form an acronym that can help us remember how destructive this trait can be if we allow it to go untreated. Denial will always:

Destroy our ability to see those traits in us that God would like to change;

Erase whatever progress we manage to make by causing us to slip back into the same old destructive behaviors and thinking patterns that negatively impact our lives;

Negate our ability to hear from God by keeping us deaf to those things He is trying to tell us;

Isolate us from others by making us believe they are the ones who need to change, not us.

Alienate us from God by convincing us that our problems stem from the fact that He either doesn't care about us or is mad at us;

Leave us lonely and frustrated as a result of the negative impact it has on our relationships with others.

What is the remedy for denial? One of the best remedies is to become accountable. Being accountable means being honest about what is really happening in our lives with an individual or a group. It is important, if we do choose to share ourselves with another, that the person is trustworthy and able to keep a confidence. Being accountable also means we are willing to receive feedback from that person, provided we know he or she has our best interests at heart.

Being accountable takes courage, but once we begin, we'll find our denial will begin to recede and our lives will begin to change. We'll discover that coming out of denial doesn't destroy us. It sets us free. Denial may be a stubborn defect, but God can remove it. And He will, if we will let Him. In doing so, He will also set us free from those attitudes and behaviors that have impaired our ability to be completely surrendered to Him.

JUNE 10 --

"I dwell in the high and holy place, with him also that is of a contrite and humble spirit, to revive the spirit of the humble, and to revive the heart of the contrite ones." (Is 57:15)

The humble heart is a precious thing to God. He so loves a humble spirit that He states it is His desire to come and dwell with the one who possesses a spirit of humility.

What is it that characterizes a humble heart?

The word "humble" is derived from the Latin word "humus," which means "fertile ground." Humus is the organic material within the soil that enables it to nourish and promote life. When the earth is fertile, it has within it the power to transform.

At the end of the growing year, all kinds of matter are cast upon the earth: dead leaves, broken branches, wilted vines. These are operated on by the natural elements – wind and sunlight, rain and snow -- and are gradually broken down and absorbed into the earth. Eventually, they become substances that provide nourishment for plants and trees. They become life-sustaining materials for the growing season ahead. Have you ever noticed how the earth is able to receive even man's refuse – our garbage and our discards – and transform it into organic, life-sustaining humus? This is an example of the "humility" of the earth.

Our lives are to be like the humble condition of the earth. In our journey we may discover that many of the things we receive are not much to our liking. They may feel a lot more like refuse and discards than blessings, but, like the earth, we can respond by allowing God to transform them. Our difficulties can be changed from negative experiences into those which are life-sustaining and life-affirming, and which will work for good, either in our lives or in the lives of others. This is not a process we can perform on our own. It is something only the Holy Spirit can accomplish; but, if we are willing, God will impart to us the quality of humility. He will make us "fertile," like the earth. When we have this kind of humility, God can use us to bring good out of seemingly negative or tragic situations. He can show us how to respond to events so our lives bring glory to Him.

"...and be clothed with humility: for God resisteth the proud, and giveth grace to the humble. Humble yourselves therefore under the mighty hand of God, that he may exalt you in due time." (I Pe 5:5-6)

JUNE 11 ---

"In whom ye also trusted, after that ye heard the word of truth, the gospel of your salvation: in whom also after that ye believed, ye were sealed with that holy Spirit of promise." (Eph 1:13)

"We hear Jesus saying to the multitude that sought him for the loaves and fishes, 'Labor not for the meat which perisheth, but for that meat which endureth unto eternal life, which the Son of man shall give unto you, for him hath God the Father sealed' (John 6:27).

This sealing must evidently refer back to his reception of the Spirit at the Jordan. One of the most instructive writers on the Hebrew worship and ritual tells us that it was the custom for the priest, having selected a lamb from the flock, to inspect it with the most minute scrutiny in order to discover if it was without physical defect, and then to seal it with the temple seal, thus certifying that it was fit for sacrifice and for food. Behold the Lamb of God, presenting himself for inspection at the Jordan! Under the Father's omniscient scrutiny he is found to be 'a lamb without blemish and without spot.' From the opening heaven God gives witness to the fact in the words: 'This is my beloved Son in whom I am well pleased,' and then he puts the Holy Ghost upon him, the testimony to his sonship, the seal of his separation unto sacrifice and service.

The disciple is as his Lord in this experience. 'In whom having also believed ye were sealed with the Holy Spirit of promise' (Eph. 1:13). As always in the statements of Scripture, this transaction is represented as subsequent to faith. It is not conversion, but something done upon a converted soul, a kind of crown of consecration put upon his faith. Indeed the two events stand in marked contrast. In conversion the believer receives the testimony of God and 'sets his seal to it that God is true' (John 3:33). In consecration, God sets his seal upon the believer that he is true. The latter is God's 'Amen' to the Christian, verifying the Christian's 'Amen' to God. 'Now he which stablisheth us with you in Christ, and anointed us, is God; who also sealed us and gave us the earnest of the Spirit in our hearts' (2 Co 1:21-22).'" – A. J. Gordon

"Note: The allusion to the seal as a pledge of purchase would be peculiarly intelligible to the Ephesians, for Ephesus was a maritime city, and an extensive trade in timber was carried on there by the ship-masters of the neighboring ports. The method of purchase was this: The merchant, after selecting his timber, stamped it with his own signet, which was an acknowledged sign of ownership. He often did not carry off his possession at the time; it was left in the harbor with other floats of timber; but it was chosen, bought, and stamped; and in due time the merchant sent a trusted agent with the signet, who, finding that timber which bore a corresponding impress, claimed and brought it away for the master's use. Thus the Holy Spirit now impresses on the soul the image of Jesus Christ; and this is the sure pledge of the everlasting inheritance." — E. H. Bickersteth

JUNE 12 --

"For it is God which worketh in you both to will and to do of his good pleasure." (Ph 2:13)

"That God should love me enough to care about the details of my life is perfectly wonderful. And then, that He should be willing to tell me all about it, and to let me know just how to live and walk so as to perfectly please Him, seems almost too good to be true. We never care about the little details of people's lives unless we love them. It is a matter of indifference to us with the majority of people we meet as to what they do or how they spend their time; but as soon as we begin to love anyone, we begin at once to care. That God cares, therefore, is just a precious proof of His love; and it is most blessed to have Him speak to us about everything in our lives, about our duties, about our pleasures, about our friendships, about our occupations, about all that we do, or think, or say. You must know this in your own experience, dear reader, if you would come into the full joy and privilege of this life hid with Christ in God, for it is one of its most precious gifts!

God's promise is that He will work in us to will as well as to do of His good pleasure. This, of course, means that He will take possession of our will, and work it for us, and that His suggestions will come to us, not so much as commands from the outside, as desires springing up within. They will originate in our will; we shall feel as though we wanted to do something, not as though we must. And this makes it a service of perfect liberty; for it is always easy to do what we desire to do, let the accompanying circumstances be as difficult as they may. Every mother knows that she could secure perfect and easy obedience in her child if she could only get into that child's will and work it for him, making him want himself to do the things she willed he should. And this is what our Father does for His children in the new dispensation; He writes His laws on our hearts and on our minds, and we love them, and are drawn to our obedience by our affections and judgment, not driven by our fears."

--Hannah Whitall Smith

JUNE 13 --

"Jesus answered and said unto him, What I do thou knowest not now; but thou shalt know hereafter." (Jo 13:7)

"This passage furnishes the key to many of the perplexities in all our lives. We do not understand them at the time. We do not see how they can have any blessing in them for us. They seem altogether dark. But we have no right to judge of our Master's work in us or with us until it is finished. 'What I do thou knowest not now.' How could we be expected to understand all the Master's great thoughts? Yet this is not the end. 'Thou shalt know hereafter.' This mystery is to be explained. This perplexity is to be resolved into the clearness of noonday. You do not understand now because you cannot yet see the end, cannot perceive the blessing and the beauty. The Master Himself knows just what He is going to bring out of each strange work of His, and therefore He is not perplexed. Then, He says that we also shall know hereafter. We shall see the cloud as it departs, glorified by the rainbow arching its dark folds. We shall see the tangles resolving into lovely grace and beauty.

> Some time, when all life's lessons have been learned,
> And sun and stars for evermore have set,
> The things which our weak judgments here have spurned,
> The things o'er which we grieved with lashes wet,
> Will flash before us, out of life's dark night,
> As stars shine most in deeper tints of blue;
> And we shall see how all God's plans were right,
> And how what seemed reproof was love most true.

What is the lesson? That we should trust God when we cannot understand His ways with us. No doubt love has planned them all. No doubt there is blessing in the outcome as it lies now in God's mind. No doubt we shall see the blessing, too, hereafter."   – J. R. Miller

JUNE 14 --

"My son, despise not the chastening of the Lord; neither be weary of his correction:" (Pr 3:11)

Many of the experiences that perplex us in life are in truth the answers to our prayers.

We pray to be able to surrender our lives to God and in return He asks us to lay at His feet some cherished plan or treasured possession. We tell God we want to become more patient or kind, and discover our lives are flooded with troubles and irritations. We yearn to be more loving and ask God for this grace, then are appalled at the way our plans and preferences are turned upside down at every turn. We intercede for those we love and find their lives, too, are suddenly submerged in upheaval, and we wonder, how could all this happen? It happens because God answers prayer. Our perplexity is due, more often than not, to our failure to view God's dealings with eyes that are able to see beyond the surface into the depths of the heart where God is busily at work.

Trials will continue for as long as we mean business with God. The more we desire to be fashioned into His likeness, the more we can expect His hand to be upon us, molding and forming us according to His plan. His constant processing will baffle us unless we have settled it in our hearts that God does indeed answer prayer, not with an indulgent smile and permission to stay as we are, but with circumstances that will mold and shape us into the kind of people He means for us to be. As we trust Him more and more, we will develop the kind of vision that will enable us to see beneath the surface of our circumstances into the heavenly realm, where we shall discern His mighty hand at work, even though we may not always understand exactly what it is He is doing.

Each time God allows us to deal with a problem, He is taking us through one more process meant to enlarge and perfect us. At times, He may remove a problem upon our praying over it. At other times, He may allow us to keep it for a while – sometimes, a good long while -- if, by keeping it, we will be led to come to know Him, and ourselves, more intimately. Our suffering is never by mistake, nor is it a result of God's not caring for us. It is, rather, a place to which our journey must take us so that we may be strengthened in fortitude, perfected in character, delivered from our defectiveness and matured in faith.

JUNE 15 --

"From that time many of his disciples went back, and walked no more with him." (Jo 6:66)

How to Preach Without Converting Anybody:

Preach about every doctrine that makes man the center of God's attention rather than God the center of man's devotion.

Tell people only what God will do for them and say nothing of any need on their part to change; let your motive be to become popular with all people.

Avoid preaching anything that is offensive to the carnal mind.

Do not disturb the consciences of your hearers so that they become alarmed about their souls.

Avoid all enthusiasm in your delivery or you may give the impression that you really believe what you say.

Avoid sharing your own personal experience of the power of Christ or your hearers may infer that you think you have something they need.

Do not stir up uncomfortable memories by reminding your hearers of their past sins.

Do not let them think that you expect them to commit themselves right on the spot to God.

Preach the gospel only as a cure for problems, not as something sinners need to attain salvation.

Make no appeals to your hearers' fears; instead, give them the impression everything is all right, no matter what they do.

Preach Christ only as an infinitely friendly and good-natured being. Ignore the fact that His rebukes to sinners and hypocrites often made them tremble.

Do not rebuke the worldly tendencies of your members, lest you hurt their feelings.

Say so little of hell that your hearers will think you don't really believe in it.

Make no references to things like self-denial, cross-bearing, and crucifixion to the world -- otherwise you might actually convict and convert some of your listeners.

Aim to make your hearers pleased with themselves and pleased with you; be especially careful not to hurt anyone's feelings.

Never tell people that they must cease from serving self and instead serve God; rather, allow them to believe they can take their time about turning from sin.

Go along with the fashionable belief that says a person can be saved without making Jesus his Lord.

Preach that Christians don't really need to do anything.

–Adapted from a sermon by Charles Finney

JUNE 16 --

"Then came to Him the mother of the sons of Zebedee, with her sons, worshipping Him, and asking a certain thing of Him." (Ma 20:20)

"The mother of James and John came before the Lord and said: 'Grant that these my two sons may sit, the one on thy right hand, and the other on the left, in thy kingdom.' Jesus answered by telling her: 'Ye know not what ye ask.' Addressing his two disciples, He asked them: 'Are ye able to drink of the cup that I shall drink of, and to be baptized with the baptism that I am baptized with?' Both of them, full of the self-confidence of youth and inexperience, responded: 'We are able.' (Jo 20:22) Jesus told them: 'Ye shall drink indeed of my cup...', yet it could not have occurred to them at that moment what it was the Lord really meant by His saying.

We, too, tend to ask God to allow us to go with Him to the high places, and then we wonder why He does not immediately take us there. He may also answer us with an answer we do not fully understand. Then He bids us to travel along a narrow, arduous road, and we fear He may not have heard our request, when in fact He has heard, and is leading us along the very path that will eventually lead us to the heights...

You ask your Lord for sovereign joy. You know not what you ask. Deeper joy requires deeper refinement, and so, instead of immediate joy, the Lord leads you into the discipline of severity, that your soul might be rendered more sensitive.

You ask that the beauty of the Lord might be upon you. You know not what you ask; for between you and that beauty there lies Gethsemane, with its exhausting ministries of intercessory prayer and sacrifice. In truth, you are asking for Heaven, for a place among the seating of the blessed. You know not what you ask!

> They climbed the steep ascent of heaven,
> Through peril, toil, and pain!

Heaven is the home of those who have sacrificed, who have been crusaders; the secret of Heaven's glory is to be found in the glorious character that has been fashioned in us along the way.

And so the gist of it all is this: thrones are for those who are fit to sit on them; we arrive at our throne when we are ready to rule. The sons of Zebedee came to the throne, but by ways which they had never dreamed. Herod killed James the brother of John with the sword. John spent his evening days in a painful exile. Yet through it all, both were sustained by the inexpressible fellowship of their Lord."

–Compiled from a message by J. H. Jowett

JUNE 17 --

"Praying always with all prayer and supplication in the Spirit, and watching thereunto with all perseverance and supplication for all saints;" (Ep 6:18)

"Prayer is really projecting my spirit, that is, my real personality, to the spot concerned, and doing business there with other spirit beings.

For example, there is a man in a city on the Atlantic seaboard for whom I pray daily. It makes my praying for him very tangible and definite to recall that every time I pray, my prayer is a spirit force instantly traversing the space between us, and going without hindrance through the walls of the house where he is, and influencing the spirit beings surrounding him, and so influencing his own will.

When it became clear to me some few years ago that [the Lord] would not have me go to those parts of the earth where the need is greatest, a deep tinge of disappointment came over me. Then, as I realized the wisdom of His sovereignty in service, it came to me anew that I could exert a positive influence in those lands for Him by prayer. As many others have done, I marked out a daily schedule of prayer. There are certain ones for whom I pray by name, at certain intervals. And it gives great simplicity to my faith, and great gladness to my heart to remember that every time such prayer is breathed out, my spirit personality is being projected ...and, in effect, I am standing in Shanghai, and Calcutta and Tokyo, and pleading the power of Jesus' victory over the evil one there, and on behalf of those faithful ones standing there for God.

It is a fiercely contested conflict. Satan is a trained strategist, and an obstinate fighter. He refuses to acknowledge defeat until he must. It is the fight of his life. Strange as it must seem, and perhaps absurd, he apparently hopes to succeed... Prayer is insisting upon Jesus' victory, and the retreat of the enemy on each particular spot, and heart and problem concerned."

– S. D. Gordon

JUNE 18 --

"That the God of our Lord Jesus Christ, the Father of glory, may give unto you the spirit of wisdom and revelation in the knowledge of him:" (Eph 1:17)

"We cannot trust a person if we do not know him. At least, it is safer for us not to do so; and as a rule we do not. But on the other hand, when we know a person thoroughly, we cannot help trusting him. No effort to trust is required when we perfectly know a person. The difficulty then is, not to trust. Why, then, do we not thus trust God? Is not the answer clear? It is because we do not know Him.

Thus we see how this knowledge of God is our greatest need; the very first step of our Christian course. Our trust will ever be in proportion to our knowledge.

If we knew, for example, a billionth part of God's infinite wisdom, we should see our own to be such utter folly that we should not merely be 'willing' for His will, but we should desire it. It would be our greatest happiness for Him to do and arrange all for us. We should say, 'Lord, I am so foolish and ignorant; I know nothing, and can do nothing; I can see only this present moment; I know nothing of tomorrow. But You can see the end from the beginning... Do, then, Your own will. This is the desire of my heart. This is what I long for above all things...

Not knowing this secret, Christians everywhere are striving and laboring to be 'willing' by looking at themselves; and by some definite act of faith to do something of themselves. Instead of thinking of His wisdom and His love, they are thinking of themselves and of their surrender.

But this is labor in vain. Even if it should seem to accomplish something, it is only like tying paper flowers on a plant. They may look natural and fair; but they have no scent, and no life; no fruit, and no seed. It is an artificial attempt to produce that which, if we did but know God, would come of itself, without an effort. The effort would be to stop or hinder the mighty power of a true knowledge of God.

The trouble with us is that we think we know better. We would not say it for the world, we would hardly admit it to ourselves. But there it is; and the difficulty of being 'made willing' is the proof of it....

If we really knew Him, and believed that He knows better than we do what is good for us, there would be no effort whatever, but only a blessed, irrepressible desire for His will." – E. W. Bullinger

JUNE 19 --

"Then shall ye remember your own evil ways, and your doings that were not good, and shall lothe yourselves in your own sight for your iniquities and for your abominations" (Ez 36:31)

One might expect that the severest accusations of conscience would come when we first turn our lives over to the Lord. After all, it is then that many of us feel most deeply the effects of our sinfulness. But frequently this is not the case. Though sorrow for our failures may spur us to seek salvation, we seldom have the ability at the beginning of our walk with God to understand the true nature of our separation from Him or the extent of our sinfulness. This depth of understanding can only come later, after we have walked with the Lord for a period of time.

The prophet Ezekiel revealed that man doesn't become aware of the extent of his sin until he has embarked on the process of sanctification. Bad men cannot understand their own badness. It is only after God has given man a new heart ('a new heart also will I give you;' Ez 36:26) and His own spirit ('and I will put my spirit within you;' v. 27) that man is able to discern, at least in part, how far he has strayed from his Lord: "then shall ye remember your own evil ways, and your doings that were not good, and shall lothe yourselves" (v. 31).

Surely most of us can heartily agree with the prophet's words. We know that the closer we get to the Lord the more we shudder at the sins we once committed, and at the sins we still commit. What wonderful grace it is that

God does not burden the newcomer with the sight of his true self. It would be almost too much to bear. Instead, God reassures him. He tells him to forget the things which are behind (Ph 3:13). It is only later, when we have grown stronger in our faith, that we are allowed to look back and take a clearer look at our pasts. Then we are likely to see more clearly the selfishness that motivated many of our actions. We are likely to want to hang our heads and say, "Father, I hate the sins I have committed and yearn to be made clean." Along with Paul, we will cry: "O wretched man that I am! who shall deliver me from the body of this death?" (Ro 7:24). Yet this greater understanding of our sins will also be a cause for rejoicing, because we will recognize that through the magnificent grace of God, which translated us into the kingdom of His dear Son, we have been freed from the bondage of sin. We can say with confidence: "I thank God through Jesus Christ our Lord....There is therefore now no condemnation to them which are in Christ Jesus, who walk not after the flesh, but after the Spirit" (Ro 7:25, 8:1); "For as many as are led by the Spirit of God, they are the sons of God...The Spirit itself beareth witness with our spirit, that we are the children of God" (Ro 8:14, 16).

JUNE 20 --

"God is in the midst of her, she shall not be moved; God shall help her, and that right early." (Ps 46:5)

"What does a little child do when he sees something that frightens him or confuses him? He doesn't stand there and try to fight the thing. He will, in fact, hardly look at the thing that frightens him. Rather, the child will quickly run into the arms of his mother. There, in those arms, he is safe. In exactly the same way, you should turn from the dangers of temptation and run to your God!

You and I are very weak. At our best we are very weak. If you, in your weakness, attempt to attack your enemies, you will often find yourself wounded. Just as frequently, you will even find yourself defeated.

There is another way. In times of temptation and distraction, remain by faith in the simple presence of Jesus Christ. You will find an immediate supply of strength. This was David's resource and support."

– Jeanne Guyon

I have set the Lord always before me: because he is at my right hand, I shall not be moved. Therefore my heart is glad, and my glory rejoiceth: my flesh also shall rest in hope. (Ps 16: 8-9)

"Charity...is not easily provoked, thinketh no evil; rejoiceth not in iniquity, but rejoiceth in the truth." (I Co 13:4,5,6)

"The peculiarity of ill temper is that it is the vice of the virtuous. It is often the one blot on an otherwise noble character. You know men who are all but perfect, and women who might be entirely perfect, but for an easily ruffled, quick-tempered, or 'touchy' disposition. This compatibility of ill temper with high moral character is one of the strangest and saddest problems of ethics. The truth is there are two great classes of sins – sins of the Body, and sins of the Disposition. The Prodigal Son may be called a type of the first, the Elder Brother of the second.

Now society has no doubt whatever as to which of these is the worse. It determines it is the Prodigal. But are we right? To the eye of Him who is Love, a sin committed against Love may seem a hundred times more base than that of the flesh. No form of vice, not worldliness, not greed, not drunkenness itself, does more to un-Christianize society than evil temper. For embittering life, for breaking up communities, for destroying relationships, for devastating homes, for withering up men and women, for wounding children; in short, for sheer gratuitous misery-producing power, this sin stands alone.

Look at the Elder Brother; moral, hard-working, patient, dutiful – let him get all credit for his virtues – look at this man, this baby, sulking outside his own father's door. 'He was angry,' we read, 'and would not go in.'

Look at the effect upon the father, upon the servants, upon the happiness of the guests. Judge the effect upon the Prodigal – and how many prodigals are kept out of the Kingdom of God by the unlovely characters of those who profess to be inside? Analyze, as a study in Temper, the thunder-cloud itself as it gathers upon the Elder Brother's brow. What is it made of? Jealousy, anger, pride, uncharity, cruelty, self-righteousness, touchiness, doggedness, sullenness – these are the ingredients of this dark and loveless soul....

You will see then why Temper is significant. It is not in what it is alone, but in what it reveals. It is a test for love, a symptom, a revelation of an unloving nature at bottom, a sample of the most hidden part of the soul exposed involuntarily when off one's guard... Christ, the Spirit of Christ, interpenetrating ours, sweetens, purifies, transforms all. Will-power does not change men. Time does not change men. Christ does."

-- Henry Drummond

"He that in these things serveth Christ is acceptable to God." (Rom. 14:18)

"God can only use us while we are trusting Him completely. Satan cared far less for Peter's denial of his Master than for the use he made of it afterwards to destroy his faith. So Jesus said to him: 'I have prayed for thee that thy faith fail not' (Lu 22:32). It was Peter's faith Satan attacked, and so it is our faith that he contests. 'The trial of our faith is much more precious than gold that perisheth' (I Peter 1:7).

Whatever else we let go of, let us hold steadfastly to our trust. 'Cast not away therefore your confidence' (He 10:35), and 'hold fast the confidence and rejoicing of the hope firm unto the end' (He 3:6). And if you would hold onto your trust then hold onto your sweetness, your right spirit, your obedience, your victory in every way.

Whatever comes, regard it as of less consequence than that you should triumph and remain steadfast. Accept every circumstance as something God is permitting to touch your life. Wave the banner of your victory in the face of every foe. Go on, shouting in Jesus' name, 'Thanks be unto God, which always causeth us to triumph in Christ' (II Cor 2:14)."   – A. B. Simpson

JUNE 23 --

"The Lord is nigh unto all them that call upon him, to all that call upon him in truth. He will fulfil the desire of them that fear him: he also will hear their cry, and will save them." (Ps 145:18-19)

Nothing passes into the life of the believer unless God has first examined every aspect of the trial and deemed it something He shall permit as part of His 'permissive' will. It doesn't matter how difficult the circumstance may be, or how perplexing to our finite minds; it has not caught our Father by surprise, nor is its purpose to permit evil to overcome us.

It may be that you are facing something unjust. It may be you have been hurt by another's sinful behavior. It may be you have encountered a time of deep suffering, an attack from the evil one, a troubling and unexpected change in your circumstances. It may be completely beyond your ability to understand or fathom why this thing has come about, but you can be sure that by the time it reached you God had already examined it and created a plan by which it may ultimately work for your good. It may take time to see the victory manifested. It may take a very long time. But it will happen, if you persevere and cling to God. In the meantime, dear one, turn with trust to our God, obey His Word and allow Him to guide you through the situation step by step, as He sees fit.

Has the way grown dark and dismal?
Is your heart bent low by fears?
Do you catch yourself believing
The future holds only tears?

Are you wondering if it's possible
That things will turn out right?
Are you questioning God's ability
To put enemy forces to flight?

Then know this is surely the moment
When faith, though seeming to fail,
May rise up bravely and stand its ground,
Knowing God is sure to prevail.

He will work, of this be certain,
His power will come through,
He will act at just the right moment,
He will prove His Word is true.

JUNE 24 --

"...so let him give; not grudgingly, or of necessity: for God loveth a cheerful giver."
(II Co 9:7)

God's economy operates in a manner that is diametrically opposed to the
world's economy. The world says: "Be competitive, strive to get ahead, beat
out the other guy, push hard so you can succeed." God's economy says the
opposite: "Give, and it shall be given unto you; good measure, pressed
down..." (Lu 6:38); "he which soweth bountifully shall reap also bountifully"
(II Cor 9:6); "whosoever shall give to drink...shall in no wise lose his reward"
(Ma 10:42).

One woman tells of the first time she put into practice living by God's
economy.

"I had just come to know the Lord and He began to reveal to me how
fearful I was about money. Most of my fears stemmed, I knew, from some
frightening financial problems that had affected my family when I was a
child. It was hard for me to believe that I would ever have enough. But God
began to work with me. He started to show me it was time for me to stop
operating out of my fear of lack and learn how to give to others.

I became aware of a ministry that helped children in need of medical
care so I decided to make a donation. I made the decision to give twenty
dollars, which may not sound like a lot now but at the time it was a very
significant portion of my weekly take-home pay. As I was about to make out
the check, I felt something urge me to give more: the amount that kept
coming into my mind was $35. At first, I dismissed the thought, but I
couldn't shake the feeling that I should give $35. Finally I decided to risk it.
I wrote out a check for that amount and mailed it off, wondering why I had
been so extravagant.

Two days later an envelope came in the mail. It was from a company for which I had done some volunteer work in the past. The company did not owe me any money; we had agreed I would do the work for free. But inside the envelope was a check, made out to me. The amount of the check was $35. There was no note, nothing whatsoever to explain why the check had been sent. There was only the check. I never again received anything from that company. I never heard from it again.

I know some might dismiss this experience as northing more than a coincidence, but I knew in my heart it was not a coincidence. I knew when I looked at the amount of the check – exactly $35 – that something significant had happened to me.

As I continued to give to God's work my financial life improved and my extreme fears about money began to subside. But the important lesson for me was not about money at all. It was about my need to learn how God's economy works. He wants us to give. He wants us to live with a sense of abundance. He wants us to be free, of fear and of selfishness. All these years later, I am still giving and trusting God to provide for me. And I am still learning about trust. But I have found, on countless occasions, that God is always faithful to provide for every one of my needs."

God wants us to give, not just so that others' needs can be met but so He can give more generously into our lives. And as we become willing to give we will discover that God will always meet our needs, even if He has to engineer a miracle to do it.

"Fear not, little flock; for it is your Father's good pleasure to give you the kingdom." (Lu 12:32)

JUNE 25 --

"And when he had given thanks, he brake it, and said, Take, eat: this is my body, which is broken for you: this do in remembrance of me." (I Co 11:24)

"Verily, verily, I say unto you, He that believeth on me hath everlasting life. I am that bread of life. Your fathers did eat manna in the wilderness, and are dead. This is the bread which cometh down from heaven, that a man may eat thereof, and not die. I am the living bread which came down from heaven: if any man eat of this bread, he shall live for ever: and the bread that I will give is my flesh, which I will give for the life of the world" (Jo 6:47-51).

"The most devout King David danced before the ark of God with all his might, commemorating the benefits bestowed in times past on his fathers. He made musical instruments of different kinds; he composed psalms and appointed them to be sung with joy; he himself likewise often sang them, playing upon his harp, inspired with the grace of the Holy Ghost. He taught the people of Israel to praise God with their whole heart, and to join their voices in blessing and magnify Him every day.

If such great devotion was displayed by him, and such a memorial of the praise of God made in the presence of the Ark of the Covenant, how great a reverence and devotion ought I and Christians everywhere have in the presence of this Sacrament, and in receiving the most precious Body of Christ!...

It is greatly to be lamented that we should be so lukewarm and negligent as not to be drawn with greater affection to the receiving of Christ, in Whom consists all the hope and merit of those that shall be saved. For He is our sanctification and our redemption; He is our comfort in our pilgrimage, and the eternal beatitude of the saints.

Oh, the blindness and hardness of the heart of man that does not more highly prize so unspeakable a gift...

Thanks be to Thee, O good Jesus, eternal Shepherd, Who has fed us poor exiles with Thy precious Body and Blood, and invited us to the receiving of these mysteries, even by the saying from Thine own mouth: 'Come to Me, all you that labor and are burdened, and I will give you rest.'"

--Thomas a' Kempis

Jesu, Savior, wholly Thine,
I partake the bread and wine,
Fleeing from my Vanity
To enter immortality,
Yearning for Thy precious grace.

Thy blood and body glorified,
Now seated by our Father's side,
Redeemer of my desperate fall,
Now become my All-in-All,
Here I welcome Your embrace.

JUNE 26 ---

"O Jerusalem, Jerusalem, which killest the prophets, and stonest them that are sent unto thee; how often would I have gathered thy children together, as a hen doth gather her brood under her wings, and ye would not!" (Lu 13:34)

"When we resist [the inspirations of God] we find pretexts for covering up and justifying resistance, but however much we try to deceive ourselves, we are not happy; there is ever at the bottom of our conscience an indefinable something that rebukes us for having failed towards God. The soul is no longer at peace, but it does not seek true peace; on the contrary, it gets farther and farther away from it by looking for it where it is not. It is like a bone which is out of joint, always causing a hidden pain; but however much it may hurt out of place, it is not in the way to get straight again; on the contrary, it gets fixed in its crooked condition."   – Francois Fenelon

"The whole question is this: What shall I do with these impulses from God? What shall I do with the beginnings and the germinations which are always working in me, which follow each other like waves, or rather like a sustained voice? Will the voice cry in the desert? Shall I reject the voice, stifle the inspiration, trample the beginnings under foot, pervert and turn aside the first enthusiasms? Am I, in short, going to stone the prophets and kill the messengers of God? Yes, such is the way of souls. The soul is a free being who stones the prophets and kills the messengers of God. A soul who knew how to listen, follow, obey, carry out, and develop, within reason and liberty, what is inspired and begun by God, would be too lovely and too divine. What then? Is this habit of murdering and strangling the gifts of life going to repel God and conquer his endeavors? No, for while the forces, and desires, and flights, and thoughts, and acts of the soul unceasingly remove it from God and dissipate it in egoism and sensuality, and the surface inhabited by the soul becomes more and more unproductive; while the soul adorns herself outwardly and neglects herself inwardly; while she builds and whitens the sepulcher beneath which death is at work, even at that very time God, full of love, by some fresh exertion, some mighty cry, some lightning flash, is ever calling back to himself the soul and its forces. 'How often would I have gathered thy children together, as a hen doth gather her brood under her wings.'"   – Alphonse Gratry

JUNE 27 --

"...Hallowed be Thy name." (Matt 6:9)

Two of the precious names of God:
1) "And Abraham called the name of that place Jehovah-jireh: as it is said to this day, In the mount of the LORD it shall be seen," (that is to say, the Lord shall provide; Ge 22:14).
What scene could impact the human heart more than this one? God had commanded Abraham to offer up his beloved son, Isaac, as a sacrifice, and Abraham, true to this test of faith, was ready to obey his God. The place was selected, the alter was built and Isaac was bound, ready to be sacrificed, when the Angel of the Lord spoke out of heaven and prevented Abraham from carrying out the deed. Abraham looked up to see a ram caught in a nearby thicket. God, he realized, had accompanied him to the mountain and was Himself providing a sacrifice to replace Isaac – a beautiful picture of John 1:29, which says: "Behold the Lamb of God, Which taketh away the sin of the world." Abraham named the place "Jehovah-Jireh," which means, "The Lord

Provides." The Lord is the One who provides our sin-offering for us. He is the One who bore the stripes we rightly deserve; He is the Savior Who went to the Cross to pay for our sins.

2) "And Moses built an altar, and called the name of it Jehovah-nissi:" (Ex 17:15)

The seventeenth chapter of Exodus explains to us that Amalek was waging a fierce battle with Moses and those who followed him. Joshua was the leader of the army of Israel. When Moses lifted up his hands, Joshua managed to prevail, but when Moses lowered his hands, Amalek prevailed. Moses' hands became heavy, so Aaron and Hur came alongside him and helped raise his hands, that they might continue to be held high, as a banner of victory. They assisted Moses in this way until sunset and, as a result, Joshua managed to win the battle. Then Moses built an alter and called the name of it "Jehovah-Nissi" (The Lord, my Banner). Jesus Christ is our Banner of victory over the enemy. Knowing this, we should look to Him each day, lift up His Name and declare by faith His everlasting victory in our lives.

JUNE 28 ---

"Therefore take no thought, saying, What shall we eat? or, What shall we drink? or, Wherewithal shall we be clothed? (For after all these things do the Gentiles seek:) for your heavenly Father knoweth that ye have need of all these things. But seek ye first the kingdom of God, and his righteousness; and all these things shall be added unto you." (Ma 6:31-33)

"Don't worry! That is the lesson. It is set for us in our text-book. We are not likely to live thus, naturally. We have to learn to do it, and the learning is not easy. St. Paul was an old man when he said he had learned, in whatsoever state he was, therein to be content; and his language seems to imply that the lesson had not been easily learned. Nor shall we find it less difficult. But however hard it may be, we should strive to learn it, for it is the ideal Christian life....

George Macdonald tells of a castle in which lived an old man and his son. Though they owned the castle, they were yet very poor. They could scarcely get enough bread to keep them from starving. Yet all the time there was great wealth, which, if they had known of it, would have supplied all their wants. Through long generations there had been concealed within the castle very valuable jewels, which had been placed there by some remote ancestor, so that if he or any of his descendants should be in need there would be something in reserve.

For a long time the old man and his son suffered for want of food, not knowing of the hidden treasures. At last, however, they learned in some way of the concealed jewels, and at once found themselves in the enjoyment of great riches. Instantly their distress was ended. Yet during all the years of their pinching poverty these treasures had lain there, belonging to them, ready to furnish them all the comforts of life, laid up there for this very purpose. They suffered, close to this abundant provision, because they did not know of it.

This story illustrates the case of many Christians. They are living in their Father's house, in which are stored the rich treasures of divine love. Yet many of them seem not to know of these treasures, and live in distress, as if no provision were made for their wants. There really never is any reason why a child of God should worry about anything. This is the lesson which Jesus sets for us in His wonderful teaching.

One of the reasons He gives is that anxiety about food and raiment and the world's things is serving mammon, and we cannot serve God and mammon at the same time. The mind must be centered before it can have perfect peace. It must have one motive, one aim, one allegiance, one ground of confidence. If it is divided between two interests, there will be distraction, and the peace will be broken. Anxiety is a sin, because it is not trusting God fully and wholly. It is trusting money to provide for our wants, instead of trusting God. When money fails, then we are in distress.

George Macdonald says again: 'How often do we look upon God as our last and feeblest resource! We go to Him because we have nowhere else to go.'

We feel safe enough when mammon's abundance fills the pantry and the wardrobe. But when mammon's supplies are exhausted, and we have only God, we worry. What we need is to train ourselves to such trust and confidence in God, that, though mammon's resources fail us altogether, we shall not be afraid, because we have God. A man is in a pitiful plight when mammon is his God. Money is a good thing, in its place. It is one of God's blessings. But when it gets to be a man's master it is turned into a curse. We all need to guard ourselves from the peril of worshiping mammon."

-- J. R. Miller

JUNE 29 --

"...but as for me and my house, we will serve the Lord." (Joshua 24:15)

Here are three suggestions from George Whitefield to help us honor God in our homes:

"1. Read the Word of God. This is a duty incumbent on every believer. The head of every Christian home is bound to instruct those in his charge in the word of God. God said in Deuteronomy 6:6-7, that His words 'shall be in thine heart:' you shall teach them with diligence to your children, and talk of them when you sit in your house, and when you walk by the way, and when you lie down, and when you rise up.

2. Pray together as a family. This is as absolutely necessary as the former. Reading is a good preparation for prayer, just as prayer is an excellent means to render reading effective. And the reason why every head of a family should join both these exercises together is plain, because the head of a family cannot perform his or her priestly office without performing this duty of family prayer.

3. Instruct children in God's Word. Every head of a Christian household, along with reading the Word and holding family prayer, should also make sure the Word of God is taught to the members of the household. God registered His approval of Abraham when He said of him: 'I know that he will command his children and his household after him, to keep the way of the Lord, to do justice and judgment.' Parents are commanded in the New Testament, to 'bring up their children in the nurture and admonition of the Lord.'

Remember, the time will come, and that perhaps very shortly, when we must all appear before the judgment-seat of Christ; where we must give a solemn and strict account of how we have had our conversation in our respective families in this world. How will you endure to see your children coming out as so many swift witnesses against you; rather will we hope that we will be ready to say, 'God forbid that we should forsake the Lord,' (Joshua 24:16) and again, in verse 21, 'Nay; but we will serve the Lord.'"

JUNE 30 ---

"Then said Jesus again unto them, I go my way, and ye shall seek me, and shall die in your sins: whither I go, ye cannot come." (Jo 8:21)

"The Lord Jesus plainly told his disciples in their private conversations that he should be crucified; but he did not speak so plainly to his enemies — he only gave them hints concerning his approaching death. When he said, 'I go my way,' they understood him not. At last they formed a conjecture concerning his meaning, and said, 'Will he kill himself?' They did not venture to put the question to the Lord himself, but consulted with each other on the subject. He knew their thoughts, and by his reply showed that he had alluded to his death. He would not indeed kill himself. Those who with wicked tongues now insulted him, with wicked hands would slay him. He would die upon the cross, but far worse would be the manner of their death — they would die — perhaps, in a bed, surrounded by weeping friends, but — in their sins.

When the Lord said to his enemies, 'You are from beneath,' he did not mean to say that they had ever lived with Satan in hell; but he meant that they partook of the nature of Satan, and were like him in pride, and hatred, and unbelief. All the inhabitants of this world are divided into two classes — of one it may be said, they are from beneath; of the other it may be declared, they are from above, having been born again by the Holy Spirit. An old writer observes, that though the children of different families are mingled in the day, when night comes on they return home to their fathers' houses. When the night of death comes, the children of Satan will go to their father's dark and horrible abode, and the children of God will go to their Father's light and glorious abode. And where shall we go? Remember the words of Jesus, 'If you believe not that I am he, you shall die in your sins.'

There is only one way of becoming the child of God — it is by believing in Jesus. The Jews scornfully inquired, 'Who are you?' Let us humbly ask the same question. Let us say as Saul did when Jesus spoke to him from heaven, 'Who are you, Lord?' He will reveal himself to all who desire to know him. He left his Father's house to seek us who were wandering about this world. He desires to bring us to his home. There is room for us, as well as for Him, in the palace of the great King. He said to his beloved apostles, 'In my Father's house are many mansions.' When night comes on it will be delightful to go to such a home. But what would it be to feel in dying that we were not going to God!"   – F. L. Mortimer

JULY 1 ---

"And Jesus, when he came out, saw much people, and was moved with compassion toward them, because they were as sheep not having a shepherd: and he began to teach them many things." (Mark 6:34)

Nothing moves the Divine Heart as deeply as the sight of His children wandering without Him among the dangers and deceptions of the world. His heart yearns for those who have not yet found their Father. When a believer comes to the place where "the mind of Christ" gets hold of him, he, too, will pity the sad condition of those who have not yet found a relationship with the true God, and will yearn to help them find it.

Nowadays people race about at a frantic pace in search of peace and contentment, but they will never find these things until they enter into the Kingdom that Christ offers them. In the end, it will not matter whether they have achieved wealth or power, or been widely respected or praised. It won't matter that they have attained high goals or won coveted awards. Unless they come to know the Father, they will still be only defenseless lambs wandering dangerously close to the precipice as night closes over the trail.

Let us look upon the sheep that are yet without a Shepherd. We may think our efforts cannot accomplish much but it is amazing what God can do through one surrendered soul. If we will do what we can, our Father will be well pleased. To Him, it is no small thing to help even one lost sheep find its way into the fold. It is, to the contrary, the noblest work we can do for Him. It is the reason why Christ, our Shepherd, stepped out of Heaven and into the pastures of Earth.

Many the starving souls
Now waiting to be fed,
Needing, though knowing not their need
Of Christ, the living Bread.
Oh, hast thou known His love?
To others make it known;
Receiving blessings, others bless,
No need abides alone.

And when thine eyes shall see
The holy, ransomed throng
In heavenly fields, by living streams,
By Jesus led along,
Unspeakable thy joy shall be,
And glorious thy reward,
If by thy barley-loaves one soul
Has been brought home to God.
                                        – J. R. Miller

JULY 2 --

"Heal me, O Lord, and I shall be healed; save me, and I shall be saved: for thou art my praise." (Jer 17:14)

"It is the sole prerogative of God to remove spiritual disease. Natural disease may be instrumentally healed by men, but even then the honor is to be given to God, who gives virtue unto medicine, and bestows power unto the human frame to cast off disease. As for spiritual sicknesses, these remain with the great Physician alone; He claims it as His prerogative, 'I kill and I make alive, I wound and I heal;' and one of the Lord's choice titles is Jehovah-Rophi, the Lord that healeth thee. 'I will heal thee of thy wounds' is a promise which could not come from the lips of man but only from the mouth of the eternal God. On this account the psalmist cried unto the Lord, 'O Lord, heal me, for my bones are sore vexed;' and again, 'Heal my soul, for I have sinned against Thee.' For this also the godly praise the name of the Lord, saying, 'He healeth all our diseases.' He who made man can restore man; He who created our nature can newly create it.
        What a transcendent comfort it is that in the person of Jesus dwells all the fullness of the Godhead bodily. My soul, whatever your disease may be, this great Physician can heal you. If He be God, there can be no limit to His power. Come, then, with the blind eye of darkened understanding, come with the limping foot of wasted energy, come with the maimed hand of weak faith, the fever of an angry temper, or the fever of despondency, come just as you are, for He who is God can certainly restore you from your plague... All

His patients have been cured in the past, and shall be in the future, and you shall be one among them, my friend, if you will but rest yourself in Him."

-- Charles Spurgeon

"And because ye are sons, God hath sent forth the Spirit of His Son into your hearts, crying, Abba, Father." (Ga 4:6)

"The deepest conviction often occurs after conversion. To the young convert we simply have to say let the Spirit who is in you always convince you of sin. He will make you hate sin, which formerly you knew only by name. He will make you know – and with shame confess – your sin, which you had not seen in the hidden depths of your heart. He will point out to you sin, which you fancied was not with you, and which you had judged severely in others. With repentance and self-condemnation, He will teach you to cast yourself upon grace as being entirely sinful. In this way, you will be redeemed and purified from sin.

Beloved brothers and sisters, the Holy Spirit is in you as the light and fire of God to unveil and to consume sin. The temple of God is holy, and you are this temple. Let the Holy Spirit in you have full mastery to point out and expel sin. After He makes you know sin, He will, at every turn, make you know Jesus as your life and your sanctification.

And then the Spirit, who rebukes, will also comfort. He will glorify Jesus in you, and will take what is in Jesus and make it known to you. He will give you knowledge concerning the power of Jesus' blood to cleanse and the power of Jesus' indwelling to keep. He will make you see how literally, how completely, how certainly Jesus is with you every moment, so that He may do all his own Jesus-work in you. Yes, in the Holy Spirit, the living, almighty, and ever-present Jesus will be your portion. You will also know this, and have the full enjoyment of it. The Holy Spirit will teach you to bring all your sin and sinfulness to Jesus. He will teach you to know Jesus with His complete redemption from sin as your own. As the Spirit of sanctification, He will drive out sin in order that He may cause Jesus to live within you.

Father, I thank You for this gift which Jesus sent to me from You. I thank You that I am the temple of Your Spirit, and that He dwells in me. Lord, teach me to believe this with my whole heart, and to live in the world as one who knows that the Spirit of God is in him to lead him. Teach me to think on this with deep reverence and loving awe, that God is in me. Lord, in that faith I have the power to be holy. Holy Spirit, reveal to me all that is sin in me. Holy Spirit, reveal to me all that is Jesus in me. Amen."

– Andrew Murray

"Thus saith the Lord; Cursed be the man that trusteth in man, and maketh flesh his arm, and whose heart departeth from the Lord." (Jer 17:5)

Many people pride themselves on being independent and having the freedom to choose what they will do with their lives. Some are grateful to God for their blessings. Others care little about Him, and deep down inside they think their blessings are a result of their own inherent goodness and worth. Each of us has a choice to make: We may decide to bow to no one; or we may bow before God and acknowledge that every good gift we possess is only because of His goodness. Either way, we will surely reap the results of whatever course we choose.

"For this cause I bow my knees unto the Father of our Lord Jesus Christ, Of whom the whole family in heaven and earth is named, That He would grant you, according to the riches of His glory, to be strengthened with might by his Spirit in the inner man; That Christ may dwell in your hearts by faith; that ye, being rooted and grounded in love, May be able to comprehend with all saints what is the breadth, and length, and depth, and height; And to know the love of Christ, which passeth knowledge, that ye may be filled with all the fulness of God... Unto him be glory in the church by Christ Jesus throughout all ages, world without end. Amen." --(Eph 3:14-19, 21)

"If religious books are not widely circulated among the masses in this country, I do not know what is going to become of us as a nation. If truth be not diffused, error will be; if God and His Word are not known and received, the devil and his works will gain the ascendancy; if the evangelical volume does not reach every hamlet, the pages of a corrupt and licentious literature will; if the power of the Gospel is not felt throughout the length and breadth of the land, anarchy and misrule, degradation and misery, corruption and darkness, will reign without mitigation or end."   – Daniel Webster

"Evening, and morning, and at noon, will I pray, and cry aloud: and he shall hear my voice." (Ps 55:17)

"It is not necessary to make long prayers, but it is essential to be much alone with God; waiting at His door; hearkening for His voice; lingering in the garden of Scripture for the coming of the Lord God in the dawn or cool of the day. No number of meetings, no fellowship with Christian friends, no amount of Christian activity can compensate for the neglect of the still hour.

When you feel least inclined for it, there is most need to make for your closet and shut the door. If you will do for duty's sake what you cannot do as a pleasure, you will find it shall end up being a delight. You could better thrive without nourishment than become happy or strong in your Christian life without fellowship with God.

When you cannot pray for yourself, begin to pray for others. When your desires flag, take the Bible in hand, and begin to turn each text into petition; or take up the tale of your mercies, and begin to translate each of them into praise. When the Bible itself becomes irksome, inquire whether you have not been spoiling your appetite by things that are not of God and renounce them; and believe that the Word is the wire along which the voice of God will certainly come to you if the heart is hushed and the attention fixed. 'I will hear what God the Lord shall speak.'

More Christians than we can count are suffering from a lack of prayer and Bible study, and no revival is more necessary that of private time with God. There is no method of godliness which can dispense with this."

– F.B. Meyer

JULY 6 --

"If ye then be risen with Christ, seek those things which are above, where Christ sitteth on the right hand of God. Set your affection on things above, not on things on the earth. For ye are dead, and your life is hid with Christ in God." (Co 3:1-3)

"There is a great difference between risen and resurrected. One may rise from one level to another; but when one is resurrected he is brought from nothing into existence, from death to life, and the transition is simply infinite. A true Christian is not raised, but resurrected. The great objection to all the teachings of mere natural religion and human ethics is that we are taught to rise to higher planes. The glory of the Gospel is that it does not teach us to rise, but shows our inability to do anything good of ourselves, and lays us at once in the grave in utter helplessness and nothingness, and then raises us up into new life, born entirely from above and sustained alone from heavenly sources.

The Christian life is not self-improving, but it is wholly supernatural and divine. Now, the resurrection cannot come until there has been the death. This is presupposed, and just as real as the death has been, will be the measure of the resurrection life and power. Let us not fear, therefore, to die to ourselves and really cease to be. We lose nothing by letting go and we cannot enter in till we come out. If we be dead with Him, we shall also live with Him....

Perhaps you say, 'How can I reckon myself dead when I find so many evidences that I am still alive, and how can I reckon myself risen when I find so many things that pull me back again to my lower plane?' It is your failure to reckon and abide that drags you back. It is the recognizing of the old life as still alive that makes it real and keeps you from overcoming it. This is the principle which underlies the whole Gospel system, that we receive according to the reckoning of our faith. The magic wand of faith will slay all the ghosts that can rise in the cemetery of your soul; and the spirit of doubt will bring them up from the grave to haunt you as long as you continue to question. The only way you can ever die, is by surrendering yourself to Christ and then reckoning yourself dead with Him."   – A. B. Simpson

JULY 7 --

"The spirit of man is the candle of the Lord,..." (Pr 20:27)

"The nighttime traveler in the snow has sometimes caught sight of a candle in a shepherd's hut. It has been to him the most joyful of all moments; it is the promise of rest. Even such, I think, is the thought of this proverb. The man who uttered it knew well the saying of the old book of Genesis, that when God had wandered six days through creation He rested in man. He had been led on by the glimmer of one candle – the light of the human soul. It was the only place of rest the Father saw in all the vast expanse. There was no other dwelling for the spirit of my Father but my spirit. He could not find shelter in any other home. Not where the bee hums could my Father dwell. Not where the bird sings could His heart be glad. Not where the cattle graze could His life repose. Not where the stars shine could He find His household fire. One far-off candle alone gave the sign of home. It was my spirit.

My Father, I have often asked You to be my light; what a wondrous thought that I once was Yours! I have been Your candle in the dark and cold; You were moving toward me. When the breath of life appeared You were moving toward me. The sixth morning was the last from Your hand, but it was the first in Your heart. The candle was more to You than the sunlight. You were in search of a light, not brighter, but better than the sun – the sparkle of a human eye, the radiance of a human face -- that was the candle that beckoned You. It said to You through the night, 'Come here, and rest.' It offered You what all past creation could not offer --communion. The brightness of the sun could not give it. The beauty of the flower could not give it. The song of the bird could not give it… You were like a dove on the face of the waters till the light in my dwelling appeared. But that candle brought You joy – joy unspeakable and full of glory. It was the first sound of home amid the waste of waters – the earliest voice that bore the invitation, 'Abide with me!' Even more, my Father, may I give You this welcome home."   – George Matheson

JULY 8 --

"In your patience possess ye your souls." (Lu 21:19)

There is an old story told about a woman who went to her room to pray. She was a very busy person, with a husband, several children and many responsibilities, but each morning she made it a priority to spend time with the Lord. She had just knelt down and started to say the Lord's Prayer when her husband interrupted her with a request to help him with an important task. She immediately stopped, gave him the assistance he needed and returned to her prayers.

Scarcely had she knelt down the second time when she was again interrupted, this time by one of her children who needed immediate help to deal with a minor emergency. Once more she gave assistance, then returned to her praying. Within minutes a neighbor came unexpectedly to the door. Then a workman arrived seeking her direction on a job he was to perform. Six times she was interrupted like this, but she did not become disturbed. Instead, she handled each task that demanded her attention. At last she returned to her room and was able to finish the Lord's Prayer without interruption. Then she opened her Bible and turned to the place where the prayer is recorded, in Luke 11:2-4. She discovered to her amazement that the letters of the prayer had entirely changed. Instead of being printed in black ink, as before, they had been transformed into letters of gold.

Most of us could probably come up with a long list of frustrating duties and annoying responsibilities that constantly interfere with our daily schedules. We are always being interrupted and disturbed! Always. And why should it be otherwise? That is life. Those situations that irritate us and tempt us to blow up are often the very means God uses to help us grow. When interruptions come along in my life, do I demand my own way or am I growing more adaptable, flexible and patient? Have I learned that God is not so much concerned with the completion of all my tasks as with the way in which I respond to the events of my day?

Do you feel like you're always being called on to stretch yourself and practice more tolerance and patience than you actually possess? Then rejoice and praise God for His kindness. He is working on your character and He will do wonders, if only you will let Him. Don't be discouraged if you don't change overnight. Transformation takes time, but it will happen. We will all be changed to become more like Christ, if only we will surrender ourselves into His care.

JULY 9 --

"My help [cometh] from the Lord, which made heaven and earth. He will not suffer thy foot to be moved: he that keepeth thee will not slumber." (Ps 121:2-3)

When Sir Edmund Hillary and Tenzing Norgay became the first men to climb to the top of Mount Everest, they discovered that some of the most treacherous obstacles they had to face lay just beneath the summit. One was a long, razor-thin ridge called the Cornice traverse. Composed of jagged rock covered by snow, the ridge was fraught with danger. One false step could result in a fall of 10,000 feet down the mountain's Kangshung face.

Norgay and Hillary inched their way along the traverse and made it to the other side, but almost immediately they encountered another problem: a sheer forty-foot rock wall jutting out of the mountain. The only way over the wall was to climb along its inner edge; again, one wrong step could mean disaster. Using what would now be considered rather primitive ice climbing equipment, the two maneuvered their way over the rock, which was later named the "Hillary Step." Once on top of the step they were finally able to see the summit: it lay just a few steps ahead. Minutes later they reached the top, making news that was beamed around the world.

Our climb of faith is often like the journey of Hillary and Norgay. Sometimes the largest obstacles appear just as we are nearing the top. Because we are so close to them, they block our view of the goal we are trying to reach; we may become discouraged and want to turn back. But obstacles and problems are part of the spiritual climb. They may seem overwhelming when we come up against them, but God will always show us how to either get around them or climb over them. Even when we feel we can't go on, He will revive us. It may take a while, but He will always show us the way. He will never abandon us until we reach the top.

Dear one, don't stop climbing just because you have encountered obstacles. God has called to you to scale the heights and He will show you how to surmount anything that is blocking your way. Let Him lead you. Let Him guide you. Trust Him to show you the way to the top.

From John Gill's Commentary on the Bible: Psalm 121:3:
"The Lord keeps the feet of his saints from falling: he will not suffer them to be moved out of the spiritual estate in which they stand; nor off of the Foundation and Rock of ages, on which their feet are set, and their goings established; nor out of the house of God, where they are as pillars; nor out of his ways, where he upholds their goings; moved in some sense they may be, yet not 'greatly moved'... neither angels nor men are the keepers of the saints, but the Lord himself; he is the keeper of every individual saint, of every regenerate person, of every one of his sheep, of every member of his church; he keeps them by his power, he preserves them by his grace, he holds them with his right hand; guides them by his counsel, keeps their feet from falling, and brings them safe to glory: and a watchful keeper he is; he does not so much as slumber; he keeps them night and day, lest any harm them..."

JULY 10 --

"And he said unto me, My grace is sufficient for thee: for my strength is made perfect in weakness. Most gladly therefore will I rather glory in my infirmities, that the

power of Christ may rest upon me. Therefore I take pleasure in infirmities, in reproaches, in necessities, in persecutions, in distresses for Christ's sake: for when I am weak, then am I strong." (II Co 12:9-10)

We can have a great deal of head knowledge about our need to depend on God for everything. We may have read many books, gone to numerous meetings, studied many passages of Scripture, and still not realize how dependent we are on God. We may even be teaching others about dependence, but until we personally experience our frailty, through circumstances that God allows to emerge in our lives, we will never have a heart understanding of how deeply we need the Lord.

How will we be able to recognize God as our sovereign Lord if we still believe we are the best judges of what should happen in our lives or in the lives of others? How can we know God as our powerful deliverer if we're still under the illusion that we can overcome our failings in our own strength? How can we go to God as our Healer, our Guide, our Deliverer, if we still believe that with a little more effort we can manage our own lives? No. There is no other way but the way of surrender. This is the one road we will all have to travel, sooner or later. Our trials and challenges are our companions along this road. God uses them to teach us how dependent upon Him we really are.

"We often ask the question, 'Why didn't God help me sooner?' It is not His order. He must first adjust us to the situation and cause us to learn our lesson from it. His promise is, I will be with him in trouble; I will deliver him, and honor him. He first must be with us in the trouble until we grow quiet. Then He will take us out of it. This will not come until we have stopped being restless and fretful about it and have become calm and trustful. Then He will say, 'It is enough.'

God uses trouble to teach His children precious lessons. They are intended to educate us. When their good work is done, a glorious recompense will come to us through them. He does not regard them as difficulties but as opportunities. They have come to instill more of God into us and to show how he can deliver us from them. Without difficulties we cannot have a mercy worth praising God for. God is just as deep, and long, and high as our little world of circumstances."   – A. B. Simpson

"Paul's thorn was not pleasant to him. He prayed to be rid of it. But when he found it had come to stay, he made friends with it swiftly. It was no longer how to dismiss, but how to entertain. He stopped groaning, and began glorying. It was clear to him that it was God's will, and that meant new opportunity, new victory, new likeness to Christ. What God means is always too good to be lost, and is worth all it costs to learn. Let us learn as swiftly as we may."   – Maltbie Davenport Babcock

"Jesus saith unto them, My meat is to do the will of him that sent me, and to finish his work." (Jo 4:;34)

"True conversion is turning away from our self-will and giving ourselves to the will of God as our duty and our only blessedness. I ask every believer who reads this to inquire whether he thinks that the doing of the Father's will has taken the place in his life and faith and conduct that it had in the life and conduct and teaching of Jesus Christ. Read the question over again, and pause; it is worthwhile giving a careful answer.

All salvation on earth or in heaven is -- doing the will of God. If we find that this blessed truth has never shone with its full heavenly light into our souls, let us at once turn to our Lord Jesus and ask Him to teach us. Let us give ourselves up to it, to study, to believe, to practice, to rejoice in it. Let us each day choose the will of God, His whole will, and nothing but His will, to have rule over us and dwell within us. The living Father whose love can make it our blessedness, through the living Christ, who loves to teach it to us and work it in us, will enable us to do His will." – Andrew Murray

Jesus, Thy life is mine,
Dwell evermore in me,
And let me see
That nothing can untwine
My life from Thine.
-Frances Ridley Havergal

"I am the true vine, and my Father is the husbandman…I am the vine, ye are the branches: He that abideth in me, and I in him, the same bringeth forth much fruit: for without me ye can do nothing" (Jo 15:1, 5).

Grafting is a radical process -- it involves trauma for both the vine and the branch, but it also serves as a beautiful example of the love of Christ and the extent to which He was willing to sacrifice Himself so that we might have eternal life.

Many fragile varieties of grapes are commonly grafted onto root stock that is strong and sturdy because they would otherwise be destroyed by pests, diseases and inclement weather conditions. We are much like fragile grapevines. We have been weakened by the disease of sin. For us, it is a terminal condition and unless we can be grafted onto studier stock we are destined to perish.

Sin is something we can never get rid of on our own. Like those delicate varieties of grapes, we need to be removed from our original rootstock and grafted into a healthy vine. That Vine is Christ. He is our hope because His life, unlike ours, has never been tainted by sin. When we become joined to Him, His perfect nature begins to flow into us, just like a properly grafted branch receives its life from a healthy vine.

The grafting process always starts with the healthy parent vine. The procedure is a drastic one. With one massive stroke, the trunk is "cut off" at a point only two to three feet from the ground. The fruit-bearing wood of the parent-vine is removed and incisions are made into its exposed surface. These incisions cause the parent vine to "bleed." Then the branches that are to be grafted into the vine are carefully trimmed and placed into these incisions. The branches must be inserted in such a way that they touch the cambium of the parent vine. The cambium is the area in the trunk through which the life force flows. After the graft is completed the area is securely wrapped. The wrapping stays in place until the branches and the parent vine grow together, becoming as one.

Grapevines are known as "lianas," a term that means "woody tree climber." Grapevines must lean on something if they are to grow properly. A good husbandman always provides a trellis to support his vines. We are like lianas. God didn't design us to grow without support. He made us to cling to Him at every stage of our development. He wants to be our strong support and promises to always be there for us: "Never will I leave you; never will I forsake you..." (He 13:5)

After being grafted into the parent vine and given a trellis for support there is still one more thing a grapevine needs if it is to thrive and become fruitful. It will have to be pruned.

Some kinds of fruit trees are pruned a little each year. Some have to be pruned extensively. But the grapevine must be pruned more heavily than almost any other crop. It is common for 85 to 90 percent of a grapevine's year-old wood to be removed during pruning. Pruning is essential if a grapevine is going to produce the right kind and quantity of fruit and to make sure the plant stays healthy. Jesus said the Father "cuts off every branch in me that bears no fruit, while every branch that does bear fruit he prunes so that it will be even more fruitful" (Jo 15:2). When the good husbandman prunes his vines they may appear at first to be almost stripped bare and practically lifeless, but this heavy pruning is actually good for them. It's the same with us. When God prunes us it doesn't feel good and we're apt to think He's taken away the most productive parts of us, but God knows what He is aiming at. He's intent upon seeing us become even more productive and mature as believers. He knows which branches of our lives need to be pruned back, which need to be redirected and which need to be entirely removed. He is the One who knows the long-range plans for productivity He has for us.

Because God loves us, He never just thinks about how much fruit we will bear. He also cares about what is best for us. The good husbandman never cuts back so much wood that the vine is damaged, nor does he leave so much wood that the vine will produce too much fruit during the coming year and thus be over-taxed and possibly damaged. Instead, he adapts the amount of pruning to fit the need of each individual vine. Sometimes he will only permit a vine to produce a modest harvest for a year or two, until it is mature enough to support a larger crop.

Our Father is a perfect Husbandman, and Christ, our Savior, is a perfect Vine. We, the branches, are far from perfect, but we can trust the Lord to continually work with us until we are one day made perfectly fruitful in Him. From the moment we first believe upon Christ, until our last season on earth, we can trust that we have a Perfect Husbandman overseeing everything that concerns us.

JULY 13 --

"...every devoted thing is most holy unto the Lord." (Le 27:28)

"The very essence of prayer is a spirit of devotion. Without devotion prayer is an empty form, a vain round of words. Sad to say, much of this kind of prayer prevails today in the church. This is a busy age, bustling and active, and this bustling spirit has invaded the church of God. Its religious performances are many. The church works at religion with the order, precision and force of real machinery. But too often it works with the heartlessness of the machine. There is much of the treadmill movement in our ceaseless round and routine of religious doings. We pray without praying. We sing without singing in the Spirit. We have music without the praise of God being in it. We go to church by habit, and come home all too gladly when the benediction is pronounced. We read our accustomed chapter in the Bible, and feel quite relieved when the task is done. We say our prayers by rote, as a schoolboy recites his lesson, and are not sorry when the 'Amen' is uttered.

Religion has to do with everything but our hearts. It engages our hands and feet; it takes hold of our voices; it lays its hands on our money; it affects even the postures of our bodies, but it does not take hold of our affections, our desires or our zeal, or make us desperately in earnest and desirous of being quiet and worshipful in the presence of God.

Activity is not strength. Work is not zeal. Moving about is not devotion. Activity often is the unrecognized symptom of spiritual weakness...The colt is much more active than its mother, but she is the wheel-horse of the team, pulling the load without noise or bluster or show... Why this modern perversion of the true nature of the religion of Jesus Christ? Why is the modern type of Christianity so much like a jewel-case with the precious jewels gone? The great lack of the modern Church is the spirit of devotion. We hear sermons in the same spirit with which we listen to a lecture or hear a speech. We visit the house of God just as if it were a common place, on a level with the theater, the lecture-room or the forum... We need the spirit of devotion to remind us of the presence of God, to be always doing the will of God, to direct all things always to the glory of God."   --E. M. Bounds

JULY 14 ---

"...For if through the offence of one many be dead, much more the grace of God, and the gift by grace, which is by one man, Jesus Christ, hath abounded unto many." (Ro 5:15)

"I wish I could only show to every one the unfathomable sweetness of the will of God. Heaven is a place of infinite bliss because His will is perfectly done there, and our lives share in this bliss just in proportion as His will is perfectly done in them. He loves us -- loves us -- and the will of love is always blessing for its loved one. Some of us know what it is to love, and we know that could we only have our way, our beloved ones would be overwhelmed with blessings. All that is good, and sweet, and lovely in life would be poured out upon them from our lavish hands, had we but the power to carry out our will for them. And if this is the way of love with us, how much more must it be so with our God, who is love itself....

A great many Christians actually seem to think that all their Father in heaven wants is a chance to make them miserable, and to take away all their blessings, and they imagine, poor souls, that if they hold on to things in their own will, they can hinder Him from doing this. I am ashamed to write the words, and yet we must face a fact which is making wretched the lives of many.

A Christian woman who had this feeling was once expressing to a friend how impossible she found it to say, 'Thy will be done,' and how afraid she was to do it. She was the mother of one child, and after she had stated her difficulties her friend said, 'Suppose your little Charley should come running to you tomorrow and say, 'Mother, I have made up my mind to let you have your own way with me from this time forward. I am always going to obey you, and I want you to do just whatever you think best with me.' How would you feel towards him? Would you say to yourself, 'Ah, now I shall have a chance to make Charley miserable. I will take away all his pleasures and fill his life with every hard and disagreeable thing I can find. I will compel him to do just the things that are the most difficult for him to do, and will give him all sorts of impossible commands.' 'Oh, no!' exclaimed the indignant mother. 'You know I would not. I would want to fill his life with all that was sweetest and best.' 'And are you more tender and more loving than God?' asked her friend. 'I see my mistake,' was the reply, 'and from

168

now on I will not be afraid of saying 'Thy will be done' to my Heavenly Father, any more than I would want my Charley to be afraid of saying it to me.'" – Hannah Whitall Smith

"In order for a lump of clay to be made into a beautiful vessel, it must be entirely abandoned to the potter. It must lie passive in his hands."

--H. W. S.

JULY 15 ---

"Now no chastening for the present seemeth to be joyous, but grievous: nevertheless afterward it yieldeth the peaceable fruit of righteousness unto them which are exercised thereby." (He 12:11)

"Ah, the evil of our nature is deeply rooted and very powerful, or such repeated, continual corrections and chastisements would not be necessary; and were they not necessary, we should not have them. But such we are, and therefore such must be our treatment; for though the Lord loves us with a tenderness beyond what the mother feels for her nursing child, yet it is a tenderness directed by Infinite Wisdom.

This kind of wisdom is very different from that weak indulgence which in parents we call fondness, which leads them to comply with their children's desires and inclinations rather than to act with a steady view to their true welfare. The Lord loves his children, and is very indulgent to them so far as they can safely bear it, but he will not spoil them.

Their sin-sickness requires medicines, some of which are very unpalatable; but when the case calls for such things no short-sighted pleadings of ours can excuse us from taking what he prepares for our good. Every dose is prepared by his own hand, and not one is administered in vain, nor is it repeated any oftener than is needed to achieve the purposed end. Till then, no other hand can remove what he lays upon us; but when his merciful design is accomplished he will bring us relief himself, and in the meantime he will either temper the experience or increase our ability to bear it, so that we will not be overpowered.

It is true, without a single exception, that all his paths are mercy and truth to them that fear him. His love is the same when he wounds as when he heals, when he takes away as when he gives. We have reason to thank him for all, but most of all we should thank him for the severe."

--John Newton

JULY 16 ---

"For whosoever will save his life shall lose it: and whosoever will lose his life for my sake shall find it." (Ma 16:25)

If I take God's Word to be true, and it tells me Christ learned obedience by the things that he suffered (Heb 5:8), do I believe I can avoid having to learn obedience in any other way? If I want the Lord to use me, do I think I can avoid being shaped and molded in order to fit the purposes He has in mind? If my desire is to bear fruit in the service of the Lord, do I think I can escape being pruned? If I desire to be made alive in Christ, do I believe I can escape the need to die to self?

> There is no death for me to fear,
> For Christ, my Lord, hath died;
> There is no curse in this my pain,
> For he was crucified.
> And it is fellowship with Him
> That keeps me near His side.
>
> My heart is fixed on God, my strength,
> My heart is strong to bear;
> I will be joyful in Thy love;
> And peaceful in Thy care.
> Deal with me, for my Savior's sake,
> According to His prayer.
>   --Anna Waring

"Verily, verily, I say unto you, Except a corn of wheat fall into the ground and die, it abideth alone: but if it die, it bringeth forth much fruit." (Jo 12:24)

When a bud bursts into bloom, it fulfills its destiny. When a soul goes home to God it has not died -- to the contrary – it has opened into everlasting life. Like the bud, it has blossomed, at last, and become that which God created it to be.

JULY 17 --

"And as it was in the days of Noe, so shall it be also in the days of the Son of man. They did eat, they drank, they married wives, they were given in marriage, until the day that Noe entered into the ark, and the flood came, and destroyed them all." (Lu 17:26-27)

Speaking about the time of His return, Jesus said to His disciples, "...as it was in the days of Noe, so shall it be also in the days of the Son of man. They did eat, they drank, they married wives, they were given in marriage, until the day that Noe entered into the ark, and the flood came, and destroyed them all."

In Noah's time, evil was out of control and things just kept getting worse every day. Sin always leads to brokenness: it leads to broken hearts, broken relationships and broken lives. It not only breaks the lives of those who commit sin, it also wounds those who are close to them: mates, children, friends, relatives, neighbors, business associates. This is how the enemy works. He is so foul that he isn't content to just take down the sinner. He wants to take down any innocent bystanders around him.

When sin spins out of control in a culture, the society ceases to function properly and after a while it begins to deteriorate. Things stop working; the dysfunction within individuals begins to manifest itself in the behavior of the society as a whole. When things are in a crisis state of deterioration, good begins to be regarded as evil, and evil as good. This is the state in which the culture of Noah's day found itself. The people of that culture had been warned for a hundred years that judgment was going to come, but their ability to hear the truth had been dulled and they didn't believe that judgment would come. After Noah built the ark the people in his culture said he was crazy. They laughed him to scorn. Then Noah was instructed by God to take the animals and his family into the ark. He did as God told him to do, but still the people did not believe. Then, after seven days, the waters of the flood came upon the earth.

God has opened the door of grace to everyone. It is not His will that any should perish. His way of salvation is not through rules or regulations or performance, but by grace and grace alone. It is available to anyone who will repent and believe upon Jesus Christ as the Savior. But the door of grace cannot stay open forever. There will come a time when God, out of His mercy and kindness, will put an end to the sin that is enveloping the world. We can rejoice, because there is still time to turn to God. It doesn't matter where we come from or who we are. He is still welcoming His children with open arms.

JULY 18 --

"So then faith cometh by hearing, and hearing by the word of God." (Ro 10:17)

"I prayed for faith, and thought that some day faith would come down and strike me like lightning. But faith did not seem to come. One day I read in the tenth chapter of Romans, 'Now faith comes by hearing, and hearing by the Word of God.' I had closed my Bible and prayed for faith. I now opened my Bible and began to study, and faith has been growing ever since."

--D. L. Moody

"The vigor of our spiritual life will be in exact proportion to the place held by the Bible in our life and thoughts.... I have read the Bible through one-hundred times, and always with increasing delight. Each time it seems like a new book to me. Great has been the blessing from consecutive, diligent, daily study. I look upon it as a lost day when I have not had a good time over the Word of God." – George Mueller

Oh, there is more than ear hath heard,
Light of the World, in this Thy Word.
It speaks the living soul to win,
It claims the loving heart within;
It tells us we are understood,
That Thou art God, that Thou art good.
Here our fallen nature raised we see,
Here our lost glory shines in Thee,
And man sees man in mortal strife,
A witness that to love is life.
--Anna Waring

JULY 19 --

"This is the day which the Lord hath made; we will rejoice and be glad in it." (Ps 118:24)

Many self-help groups have come up with what are called "Just For Today" lists. These lists are intended to help members remember that they don't have to get all their problems fixed in one day and that it's a good idea to take things a little easy, rather than trying to do everything at once. Just-For-Today lists can be helpful to almost all of us. They can help us to keep our goals realistic and our attitudes positive. Perhaps we need to remind ourselves to be less compulsive. Maybe we need to stop pushing ourselves so hard. Whatever our goal may be, a Just-For-Today List can be a practical way to help us work on the things in our lives that we want to change. Here's one example of a "Just for Today" list. You might want to consider coming up with one of your own.

Just for Today...
I will live in the here and now; I won't live in the past, with its tendency to pull me into regrets, or in the future, with its nameless fears.
I will focus on my blessings and not on my difficulties.
I will resist the temptation to be critical of others and concentrate instead on what I might do to change myself for the better.
I will remember that life is what it is, not what I think it should be. I will take things as they come and ask for God's help to respond to events as He would desire. If I get disturbed, I'll try to pray before I act.
I will say something encouraging to someone else. I'll work on being a blessing to others rather than thinking of how I would like to be blessed.

"...for I am the Lord that healeth thee." (Ex 15:26)

Dr. Alexis Carrel was a Nobel Prize-winning physician who had an amazing experience with divine healing. Carrel had heard of people being healed at the well-known shrine of Lourdes, France, but his opinion was that such claims were unfounded; he believed healing did not occur outside of traditional medical means and felt it was cruel to encourage people to believe that they could pray to God and receive healing directly from Him.

Describing himself as a "tolerant skeptic," Carrel decided he wanted to learn more about the subject of healing, so, in 1903, he arranged to travel by train to Lourdes and study the issue for himself.

On the train to Lourdes, he met a number of people who were seriously ill. Some of them were in great pain and entreated him to give them medication for their pain. One young woman named Marie Ferrand, who was extremely ill with tuberculosis, attracted his attention. He examined her and found that she had a distended abdomen and a number of growths in her stomach. It was clear to him she was suffering from tubercular peritonitis. He was certain she had only a few days to live.

Upon arriving at Lourdes, Carrel was struck by the good cheer of most of the patients who were seeking healing. Still, he believed their faith was misplaced. He was convinced the stories of cures were nothing but "hysterical cases" and "pious propaganda." Yet something deep inside him yearned to believe that God would indeed heal. Meanwhile, Marie Ferrand received prayer, but her condition grew worse by the hour. Her pulse rate increased to 150; her pain required injections of morphine. After another thorough examination, Dr. Carrel determined the girl was near death.

Then something odd happened. Marie's abdomen began to flatten out a little. "Her eyes," recalled Carrel, became "wide with ecstacy." He didn't know what to make of what was happening. Within a few more minutes the bloating completely disappeared and her abdomen returned to a normal state. Dr. Carrel remembered he "felt as though he were going mad." Marie was still terribly weak, but she managed to tell him that she thought she had been healed. Upon examination he discovered her pulse had somehow returned to a normal 80. The hard masses he had earlier felt in her stomach had entirely disappeared. All the symptoms of tubercular peritonitis, a condition which Carrel had personally diagnosed, had vanished. Marie was still fragile and emaciated from lack of proper nourishment, but other than that she appeared to be completely healed. Everything this great physician had believed about healing had suddenly been turned upside down.

Carrel still had trouble believing what he had seen. All that night he struggled to come up with some other explanation for Marie's healing but he could not. Putting aside what he termed his "intellectual pride," he asked

173

God to help him believe in what he had seen. Walking through the darkness, he prayed and struggled with his unbelief. By 3 a.m., his struggle was over. He knew in his heart he had witnessed a divine miracle. Carrel went to bed that night and slept like a little child.

Carrel knew he had to publish his findings to inform the medical community of what he had seen. He wrote a report about his experience, but, afraid of professional repercussions, he published the account under another name. After his death, however, his widow published the full account of Carrel's experience with healing under the title, "A Journey to Lourdes."

Does the Lord still heal? The answer is yes. He not only heals the bodies, but also the hearts, minds and emotions of His children. And He still delights in helping "tolerant skeptics" overcome their unbelief so that they, too, can know the joy and peace that comes from believing in the healing power of God.

JULY 21 --

"Persecuted, but not forsaken; cast down, but not destroyed." (II Cor 4:9)

"You may be cast down by many doubts and fears, and lose the sense of the Lord's love for your soul, but you cannot lose the reality of it, nor is your faith destroyed by the hottest flame. It is like gold; the fire melts away and separates the dross and tin, but never touches the gold. In your hottest trials your true faith will not have lost a particle. Neither will your hope be destroyed, no matter how you may be cast down about your state or standing; for not a particle of hope, or of any other Christian grace, can ever be lost. They may seem to suffer diminishment, as the apostle says: 'If a man's work shall be burned, he shall suffer loss' (I Co 3:15), but it is not a real loss--it is merely the dross being removed so the vessel may be purified.

The work of the Holy Spirit is as indestructible as the work of Christ; and thus every grace which he implants in the soul remains there untouched, unharmed in all its divine integrity. Love, patience, submission, and humility all remain unhurt in the flame, though the dross which is mixed with them is taken from them, that they may shine all the brighter. Thus, though you may be plunged into the hottest fires, you will not be destroyed, any more than the three Hebrew children were destroyed in Nebuchadnezzar's furnace, or Jonah in the belly of the whale."

– Joseph Philpot

JULY 22 --

"Ye have not chosen me, but I have chosen you, and ordained you, that ye should go and bring forth fruit, and that your fruit should remain: that whatsoever ye shall ask of the Father in my name, he may give it you." (Jo 15:16)

"The greatest thing any one can do for God and for man is to pray. It is not the only thing. But it is the chief thing. If a man is to pray right, he must first be right in his motives and life. And if a man be right, and put the practice of praying in its right place, then his serving and giving and speaking will be fairly fragrant with the presence of God.

The great people of the earth today are the people who pray. I do not mean those who talk about prayer; nor those who say they believe in prayer; nor even those who can explain about prayer, but I mean those people who take time and pray. They often do not have the time. It must be taken from something else. This something else is important. Very important, and pressing, but still less important and less pressing than prayer. There are people that put prayer first, and group the other items in life's schedule around and after prayer.

These are the people today who are doing the most for God; in winning souls; in solving problems; in awakening churches; in supplying both people and money for mission posts; in keeping fresh and strong these lives far off in sacrificial service on the foreign field where the thickest fighting is going on; in keeping the old earth a little sweeter for a little while longer.

It is wholly a secret service. We do not know who these people are, though sometimes shrewd guesses may be made. I often think that sometimes we pass by some rather plain looking people who quietly slip out of church and we hardly give them a passing thought, and do not know, nor guess, that perhaps they are the ones who are doing far more for their church, and for the world and for God, than a hundred who would claim more attention, because they pray -- truly pray -- as the Spirit of God inspires and guides.

Let me put it this way: God will do as a result of the praying of the humblest one here what otherwise he would not do. Yes, I can make it stronger than that, and I must make it stronger, for the Book does. God will do in answer to the prayer of the weakest one here what otherwise He could not do.

'Oh,' someone says, 'you are saying that too strong.' Well, you listen to Jesus' own words in that last, long quiet talk He had with the eleven men between the upper room and the olive grove. John preserves much of that talk for us. Listen: 'Ye did not choose Me, but I chose you, and appointed you, that ye should go and bear fruit, and that your fruit should abide' -- listen, this is part of the purpose of why we have been chosen -- 'that whatsoever ye shall ask of the Father in My name, He may give it you.' Mark that word 'may;' not 'shall,' but may. 'Shall' throws the matter over on God -- His purpose. 'May' throws it over upon us -- our cooperation. That is to say our praying makes it possible for God to do what otherwise He could not do."   --S. D. Gordon

"Is not this the carpenter's son?" (Ma 13:55)

"[This question in Scripture] invites us to consider Jesus as the Son of man, as the son of a carpenter, and in all probability, as one who assisted Joseph in his humble calling until He began to be about thirty years of age. Hence it was asked concerning Jesus, 'Is not this the carpenter?' How truly did the Son of God identify Himself with the humanity and the curse He came to ransom and remove. And when we see those hands which built the universe building earthly dwellings for man--squaring the beam, plying the saw, working the plane, driving the nail, constructing and raising the framework--we personally behold Him tasting the bitterness of that part of the curse which stated, 'In the sweat of your face shall you eat bread.'

We learn from this that obscurity of birth and lowliness of craft are no dishonor; to the contrary, they are often the condition of many who exhibit true greatness of character, real devotion to God and noble and useful deeds for man. God, who is no respecter of persons, looks upon man's outward estate with a very different eye than that with which the world looks upon it. You ask for proof? Behold the Incarnate Son of God. Instead of selecting, as He might have done, a princess for His mother and a palace for His birth, His reputed father was a carpenter, His mother, though of royal lineage, was too poor to present on the day of her purification an offering more costly than 'a pair of turtle-doves,' and the scene of His wondrous advent was among the beasts of the field feeding quietly at their troughs.

Perhaps you have been taunted for your obscure birth, looked down upon for your humble calling, slighted for your social position and even discouraged from believing that you could rise above them. Learn from Jesus that there is no dishonor in humble parentage, that true dignity belongs to honest work, and that personal piety, consecration to God, and far-reaching usefulness to man often belong to those whose niche in society is low in the scale and whose walk through life is along its more shaded paths.

Consider Jesus. He knows your walk. He will sympathize with, and give you grace for, the difficulties and discouragements, the temptations and trials of your life. And, however obscure your birth, lowly your calling or cramped your powers, strive to imitate and glorify Him. Your trust in God, your resemblance to Christ, the example of your honest hard work and patient endurance ... will be a wonderful influence on all whose privilege it may be to know, admire and love you."   – Octavius Winslow

"The little troubles and worries of life may be as stumbling blocks in our way, or we may make them stepping-stones to a nobler character and to Heaven. Troubles are often the tools by which God fashions us for better things."   – Henry Ward Beecher

"The pillar of cloud moved from in front of them and stood behind them." (Ex 14:19)

"It is not always guidance that we most need. Sometimes we must stand still, with danger all around us, and then God goes behind us to shelter us. He always suits himself to our need. When we require guidance, he leads us. But when we need protection, he puts himself between us and the danger.

There is something very striking in this picture: the divine presence moving from before and becoming a wall between Israel and their enemies. There are some mother-birds – storks for instance – which cover their young with their own body in time of peril, to shield them, receiving the dart themselves. Human love often interposes itself as a shield to protect its own. On the cross, Jesus bared his own bosom to receive the storm of wrath, that no blast of the awful tempest might strike his own people!

But not only does Christ put himself between us and our sins; he puts himself also between us and danger. The Lord God is our shield. Many of our dangers come upon us from behind. They are stealthy, insidious, assaulting us when we are unaware of their nearness. The tempter is cunning and shrewd. He does not meet us from the front. It is a comfort to know that Christ comes up behind us when it is there we need the protection."   -- J. R. Miller

"For sin shall not have dominion over you: for ye are not under the law, but under grace." (Ro 6:14)

"Sin's a hard master. It snaps a long whip with a stinger on the end. It exacts slavish obedience. Jesus breaks sin's hold. He cuts off that stinger and breaks the whip. He asks obedience, too, but how different. Obedience is really a music word. It's the rhythm of your will, at its strongest, with Jesus' will. Obedience is best when you're not thinking so much about obeying as about pleasing your Friend.

Jesus undoes sin's work. He unties sin's knots, tears away the bonds, sets the man free, and flushes in new life. Sin cripples the body with weakness and disease, the mind with stupidity and prejudice, the spirit with selfishness and self-will, and the life with stain and evil habit. When Jesus is allowed free swing he frees body, mind, spirit, and life of all that hurts, and gives new life in flood-tide measure."   – S. D. Gordon

"Having eyes, see ye not? and having ears, hear ye not? and do ye not remember? When I brake the five loaves among five thousand, how many baskets full of fragments took ye up? They say unto him, Twelve. And when the seven among four thousand, how many baskets full of fragments took ye up? And they said, Seven. And he said unto them, How is it that ye do not understand?" (Mark 8:18-21)

"The lesson Christ would have his disciples learn from this miracle was that God cared for his children, and could, did, and would, provide for their necessities. This lesson they had not learned. The ground of the Master's up-braiding is not that they did not understand him, but that they did not trust God; that, after all they had seen, they still troubled themselves about bread.

Because we easily imagine ourselves in want, we imagine God ready to forsake us. The miracles of Jesus were the ordinary works of his Father, performed in a small and swift manner, so that we might take them in. The lesson of them was that help is always within God's reach when his children want it. Their purpose was to show who God is. The mission undertaken by the Son was not to show himself as having all power in heaven and earth, but to reveal his Father, to show him to men such as he is, that men may know him, and by knowing him, that they would trust him....

The next hour, the next moment, is as much beyond our grasp and as much in God's care as the hour which is a hundred years away. Care for the next minute is just as foolish as care for the morrow, or for a day that will occur a thousand years from now. We can do nothing about either and in both cases God shall do everything for us.

With the disciples, as with the rich youth, it was Things that prevented the Lord from being understood. Because of possessions, the rich young man had no idea of the grandeur of the call with which Jesus honored him. Things barricaded his door, so that God could not enter in.

The disciples were a little further on than he; they had left all and followed the Lord; but neither had they yet got rid of Things. The paltry solitariness of a loaf of bread was enough to hide the Lord from them, to make them unable to understand him. In the former case it was the possession of wealth, in the latter the not having more than a loaf, that rendered them incapable of receiving the word of the Lord. The evil principle was precisely the same. If it be Things that slay you, what does it matter whether they be things you have, or things you do not have?

Distrust is atheism, and the barrier to all growth. The care that is filling your mind at this moment, or waiting until you lay this book aside to leap upon you, is a demon sucking at the spring of your life.

'No,' you say, 'mine is a reasonable care, an unavoidable care.'
'Is it something you have to do this very moment?'
'No.'
'Then don't allow it to usurp what is required of you at this moment.'
'There is nothing required of me at this moment.'
'But there is. The greatest thing that can be required of man.'
'What is that?'
'Trust in the living God. His will is your life.'"

--George MacDonald

JULY 27 ---

"But the anointing which ye have received of him abideth in you, and ye need not that any man teach you: but as the same anointing teacheth you of all things, and is truth, and is no lie, and even as it hath taught you, ye shall abide in him." (I Jo 2:27)

"If the reader understands very little of the word of God, he ought to read it very much; for the Spirit explains the Word by the Word. And if he enjoys reading the Word only a little, that is just why he should read it a great deal; for the frequent reading of the Scriptures creates a delight in them, so that the more we read them, the more we desire to do so.

Above all, he should seek to have it settled in his own mind that God alone by His Spirit can teach him, and that therefore, as God will be inquired of for blessings, it becomes him to seek God's blessing before reading, and also while reading.

He should also have it settled in his mind that although the Holy Spirit is the best and most sufficient Teacher, He does not always teach us immediately upon our desiring it; and that therefore we may have to entreat Him again and again for the explanation of certain passages; but we can be assured He surely will teach us at last, if we seek for the light prayerfully, patiently and with a view to the glory of God." – George Mueller

JULY 28 ---

"Fight the good fight of faith, lay hold on eternal life, whereunto thou art also called, and hast professed a good profession before many witnesses." (I Ti 6:12)

"If the tradition of the Church is harmonious and conclusive on any one point concerning the spiritual life, it is that it is a struggle, a strife, a battle, warfare, whichever word you may choose. No one doubts it. A man would be out of his senses who should doubt it. Reason proves it, authority proves it, experience proves it. Yet see what an awkward practical question for each one of us rises out of this universal admission. At any moment we may turn round upon ourselves and say, Is my religious life a struggle? Do I feel it to be so? What am I struggling against? Do I see my enemy? Do I feel the weight of his opposition? If my life is not sensibly a fight, can it be a spiritual life at all?... These are very serious questions to ask ourselves, and we ought to be frightened if at any time we cannot obtain satisfactory answers to them. A good frightening! What an excellent thing that is now and then in the spiritual life!"   – Frederick William Faber

"In every believer's heart there is a constant struggle between the old nature and the new. The old nature is very active, and loses no opportunity of plying all the weapons of its deadly armory against newborn grace; while on the other hand, the new nature is ever on the watch to resist and destroy its enemy. Grace within us will employ prayer, and faith, and hope, and love, to cast out the evil; it takes up the 'whole armour of God,' and wrestles earnestly. These two opposing natures will never cease to struggle so long as we are in this world.... The enemy is so securely entrenched within us that he can never be completely driven out while we are in this body. But although we are closely beset, and often in sore conflict, we have an Almighty helper, even Jesus, the Captain of our salvation, who is ever with us, and who assures us that we shall eventually come off more than conquerors through Him. With such assistance the new-born nature is more than a match for its foes.

Are you fighting with the adversary today? Are Satan, the world, and the flesh all against you? Do not be discouraged nor dismayed. Keep on fighting, for God Himself is with you; Jehovah Nissi is your banner, and Jehovah Rophi is the healer of your wounds. Do not fear; you shall overcome, for who can defeat Omnipotence?"   --Charles Spurgeon

JULY 29 ---

"For ye were sometimes darkness, but now are ye light in the Lord: walk as children of light:" (Eph 5:8)

"Our heavenly Father has a way of looking at us, his children, that ought to be a great comfort and incentive to us. He sees, not merely what we are, but what we shall be. And, for the joy set before Him of the perfected work, He endures the days of crudeness and mistake. He sees the man in the child, the painting in the sketch, the angel in the marble. If He saw us only in ourselves, He would see us only as we are; but, seeing us in Christ, He sees beyond repentance and trust and struggle, beyond justification and sanctification and glorification, to the cap-stone of Christ-likeness; and 'let every man that hath this hope in him purify himself, even as he is pure.'"
                                --Maltbie Davenport Babcock

"So then, when you have fallen, lift up your heart in quietness, humbling yourself deeply before God by reason of your frailty, without marveling that you fell; there is no cause to marvel because weakness is weak, or infirmity infirm. Heartily lament that you should have offended God, and begin anew to cultivate the lacking grace, with a very deep trust in His mercy, and with a bold, brave heart." --St. Francis de Sales

Oh, Thou art very great
To set Thyself so far above,
But we partake of Thine estate,
Established in Thy strength and in Thy love:
That love hath made eternal room for me
In the sweet vastness of its own eternity.

Oh Thou art very meek
To overshade Thy creatures thus,
Thy grandeur is the shade we seek;
To be eternal is Thy use to us:
Ah, Blessed God, what joy it is to me
To lose all thought of self in Thine eternity.
--Frederick William Faber

JULY 30 --

"I therefore, the prisoner of the Lord, beseech you that ye walk worthy of the vocation wherewith ye are called, With all lowliness and meekness, with longsuffering, forbearing one another in love;" (Eph 4:1-2)

"Love will rebuke evil, but will not rejoice in discovering it. Love will be impatient of sin, but patient with the sinner. To form the habit of finding fault constantly is very damaging to spiritual life; it is about the lowest and meanest position that a man can take. I never saw a man who was aiming to do the best work but there could have been some improvement; I never did anything in my life, I never addressed an audience, that I didn't think I could have done better and I have often upbraided myself that I had not done better; but to sit down and find fault with other people when we are doing nothing ourselves, not lifting our hands to save someone, is all wrong -- is the opposite of holy, patient, divine love.

Love is forbearance; and what we want is to get this spirit of criticism and fault-finding out of the Church and out of our hearts; and let each one of us live as if we had to answer for ourselves, and not for the community, at the last day. If we are living according to the thirteenth chapter of Corinthians, we will not be all the time finding fault with other people. 'Love suffereth long, and is kind.' Love forgets itself, and doesn't dwell upon itself.

181

The woman who came to Christ with that alabaster box, I venture to say, never thought of herself. Little did she know what an act she was performing. It was just her love for the Master. She forgot the surroundings, she forgot everything else that was there; she broke that box and poured the ointment upon Him, and filled the house with its odor. The act, as a memorial, has come down through these [2,000] years... That ointment was worth $40 or $50; no small sum in those days for a poor woman. Judas sold the Son of God for about $15 or $20. But what this woman gave to Christ was everything that she had, and she became so occupied with Jesus Christ that she didn't think what people were going to say. So when we act with a single eye for the glory of our lord, not finding fault with everything about us, but doing what we can in the power of this love, then will our deeds for God speak, and the world will acknowledge that we have been with Jesus, and that this glorious love has been shed abroad in our hearts."

-- D. L. Moody

JULY 31 --

"Forbearing one another, and forgiving one another, if any man have a quarrel against any; even as Christ forgave you, so also [do] ye." (Co 3:13)

"Some people seem able to maintain a superior attitude to insults and disgrace, but this trait proceeds from a callous and indifferent temperament; they are cold and insensible to both kindness and unkindness. This was not the case with Jesus.

The tender sensibilities of His holy nature rendered Him keenly sensitive to ingratitude and injury, whether this was manifested in the malice of undisguised enmity or the treachery of trusted friends. To a noble nature the latter of these is often the more wounding. Many are inclined to forgive an open and unmasked antagonist, who are not so willing to forgive heartless faithlessness or unrequited love. But notice, too, in this respect, the conduct of the blessed Redeemer. Watch how He deals with His own disciples who had basely forsaken Him and fled, and that, too, in the hour He most needed their sympathy. No sooner does He rise from the dead than He hastens to disarm their fears and assure them of an unaltered and unalterable affection.

'Go tell my brethren,' is the first message He sends; 'Peace be unto you,' is the salutation at the first meeting; 'Children,' is the word with which He first greets them on the shores of Tiberias. Even Joseph (the Old Testament type and pattern of generous forgiveness), when he makes himself known to his brethren, recalls the bitter thought, 'Whom you sold into Egypt.' The true Joseph, when He reveals Himself to His disciples, buries in oblivion the memory of bygone faithlessness. He meets them with a benediction. He leaves them at His ascension with the same: 'He lifted up His hands and blessed them!'

Follow in all this the spirit of your Lord and Master. Seek to feel that with you there should be no such word as 'enemy.' Do not harbor resentful thoughts or indulge in bitter recriminations. Don't surrender to sullen fretfulness. Put the best construction on the failings of others and make no injurious comments on their frailties. 'Consider yourself, lest you also be tempted.' When tempted to cherish an unforgiving spirit towards a brother, think, if your God had retained His anger, where would you be? If He has had patience with you, and forgiven you all, will you, on account of some petty grievance, which your calmer moments would pronounce unworthy of a thought, indulge in the look of cold estrangement? 'If any man have a quarrel against any, even as Christ forgave you, so also do you.'"

--John MacDuff

AUGUST 1 --

"Then cometh Simon Peter following him, and went into the sepulchre, and seeth the linen clothes lie, And the napkin, that was about his head, not lying with the linen clothes, but wrapped together in a place by itself." (Jo 20:6-7)

"Why was the napkin 'wrapped together in a place by itself?' Because Jesus wished to show that He arose calmly: no haste, no hurry, not as if in flight from the tomb, but in solemn triumph and at leisure. So He wishes His people to be calm. 'He that believeth shall not make haste.' Yes, and see: He folded the napkin neatly and laid it by.

But far more. That napkin had been put there by Joseph and Nicodemus ... Seeing the bleeding wounds caused by the crown of thorns, they carefully and tenderly drew the napkin round His brow. When Jesus awoke on the third day He noticed this act of kindness, and folded up the napkin and laid it in a place by itself, as indeed precious to Him, because it told of the tenderness of their care for Him. They will hear more about this napkin when He returns.

Thus He cares for the smallest acts of kindness we do for Him and to Him; how much more for what we do under difficulties and in suffering, and not least, for our efforts to win souls." --Andrew Bonar

"But God forbid that I should glory, save in the cross of our Lord Jesus Christ, by Whom the world is crucified unto me, and I unto the world." (Ga 6:14)

Souls of men, why will ye scatter
Like a crowd of frightened sheep?
Foolish hearts, why will ye wander
From a love so true and deep?

Was there ever kinder shepherd
Half so gentle, half so sweet,
As the Savior Who would have us
Come and gather round His feet?

There is plentiful redemption
In the blood that has been shed;
There is joy for all the members
In the sorrows of the Head.
                    --Frederick W. Faber

AUGUST 2 --

"But the fruit of the Spirit is love, joy, peace, longsuffering, gentleness, goodness, faith," (Ga 5:22)

"A great many of us try hard at times to love. We try to force ourselves to love, and I do not say that is wrong; it is better than nothing. But the end of it is always very sad. 'I fail continually,' many must confess. And what is the reason? The reason is simply this: they have never learned to believe and accept the truth that the Holy Spirit can pour God's love into their hearts. That blessed text has often been limited: 'The love of God is shed abroad in our hearts' (Romans 5:5). It has often been understood in this sense: It means the love of God to me. Oh, what a limitation! That is only the beginning. The love of God is always the love of God in its entirety, in its fullness as an indwelling power. It is a love of God to me that leaps back to Him in love, and overflows to my fellow men in love -- God's love to me, and my love to God, and my love to my fellow men. The three are one; you cannot separate them.

Do believe that the love of God can be shed abroad in our hearts and minds so that we can love all the day. 'Ah,' you say, 'how little I have understood that.' Why is a lamb always gentle? Because that is its nature. Does it cost the lamb any trouble to be gentle? Has a lamb to study to be gentle? No. Why does it come so easy? Because it is its nature. And a wolf -- why does it cost a wolf no trouble to be cruel, and to put its fangs into the poor lamb or sheep? Because that is its nature. It does not have to summon up its courage; the wolf nature is there.

And how can I learn to love? I cannot learn to love until the Spirit of God fills my heart with God's love, and I begin to long for God's love in a very different sense from which I have sought it so selfishly -- as a comfort, a joy, a happiness and a pleasure to myself. I will not learn it until I realize that 'God is love,' and to claim and receive it as an indwelling power for self sacrifice. I will not love until I begin to see that my glory, my blessedness, is to be like God and like Christ, in giving up everything in myself for my fellow men. May God teach us this. Oh, the divine blessedness of the love with which the Holy Spirit can fill our hearts! 'The fruit of the Spirit is love.'"

--Andrew Murray

AUGUST 3 --

"For in the time of trouble he shall hide me in his pavilion: in the secret of his tabernacle shall he hide me; he shall set me up upon a rock." (Ps 27:5)

"In the secret of God's tabernacle no enemy can find us, and no troubles can reach us. The pride of man and the strife of tongues find no entrance into the pavilion of God. The secret of his presence is a more secure refuge than a thousand Gibraltars. I do not mean that no trials come. They may come in abundance, but they cannot penetrate into the sanctuary of the soul, and we may dwell in perfect peace even in the midst of life's fiercest storms."

– Hannah Whitall Smith

"Jesus feels for you; Jesus consoles you; Jesus will help you. No monarch in his impregnable fortress is more secure than the rabbit in his rocky burrow. The master of ten thousand chariots is not one whit better protected than the little dweller in the mountain's cleft. In Jesus the weak are strong, and the defenseless are safe; they could not be more strong if they were giants, or more safe if they were in heaven. Faith gives to men on earth the protection of the God of heaven. More they cannot need, and need not wish. The rabbits cannot build a castle, but they avail themselves of what is there already. I cannot make myself a refuge, but Jesus has provided it, His Father has given it, His Spirit has revealed it, and therefore ...I enter it, and am safe from every foe." – Charles Spurgeon

AUGUST 4 --

"Come, ye children, hearken unto me: I will teach you the fear of the Lord. What man is he that desireth life, and loveth many days, that he may see good? Keep thy tongue from evil, and thy lips from speaking guile." (Ps 34:11-13)

It takes courage to do what the Lord tells us to do. To be kind when it would be so much easier to lash out. To refuse to gossip when everyone around you is enjoying the sport. To refuse to respond to criticism when you'd much rather issue a stern rebuke. Or to speak the truth in love when you'd like to make your feelings known in no uncertain terms. It takes courage to be tolerant and kind and patient and longsuffering and even-tempered; to live according to our convictions instead of our feelings. Convictions, however, are what the Christian life is all about, and so we Christians are to ask God, day by day, to give us the power to live according to our convictions, and to give us the courage to apply them to each of the situations we encounter during our day.

"Kind words do not cost much. They never blister the tongue or lips. They make other people good-natured... Kind words produce their own image in men's souls; and a beautiful image it is. They soothe and quiet and comfort the hearer. They shame him out of his sour, morose, unkind feelings. We have not yet begun to use kind words in such abundance as they ought to be used."
– Blaise Pascal

Lord, help me this day to bridle my tongue. When I'm tempted to be harsh, help me remember how it feels when someone else is harsh toward me. Keep me from speaking unkind words, and, just as important, keep me from retreating into unkind silences. When I need to confront a problem, help me to do so kindly, openly and constructively, with an attitude that seeks to find answers and better ways of communicating, rather than one that criticizes or seeks to place blame. Help me to listen to what others have to say, rather than thinking of what I want to say while they're speaking. Help me remember that my goal is to become kinder, gentler, sweeter; in other words, more like You. Amen.

AUGUST 5 ---

"Take therefore no thought for the morrow: for the morrow shall take thought for the things of itself. Sufficient unto the day is the evil thereof." (Ma 6:34)

"Be not anxious about the future; it is opposed to grace. When God sends you consolation, regard Him only in it, enjoy it day by day as the Israelites received their manna, and do not endeavor to lay it up in store. There are two peculiarities of pure faith; it sees God alone under all the imperfect envelopes which conceal Him, and it holds the soul incessantly in suspense. We are kept constantly in the air, without being allowed to touch a foot to solid ground. The comfort of the present instant will be wholly inappropriate to the next; we must let God act with the most perfect freedom, in whatever belongs to Him, and think only of being faithful in all that depends upon ourselves. This momentary dependence, this darkness and this peace of the soul, under the utter uncertainty of the future, is a true martyrdom, which takes place silently and without any stir. It is death by a slow fire; and the end comes so imperceptibly and interiorly, that it is often almost as much hidden from the sufferer himself, as from those who are unacquainted with his state. When God removes his gifts from you, He knows how and when to replace them, either by others or by Himself. He can raise up children from the very stones.

Eat then your daily bread without thought for the morrow; 'sufficient unto the day is the evil thereof.' Tomorrow will take thought for the things of itself. He who feeds you today is the same to whom you will look for food tomorrow; manna shall fall again from heaven in the midst of the desert, before the children of God shall want any good thing."

--Francois Fenelon

AUGUST 6 --

"And shall not God avenge his own elect, which cry day and night unto Him, though He bear long with them? I tell you that He will avenge them speedily. Nevertheless when the Son of man cometh, shall He find faith on the earth?" (Lu 18:7-8)

"Jesus sets forth the necessity of importunity in prayer in a startling way. The word rendered 'importunity' means literally 'shamelessness,' as if Jesus would have us understand that God would have us draw nigh to Him with a determination to obtain the things we seek that will not be put to shame by any seeming refusal or delay on God's part. God delights in the holy boldness that will not take 'no' for an answer. It is an expression of great faith, and nothing pleases God more than faith.

Jesus seemed to put the Syro-Phoenician woman away almost with rudeness, but she would not be put away, and Jesus looked upon her shameless importunity with pleasure, and said, 'O woman, great is thy faith; be it unto thee even as thou wilt' (Ma 15:28).

God does not always let us get things at our first effort. He would train us and make us strong by compelling us to work hard for the best things. So also He does not always give us what we ask in answer to the first prayer; He would train us and make us strong men and women of prayer by compelling us to pray hard for the best things. He makes us pray through.

I am glad that this is so. There is no more blessed training in prayer than that which comes through being compelled to ask again and again and again, even through a long period of years, before one obtains that which he seeks from God. Many people call it submission to the will of God when God does not grant them their requests at the first or second asking, and they say: 'Well, perhaps it is not God's will.' As a rule, this is not submission but spiritual laziness. When the man of action starts out to accomplish a thing, if he does not accomplish it the first, or second or one hundredth time, he keeps hammering away until he does accomplish it; and the strong man of prayer when he starts to pray for a thing keeps on praying until he prays it through.

We should be careful about what we ask from God, but when we do begin to pray for a thing we should never give up praying for it until we get it, or until God makes it very clear and very definite to us that it is not His will to give it.

George Mueller prayed for two men daily for upwards of sixty years. One of these men was converted shortly before his death, I think at the last service that George Muller held; the other was converted within a year after Mueller's death. One of the great needs of the present day is men and women who will not only start out to pray for things, but pray on and on and on until they obtain that which they seek from the Lord."

– Reuben Archer Torrey

AUGUST 7 ---

"The sacrifices of God are a broken spirit: a broken and a contrite heart, O God, thou wilt not despise." (Ps 51:17)

"A natural heart is offended at the preaching of the Cross. Many, I have no doubt, hate it. The preaching that we must have Another's righteousness or perish, I have no doubt, enrages many a heart. The offence of the Cross has not ceased. But a broken heart will not be offended. We cannot speak too plainly to a broken heart. A broken heart will sit forever in order to hear of the righteousness that does not require works.

Many of you may be offended when we preach plainly against sin. But a broken heart cannot be offended, for it hates sin worse than any fervent minister. Many are like those who worshiped Baal. They bow to idols. But a broken heart loves to see the idol stamped upon and beaten small. The unconverted heart is like the troubled sea. You see it going from creature to creature. But the broken heart says, 'Return unto thy rest, O my soul.' The righteousness of Christ takes away every fear; it 'casts out fear.' The broken heart casts its burden on Jesus.

To the unconverted, how dreadful are misfortunes like lack of money or death. He is tossed like a wild beast in a net. But a broken heart is satisfied with Christ. For him, Christ is enough. There is no ambition for more. Take away all else, and Christ remains." – Robert Murray McCheyne

Made pure by the blood that He shed,
My heart in His presence was free;
I was hungry and thirsty — He fed,
I was sick, and he comforted me;
He gave me the blessing complete,
The hope that is with me today,
And a quiet abode at his feet,
That shall not be taken away.
--Anna Waring

"...he will not fail thee, neither forsake thee: fear not, neither be dismayed." (De 31:8)

Letter to A Hurting Child:

My Beloved Child;

I have been waiting for you, and still you do not come to Me.

I have heard the untruths you have been told about me and seen the evil deeds performed in my name by those who do not know me. I know the hard thoughts you have harbored toward Me, because you have not understood who I am. And, since you do not come to me, I am coming after you. Hear My words. Hear the truth about your Lord.

You have believed I do not care for you, but I am the One who created you; I am He who "formed thee from the womb" (Is 44:2). You have felt yourself unloved, but the truth is, I fashioned you with tender, loving hands, and created you to live forever; you are "fearfully [and] wonderfully made" (Ps 139:14). You think I do not notice you, but the fact is you cannot escape my loving gaze: If you ascend up into heaven, I am there; if you make your bed in hell, I am there; If you take the wings of the morning and dwell in the uttermost parts of the sea, even there, my hand shall lead you and my right hand shall hold you (Ps 139:8-10). You have wondered if I care that your heart has been broken, but "The Lord is nigh unto them that are of a broken heart; and saveth such as be of a contrite spirit" (Ps 34:18). You fear I may not give you what you so desperately need, but the truth is, "He that spared not his own Son, but delivered him up for us all, how shall he not with him also freely give us all things?" (Ro 8:32)

You fear I have no plan for your life, but "I know the thoughts that I think toward you... thoughts of peace and not of evil, to give you an expected end" (Je 29:11). You question whether I can heal your diseases but I tell you, "I [am] the Lord that healeth thee" (Ex 15:26). You fear I cannot bind up your wounds, but in fact I am He Who sent my only begotten Son "to preach the gospel to the poor...to heal the brokenhearted, to preach deliverance to the captives, and recovering of sight to the blind, to set at liberty them that are bruised" (Lu 4:18). You fear that I am like those who should have cared for you but did not, but I say to you, even if there be parents who forget their children, that do not have compassion on them, "they may forget, yet will I not forget thee" (Is 49:15).

You worry that your sins may separate you from Me, but I tell you whoever shall believe on the Lord Jesus Christ shall be saved (Acts 16:31); I say to you, "neither death, nor life, nor angels, nor principalities, nor powers, nor things present, nor things to come, nor height, nor depth, nor any other creature, shall be able to separate [you] from the love of God, which is in Christ Jesus our Lord" (Ro 8:38-39). You fret there may not be enough for you, but I tell you, "Fear not, little flock; for it is your Father's good pleasure to give you the kingdom" (Lu 12:32); you fear I will not lead you, but I say "I will instruct thee and teach thee in the way which thou shalt go: I will guide thee with mine eye." (Ps 32:8)

As to the future, my child, do not fear. "Trust in the Lord with all thine heart; and lean not unto thine own understanding. In all thy ways acknowledge him, and he shall direct thy paths" (Pr 3:5-6). Though you have experienced many trials, remember, "many [are] the afflictions of the righteous: but the Lord delivereth him out of them all" (Ps 34:19). One day my children shall come to me and I will "wipe away all tears from their eyes; and there shall be no more death, neither sorrow, nor crying, neither shall there be any more pain: for the former things [will have] passed away" (Re 21:4).

My desire for you is, "That Christ may dwell in your heart by faith; that ye, being rooted and grounded in love, may be able to comprehend with all saints what is the breadth, and length, and depth, and height; and to know the love of Christ, which passeth knowledge, that ye might be filled with all the fulness of God" (Ep 3:17-19).

Signed: Your Loving Father

AUGUST 9 --

"Before I formed thee in the belly I knew thee; and before thou camest forth out of the womb I sanctified thee, and I ordained thee a prophet unto the nations." (Je 1:5)

"God has a plan for each of his children. From the foot of the Cross, where we are cradled in our second birth, to the brink of the river, where we lay down our armor, there is a path laid out for us. God prepares us for the path He has chosen. We are His workmanship, created unto the good works which He has chosen us to perform. There is no emergency in our path for which there has not been provision made. From the earliest inception of his being, God had a plan for Jeremiah's career, for which He prepared him.

Ask what your work in the world is, that for which you were born, to which you were appointed, and on account of which you were conceived in the creative thought of God. That there is a Divine purpose in your being is indubitable. Seek for it, that you may be permitted to realize it, and never doubt that you have been endowed with all the special aptitudes which that purpose may demand. God has formed you, and equipped you with all that He knew to be necessary for your life's work. It is your part to elaborate and improve to the utmost the one or two talents entrusted to your care.

Do not be jealous or covetous; do not envy another his five talents, but answer the Divine intention in your creation, redemption, and call to service. It is enough for you to be what God made you to be, and to be always at your best.

But in cases where the Divine purpose is not clearly disclosed, in which life is lived piecemeal, we must dare to believe that God has an intention for each of us; and that if we are true to our noblest ideals, we shall certainly work out the Divine pattern, and be permitted some day to see it in its unveiled symmetry and beauty. To go on occupying the position in which we have been placed by God, and to hold it for God until He bids us do something else: these are golden secrets of blessedness and usefulness."

--F. B. Meyer

AUGUST 10 --

"And saying, Repent ye: for the kingdom of heaven is at hand." (Ma 3:2)

"This was John's gospel. At first it seems very unlike the story of love which Jesus preached, and yet it is part of the same story. Repentance must always come before forgiveness and peace. Perhaps we need to be reminded of this in these days. We are in danger of making salvation too easy a matter and of being altogether too tolerant with ourselves. We forget, some of us, that sin is such a terrible thing, and we are too careless about getting rid of our sins. We misunderstand God's forgiveness if we think of it merely as an easy forgetting that we have done the wrong thing. Jesus did not come to save us merely from sin's penalties; he came to save us from the sins themselves, by leading us to forsake them forever. Unless we repent of our sins we never can have forgiveness.

We must make sure, too, that we do thorough work in our repenting. Repentance is not merely a little twinge of remorse over some wrong thing. It is not simply a gush of tears at the recollection of some wickedness. It is not mere shame at being found out in some meanness or uncleanness or dishonesty. It is the revolution of the whole life... Repentance is a change of heart, a turning of the face just the other way. It is well for us to make diligent quest to be sure that we always abandon the wrong doing which we deplore, that we quit the evil course which we regret, that we turn away from the sin which we confess.

A good many people get only half the gospel. They talk a great deal about believing, but very little about repenting. It needs to be remembered that a faith which does not lead to genuine repentance is not a faith that saves. He who bewails a sin and confesses it, secretly intending to return to it again, has no good ground to hope that he is forgiven."   – J. R. Miller

AUGUST 11 --

"Finally, brethren, whatsoever things are true, whatsoever things are honest, whatsoever things are just, whatsoever things are pure, whatsoever things are lovely, whatsoever things are of good report; if there be any virtue, and if there be any praise,

think on these things. Those things, which ye have both learned, and received, and heard, and seen in me, do: and the God of peace shall be with you." (Ph 4:8-9)

"The love spirit lives true wherever it is, and whatever the relationship. We should be rightly eager to make the most of life's opportunities, but whether one is an employee or employer, in a hidden-away corner or in the limelight, the thing that matters most is this: being true and pure just where we are, and, with this, being patiently, gently, thoughtfully loving in all personal contacts. This is what Jesus did, and so should we.

Goodness will arouse the bad in those that are bad. A piece of red-hot iron plunged into cold water makes a lively disturbance. A true Christian, living a true, consistent, loving life, will arouse antagonisms. Jesus' mere presence in the world stirred up the greatest demon activity on record. The thing is to keep strongly, steadily on being true and pure and gentle, in spite of all opposition, and to avoid extremes."   -- S. D. Gordon

AUGUST 12 --

"I will strengthen thee; yea, I will help thee; yea, I will uphold thee." (Is 41:10)

"God has three ways of helping us. First, He says, I will strengthen thee. In other words, He is saying, 'I will make you a little stronger yourself.' Second, He adds, I will help thee. By that we understand Him to say, 'I will add my strength to your strength, but you shall lead and I will help you.' Third, He says, I will uphold thee with the right hand of my righteousness, or, 'I will lift you up bodily and carry you altogether. It will be neither your strength nor My help, but My complete upholding.'

When we come to the end of our strength, we come to the beginning of His. In Him the weakest are the strongest, and the most helpless the most helped. He gives power to the faint, but to them that have no might at all He increases strength. His word is, My grace is sufficient for thee.

The answer is a paradox of contradictions, and yet the most practical of truths.

Most gladly therefore will I rather glory in my infirmities, that the power of Christ may rest upon me.

...For when I am weak, then am I strong (II Co 12:9-10)."

-- A. B. Simpson

AUGUST 13 --

"...he left nothing that is not put under him." (He 2:8)

"It is God's special prerogative to bring good out of evil, and order out of confusion. If you were to watch carefully from an astronomical observatory the movements of the planets, you would see them all in the greatest apparent disorder. Sometimes they would seem to move forward, sometimes backward, and sometimes not to move at all. These confused and contradictory movements sadly puzzled astronomers until Sir Isaac Newton explained the whole; then all was seen to be the most beautiful harmony and order, where before there was the most puzzling confusion.

Take a scriptural instance -- the highest and greatest that we can give-- to show that where, to outward appearance, all is disorder, there the greatest wisdom reigns. Look at the crucifixion of our blessed Lord. Can you not see the scene as painted in the word of truth? See those scheming priests, that wild mob, those rough soldiers, that faltering Roman governor, the pale and terrified disciples, the weeping women, and, above all, the innocent Sufferer with the crown of thorns, enduring that scene of woe which made the earth quake and the sun withdraw his light. What confusion! What disorder! What oppressed and vanquished innocence! But was it really so? Was God not accomplishing even here, by the instrumentality of human wickedness, his own eternal purposes? Hear his own testimony to this point: 'Him, being delivered by the determinate counsel and foreknowledge of God, ye have taken, and by wicked hands have crucified and slain' (Ac 2:23). If, by the wicked hands of man, God was able to accomplish His greatest and most glorious work, which was that of redemption, shall we not trust Him to also execute His will in the mysterious instances we encounter in our own lives?"

--Joseph Philpot

AUGUST 14 --

"Then said Jesus to them again, Peace [be] unto you: as [my] Father hath sent me, even so send I you." (Jo 20:21)

"Every real prayer is the soul's response to the love of God in an act of self-surrender. The life of prayer is the life of conversion -- a gradual, progressive turning from self to God. Potentially and ideally, that conversion is accomplished in the first genuine act of surrender, whereby the soul disassociates itself from sin and enters into its right relation with Eternal Love; actually it involves a lifetime of successive and increasingly complete acts of self-donation, such acts being the expression of a habit of daily self-denial and daily integration into Christ. Prayer is thus essentially an 'imitation' of Christ in his self-surrender to the Father, a yielding up of the self that it may be filled with the fullness of God, a losing of life that it may be found again in him.

But this passing from the life of the flesh to the life that is hid with Christ in God is no mere pious sentiment or vague mysticism. It means the identification of the whole personality -- mind, will and emotion -- with the mind and will and heart of God. It means loyal citizenship in the Kingdom of Love and Grace. It means making Christ's interests our own. It means to learn to think with God, to have the mind of Christ, to see the world through his eyes, to share his passion to save and redeem. It has well been said that 'the heart of Christ in the heart of the Christian is the vital center of practical Christianity, the living fountain of all its healing agencies.' And that heart is formed in us by prayer. As the soul lies open to God, his thoughts enter into us, his life of Love takes possession of us. His activity becomes ours."

--Brigid Herman

AUGUST 15 --

"The Pharisee stood and prayed thus with himself, God, I thank thee, that I am not as other men are, extortioners, unjust, adulterers, or even as this publican. I fast twice in the week, I give tithes of all that I possess. And the publican, standing afar off, would not lift up so much as his eyes unto heaven, but smote upon his breast, saying, God be merciful to me a sinner." (Lu 18:11-13)

"Our Lord with great preciseness gives us the sequel of the story of these two men, one utterly devoid of humility, the other utterly submerged in the spirit of self-depreciation and lowliness of mind.

'I tell you this man went down to his house justified rather than the other; for every one that exalteth himself shall be abased; and he that humbleth himself shall be exalted...'(Lu 18:14).

Humility is a rare Christian grace, of great price in the courts of heaven and an inseparable condition of effectual praying. It gives access to God when other qualities fail. It takes many descriptions to describe it, and many definitions to define it. It is a rare and retiring grace. Its full portrait is found only in the Lord Jesus Christ. Our prayers must be set low before they can rise to God. Our prayers must have much of the dust on them before they can ever have much of the glory of the skies in them. In our Lord's teaching, humility has such prominence in his system of religion, and is such a distinguishing feature of his character, that to leave it out of his lesson on prayer would be unseemly.

The Pharisee seemed to be inured to prayer. Certainly he should have known by that time how to pray, but, like many others, he seemed never to have learned this invaluable lesson... Words are uttered by him but words are not prayer. God hears his words only to condemn him. A death chill has come from those formal lips of prayer – a death curse from God is on his words of prayer....

On the other hand, the publican, smitten with a deep sense of his sins and his inward sinfulness, realizing how poor in spirit he is and with his pride blasted and dead, falls down with humiliation and despair before God. He utters a sharp cry for mercy for his sins and his guilt. This is the picture of humility against pride in praying. Here we see by sharp contrast the utter worthlessness of self- righteousness, self-exaltation, and self-praise, and the great value, beauty and commendation which comes to the humble of heart when a soul comes before God in prayer.

> Let the world their virtue boast,
> Their works of righteousness;
> I, a wretch undone and lost,
> Am freely saved by grace;
>
> Other title I disclaim,
> This, only this, is all my plea,
> I the chief of sinners am,
> But Jesus died for me."
> --E.M. Bounds

AUGUST 16 --

"Thy kingdom come. Thy will be done in earth, as it is in heaven." (Ma 6:10)

"How to Ascertain the Will of God:

1. I seek at the beginning to get my heart into such a state that it has no will of its own in regard to a given matter. Nine-tenths of the trouble with people generally is just here. Nine-tenths of the difficulties are overcome when our hearts are ready to do the Lord's will, whatever it may be. When it is truly in this state, it is usually but a little way to the knowledge of what His will is.

2. Having done this, I do not leave the result to feeling or simple impression. If so, I make myself liable to great delusions.

3. I seek the will of the Spirit of God through, or in connection with, the Word of God. The Spirit and the Word must be combined. If I look to the Spirit alone without the Word, I lay myself open to great delusions also. If the Holy Ghost guides us at all, He will do it according to the Scriptures and never contrary to them.

4. Next, I take into account providential circumstances. These often plainly indicate God's will in connection with the Word and Spirit.

5. I ask God in prayer to reveal His will to me rightly.

6. Thus, through prayer to God, the study of the Word and reflection, I come to a deliberate judgment according to the best of my ability and knowledge, and if my mind is thus at peace, and continues to be so after two or three more petitions, I proceed accordingly. In trivial matters, and in transactions involving important issues, I have found this method always effective." –George Mueller

"Therefore I say unto you, Take no thought for your life, what ye shall eat, or what ye shall drink; nor yet for your body, what ye shall put on. Is not the life more than meat, and the body than raiment? Behold the fowls of the air: for they sow not, neither do they reap, nor gather into barns; yet your heavenly Father feedeth them. Are ye not much better than they?" (Ma 6:25-26)

"It has been well said that no man ever sank under the burden of the day. It is when tomorrow's burden is added to the burden of today that the weight is more than a man can bear. Never load yourselves in this way, my friends. If you find yourselves so loaded, at least remember this: it is your doing, not God's. He begs you to leave the future to Him, and mind the present.

What more or what else could He do to take the burden off you? Nothing else would do it. Money in the bank wouldn't do it; He cannot do tomorrow's business for you to save you from fear about it. That would derange everything. What else is there but to tell you to trust in Him, irrespective of the fact that nothing else but trust can put our hearts at peace, from the very nature of our relationship to Him, as well as the fact that we need these things.

We think that we come nearer to God than the animals do by our foresight. But there is another side to it. We are like Him with whom there is no past or future, with whom a day is as a thousand years and a thousand years as one day, when we live with large, bright spiritual eyes, doing our work in the present and leaving both the past and future to Him to whom they are ever present. We should fear nothing, because He is in our future as much as in our past and present. As partakers of this divine nature we may rest in that perfect All-in-All, in whom our nature is eternal, too; we may walk without fear, full of hope and courage and strength to do His will, as we wait for the endless good which He is always giving, as fast as He can get us able to take it in." -- George MacDonald

"And one cried unto another, and said, Holy, holy, holy, is the Lord of hosts: the whole earth is full of his glory." (Is 6:3)

When we pray, and keep on praying, the door opens for God to reveal reality to us. As we pray, He is able to impart to us a thirst for righteousness and purity, and a deeper revelation of just how sinful we are.

In the year that king Uzziah died, the prophet Isaiah went into prayer and saw the Lord situated upon a throne. Above it stood the seraphim, one of whom cried unto another and said, "Holy, holy, holy, is the Lord of hosts;

the whole earth is full of his glory" (Is 6:3). The posts of the door moved at the voice of the seraph and the house was filled with smoke. Then Isaiah said, "Woe is me! for I am undone; because I am a man of unclean lips, and I dwell in the midst of a people of unclean lips; for mine eyes have seen the King, the Lord of hosts" (v. 5).

As we draw closer to the Lord we are bound to become more and more aware of our utter inability to be holy. As we advance nearer to His presence we will be struck with the truth of our frailty and our powerlessness to cease from sin. Like Isaiah, we will cry "Woe is me." And yet, this painful realization is a sign of progress. When we become disturbed and frustrated at the depth of our sin and our inability to achieve, in our own strength, the righteousness God intends to instill in us, we becoming more aware of our own personal littleness and the immensity of God. When one draws close to a bright light, the shadow he casts grows darker. So it is with us; the closer we draw to God, the more we will become aware of the darkness within us, and of our need to go to the Lord -- not for some grace, not for much grace, but for all the grace we need.

Fierce may be the conflict,
Strong may be the foe,
But the King's own army
None can overthrow.
Round His standard ranging,
Victory is secure,
For His truth unchanging
Makes the triumph sure.
Joyfully enlisting
By Thy grace divine,
We are on the Lord's side;
Saviour, we are Thine.
          --Frances Havergal

AUGUST 19 --

"A living dog is better than a dead lion." (Ec 9:4)

"A living dog keeps better watch than a dead lion, and is of more service to his master; and so, the poorest preacher who is spiritually connected to his Lord is infinitely to be preferred to the exquisite speaker who has no wisdom but that of words, no energy but that of sound.

The like holds true of our prayers; if we are quickened in them by the Holy Spirit, they are acceptable to God, though we may think them to be worthless things; while our grand performances, in which our hearts are absent, like dead lions, will lie before God like so much decaying flesh.

Oh, for living groans, living sighs, living despondencies, rather than lifeless songs and dead calms. Better anything than death. The snarls of the dogs of hell will at least keep us awake, but dead faith and dead profession, what greater curses can a man have? Oh Lord, do please quicken us."

-- Charles Spurgeon

AUGUST 20 ---

"Brethren, pray for us." (I Th 5:25)

"The enemy yields only what he must. He yields only what is taken. Therefore the ground must be taken step by step. He continually renews his attacks; therefore, the ground taken must be held against him in the Victor's name. This helps us to understand why prayer must be persisted in after we have full assurance of the result, and even after some immediate results have come, or, after the general results have commenced coming.

The Victor's best ally in this conflict is the man, who, while he remains down on the battlefield, puts his life in full touch with his Saviour, and then incessantly, insistently, believingly claims victory in Jesus' name. He is the one foe among men whom Satan cannot withstand. He is projecting an irresistible spirit force into the spirit realm. Satan is obliged to yield.

We are so accustomed through history's long record to seeing victories won through force, physical force alone, that it is difficult for us to realize that moral force defeats as the other never can. Witness the demons in the gospels; clearly against their own set purpose, notwithstanding the most intense struggle on their part, they had to admit defeat and even to ask favors of their Conqueror. The records of personal Christian service give fascinating instances of fierce opposition utterly subdued and individuals transformed through such influence.

Had we eyes to see spirit beings and spirit conflicts we would constantly see the enemy's defeat in numberless instances through the persistent praying of someone allied to Jesus in the spirit of His life. Every time such a person prays it is a waving of the red-dyed flag of Jesus Christ above Satan's head in the spirit world. Everyone who freely gives himself over to God and up to prayer, is giving God a new spot in the contested territory on which to erect His banner of victory. The individual wholly given over to God gives Him a new headquarters on the battlefield from which to work. And the Holy Spirit within that person, upon that new spot, will insist on the enemy's retreat in Jesus the Victor's name. That is prayer. Shall we not, every one of us, increase God's footing here upon His prodigal earth?"

--S. D. Gordon

AUGUST 21 --

"Therefore, behold, I will allure her, and bring her into the wilderness, and speak comfortably unto her. And I will give her vineyards from thence, and the valley of Achor for a door of hope: and she shall sing there, as in the days of her youth, and as in the day when she came up out of the land of Egypt." (Ho 2:14-15)

"This is still the way God deals with His people. They often forget Him in the glare and glitter of prosperity. He hushes the din of the world – takes them out into the solitudes of trial, and there, while abased, humbled and chastened He speaks to them of His love, forgiveness, and comfort. What infinite tenderness characterizes the dealings of this Heavenly Lord when He chastens. How slow to abandon those who have abandoned Him! Every means and instrument is employed rather than leave them to the bitter fruits of their own guilty deeds.

Has God dealt with you by affliction? Did He blight your earthly hopes, cause your gladness to cease, destroy your vines and fig-trees, make all around you a desert? Think what it might have been, had He allowed you to go on in your course of estrangement, allowed your truant heart to plunge deeper and deeper into its career of sin. Is it not His mercy that has dimmed that false and deceptive glitter of earth? He has brought you into the wilderness. As Jesus did with His disciples of old when He would nerve them for the coming trial, He has taken you to 'a high mountain alone,' apart from the world. He has humbled you and proved you. He may have touched you to the quick – touched you in your tenderest point, severed precious companionships, leveled idols – but it was all His doing. 'Behold, I will allure' – 'I will bring into the wilderness' – 'I will comfort.' He leads us into the wilderness, and He leads us up, and He leads us through."

--John MacDuff

AUGUST 22 --

"Wherefore (as the Holy Ghost saith, Today if ye will hear his voice, Harden not your hearts, as in the provocation, in the day of temptation in the wilderness:" (He 3:7-8)

"Today! It is a word of wonderful promise. It tells that Today, this very moment, the wondrous love of God is for you. It is even now waiting to be poured out into your heart; that Today - all that Christ has done, and is now doing in heaven, and is able to do within you -- this very day, it is within your reach. Today the Holy Ghost, in whom there is the power to know and claim and enjoy all that the Father and the Son are waiting to bestow, today the Holy Ghost is within you, sufficient for every need, equal to every emergency. With every call we find in our Bible to full and entire surrender; with every promise we read of grace for the supply of temporal and spiritual need; with every prayer we breathe, and every longing that rules in our heart, there is the Spirit of promise whispering, 'Today.' Even as the Holy Ghost saith, Today.

Today! It is a word of solemn command. It is not here a question of some higher privilege which you are free to accept or reject. It is not left to your choice, Dear Believer, whether you will receive the fulness of blessing the Holy Spirit offers. That Today of the Holy Ghost brings you under the most solemn obligation to respond to God's call, and to say, 'Yes, today, Lord, complete and immediate submission to all of Your will; today, the surrender of a present and a perfect trust in all Your grace.' Even as the Holy Ghost saith, Today."
— Andrew Murray

AUGUST 23 --

"For yet a little while, and he that shall come will come, and will not tarry." (He 10:37)

"The grandest fact in history is that Jesus Christ, the Lord of Glory, has been in this world. And the most important fact of the present is that He is now in Heaven making intercession for us. And the greatest prophesied event of the future is, that He is coming again.

These three appearings are beautifully set forth in the ninth chapter of Hebrews: His appearing upon earth 'to put away sin by the sacrifice of Himself' (verse 26); His entering 'into Heaven itself, now to appear in the presence of God for us' (verse 24); and His being 'once offered to bear the sins of many; and unto them that look for him shall he appear the second time without sin unto salvation' (verse 28).

While He was here upon earth He said: 'It is expedient for you that I go away,' and He went away. He said, 'I go to prepare a place for you,' then promised, 'If I go and prepare a place for you, I will come again, and receive you unto myself; that where I am, there ye may be also' (Jo 14:2-3). He gave us this promise as our hope and comfort while He is away. He said: 'In the world ye shall have tribulation' (Jo 16:33), 'ye [shall] have sorrow: but I will see you again, and your heart shall rejoice, and your joy no man taketh from you' (Jo 16:22). Nothing can be more comforting to the Church, the bride of Christ, than this precious promise which our absent Lord has left us, that He will come and receive us unto Himself, and that we shall be with Him, to behold His glory.

He has given us The Lord's Supper, that we should take the bread and the cup in remembrance of Him, and to show His death until He come. We have this simple and loving memorial for a continual sign of this promise during all the earthly pilgrimage of the Church, and through it we look forward from the Cross to His coming, when He will drink it anew with us, in His Father's kingdom, at the marriage feast of the Lamb.

It is a constant reminder of His promise, pointing our eye of faith to His coming again. 'He is faithful that promised,' and we are exhorted to have confidence and patience, that we may 'receive the promise,' 'for yet a little while, and He that shall come, will come, and will not tarry.'"

-- William Blackstone

AUGUST 24 --

"Know ye not that they which run in a race run all, but one receiveth the prize? So run, that ye may obtain." (I Cor 9:24)

"Our business in life is not to get ahead of other people, but to get ahead of ourselves. To break our own record, to outstrip our yesterdays by todays, to bear our trials more beautifully than we ever dreamed we could, to whip the tempter inside and out as we never whipped him before, to give as we never have given, to do our work with more force and a finer finish than ever -- this is the true idea -- to get ahead of ourselves. To beat someone else in a game, or to be beaten, may mean much or little. To beat our own game means a great deal. Whether we win or not, we are playing better than we ever did before, and that's the point after all -- to play a better game of life.

O Lord, I pray that for this day I may not swerve
By foot or hand from Thy command, not to be served, but to serve.
This, too, I pray, that for this day no love of ease
Nor pride prevent my good intent, not to be pleased, but to please.
And if I may, I'd have this day strength from above
To set my heart in heavenly art, not to be loved, but to love."

-- Maltbie Davenport Babcock

AUGUST 25 --

"Trust in the Lord with all thine heart; and lean not unto thine own understanding. In all thy ways acknowledge him, and he shall direct thy paths." (Pr 3:5-6)

"I surrender and abandon myself entirely to Divine Providence from one day to the next. You do the same as far as you are able. There's nothing better. It is only in total obedience that we are able to find and experience an unfailing peace within. The greatest good fortune for the next life is to die to everything in this one. Happy is he who, by his daily death, prepares for the true death through which we enter the true life.

Likewise, let us abandon ourselves to every wish of God, and we shall soon be relieved of our burden. Then we shall see that in order to make progress in the paths of salvation and perfection, there is, in the end, little to be done. Without worrying about the past or the future, we must look to

God in trust, as to a Loving Father who leads us by the hand through the present moment.

I do not know what my future is to be, and I am very relieved. This total ignorance leaves me completely submitted to Divine Providence, where I am utterly at peace and in my element, without a care, like a little child sleeping gently on its tender mother's bosom, wanting all and wanting nothing, that is to say, everything that God wills and nothing that He does not will.

In this happy abandonment I find peace and a profound repose of heart and spirit which sets me free from a thousand vain thoughts, hundreds of disquieting ambitions and of every care I might have about the future."

– Jean-Pierre de Caussade

AUGUST 26 --

"I the Lord do keep it; I will water it every moment: lest any hurt it, I will keep it night and day." (Is 27:3)

California's great Central Valley is home to countless vineyards. During the long summers the days are hot, often reaching over 100 degrees. Such intense heat can damage the vines unless they are regularly watered.

We are like these grapevines. Unless we receive regular refreshings from the life-giving water of the Holy Spirit, we are likely to wilt under the heat of trials, temptations and attacks by the enemy. Every moment of the day, or, as F. B. Meyer once put it, "every time the eye twinkles," God is watering us with His grace. Sometimes we will be aware of what He is doing. Sometimes we won't, but God's soul-freshening activity is always going on whether or not we are conscious of it.

At times, He will send us showers of blessings. At others, gentle mists of mercy. Sometimes he will flood us with the awareness of His love and care, or He may apply drops of comfort to our hearts when we must bear up under the drought of sorrow or pain. During dry days He may send the moisture of a friend's encouragement, a stranger's help, a passage of Scripture to cheer us, a book to lift our spirits, a neighbor to do us a favor, or, perhaps, He may call upon us to see to the needs of another and thereby bring encouragement and refreshing to our own hearts.

God knows just how to impart the spiritual moisture we need. Because He is all-wise, He knows exactly how much Living Water to apply and at what intervals. In addition, He knows how to meet all our other needs. He will protect us from the heat of our trials and watch over us, both night and day, so the enemy cannot damage the fruit He is developing within us. The Lord has committed Himself to keeping His children safe. If we will cling to him, as clusters of grapes cling to the vine, we will be protected by the shade of His overshadowing love, and refreshed by the water of His Life-giving Spirit.

Jesus, grace for grace outpouring,
Show me ever greater things;
Raise me higher, sunward soaring,
Mounting as on eagle-wings.
By the brightness of Thy face,
Jesus, let me grow in grace.

Let me grow by sun and shower,
Every moment water me;
Make me really hour by hour
More and more conformed to Thee,
That Thy loving eye may trace,
Day by day, my growth in grace.
                    --Frances Ridley Havergal

AUGUST 27 --

"And they said among themselves, Who shall roll us away the stone from the door of the sepulchre? And when they looked, they saw that the stone was rolled away: for it was very great." (Mark 16:3-4)

"We are all alike. Even these holy women on this most sacred errand went forward to borrow trouble. There was a stone in the way that must be rolled aside, and they had not strength to do it. Naturally enough, they began to be anxious as to the removal of this obstacle. When they came near they saw that the obstacle had been already removed. The Divine love had been beforehand in preparing the way for them. Angels had rolled the stone aside. The lesson is very simple and beautiful. We go forward worrying about the difficulties that lie before us, wondering how we can ever get through them, or who will remove them out of our way. Then when we come up to them we find that they are gone. Someone has been there before us and has taken them away. God always opens the way of duty for us if we quietly move on.

This applies to one beginning a Christian life. Many persons shrink from it. They say, 'I never can be faithful. I never can do the duties. I never can bear the burdens.' But as they enter and go on they find that an unseen and mighty Helper goes on before and prepares the way. The hard tasks become easy, and the heavy burdens grow light. It is so all through the Christian life. God's commandment seems impossible of obedience. Walls of stone seem built across the path we are required to walk over. But as we go on the commandment is easy, and a gateway is opened in the wall. Love and faith always have an advance of angels to roll away stones. The practical lesson is, that we are never to hesitate nor shrink back because obstacles seem to lie before us; we are to go right on, and God will take them away for us. When

He wants us to go anywhere He will open the path for our feet. Knowing this, we may go on feeling confident of our own safety." – J. R. Miller

AUGUST 28 --

"And the angel of the Lord came again the second time, and touched him, and said, Arise [and] eat; because the journey is too great for thee. And he arose, and did eat and drink, and went in the strength of that meat forty days and forty nights unto Horeb the mount of God." (I Ki 19:7-8)

We are all prone to suffer from HALT now and then. HALT is an acronym that stands for being too Hungry, too Angry, too Lonely or too Tired. Suffering from just one of these difficulties can cause us problems; when we have more than one going on at the same time, it can dampen our faith and make us feel like all the cards are stacked against us. HALT can affect anyone, even the most mature among us. Our flesh is weak, even under the best of circumstances, and when we're worn out or overwhelmed it can make us feel like giving up.

Look at the prophet Elijah. As much as he loved God, he almost gave up because he became too hungry, too tired and felt utterly alone.

After he confronted the prophets of Baal, and proved how superior the Lord was to the gods they worshiped, Elijah ordered their destruction. As a result, he became a wanted man. Jezebel swore she would search him out and kill him. He escaped into the desert, but there, afraid for his life and exhausted from his journey, he collapsed under a juniper tree. He poured out his frustration and anxiety to God: "It is enough; now, O Lord, take away my life; for I am not better than my ancestors." God's response was to ignore Elijah's request; instead, he sent an angel who roused Elijah and entreated him to "get up and eat." Elijah discovered a cake of bread and jar of water had miraculously been provided for him. He did as he was told. He ate and rested. Then he ate again. His strength returned, so much so that he was able to travel forty days and forty nights to Horeb, the mountain of God, and thereby escape Jezebel's wrath.

When we are suffering from HALT, we may feel like we will never be able to overcome our challenges, but most of the time it only means we need to take care of ourselves or take a break. If we are hungry or ill, we may need to stop what we're doing and tend to our health. If we're angry, we may want to share our feelings with someone who will listen to us and give us sound counsel. If we're lonely, we may need to reach out to another person or see how we can bless someone else who may be facing even bigger battles than we are. If we're tired, we should get some rest. Struggles don't always indicate we need to bear down harder. Sometimes they simply mean we need to reach out for some encouragement or take time to see to our physical needs.

"Continue in the faith..." (Ac 14:22)

"Perseverance is the badge of true saints. The Christian life is not only a beginning in the ways of God but is also a continuance in them as long as life lasts. It is with a Christian as it was with Napoleon: he said, 'Conquest has made me what I am, and conquest must maintain me.'

So, under God, dear one, conquest has made you what you are and conquest must sustain you. He only is a true conqueror who continues until the trumpet of war ceases to blow. Perseverance is, therefore, the target of all our spiritual enemies.

The world does not object to your being a Christian, for a time, if she can tempt you to cease your pilgrimage at some point and settle down to buying and selling along with her. The flesh will also seek to ensnare you and prevent you from passing on to glory. It will say, 'It is weary work being a pilgrim; come, give it up. Am I always to be mortified? Am I never to be indulged? Give me at least a furlough from this constant warfare.' In addition, Satan will make many a fierce attack on your perseverance; it will be the mark for all his arrows. He will strive to hinder you in service; he will insinuate that you are doing no good, and that you must have rest. He will endeavor to make you weary of suffering. He will whisper, 'Curse God, and die.' Or he will attack your steadfastness: 'What is the good of being so zealous? Be quiet, like the rest; sleep, as the others do, and let your lamp go out, as the other virgins do.' Or he will assail your doctrinal sentiments: 'Why do you hold to these denominational creeds? Sensible people are getting more liberal; they are removing the old landmarks; why don't you fall in with the times?'

Wear your shield, then, Christian, and hold it close upon your armor, and cry mightily unto God, that by His Spirit you may endure to the end."

–Charles Spurgeon

"For what if some did not believe? Shall their unbelief make the faith of God without effect? God forbid: yea, let God be true, but every man a liar; as it is written, That thou mightest be justified in thy sayings, and mightest overcome when thou art judged." (Ro 3:3-4)

"God loves us so well that He will not permit us to take less than His highest will. Some day we shall thank our faithful Teacher who kept the standard inflexible and then gave us the strength and grace to reach it. We shall thank Him who would not excuse us until we had accomplished all His glorious will. Let us be unyielding with ourselves. Let us mean exactly what

God means, and have no discounts upon His promises or commandments. Let us keep the standard up, and never rest until we reach it. Let God be true, but every man a liar. Even if we fail a hundred times, let us not accommodate God's ideal to our thinking, let us rather be like the brave ensign who stood in front of his company waving the regimental banner. When the soldiers tried to call him back, he only waved the banner higher and cried, 'Don't bring the colors back to the regiment; bring the regiment up to the colors.'

> Forward, forward, leave the past behind thee,
> Reaching forth unto the things before;
> All the Land of Promise lies before thee,
> God has greater blessings yet in store."
> —A.B. Simpson

AUGUST 31 --

"Wherefore the Lord God of Israel saith, I said indeed that thy house, and the house of thy father, should walk before me for ever: but now the Lord saith, Be it far from me; for them that honour me I will honour, and they that despise me shall be lightly esteemed." (I Sa 2:30)

"To cast a doubt upon the truth of God's Word is to cast the highest dishonor upon God himself. We must remind ourselves to beware of tampering with the Bible or raising trivial objections to its revealed truths; instead, we should stand in awe of its divinity, adore its majesty, and bow unquestioningly to its authority. Then will God honor us by making His Word our light in darkness, our joy in grief, our strength in service, our hope in despondency and despair...

I honor God by trusting Him. As there is not a more God-dishonoring principle than unbelief, so there is not a more God-glorifying grace than the faith that rests in Him with a childlike and unquestioning confidence--a faith that trusts His power to perform all that He has pledged in His covenant and Word to do. If your soul is tried, burdened, and in need, have faith in God. Now is the time to bring honor and glory to His great Name by a simple, unhesitating trust in His power, faithfulness, and love."

– Octavius Winslow

SEPTEMBER 1 --

"Though I speak with the tongues of men and of angels, and have not charity, I am become as sounding brass, or a tinkling cymbal. And though I have the gift of

prophecy, and understand all mysteries, and all knowledge; and though I have all faith, so that I could remove mountains, and have not charity, I am nothing." (I Co 13:1-2)

"A great many are praying for faith; they want extraordinary faith; they want remarkable faith. They forget that love exceeds faith. The Charity spoken of in the above verses is love, the fruit of the Spirit, the great motive-power of life. What the Church of God needs today is love: more love to God and more love to our fellow-men. If we love God more, we will love our fellow-men more. There is no doubt about that. I used to think that I should like to have lived in the days of the prophets; that I should like to have been one of the prophets, to prophesy, and to see the beauties of heaven and describe them to men. But, as I understand the Scriptures now, I would rather live in the thirteenth chapter of First Corinthians and have this love that Paul is speaking of, the love of God burning in my soul like an unquenchable flame, so that I may reach men and win them for heaven.

A man may have wonderful knowledge that can unravel the mysteries of the Bible, and yet be as cold as an icicle. He may glisten like the snow in the sun. Sometimes you have wondered why it was that certain ministers who have had such wonderful magnetism, who have such a marvelous command of language and who preach with such mental strength, haven't had more conversions. I believe, if the truth be known, it is because there is no divine love back of their words, no pure love in their sermons. You may preach like an angel, Paul says, 'with the tongues of men and of angels,' but if you have not love, it amounts to nothing. A man may be very charitable and give away all his goods, a man may give all he has, but if it is not the love of God which prompts the gift, it will not be acceptable with God. A man may go to the stake for his principles; he may go to the stake for what he believes, but if it is not love to God which motivates him, it will not be acceptable to God."   – D. L. Moody

SEPTEMBER 2 --

"But while men slept, his enemy came and sowed tares among the wheat, and went his way." (Ma 13:25)

"How clearly our Lord taught the personality of Satan! In His explanation of this parable, He said distinctly, 'The enemy that sowed them is the devil.' He knew that in every heart, in the Church as well as in the world, the great enemy of God's Kingdom, and of human happiness, is always at work, sowing tares. The seed may be very small, but in a single night irreparable injury may be inflicted.

Notice that we become as the seed we receive. Those who receive the wheat-seed become wheat; those who receive the tare-seed become tares. 'As a man thinketh in his heart, so is he.' How careful we should be over the books we read, the companionship and friendship that we form, the activities we take part in. Such are some of the processes by which our characters are being made. If we are thoughtless and careless, we expose ourselves to the reception of tare-seed, which germinates into weeds and rubbish. Of course, if our necessary duties take us into scenes where evil is rife, we may claim the keeping power of Christ, and hide ourselves in Him. As a doctor will use disinfectant when working with a patient who is contagious, so the Holy Spirit, in whom we may bathe our souls, will be as a disinfectant, and deliver us from the microbes of temptation (Ga 5:16-17).

There is not much difference, it is said, between wheat and tares in the earlier stages of their growth; it is only when the harvest comes that the distinction is clearly defined. So it is in the Church and the world. There are many counterfeits, people who seem to be good and true, but they are not what they seem, and in the day of reckoning they will be rooted up and cast forth as rubbish. The two classes that will be rejected at last are, 'All that cause stumbling, and them that do iniquity' (Ma 13:41).

It may be that you are not amongst those that do iniquity, in any of its glaring forms, but are you causing others to stumble by your inconsistent behaviour or worldliness? Let each of us carefully examine ourselves, and open our hearts to receive from the hand of the Lord Jesus the incorruptible seed which He waits to implant by His Word."   – F. B. Meyer

SEPTEMBER 3 --

"Think not that I am come to destroy the law, or the prophets: I am not come to destroy, but to fulfil. For verily I say unto you, Till heaven and earth pass, one jot or one tittle shall in no wise pass from the law, till all be fulfilled." (Ma 5:17-18)

"If [Jesus] came and literally fulfilled the prophecies of a suffering Messiah, will He not as surely come and likewise fulfill the prophecies of a glorified Messiah reigning in victory and majesty? Think of the many prophecies descriptive of a suffering Messiah, which we have seen literally fulfilled, and upon which we rest, as strong evidence for the truth and inspiration of the Word. These include the fact that He was:

Born of a virgin (Is 7:14); born at Bethlehem (Mi 5:2); called out of Egypt (Ho 11:1); anointed with the Spirit (Is 11:2); betrayed by a friend (Ps 41:9; 55:12-14); forsaken by the disciples (Ze 13:7); sold for thirty pieces of silver (Ze 11:12); spit on and scourged (Is 50:6); crucified but without a bone broken (Ps 34:20); and with His hands and feet pierced (Ps 22).

All these were literally fulfilled when Christ came. Do not, then, reject the literal fulfillment of those numerous prophecies which describe His future coming, and His glorious reign upon the earth. Namely, that:

He shall come Himself (I Th 4:16); He shall shout (I Th 4:16); the dead will hear His voice (Jo 5:28); the raised and changed believers will be caught up to meet Him in the air (I Th 4:17); He will receive them to Himself (Jo 14:3); He will come to earth again (Ac 1:11); He shall set foot upon the same Mount Olivet from which He ascended (Ze 14:4); His saints (the Church) will come with Him (De 33:2; I Th 3:13; Ju 14); every eye shall see Him (Re 1:7); He shall destroy the Antichrist (II Th 2:8); He shall sit on His throne (Ma 25:31); all nations will be gathered before Him and He will judge them (Ma 25:32); He shall have a kingdom (Da 7:13-14); He shall rule over it with His saints (Da 7:18-27; Re 5:10); all kings and nations shall serve Him (Ps 72:11; Is 49:6-7; Re 15:4); every knee shall bow to Him (Is 45:23); He shall build up Zion (Ps 102:16); His throne shall be in Jerusalem (Je 3:17); He shall rule all nations (Ps 2:8-9); His glory shall be revealed (Is 40:5); His rest shall be glorious (Is 11:10); and so many more...

Surely there is not symbolism in these clear prophecies. Rather, let us expect that He will as literally fulfill these as He did the others at His first coming."   – William Blackstone

SEPTEMBER 4 --

"Furthermore we have had fathers of our flesh which corrected us, and we gave them reverence: shall we not much rather be in subjection unto the Father of spirits, and live? For they verily for a few days chastened us after their own pleasure; but he for our profit, that we might be partakers of his holiness." (He 12:9-10)

Walking with the Lord is a little like being an onion that gets peeled one layer at a time. When the first layer is peeled away we may discover for the first time in our lives that we have some major defects lying beneath the surface of our personalities. Generally we are disturbed at the revelation of these defects, but we usually respond by saying something like, "Sure, I have flaws, everybody does, but I try to be a good person. And I really do mean well. I don't think I'm all that bad."

Then God takes us on a little farther in the spiritual life. He may lead us through circumstances that overwhelm us so we have to recognize that all the strength we thought was ours by nature was merely a facade. Or he may allow us to undergo disappointments that dash some of our most precious hopes and dreams, causing us to realize we can't control life the way we once thought we could. As layer after layer is peeled away, we come to recognize that we don't have the resources to handle life in our own strength and according to our own wills. We need God's help. Over time, we discover it no longer works to allow God to only be a part of our life; He must become all of our life. He is the Alpha and Omega, the only Source of real spiritual power, while we are merely fragile reeds.

Let us not despise those times of trial that God allows to come into our lives. They act as paring knives; they peel back the layers of self that must eventually be removed if we are to draw close to God.

"God did not bring you into the world because He had any need of you... but solely that He might show forth His Goodness in you, giving you His Grace and Glory. And to this end He gave you understanding that you might know Him, memory that you might think of Him, a will that you might love Him, imagination that you might realize His mercies, sight that you might behold the marvels of His works, speech that you might praise Him, and so on with all your other faculties... Consider how unhappy they are who do not think of all this, who live as though they were created only to build and plant, to heap up riches and amuse themselves with trifles."

--St. Francis de Sales

SEPTEMBER 5 --

"He that loveth not knoweth not God; for God is love." (I Jo 4:8)

"'God is love.' That sums up the whole contents of the Bible. If I were asked for a sentence to print in letters of gold on the outside of our Bible, a sentence that summed up the whole contents of the Book, it would be this one, 'God is love.' That is the subject of the first chapter of Genesis, it is the subject of the last chapter of Revelation, and it is the subject of every chapter that lies in between.

The Bible is simply God's love story, the story of the love of a holy God to a sinful world. That is the most amazing thing in the Bible. People tell us the Bible is full of things that it is impossible to believe. I know of nothing else so impossible to believe as that a holy God should love a sinful world, and should love such individuals as you and me, as the Bible says He does. But impossible as it is to believe, it is true. There is mighty power in that one short sentence, power to break the hardest heart, power to reach individual men and women who are sunk down in sin, and to lift them up until they are fit for a place beside the Lord Jesus Christ upon the Throne."

--Reuben Archer Torrey

Finish, then, Thy new creation;
Pure and spotless let us be.
Let us see Thy great salvation
Perfectly restored in Thee;
Changed from glory into glory,
Till in heaven we take our place,

Till we cast our crowns before Thee,
Lost in wonder, love, and praise.
                    --Charles Wesley

"And we have known and believed the love that God hath to us. God is love; and he that dwelleth in love dwelleth in God, and God in him. Herein is our love made perfect, that we may have boldness in the day of judgment: because as he is, so are we in this world." (I Jo 4:16-17)

SEPTEMBER 6 --

"...and we shall be changed." (I Co 15:52)

"Look at the story of the butterfly -- so plain that the pagan Greeks called both it and the soul by one name: Psyche. Look at the creeping thing, so ugly to us that we can hardly handle it without a shudder. When it begins to find itself growing sick with age it falls to spinning and weaving its own shroud, coffin and grave, all in one. Thus it prepares itself for its own resurrection; for it is for the sake of the resurrection that death exists.

Patiently it spins its strength away, but not its life. It folds itself up decently, that its body may rest in quiet until the new body is formed within it. And at length, when the appointed hour has arrived, out of this formerly crawling thing breaks forth the winged splendor of the butterfly; not the same body but a new one built out of the ruins of the old, even as Paul tells us that it is not the same body which we will have at the resurrection but a nobler one, like ourselves, with all the imperfect and evil taken out of it.

No more creeping for the butterfly. No, it makes its way upon wings of splendor. Think of it. No longer a tiring journey over low ground, exposed to the foot of every passer-by; no more eating by the destruction of lovely leaves and the fruit they shelter. Instead, up to the pathways in the air, and to the gathering of food which never destroys its source -- a food which is like a tribute from the loveliness of the flowers to the higher loveliness of the flower-angel. Is this not a resurrection? And this being's children, too, shall pass through this same process, to wing the air of a summer noon and rejoice in the ethereal and the pure."   – George MacDonald

SEPTEMBER 7 --

"Give, and it shall be given unto you; good measure, pressed down, and shaken together, and running over, shall men give into your bosom. For with the same measure that ye mete withal it shall be measured to you again." (Lu 6:38)

The God that Jesus introduced to his disciples was a God who loved to give to His children. This assertion – that God was a giving God rather than

211

a demanding, punishing God -- was a revolutionary idea at the time; it flew in the face of almost all the people had been taught about the nature of their Lord. In the past, they had been rigorously educated about the things God demanded of them. Since God was perfect, He demanded either perfection or a sacrifice to atone for their inability to fulfill the law. Since God was all-powerful, He demanded submission. Because He was holy, He demanded reverence. It seemed almost a blasphemy, then, when Jesus announced that the God He served was a loving Father who desired to give good gifts to His children.

Jesus told them God had a storehouse of riches He wished to share with His children. He wanted to bestow upon them His gifts of grace, forgiveness, salvation and love. And He wanted his children to learn how to give, too. Many of Jesus' listeners were amazed at this new vision of God, but when they saw how Jesus gave to others, how He healed and delivered and forgave, they began to recognize what He said was true.

Today it is still hard for many of us to recognize that God offers us a new way of life -- a life of giving instead of taking -- as the way to spiritual abundance. This new way of life requires us to toss aside much of what we have been taught about the Lord, and about how we are to live.

Are we willing to learn how to live according to this new system? Are we willing to let God remake our hearts so that we, too, become givers? It will require that we become willing to take risks. In fact, Christ's way will require us to risk everything we have. We will need to become willing to trade in our old, grasping natures for God's new, giving nature. We will need to reject the world's way of doing things – the way of self seeking and self promotion -- and substitute in its place God's way – the way of forsaking our own interests and caring for the needs of others. These two ways of life are diametrically opposed.

If we wish to enter this new world, God will show us how. He will teach us, one step at a time, how to become givers, and will place in front of us opportunities to give of our time, our love, our money, our prayers, our possessions, our encouragement, our blessings, our patience, our long-suffering, our forgiveness, our very selves. Our part is to welcome these opportunities and to look for them, not with our physical eyes only, but with the spiritual sight God will instill in us. As we become willing to give, God will give to us, good measure, pressed down, running over, in amazing abundance. It will happen because it is the law of God's eternal, divine economy.

SEPTEMBER 8 ---

"What is it then? I will pray with the spirit, and I will pray with the understanding also: I will sing with the spirit, and I will sing with the understanding also." (I Co 14:15)

"How few there are who pray, for there are few who desire what is truly good. Crosses, external and internal humiliation, renouncement of our own wills, the death of self and the establishment of God's throne upon the ruins of self love, these are indeed good; when we do not desire these things we will not pray for them, not desire them seriously, soberly, constantly, and with reference to all the details of life. When we will not desire them, and yet suppose to ourselves that we pray, we are under an illusion like that of the wretched who dream themselves happy. How many souls there are who are full of self and imagine that they desire personal perfection when they voluntarily maintain a host of imperfections. It was in reference to this that St. Augustine said: 'He that loveth little, prayeth little; he that loveth much, prayeth much.'

On the other hand, the heart that truly loves God never ceases to pray. Love, hidden in the bottom of the soul, prays without ceasing, even when the mind is drawn another way. God continually beholds the desire which He has himself implanted in the soul, though it may at times be unconscious of its existence; his heart is touched by it; it ceaselessly attracts his mercies; it is that Spirit which, according to St. Paul, 'helpeth our infirmities' and 'maketh intercession for us with groanings which cannot be uttered' (Ro 8:26)."

– Francois Fenelon

"Faith in a prayer-hearing God will make a prayer-loving Christian."

--Andrew Murray

SEPTEMBER 9 --

"Behold, what manner of love the Father hath bestowed upon us, that we should be called the sons of God: therefore the world knoweth us not, because it knew him not. Beloved, now are we the sons of God, and it doth not yet appear what we shall be: but we know that, when he shall appear, we shall be like him; for we shall see him as he is." (1 Jo 3:1-2)

"Behold, what manner of love the Father has bestowed upon us. Consider who we were, and what we feel ourselves to be even now when corruption is powerful in us, and you will wonder at our adoption. Yet we are called 'the sons of God.'

What a high relationship is that of a son, and what privileges it brings. What care and tenderness the son expects from his father, and what love the father feels towards the son. But all that, and more than that, we now have through Christ. As for the temporary drawback of suffering with the elder brother, this we accept as an honour: 'Therefore the world knoweth us not, because it knew him not.' We are content to be unknown with him in his humiliation, for we are to be exalted with him.

'Beloved, now are we the sons of God.' That is easy to read, but it is not so easy to feel. How is it with your heart this day? Are you in the lowest depths of sorrow? Does corruption rise within your spirit; does grace seem like a poor spark trampled under foot? Does your faith almost fail you? Do not fear, it is neither your graces nor feelings on which you are to live: you must live simply by faith in Christ. With all these things against us, now, even in the very depths of sorrow, wherever we may be, now, as much in the valley as on the mountain, Beloved, we are 'the sons of God.'

'Yes,' you may argue, 'but don't you see, my graces are not bright, my righteousness does not shine.' But read the next: 'It doth not yet appear what we shall be: but we know that, when he shall appear, we shall be like him.'

The Holy Spirit shall purify our minds, and divine power shall refine our bodies; then shall we see him as he is."   --C. H. Spurgeon

SEPTEMBER 10 ---

"I delight to do thy will, O my God: yea, thy law is within my heart." (Ps 40:8)

"I believe that people trying to be holy would be saved a lot of trouble if they were taught to follow the right path, and I am writing of people who live ordinary lives in the world and of those specially marked by God.

Let the former realize what lies hidden in every moment of the day and the duties each one brings, and let the latter appreciate the fact that things they regard as trivial and of no importance are essential to sanctity. And let them both be aware that holiness means the eager acceptance of every trial sent them by God.

This is vastly superior to the enjoyment of all extraordinary experiences. It is the philosophers' stone which changes into gold all their worries, all their troubles, all their sufferings. Let them realize this, and then how contented they will be. Let them realize that all they have to do to achieve the height of holiness is to do only what they are already doing and endure what they are already enduring, and to realize, too, that all they count as trivial and worthless is what can make them holy."   – Jean-Pierre de Caussade

SEPTEMBER 11 ---

"And he said unto them, When ye pray, say, Our Father which art in heaven, Hallowed be thy name. Thy kingdom come. Thy will be done, as in heaven, so in earth. Give us day by day our daily bread. And forgive us our sins; for we also forgive every one that is indebted to us. And lead us not into temptation; but deliver us from evil." (Lu 11:2-4)

"This wonderful prayer was dictated by our Lord in reply to the question on the part of His disciples, 'Lord, teach us to pray.' His answer was to bid them pray. This is the only way we shall ever learn to pray, by just beginning to do it. And as the babbling child learns the art of speech by speaking, and the lark mounts up to the heights of the sky by beating its little wings again and again upon the air, so prayer will teach us how to pray; and the more we pray, the more shall we learn the mysteries and heights and depths of prayer. And the more we pray, the more we shall realize the incomparable fullness and completeness of this unequaled prayer, the prayer of universal Christendom, the common liturgy of the Church of God, the earliest and holiest recollection of every Christian child, and the last utterance often of the departing soul. We who have used it most have come to feel that there is no want which it does not interpret and no holy aspiration which it may not express. There is nothing else in the Holy Scriptures which more fully evolves the great principles that underlie the divine philosophy of prayer....

It is not the cry of nature to an unknown God, but the intelligent converse of a child with his heavenly Father. It presupposes that the seeker has become a child, and it assumes that the mediation of the Son has preceded the revelation of the Father. No one, therefore, can truly pray until he has accepted the Lord Jesus Christ as Savior and received through Him the child-heart in regeneration, and then been led into the realization of sonship in the family of God. The Person to whom prayer is directly addressed is the Father as distinguished from the Son and the Holy Ghost. The great purpose of Christ's mediation is to bring us to God and reveal to us the Father as our Father in reconciliation and fellowship."

--A.B. Simpson

"This is our Lord's will, that our prayer and our trust be, alike, large. For if we do not trust as much as we pray, we fail in fully worshiping our Lord; we hinder and hurt ourselves. The reason is that we do not recognize that our Lord is the ground from which our prayer springs; nor do we know that it is given to us by his grace and his love. If we knew this, it would make us trust to have all of our Lord's gifts. For I am sure that no man who sincerely asks God for mercy and grace has not already received mercy and grace from God." – Juliana of Norwich

SEPTEMBER 12 --

"A time to rend, and a time to sew; a time to keep silence, and a time to speak;" (Ec 3:7)

"We can draw much instruction from Christ's silence. A Moravian hymn says: 'Let Christ's word, and silence, too, dwell in thy heart...'

Let us notice two instances of Christ's silence.

1) His silence at Nazareth for thirty years. There was no noise made about His coming into the world. He slipped into it, we may say, until a choir of angels made it known. A few weeks after, we hear the tramp of Herod's horsemen, and we see the babe fleeing into Egypt. Then we hear nothing of Him (with one exception) for thirty years. He grew up silently before the Lord. He did all for God only, and this is true service for child or man. He broke the silence once that He might tell us what He was engaged in. 'Wist ye not that I must be about my Father's business?' Christ never refers to these thirty years. Why did He keep silence? To teach us the real nature of obedience. Is it not doing everything under God's eye and for Him, not drawing the attention of others to what we are, and to what we are doing? He was teaching us to be content with the Father's approval, that the way to please the Lord is by our obedience. Is God's approval enough for you, though all men should ignore you or even despise you? Christ lived for thirty years with the two tables of the law unbroken... These thirty years ended at Christ's baptism, when the heavens were opened and the voice said, 'This is My beloved Son, in whom I am well pleased.' This was the Father's seal to the Son's thirty years of obedience.

2) His silence at the marriage in Cana. He says nothing to the guests, as we would have expected Him to do. Sitting in the midst of them the first of His miracles is done in silence. He spoke by His presence. A good man's presence in a company may be a great blessing, if his presence is also the presence of the Master. As Christ sat there He silently changed the water into wine. He was teaching the secret of power. It is the presence of the Lord that is the secret of power. It is that which we need in order to have blessing. Real conviction comes when the soul is quietly alone with God. No one in the church knows what you are feeling, but the Lord is working in the might of His divinity. We are to stand under the cross and look at the Crucified One. 'Behold Me! Behold Me!' And so, looking quietly on the Lord Jesus, the water may be changed into wine, and the hard heart may be melted!"

--Andrew Bonar

SEPTEMBER 13 --

"Cast your burden upon the Lord – and He shall sustain you!" (Ps 45:22)

"There are currently some mistaken notions concerning the ways in which God would help us. People think that whenever they have a little trouble, a bit of a hard path to go over, a load to carry, a sorrow to endure, that all they have to do is to call upon God, and He will at once take away their sorrow, or free them from the trouble. But this is not the way God helps us. His purpose of love concerning us is not to make all things easy for us but to make something of us.

When we ask God to save us from our trouble, to take the struggles out of our life, to lift off every heavy load, He will not do it! It would be most unloving in Him to accommodate us. We must carry the burden ourselves. All God promises is to sustain us as we carry it. He wants us to learn life's lessons and to do this we must be left to work out the problems for ourselves.

There are rich blessings which can be gotten only in sorrow. It would be short-sighted love indeed which would heed our cries and spare us from sorrow and thus deprive us of the wonderful blessings which can be gotten only in sorrow. God is too good to us to answer our prayers which would save us from pain, cost, and sacrifice today, at the price of a holier, better, truer life in the end. He is not going to rob us of the blessing that is in the burden, which we can get only by carrying it."   – J. R. Miller

SEPTEMBER 14 --

"Are not five sparrows sold for two farthings, and not one of them is forgotten before God? But even the very hairs of your head are all numbered. Fear not therefore..." (Lu 12:6-7)

"To the children of God, everything comes directly from their Father's hand, no matter who or what may have been the apparent agents. There are no 'second causes' for them. The whole teaching of the Bible asserts and implies this. Not a sparrow falls to the ground without our Father. The very hairs of our head are all numbered. We need not be careful for anything, for our Father cares for us....

To my own mind, these Scriptures, and many others like them, settle forever the question as to the power of second causes in the life of the children of God. They are all under the control of our Father, and nothing can touch us except with His knowledge and by His permission. It may be the sin of man that originates the action, and therefore the thing itself cannot be said to be the will of God, but by the time it reaches us, it has become God's will for us, and must be accepted as directly from His hands. No man or company of men, no power in earth or heaven, can touch that soul which is abiding in Christ, without first passing through Him, and receiving the seal of His permission. If God be for us, it matters not who may be against us; nothing can disturb or harm us, except He shall see that it is best for us, and shall stand aside to let it pass."   – Hannah Whitall Smith

SEPTEMBER 15 --

"Work out your own salvation with fear and trembling." (Ph 2:12)

"None but God's people under the teachings of the Spirit know what it is to 'work out their own salvation.' And all who work out their own salvation will work it out 'with fear and trembling.' For when a man is taught by God to know what he is; when he feels what a deceitful heart is in him; when the various snares, temptations, and corruptions by which he is daily encompassed are opened up to him; when he knows and feels what a ruined wretch he is in himself, then he begins to fear and tremble, lest he should be damned at the last. He cannot go recklessly and carelessly on without 'making straight paths for his feet,' without 'examining himself whether he be in the faith.'

Whenever a man's dreadfully deceitful heart is opened up to him; whenever he feels how strait is the path, how narrow the way, and how few there are that find it; whenever he is brought to see how easily a man is deceived, and how certainly he must be deceived unless God teaches him in a special manner; whenever a man is brought to this point, to see what a rare and sacred and spiritual a thing religion is and that God himself is the author and finisher of it; when he stands on this solemn ground, and begins to work out that which God works in, it will always be 'with fear and trembling.' And there will yet be some 'fear' until God assures him by His own blessed lips that he is not deluded; and some 'trembling,' for he will know that he is standing in the immediate presence of God, and under his heart-searching eye."   -- J. C. Philpot

SEPTEMBER 16 --

"Believe me that I [am] in the Father, and the Father in me:" (Jo 14:11)

"What a blessed Revealer of God is Jesus. He lifts the veil and shows me the Father as no planet in its glory could, as no mountain in its magnitude could, as no flower in its beauty could. No, not even the greatest, most sublime object in nature could reveal the Lord as Jesus does. 'He that has seen me, has seen the Father' (Jo 14:9).

He is also a very human Teacher. We could not learn from angels. Our dullness would weary their patience, our waywardness would exhaust their love, our questions would baffle their knowledge. Our Teacher must be like ourselves, human. 'And because he is human, he (the Old Testament high priest) is able to deal gently with the people, though they are ignorant and wayward. For he is subject to the same weaknesses they have' (He 5:2). He must be gentle, long-suffering, and infinite in knowledge. Such is Jesus. With what unfaltering love and unwearied patience, bearing with our dullness, indifference, and ingratitude, does Jesus teach us the precious things of His Word, and the yet more glorious and precious things of Himself.

And what does Jesus teach us? He teaches the plague of our own heart, the exceeding sinfulness of sin, the hatefulness and nothingness of self, the emptiness of the creature, and the insufficiency of the world. He makes us acquainted with the heart and character of our Father -- His thoughts of peace, His purposes of grace, and designs of mercy. He reveals to us His own glory and beauty, fullness and preciousness. In a word, He teaches every spiritual truth and holy lesson essential to the completeness of our education for a heaven of perfect knowledge, purity, and love.

And how does Jesus teach us? He teaches by the illumination of the Spirit, by the letter of the Word, by the dispensations of His providence, and by the communications of His grace; yes, by all the events and circumstances, joys and sorrows, lights and shadows of our solemn and checkered life. He is teaching you, dear one, more of your own nothingness and of His all-sufficiency, by one hallowed sorrow, by one fiery temptation, than, perhaps, you have ever learned in all your previous history, for 'who teaches like Him?' What a university in the believer's training for heaven is Jesus' school.

O Lord: Give Your servant a lowly, meek, and teachable spirit, willing to learn any lesson or truth in any school or way Your infinite wisdom and love may appoint.

Your way, not mine, O Lord,
However dark it be!
Lead me by Your own hand,
Choose out the path for me."
--Octavius Winslow

SEPTEMBER 17 --

"The very hairs of your head are all numbered." (Ma 10:30)

"What a 'word' this is to us: All that befalls you, to the very numbering of your hairs, is known to God. Nothing can happen by accident or chance. Nothing can elude His inspection. The fall of the forest leaf, the fluttering of the insect, the annihilation of a world -- all are equally noted by Him. Man speaks of great things and small things: God knows no such distinction.

How especially comforting to think of this tender solicitude with reference to His own covenant people, that He metes out their joys and their sorrows. Every sweet, every bitter, is ordained by Him. Even 'wearisome nights' are 'appointed.' Not a pang that I feel, not a tear that I shed, is unknown to Him. What are called 'dark dealings' are the ordinations of undeviating faithfulness. Man may err: his ways are often crooked. But as for God, His way is perfect. He puts my tears into His bottle. Every moment the everlasting arms are underneath and around me. He keeps me 'as the apple of His eye.' He bears me as a man bears his own son.

Do I look to the future? Is there much of uncertainty and mystery hanging over it? Trust Him. All is marked out for me. Dangers will be averted; bewildering mazes will show themselves to be interlaced and interweaved with mercy. He keeps the feet of His saints. A hair of their head will not be touched. He leads sometimes darkly, sometimes sorrowfully; most frequently by circuitous ways we ourselves would not have chosen; but always wisely, always tenderly. With all its mazy windings and turnings, its roughness and ruggedness, the believer's is not only a right way, but the best way which love and wisdom could select.

Well may I commit the keeping of my soul to Jesus, Who is a faithful Creator. He gave Himself for me. This transcendent pledge of love is the guarantee for the bestowment of every other needed blessing. What a blessed thought. My sorrows are numbered by the Man of Sorrows; my tears are counted by Him who shed first His tears and then His blood for me. He will impose no needless burden, and exact no unnecessary sacrifice. There was no unnecessary drop in the cup of His own sufferings; neither will there be in that of His people. 'Though He slay me, yet will I trust in Him.'"

--John MacDuff

SEPTEMBER 18 ---

"Fear not, little flock: for it is your Father's good pleasure to give you the kingdom."
(Lu 12:32)

Think upon this marvelous verse for just a moment or two. Think of all the trials you have experienced, the sins you have committed and now regret, the disappointments you have known, the difficulties you have encountered, the failings you have discovered within yourself, and realize that transcending them all is the Lord's assurance that you need not fear.

If you have accepted Christ then you, dear reader, are part of God's little flock. You are precious to Him and these words are as much for you as for any other person, living or dead, who has ever walked the earth. His words are to be a comfort to you, to reassure you, to remind you that you have nothing to fear, for you are a member of the flock He is leading to the home He has prepared for you. No matter who you are, what you have done, how many times you have failed or how many wrong turns you have made along the way, it is His good pleasure -- that means His delight, His full intention -- to give you the Kingdom.

How can this be? How can the Lord so willingly and lovingly bequeath His kingdom to a fallen race like ours? Because of His love. Amazing as this may seem, once a soul believes upon Christ and enters into relationship with Him, there is no power on earth that can prevent his receiving the Kingdom of God.

Think upon this gift today, and marvel at what it means to you. Even though you cannot fully understand all its meanings, dwell upon it. Yes, you will have trials. Yes, you will have mountains to climb as you make your way to the high places. But you do not have to fear. You shall inherit all He has prepared for you. You are now, and always will be, the object of His love and His delight. Your inheritance is assured. You are a child of the King.

SEPTEMBER 19 ---

"...and His communication is with the simple." (Pr 3:32; Douay-Rheims Translation)

"Let us recognize the fact that God is incessantly speaking in us. He speaks in the impenitent, but, stunned by the noise of the world and their passions, they cannot hear Him; the interior voice is to them a fable... God speaks, too, in wise and enlightened persons, whose lives, outwardly correct, seem adorned with many virtues. But such are often too full of themselves and their own thoughts to listen to God. Everything is turned into reasoning; they substitute the principles of natural wisdom and the plans of human prudence for what would come infinitely better through the channel of simplicity and docility to the word of God. They seem to be good, sometimes better than others; and they are, perhaps, up to a point; but it is a mixed goodness. They are still in possession of themselves, and desire always to be so. They love to be in the hands of their own counsel, and to be strong and great in their own eyes.

I thank You, O my God with Jesus Christ, that You have hidden Your ineffable secrets from these great and wise ones, while revealing them to feeble and humble souls. It is with babes alone that You are wholly unreserved; the others You treat in their own way. They desire knowledge and great virtues, and You give them dazzling illuminations and convert them into heroes. But this is not the better part. There is something more hidden for Your dearest children. They lie with John upon Your breast.

As for the great ones who are constantly afraid of stooping and becoming lowly, You leave them to their greatness. But they shall not experience Your caresses or Your intimacy, for to deserve these they would have to become as little children, and play upon Your knees.

I have often observed that a rude, ignorant sinner, just beginning to be touched by a lively sense of the love of God, is much more disposed to listen to the inward language of the Spirit of Grace, than those enlightened and learned persons who have grown old in their own wisdom. God, whose sole desire is to communicate Himself, cannot, so to speak, find where to set his foot in souls so full of themselves, who have grown fat upon their own wisdom and virtues; but, as says the Scripture, 'his secret is with the simple.'"

-- Francois Fenelon

"Thy sun shall no more go down; neither shall thy moon withdraw itself: for the Lord shall be thine everlasting light, and the days of thy mourning shall be ended." (Is 60:20)

"Just as the sun shines its beautiful, life-giving light on and into our earth, so God shines into our hearts the light of His glory, of His love and of Christ His Son. Our heart is meant to have that light filling and gladdening it all day. It can have it because God is our sun, and it is written, 'Thy sun shall no more go down.' God's love shines on us without ceasing.

But, can we indeed enjoy it all day? Yes, we can. And how can we? Let nature give us the answer.

Those beautiful trees and flowers, with all the green grass, what do they do to keep the sun shining on them? They do nothing; they simply bask in the sunshine when it comes. The sun is millions of miles away, but over all that distance it comes, its own light and joy. And, the tiniest flower that lifts its little head upward is met by the same exuberance of light and blessing as flood the widest landscape. We do not have to care for the light we need for our day's work. The sun cares, and provides and shines the light around us all day. We simply count upon it, receive it, and enjoy it.

The only difference between nature and grace is this: that what the trees and the flowers do unconsciously, as they drink in the blessing of the light, is to be, for us, a voluntary and loving acceptance. Faith, simple faith in God's Word and love, is to be the opening of the eyes and the heart, to receive and enjoy the unspeakable glory of His grace. And just as the trees, day by day and month by month, stand and grow into beauty and fruitfulness, just welcoming whatever sunshine the sun may give, so it is the very highest exercise of our Christian life just to abide in the light of God. Let it, and let Him, fill us with the life and the brightness it brings."

-- Andrew Murray

"...and the vail shall divide unto you between the holy place and the most holy." (Ex 26:33)

"The vail was rent when Jesus died, the Holy Ghost signifying that from that moment access was free into the Holiest. All believers are now welcome to draw near and live in the perpetual presence of God, their Father, even as Jesus did in His earthly life, and as He does in the Heaven of Heavens. This is the clear teaching of Hebrews 10:19-22: 'Having therefore, brethren, boldness to enter into the holiest by the blood of Jesus, by a new and living way, which He hath consecrated for us, through the vail, that is to say, His flesh; and having a High Priest over the house of God; let us draw near with a true heart, in full assurance of faith, having our hearts sprinkled from an evil conscience and our bodies washed with pure water.'

But there is a deeper significance still. The new and living way was opened through the rending of the flesh of Jesus Christ. As His flesh was rent on the Cross, the Temple vail was also rent from top to bottom. And it is only when we have chosen the Cross, with its shame and death, as the lot of our self-life, that we enter into immediate fellowship with God, which is described as 'within the vail.'

How many there are who never get beyond that dividing vail. They know the brazen altar of Atonement, the laver of daily washing, the golden altar of intercession; but they are never admitted to that blessed intimacy of communion which sees the Shekinah glory between the cherubim and blood-sprinkled mercy-seat.

Oh, Spirit of God, apply the blood to sprinkle our consciences, and the water to cleanse the habits of our daily life; and lead us where our Forerunner and Priest awaits us."   – F. B. Meyer

SEPTEMBER 22 --

"Whosoever shall receive one of such children in my name, receiveth me: and whosoever shall receive me, receiveth not me, but him that sent me." (Mark 9:37)

"How terribly...have the theologians misrepresented God! Nearly all of them represent Him as a great King on a grand throne, thinking how grand He is, and making it the business of His being and the end of His universe to keep up His glory, wielding the bolts of a Jupiter against them that take His name in vain. They would not admit to this, but if you follow out what they say it comes to this.

Brothers, have you found our king? There He is, kissing little children and saying they are like God. There He is at table with the head of a fisherman resting on His bosom, feeling somewhat heavy at heart that even he, the beloved disciple, cannot yet understand Him very well. The simplest peasant who loved his children and his sheep is a truer type of our God in comparison with that monstrosity of a monarch.

The God who is ever uttering in the profusion of nature; who takes millions of years to form a soul that shall understand him and be blessed; who never is in haste; who welcomes the simplest thought of truth or beauty; the God of music, of painting, of building, the Lord of Hosts, the God of mountains and oceans; this is the God of little children and he alone can be perfectly, abandonedly simple and devoted....

Therefore, with angels and with archangels, with the spirits of the just made perfect, with the little children of the kingdom, yes, with the Lord Himself, and for all them that do not know Him, we praise and magnify and laud His name, saying 'Our Father.' We do not draw back because we are unworthy, nor even because we are hard-hearted and care not for that which is good. For it is His childlikeness that makes Him our God and Father. The perfection of His relation to us swallows up all our imperfections, all our defects, all our evils; for our childhood is born of His fatherhood. That man is perfect in faith who can come to God in the utter dearth of his feelings and his desires, without a glow or an aspiration, with the weight of low thoughts, failures and wandering forgetfulness, and say to Him, 'You are my refuge, because you are my home.'

> Sometimes I wake, and, lo, I have forgot,
> And drifted out upon an ebbing sea,
> My soul that was at rest now resteth not,
> For I am with myself and not with thee;
> Truth seems a blind moon in a glaring morn,
> Where nothing is but sick-heart vanity:
> Oh, Thou who knowest, save thy child forlorn."
> --George MacDonald

SEPTEMBER 23 --

"Rejoice in the Lord always: and again I say, Rejoice. Let your moderation be known unto all men. The Lord is at hand." (Ph 4: 4-5)

"There is a certain border-land in which we must live no small part of our time. It is not the country of compromise, but of give and take. We are bound by conscientiousness to be truthful, but that does not mean being brutally truthful. We are bound to be polite and self-sacrificing, but bound also to let others deny themselves for us. We are bound to give, but no less to receive. We may have a right to be annoyed, but we need not wholly live up to it. We may be obliged to reprove, but we can also plan some scheme of kindness. Life demands a firm hand, but there is no law against wearing a velvet glove.

Thy will be done means more than thy will be borne. No matter what sorrow invades our life, we are still to do God's will. We shall see afterwards that the sorrow rightly accepted fitted us to do some new duty, or to do our old duty more effectively. 'Speak, Lord, for thy servant heareth,' is the right cry in the hour of bewildering grief. 'What wilt thou have me to learn and do?' It is not how we like our new lesson, but how we learn it that is of the highest importance, not how we feel at the loss of an old tool, but can we make more faithful and fruitful use of the tools that are left. Life can never be the same, we say, but it ought not to be, and what it costs to make it better we can well afford to pay. Instead, then, of a resignation, which passionately or passively, defiantly or despairingly, lets go of the prized possession, let there be the heroism of renunciation which says, 'Now that I know God's will, I lay this down of myself, to live a better life—more blessed and more of a blessing without it, than I could have been with it.' How certainly will the future justify such faith, and a braver bearing of God's will lead to a better doing of God's will." — Maltbie Davenport Babcock

SEPTEMBER 24 ---

"Casting all your care upon him; for he careth for you." (I Pe 5:7)

"It is indeed natural to us to wish and to plan, and it is merciful of the Lord to disappoint our plans, and to cross our wishes. For we cannot be safe, much less happy, except in proportion as we are weaned from our own wills and made desirous of being directed by His guidance. When we are enlightened by His Word this becomes a familiar truth to us but we seldom reduce it to practice without being trained awhile in the school of disappointment.

The schemes we form look so plausible and convenient that when they are broken, we are ready to say, 'What a pity!' We try again, and with no better success; we are grieved, and perhaps angry, and plan out another, and so on; at length, in a course of time, experience and observation begin to convince us that we are not able, nor are we worthy, to choose what is right for ourselves. Then the Lord's invitation to cast our cares upon Him, and His promise to take care of us, appear attractive to us, and as we abstain from planning, His plan in our favor gradually opens, and he does more and better for us than we could have either asked or thought.

I can hardly recall a single plan of mine that has not been satisfied that, had it taken place in the season and circumstance as I proposed, it would, humanly speaking, have proved my ruin; or at least it would have deprived me of the greater good the Lord had designed for me.

We judge of things by their present appearances, but the Lord sees them in their consequences; if we could see as He does we would also be perfectly of His mind, but, as we cannot, it is an unspeakable mercy that He manages for us, whether we are pleased with His management or not.

It is actually one of His heaviest judgments when God gives up any person or people to the way of their own hearts and to walk after their own counsels." — John Newton

SEPTEMBER 25 ---

"But as many as received him, to them gave he power to become the sons of God, even to them that believe on his name:" (Jo 1:12)

"We know that when the Lord Jesus came into the world, the greater part of men despised and rejected him; but there were a few who received him. They believed in him; that is, they received Jesus into their hearts. And now, observe what a glorious privilege God bestowed upon these believers. He gave them 'power to become the sons of God.' He adopted them as his sons and heirs. It is written in Romans 8:15, 'You have received the Spirit of adoption, whereby we cry, Abba, Father;' and again, 'If children, then heirs.' God will bestow upon his adopted children his riches in glory. 'He who overcomes shall inherit all things. I will be his God, and he shall be my son.' (Re 21:7)

But what is the reason that some believed in Jesus? Were they by nature better than others? Were their hearts softer, so that they could not reject their dying Savior? No, they were by nature like others, but they were born of God. As it is written in Jo 1:13, 'Who were born... of God;' that is, of the Spirit of God.

We are also told what they were NOT born of. Let us consider each of the expressions: 'Not of blood,' that is, they did not believe because they were of the blood of any good man, such as Abraham. Many who were of the blood of Abraham did not believe in Christ. Neither were they born of the will of the flesh. They did not believe because it was the will of their flesh, or of their nature, to believe. They did not choose Christ from their own power. If they had been left to themselves, they would have refused him; for the natural man does not receive the things of the Spirit of God (I Co 2:14). Neither were they born of the will of man. They did not believe because it was the will of any man that they should believe. Such people are not converted merely because they hear a minister speak of God. It is the will of God that makes a man believe.

If we have been born of God, we see that it was not because we were of the blood of any pious parents or ancestors; it was not because it was the will of our flesh to believe, for we were dead in sins. It was not because it was the will of man. No pious minister or friend could have made us believe. But if we have been raised from the death of sin, it was the power of God that raised us. Therefore to God be all the glory!"   – F. L. Mortimer

SEPTEMBER 26 --

"And he arose, and came to his father. But when he was yet a great way off, his father saw him, and had compassion, and ran, and fell on his neck, and kissed him." (Lu 15:20)

"This world is God's prodigal son. The heart of God bleeds over His prodigal. It has been gone so long, and the home circle is broken. He has spent all the wealth of His thought on a plan for winning the prodigal back home. Angels and men have marveled over that plan, its sweep, its detail, its strength and wisdom, its tenderness.

He needs man for His plan. He will use man. That is true. He will honor man in service. That is true. But these only touch the edge of the truth. The pathway from God to a human heart is through a human heart. When He came to the great strategic move in His plan, He Himself came down as a man and made that move. He needs man for His plan.

The greatest agency put into man's hands is prayer. To fully understand this one needs to define prayer. And to define prayer adequately one must use the language of war.

Peace language is not equal to the situation. The earth is in a state of war. It is being hotly besieged and so one must use war talk to grasp the facts with which prayer is concerned. Prayer from God's side is communication between Himself and His allies in the enemy's country. Prayer is not persuading God. It does not influence God's purpose. It is not winning Him over to our side; never that. He is far more eager for what we are rightly eager for than we ever are. What there is of wrong and sin and suffering that pains you, pains Him far more. He knows more about it. He is more keenly sensitive to it than the most sensitive one of us. Whatever of heart yearning there may be that moves you to prayer is from Him. God takes the initiative in all prayer. It starts with Him. True prayer moves in a circle. It begins in the heart of God, sweeps down into a human heart upon the earth, so intersecting the circle of the earth, which is the battle-field of prayer, and then it goes back again to its starting point, having accomplished its purpose on the downward swing."   – S. D. Gordon

SEPTEMBER 27 --

"But without a parable spake he not unto them: and when they were alone, he expounded all things to his disciples." (Mark 4:34)

"What is the exact meaning of the word 'disciple'? It means 'a learner,' one who is under a teacher, whose submissive and devoted pupil he has become, and from whom he receives continual instruction. Thus, a disciple of Christ is one who is admitted by the Lord Jesus into His school, one whom He himself condescends personally to instruct, and who therefore learns from Him to be meek and lowly of heart.

A disciple of Jesus sits meekly at the Redeemer's feet, receiving into his heart the gracious words which fall from his lips. This was Mary's happy posture, whom the Lord commended for choosing the better part. It is also the posture of all God's saints, according to the ancient declaration, 'Yes, he loved the people; all his saints are in thy hand; and they sat down at your feet, every one shall receive of thy words.' (De 33:3).

But a true and sincere disciple not only listens to his Master's instructions, he acts as He bids. So a disciple of Jesus is one who copies his Master's example, and is conformed to his Master's image. A sincere disciple is also characterized by the love which he bears to his Master; so a disciple of Jesus is one who treasures up the words of Christ in his heart, ponders over His precious promises, and takes delight in His glorious Person, love, and blood....

To select an obstinate, ungodly, perverse rebel, and place him in the School of Christ and at the feet of Jesus is the highest favor God can bestow upon any child. How great must be that kindness whereby the Lord condescends to bestow his grace on an alien and an enemy, to soften him by His Spirit and thus cause him to grow up into the image and likeness of His own dear Son. What are earthly honors and titles when compared with this kind of favor, which is conferred upon those whose foundation is in the dust? Compared with this high privilege, all earthly honors and titles sink into utter insignificance."   – Joseph Philpot

SEPTEMBER 28 ---

"For verily I say unto you, That whosoever shall say unto this mountain, Be thou removed, and be thou cast into the sea; and shall not doubt in his heart, but shall believe that those things which he saith shall come to pass; he shall have whatsoever he saith." (Mark 11:23)

"Faith deals with God, and is conscious of God. It deals with the Lord Jesus Christ and sees in Him a Saviour; it deals with God's Word, and lays hold of the truth; it deals with the Spirit of God, and is energized and inspired by its holy fire.

God is the great objective of faith, for faith rests its whole weight on His Word. Faith is not an aimless act of the soul, but a looking to God and a resting upon His promises. Just as love and hope always have an objective, so, also, has faith. Faith is not believing just anything; it is believing God, resting in Him and trusting His Word.

Faith gives birth to prayer, and grows stronger, strikes deeper, rises higher, in the struggles and wrestlings of mighty petitioning. Faith is the substance of things hoped for, the assurance and realization of the inheritance of the saints. Faith, too, is humble and persevering. It can wait and pray; it can stay on its knees, or lie in the dust. It is the one great condition of prayer; the lack of it lies at the root of all poor praying, feeble praying, little praying, unanswered praying."   – E. M. Bounds

"For whatsoever is born of God overcometh the world: and this is the victory that overcometh the world, even our faith." (I Jo 5:4)

"And this commandment have we from him, That he who loveth God love his brother also." (I Jo 4:21)

"We read that the fruit of the Spirit is love. God is love, Christ is love, and we should not be surprised to read about the love of the Spirit. What a blessed attribute is this. May I call it the dome of the temple of graces. Better still, it is the crown of crowns worn by the Triune God. Human love is a natural emotion which flows forth toward the object of our affections. But Divine love is as high above human love as heaven is above the earth. The natural man is of the earth, earthy, and however pure his love may be, it is weak and imperfect at best. But the love of God is perfect and entire, wanting nothing. It is as a mighty ocean in its greatness, dwelling with and flowing from the Eternal Spirit.

In Romans 5:5, we read: 'And hope maketh not ashamed, because the love of God is shed abroad in our hearts by the Holy Ghost which is given to us.' Now, if we are co-workers with God, there is one thing we must possess, and that is love. A man may be a very successful lawyer and have no love for his clients, and yet get on very well. A man may be a very successful physician and have no love for his patients, and yet be a very good physician; a man may be a very successful merchant and have no love for his customers, and yet he may do a good business and succeed; but no man can be a co-worker with God without love. If our service is mere profession on our part, the quicker we cease from it the better. If a man takes up God's work as he would take up any profession, the sooner he gets out of it the better.

We cannot work for God without love. It is the only fruit-producing tree on this sin-cursed earth that is acceptable to God. If I have no love for God nor for my fellow man, then my work cannot be acceptable. I am like sounding brass and a tinkling cymbal. We are told that the 'love of God is shed abroad in our hearts by the Holy Ghost.' Now, if that love has been shed abroad in our hearts, we are ready for God's service; if it has not, we are not ready. It is so easy to reach a man when you love him; all barriers are broken down and swept away." – D. L. Moody

"And the servant of the Lord must not strive; but be gentle unto all men, apt to teach, patient," (II Ti 2:24)

The Bible tells us about the traits that are important for us to acquire as Christians. One of these is gentleness.

Most of us, if we're honest, will have to admit we aren't as gentle as we'd like to be. It's easy to forget about being gentle when our day becomes crowded with responsibilities, interruptions and problems.

What does the word "gentle" actually mean? It's more than just being nice. It's more than merely trying to act like a good person. The quality of gentleness is in truth an attitude of the heart. When we are gentle, we are not striving to compete with anyone. We're not trying to get ahead of them, not focusing on what they think of us, not waiting for them to be kind to us before we become willing to be kind in return. Gentleness is willing to be the first to reach out, the first to extend concern for the welfare of others. Gentleness melts away the barrier of defensiveness and, if a problem should arise, it is willing to take the steps needed to work through conflict with a calm and measured attitude instead of an unthinking rebuke or abrupt outburst.

People sometimes mistake gentleness for weakness. The fact is that real gentleness requires a great deal more strength and courage than harshness does. Harshness is usually based on self-centeredness and fear. Gentleness requires strength of character. It requires us to be balanced and kind even when we are being opposed or criticized by others. Gentleness doesn't mean we must always give in, keep quiet or avoid conflict. It doesn't mean we have to be cowards or people-pleasers. Instead, it means we must treat others with respect even when it is important to disagree with them. It means asserting our beliefs with a posture of kindness rather than one that is overbearing or rude.

Jesus was gentle. His desire is for us to become gentle, too. His disciples didn't start out as gentle people, but over the years, as they were trained and perfected in the knowledge of God, they became more and more gentle. It was a long, arduous process for them. It will be for us, too, but we can grow in the quality of gentleness if we pray for it and are willing to let the Holy Spirit work with us. If any single trait can alleviate hard feelings, melt away misunderstandings and open the door to love, it has to be the trait of gentleness.

OCTOBER 1 --

"For He doth not afflict willingly nor grieve the children of men." (Lam 3:33)

"In our seasons of trial, when we are under some inscrutable dispensation, how apt we are to harbor murmuring thoughts: 'All these things are against me;' 'Couldn't this overwhelming blow have been spared?' 'Why wasn't this dark cloud prevented from afflicting me and my home?' 'Couldn't this trial have been less severe?' 'Surely the Lord has forgotten to be gracious.' No, these afflictions are errands of mercy in disguise.

'He does not afflict willingly.' There is nothing capricious or arbitrary about your God's dealings. Unutterable tenderness is the character of all His actions. The world may wound by unkindness; trusted friends may become treacherous; a brother may speak with unnecessary harshness; but the Lord is 'abundant in goodness and in truth.' He appoints no needless pangs. When he appears like Joseph to 'speak roughly,' there are gentle undertones of love. The stern accents are assumed because He has precious lessons that could not otherwise have been taught.

Be assured there is some deep necessity in all He does. On our calenders of sorrow we should note, 'it was needed.' Some unfruitful branch in the tree required pruning. Some wheat required to be cast overboard to lighten the ship and avert disaster....

We, in our blind unbelief, may speak of trials we imagine might have been spared, chastisements that are unnecessarily severe. But the day is coming when every step of the Lord's procedure will be vindicated; when we shall own and recognize each separate experience of sorrow to have been an important period in the history of our souls."   – John MacDuff

OCTOBER 2 --

"And Jesus said unto him, Go thy way; thy faith hath made thee whole. And immediately he received his sight, and followed Jesus in the way." (Mark 10:52)

"Christ asks [us to make the] surrender of faith. When He spoke to the impotent man His word of command was to be obeyed. The man believed that there was truth and power in Christ's word; in that faith he rose and walked. By faith he obeyed. And what Christ said to others was for him, too: 'Go thy way; thy faith hath made thee whole.'

Of us, too, Christ asks this faith, that His word may change our impotence into strength, and fit us for that walk in newness of life for which we have been quickened in Him. If we do not believe this, if we will not take courage and say, with Paul, 'I can do all things through Christ, which strengtheneth me,' we cannot obey. But if we will listen to the word that tells us of the walk that is not only possible, but has been proved and seen in God's saints from of old, if we will fix our eye on the mighty, living, loving Christ, who speaks in power, 'Rise and walk,' we shall take courage and obey. We shall rise and begin to walk in Him and His strength. In faith, apart from and above all feeling, we shall accept and trust an unseen Christ as our strength, and go on in the strength of the Lord God. We shall know Christ as the strength of our life. We shall know, and tell, and prove that Jesus Christ has made us whole.

Can it be true? Yes, it can. He has done it for many: He will do it for you. But beware of forming wrong conceptions of what must take place. When the impotent man was made whole he still had to learn how to use his new-found strength. If he wanted to dig or build or learn a trade, he had to begin at the beginning. Do not expect at once to be totally proficient in prayer or any part of the Christian life. But do expect and be confident of this one thing, that, as you have trusted yourself to Christ to be your health and strength, He will lead and teach you. Begin to pray with a sense of your ignorance and weakness, but in a joyful assurance that He will work in you what you need. Rise and walk each day in a holy confidence that He is with you and in you. Just accept Jesus Christ the Living One, and trust Him to do His work.

Will you do it? Have you done it? Even now Jesus speaks, 'Rise and walk.' Make your reply: 'Amen, Lord. At Thy word I come. I rise to walk with You, and in You, and like You.'" -- Andrew Murray

OCTOBER 3 --

"Whoso keepeth his mouth and his tongue keepeth his soul from troubles." (Pr 21:23)

Most of us can probably think of at least one individual we know who is a perfectionist. You know what a perfectionist is: it's the person who insists on taking great pains but instead just ends up being one. Of all the traits that can harm a relationship, perfectionism has to rank somewhere at the top of the list. It can end up causing hurt, frustration, resentment and even permanent damage, especially if it's exhibited by parents toward their children.

Why do some of us become perfectionists? There are many reasons. Some of us may have been raised in environments where failure or frailty were not acceptable, and we felt we had to excel at everything to either gain approval or avoid rejection. Or, we may have discovered at some point in our lives that if we were to feel safe, either physically or emotionally, we had to keep tight control over our circumstances; as a result, we became perfectionists. Some of us, on the other hand, may feel we were simply born that way. Whatever the reason, perfectionism can end up doing a lot of damage. It can drive us to try to make everyone and everything around us measure up to our high standards. Then, when family members, friends or business associates rebel against our compulsive behavior, we wonder what their problem is – weren't we merely trying to help?

One symptom of perfectionism is a critical attitude which always seems to have something discouraging to say about ourselves, about others, or about life in general. People, places and things just don't conform to the way we think they should be. Perfectionism can rear its head anywhere, even within religion. It can drive us to attempt to become "perfect" Christians. We may find ourselves constantly striving to be perfectly loving, perfectly holy, or perfectly forgiving. Then, when we fail to measure up, we wind up feeling like failures and wonder why God is so demanding of us; after all, we've been trying so hard.

How do we overcome perfectionism? It's a day by day, step by step process. One thing we can do is to resist those urges to correct, to judge, to criticize and to feel superior to others. We can stop doing for others all the time and let them have the experience of handling their own problems. We can let others be imperfect, and we can let ourselves be imperfect, too.

Most of us would probably agree it isn't the perfectionist in our lives who makes us feel loved and accepted – it's the person who treats us with respect, patience, tolerance and understanding. These are the traits that make people thrive. Perfectionism makes them wither.

Jesus was perfect, yet he was not a perfectionist. He was loving, patient and understanding of people and their shortcomings. He loved sinners before they repented, not just after. He kept encouraging his disciples to grow and pursue holiness, even though they continued to sin and make mistakes. If we will surrender ourselves to Jesus, He will help us to become less perfectionistic, and more like Him.

Father, please help me today to surrender any perfectionism that is in me and allow You to put Your personality in its place.

OCTOBER 4 --

"Blessed are the peacemakers: for they shall be called the children of God." (Ma 5:9)

"This is the seventh of the beatitudes: and seven was the number of perfection among the Hebrews. It may be that the Saviour placed the peacemaker as the seventh upon the list because he most nearly approaches the perfect man in Christ Jesus. He who would have perfect blessedness, so far as it can be enjoyed on earth, must attain to this seventh benediction, and become a peacemaker. There is significance also in the position of the text. The verse which precedes it speaks of the blessedness of 'the pure in heart: for they shall see God.' It is well to understand that we are to be 'first pure, then peaceable.' Our peaceableness is never to be a compact with sin, or toleration of evil.

We must set our faces like flints against everything which is contrary to God and his holiness: purity being in our souls a settled matter, we can go on to peaceableness. Not less does the verse that follows seem to have been put there on purpose. However peaceable we may be in this world, yet we shall be misrepresented and misunderstood. And we should not marvel at this, for even the Prince of Peace, by his very peacefulness, brought fire upon the earth. He himself, though he loved mankind and did no ill, was 'despised and rejected of men, a man of sorrows and acquainted with grief.' Lest, therefore, the peaceable in heart should be surprised when they meet with enemies, it is added in the following verse, 'Blessed are they which are persecuted for righteousness' sake: for theirs is the kingdom of heaven.' Thus, the peacemakers are not only pronounced to be blessed, but they are compassed about with blessings.

Lord, give us grace to climb to this seventh beatitude. Purify us, that we may be 'first pure, then peaceable,' and fortify us, that our peaceableness may not lead us into cowardice and despair, when for Your sake we are persecuted."   – C. H. Spurgeon

OCTOBER 5 --

"Thus saith the Lord, thy redeemer, and he that formed thee from the womb, I [am] the Lord that maketh all [things]; that stretcheth forth the heavens alone; that spreadeth abroad the earth by myself;" (Is 44:24)

"God who made us out of nothing, recreates us, as it were, every moment of the day. It does not follow that because we were here yesterday, we shall of course be here today; we should cease to exist and return into the nothingness out of which He formed us if God did not prevent it. Of ourselves we are nothing; we are but what God has made us, and only for so long a time as He pleases. He has but to withdraw the hand that sustains us and we will plunge into the abyss of annihilation, as a stone held in the air must fall when its support is removed. Life and existence, then, are only ours because they are conferred by God.

There are blessings, however, of a purer and higher order than these; a well-ordered life is better than mere life; virtue is of a higher price than health; uprightness of heart and the love of God are as far above temporal goods as the heavens are above the earth. If these lower and baser gifts, then, are held only through the mercy and at the pleasure of God, how much more must it be true of the sublime gift of his love!

They do not know You, O my God, who regard You as only an all-powerful Being, separate from themselves, giving laws to nature and only acting as the creator of everything which we behold. They know You only in part. They do not know that which is most marvelous and which most nearly concerns Your rational creatures. To know that You are the God of my heart, that You do there that which pleases You; this is the knowledge that elevates and affects me. When I am good, it is because You render me so; not only do You fashion my heart as You please, but You give me one like Your own... You are the life of my soul just as my soul is the life of my body; You are more intimately present to me than I am to myself. This self, to which I am so attached and which I have so ardently loved, should be like a stranger to me in comparison with You; You are the One who bestowed it to me; without You, it never would have existed; therefore, it is Your desire that I should love You better than I love it."   – Francois Fenelon

"For we have not an high priest which cannot be touched with the feeling of our infirmities..." (He 4:15)

"There is a beautiful touch of loving thoughtfulness in the account of Christ's miracle at Capernaum in providing the tribute money. After the reference to Peter's interview with the tax collector, the Scriptures add, when he was come into the house, Jesus prevented him (Ma 17:25); that is, anticipated him, as the old Saxon word means. Jesus arranged for the need before Peter had to speak about it at all and sent him down to the sea to find the piece of gold in the mouth of the fish. So the Lord is always thinking in advance of our needs. He loves to save us from embarrassment. He anticipates and cares by laying up His loving acts and providing before the emergency comes. Then with exquisite tenderness the Master adds: 'That, take, and give to them for me and thee.' He puts Himself first in the embarrassing need and bears the heavy end of the burden for His distressed child. He makes our cares His cares, our sorrows His sorrows, our shame His shame. He is able to be touched with the feeling of our infirmities."

– A. B. Simpson

My Lord, I find that nothing else will do,
But follow where thou goest, sit at thy feet,
And where I have thee not, still run to meet.
Roses are scentless, hopeless are the morns,
Rest is but weakness, laughter crackling thorns,
If thou, the Truth, do not make them the true:
Thou art my life, O Christ, and nothing else will do.
-- George MacDonald

"Who are kept by the power of God through faith unto salvation ready to be revealed in the last time." (I Pe 1:5)

"Are any of you who are believers afraid that you will some day bring disgrace on your profession of faith? Then study these words. 'Kept' is the whole history of a believer's life. It tells us we are very weak, for we need to be kept; but, at the same time, it is a most comforting word, for it tells us we are worth keeping.

God counts us a treasure worth keeping. This truth has a wonderful power to give energy to believers. Rightly viewed, it bears on the interests of holiness in a wonderful manner. There may be ups and downs in the degrees of our faith and of our love, but we cannot be lost, for we are 'kept by the power of God.' The word throws emphasis on the mighty power that grasps and keeps us; it means 'garrisoned by the power of God.' It is God's own power that encompasses us. None shall pluck us out of His hand.

We are kept by the power of God. We are in the arms of omniscience and omnipotence, for the term literally means 'kept in the power of God.' We are resting upon that power, and we need it all. The power of the devil is tremendous, the power of the world is tremendous. Its current often carries us away. No wonder if we sometimes say, 'I shall one day perish.' We are 'kept by the power of God.' If you want to know the workings of that power, read Ephesians 1:19-23. What a defense; better than ten legions of angels; and yet we have that, too. But Jude says, 'Keep yourselves.' We are to keep ourselves, but how? 'By faith.' God keeps us by making us keep ourselves 'by faith.'

We are kept by faith. God's part is to put forth His power; our part is to put forth faith. God enables us to have faith, and He keeps it in us continually, and not all the power of hell can pluck that faith out of our heart. It never decays. We get power continually from God to go on believing from day to day. Our faith will not vanish. It may grow weaker, but it will not disappear. If we give way to unbelief we are letting go our hold of the chain that fastens us to the omnipotent arm. Faith implies that our eye is daily looking to the Cross of Christ - not looking to our feet, not looking about at what might terrify us, but 'looking unto Jesus.' We think of the righteousness He gives us, every day. We think of the blood shed to put away our sin, every day. We think of the new and living way opened to us by Christ, every day. Faith is always looking, not only to the work of Christ, but to His Person. 'He ever liveth to make intercession for us.' He lives to keep His vine and water it every moment."   – Andrew Bonar

OCTOBER 8 --

"Lord, if thou hadst been here, my brother had not died." (Jo 11:21)

"Would Lazarus not have died if Jesus had been there? Do we not read that because Jesus loved the Bethany family, and because He learned of the sickness of Lazarus, therefore He remained two days after the messenger came? Did He not also say that He was glad He had not been there before Lazarus died?

One thing at least we know: it was better as it was — better that Lazarus should not be cured, but should die, and then that Christ's power should be shown in his resurrection. It was therefore an unbelieving 'if,' and a groundless one, which fell from Martha's lips. Yet we are all apt to let similar 'ifs' drop from our lips when trouble comes to us. If we had only tried another physician, or taken the matter in hand a little sooner, our friend had not died. We feel sometimes that sorrow is an evidence that God did not hear our prayers; if He had only heard our cry the trial would have been averted. Yet we have but to read this story through to the end to see that Christ's way was the better way here, as it always is the better way.

> We sadly watched the close of all; life balanced on a breath;
> We saw upon his features fall the awful shade of death.
> All dark and desolate we were, and murmuring nature cried —
> 'Oh, surely, Lord, hadst thou been here, our brother had not died.'
>
> But when its glance the mourner cast, on all that grace had done,
> And thought of life's long warfare passed, and endless victory won,
> The faith prevailing wiped the tears, and looking upward cried,
> 'Oh, surely, Lord, thou hast been here, our brother has not died."
> -- J. R. Miller

OCTOBER 9 --

"I am the vine, ye are the branches: He that abideth in me, and I in him, the same bringeth forth much fruit: for without me ye can do nothing." (Jo 15:5)

"The fact of our oneness with Christ contains the whole thing in a nutshell. If we are one with Him, then of course in the very nature of things we can do nothing without Him. For that which is one cannot act as being two. And if I therefore do anything without Christ, then I am not one with Him in that thing, and like a branch severed from the vine I am withered and worthless. It is as if the branch should recognize its connection with and dependence upon the vine for most of its growth and fruit-bearing and climbing, but should feel a capacity in itself to grow and climb over a certain fence or around the trunk of a certain tree, and should therefore sever its connection with the vine for this part of its living. Of course that which seeks such an independent life will wither and die in the very nature of things. And just so is it with us who are branches of Christ, the true vine. No independent action, whether small or great, is possible to us without withering and death, any more than to the branch of the natural vine....

If our religion is really our life, and not merely something extraneous tacked on to our life, it must necessarily go into everything in which we live; and no act, however human or natural it may be, can be taken out of its control and guidance.

If God is with us always, then He is just as much with us in our business times and our social times as in our religious times, and one moment is as solemn with His presence as another." – Hannah Whitall Smith

"Behold, I have refined thee, but not with silver; I have chosen thee in the furnace of affliction." (Is 48:10)

"According to God's own testimony, it is 'through much tribulation' that we are to enter into the kingdom; and therefore there is no entering into the kingdom of grace here, or the kingdom of glory hereafter, without it. But let this be ever borne in mind, that whatever affliction befalls the saints, it is laid upon them by the hand of God, and that for the express purpose of putting them into a situation and of making them capable of receiving those comforts which God only can bestow.

None but Jesus himself and the Father can comfort a truly afflicted heart. And he can and does from time to time comfort his dear people by a sense of his presence; by a word of power from his gracious lips; by the light of his countenance; by the balm of his atoning blood and dying love; and by the work and witness of the Spirit within. And as they receive this consolation from the mouth of God, their hearts are comforted. How good the Lord is of his own free grace to bestow such blessings upon his redeemed family. May he give us many of them. And may he, wherever he has bestowed upon any of us everlasting consolation, or even a good hope through grace, comfort our hearts as we journey through this valley of tears, and may our consolations be neither few nor small." – Joseph Philpot

"I am the good shepherd, and know my sheep, and am known of mine." (Jo 10:14)

"The Good Shepherd: those who know His voice can attest to the truthfulness and faithfulness of this endearing title and word. Where would they be had He not left His throne of glory, traveled down to this dark valley of the curse and given His life as a ransom for many?

Think of how He loves each separate member of the flock. Though they wander over pathless wild places he continues to pursue them with unwearied patience and care until he finds them.

Think of His love: 'I am the Good Shepherd.' His tender, watchful eye still follows those who wander. The glories of heaven and the songs of angels are unable to dim or alter His affection, His words are as sweet as when first He uttered them: 'I know my sheep.'

Every individual believer — the weakest, the weariest, the faintest — receives His attention. His loving eye follows me day by day as I go out into the wilderness, marks out my pasture and studies all my needs, my trials, my sorrows and perplexities, every steep ascent, every brook that must be crossed, every winding path, every thorny thicket.

'He goes before them.' He does not drive roughly. He guides gently. He does not take His flock over an unknown road; He himself has walked it before. He has drunk of every brook by the way; He himself has 'suffered being tempted.' He is 'able to support those who are tempted.' He seems to say, 'Fear not; I cannot lead you wrong; follow Me in the bleak waste, the blackened wilderness, as well as by the green pastures and the still waters. Do you ask why I have led you away from the sunny side of the valley to some high mountain apart, some cheerless spot of sorrow? Trust me. I will lead you by paths you have not known, but they are all known to me, and selected by me. Follow Me.'

'They know Me.' Dear Reader, can you identify with this phrase? Do you know Him in all the glories of His person, in all the completeness of His finished work, in all the tenderness and unutterable love of His every dealing towards you? Those who are familiar with life in Palestine will tell you that not only do the sheep there follow their shepherd, but even while grazing they look to him to assure themselves that they are near him. Is this your attitude: 'looking unto Jesus?' In all your ways acknowledge Him, and he will direct your paths. Leave the future to His providing.

'The Lord is my Shepherd; I shall not lack.' I shall not lack: this phrase has been beautifully called 'the bleating of Messiah's sheep.' Take it as your watchword during your wilderness wanderings, until grace be perfected in glory. Let this be the record of your simple faith and unwavering trust...the sheep follow him, for they know his voice."   – John MacDuff

OCTOBER 12 ---

"Cause me to hear thy lovingkindness in the morning; for in thee do I trust: cause me to know the way wherein I should walk; for I lift up my soul unto thee." (Ps 143:8)

"...leave to God what is his business and carry on peacefully with your work. Be quite sure that whatever happens to your spiritual life or to your activities in the world is always for the best. Let God act, and abandon yourself to him. Let the chisel and the brush do their work, even though the brush covers the canvas with so many colors that, instead of a picture, it seems there is only a daub. Let us work together with the will of God by a steady and simple submission, a complete forgetfulness of self and concentration on our duties. Let us go straight ahead. Never mind the lack of a map, ignore the lie of the land and take no notice of the places you pass through. Keep going and you will attain all you desire. Everything will be given to you if, with love and obedience, you seek God's kingdom and his righteousness. There are many people who are uneasy and ask: 'Who will guide us toward that mortification of self which will lead us to perfect holiness?' Well, leave them to ransack books in an effort to find a formula to help them. Let us stay united with God by love and let us walk blindly along

the clear straight path of duty. His angels protect you, and if he wants more
from you he will let you know." — Jean-Pierre de Caussade

OCTOBER 13 ---

*"If I take the wings of the morning, and dwell in the uttermost parts of the sea; Even
there shall thy hand lead me, and thy right hand shall hold me." (Ps 139:9-10)*

In former days, before we discovered our need of God, we sailed our
little boats along the seemingly safe shoreline of The World. We might
venture out a little way from land, but we never went far. And we would
only set sail when the sun was shining and the skies were clear. By nightfall
we always returned to The World and the safety of its harbors. We never
gave much thought to what lay beyond.

Then God came into our lives and everything changed. We made the
decision to follow Him to His Kingdom. And so we faced the fact that we
would have to leave The World. We accepted that we had to climb into our
little boats and set sail, trusting God to guide us on our way. The time had
come to embark on the journey to our True Home.

On some days the seas are calm. On others, we encounter storms.
Sometimes our boats are tossed upon the waves and the wind howls. The fog
blocks out the sun and stars; there are times when we worry that we may
have lost our way. Sometimes we wonder if we'll be able to stay afloat.

Let us take heart. God has given us a precious promise. Nothing shall
ever be able to separate us from His sight, nor from His love. Our little ship
will stay afloat and reach the safe harbor of His Kingdom, because He has
promised that it shall be so. Our boats shall never be broken upon the rocks.
They shall never overturn. They will reach His Kingdom's shores. The Lord
has promised that not one of His children shall be lost on the way to the place
He has prepared for them. We can be certain of our safe arrival because God
has already mapped our path through the waters. Our job is to keep our eyes
upon Him. If we will do this, He will guide us. If we will do this each and
every day, He will bring us safely home.

> Have mercy, Lord, on our little ship,
> Guide us on our sacred trip,
> Lead us to the Golden shores
> Where broken hearts Your love restores.
>
> The winds are strong, the way is dark,
> Nonetheless we must embark
> Upon the path, its ways unknown,
> Because Your voice has called us home.

The storms are fierce, the winds are strong,
Their terrors often drown Your song,
At certain times all one can hear
Are cries of doubt and crippling fear.

But Jesus comes miraculously,
To shine His bright divinity,
And by its Light is clearly shone
The path to our eternal Home.

OCTOBER 14 --

"Speak ye comfortably to Jerusalem, and cry unto her, that her warfare is accomplished, that her iniquity is pardoned:..." (Is 40:2)

"It has been the habit of man throughout the ages to heal people by applying some remedy to the outward body when, in fact, the disease is deep inside. Why do converts remain basically unchanged despite so much effort? It is because those over them have dealt only with the outward matters of their lives. There is a better way: Go straight to the heart. Laying down rules and trying to change the outward behavior will not produce a work that will endure in the life of a Christian.

Then what is the answer? Give the new convert the key to his spirit, to the inward parts of his being. Give this secret to him first, and you will discover that his outward life will be changed naturally and easily.

Accomplishing all this is very easy. How? By simply teaching the believer to seek God within his own heart. Show the new Christian that he can set his mind on Jesus Christ and return to Him whenever he has wandered away. Furthermore, show him he should do all and suffer all with a single eye to pleasing his God. What a difference it will make. The new convert will be led to Jesus Christ; he will discover that the Lord Jesus is the source of all grace; and he will see that in Him is everything needed for life and godliness.

Any of you who are stewards of men's souls, I urge you to lead these young ones in Christ in this very way. Why? Because this way is Jesus Christ. It is not I, but Christ Himself urging you by His own blood that was shed for believers: 'Speak ye comfortably to Jerusalem....'

I would emphasize again: The heart is the key. The heart alone can oppose His sovereignty. But conversely, in gaining the heart, the Lord's sovereignty in the believer's life is confessed and highly honored."

--Jeanne Guyon

"But let him ask in faith, nothing wavering. For he that wavereth is like a wave of the sea driven with the wind and tossed. For let not that man think that he shall receive any thing of the Lord. A double minded man [is] unstable in all his ways." (Ja 1:6-8)

"[When we pray] there must be confident, unwavering expectation. But there is a faith that goes beyond expectation, that believes that the prayer is heard and the promise granted. This comes out in the Revised Version of Mark 11:24: 'Therefore I say unto you, All things whatsoever ye pray and ask for, believe that ye *have* received them, and ye shall have them.'

But how can one get this faith?

Let us say with all emphasis, it cannot be pumped up. Many a one reads this promise about the prayer of faith, and then asks for things that he desires and tries to make himself believe that God has heard the prayer. This ends only in disappointment, for it is not real faith and the thing is not granted. It is at this point that many people make a collapse of faith altogether by trying to work up faith by an effort of their will, and as the thing they made themselves believe they would get is not given, the very foundation of faith is oftentimes undermined.

But how does real faith come?

Romans 10:17 answers the question: 'So then faith cometh by hearing, and hearing *by the Word of God.*' If we are to have real faith, we must study the Word of God and find out what is promised, then simply believe the promises of God. Faith must have a warrant. Trying to believe something that you want to believe is not faith. Believing what God says in His Word is faith. If I am to have faith when I pray, I must find some promise in the Word of God on which to rest my faith. Faith furthermore comes through the Spirit. The Spirit knows the will of God, and if I pray in the Spirit, and look to the Spirit to teach me God's will, He will lead me out in prayer along the line of that will, and give me faith that the prayer is to be answered; but in no case does real faith come by simply determining that you are going to get the thing that you want to get. If there is no promise in the Word of God, and no clear leading of the Spirit, there can be no real faith, and there should be no upbraiding of self for lack of faith in such a case. But if the thing desired is promised in the Word of God, we may well upbraid ourselves for lack of faith if we doubt; for we are making God a liar by doubting His Word."

-- Reuben Archer Torrey

"Trust in him at all times; ye people, pour out your heart before him: God [is] a refuge for us. Selah." (Ps 62:8)

"We can no more trust and keep on trusting than we can do anything else of ourselves. Even in this it must be 'Jesus only.' We are to look to Him not only to be the Author and Finisher of our faith, but we are to look to Him for all the intermediate fulfillment of the work of faith (II Thessalonians 1:11). We must ask Him to go on fulfilling it in us, committing even this to His power.

> For we both may and must
> Commit our very faith to Him,
> Entrust to Him our trust.

What a long time it takes us to come down to the conviction, and still more to the realization, that without Him we can do nothing. He must work all our works in us. 'This is the work of God, that you believe in Him whom He has sent' (John 6:29). And no less must it be the work of God that we go on believing and that we go on trusting.

Then, dear friends, if you are longing to trust Him with unbroken and unwavering trust, cease the effort and drop the burden and *now* entrust your trust to Him. He is just as well able to keep that as any other part of the complex lives that we want Him to take and keep for Himself. And do not just pass on, content with the thought, 'Yes, that is a good idea. Perhaps I should find that a great help.' Do it now. It is no help to the sailor to see a flash of light across a dark sea if he does not instantly steer accordingly."

-- Frances Ridley Havergal

OCTOBER 17 --

"[but] the LORD [was] not in the wind: and after the wind an earthquake; [but] the LORD [was] not in the earthquake: And after the earthquake a fire; [but] the LORD [was] not in the fire: and after the fire a still small voice." (I Ki 19:11-12)

"A gentleman was asked by an artist friend of some note to come to his home, and see a painting just finished. He went at the time appointed, was shown by an attendant into a room which was quite dark, and was left there. He was much surprised, but quietly awaited developments. After perhaps fifteen minutes the artist friend came into the room with a cordial greeting, and took him up to the studio to see the painting, which was greatly admired. When bidding his friend goodbye, the artist said laughingly, 'I suppose you thought it odd to be left in that dark room so long.' 'Yes,' the visitor said, 'I did.' 'Well,' said his friend, 'I knew that if you came into my studio with the glare of the street in your eyes you could not appreciate the fine coloring of the picture. So I left you in the dark room till the glare was removed from your eyes.'

The first stage of Moses' prayer-training was removing the noise of Egypt from his ears so he could hear the fine, quiet tones of God's voice. He who would become skilled in prayer must take a silence course in the University of Arabia. Then came the second stage. Forty years were followed by forty days, twice over, of listening to God's voice speaking up on the mount. Such an ear-course as that made a skilled and famous intercessor."   --S. D. Gordon

Let us then labour for an inward stillness,
An inward stillness and an inward healing;
That perfect silence where the lips and heart
Are still, and we no longer entertain
Our own imperfect thoughts and vain opinions,
But God alone speaks in us, and we wait
In singleness of heart, that we may know
His will, and in the silence of our spirits,
That we may do His will, and do that only.
                                                        --Longfellow

OCTOBER 18 ---

"That the trial of your faith, being much more precious than of gold that perisheth, though it be tried with fire, might be found unto praise and honour and glory at the appearing of Jesus Christ:" (I Pe 1:7)

Why is it that God sees fit to exercise us so continually with trials? What are we to think when life starts making us feel like we're in a pressure cooker, a marathon race, or even, on some days, a meat grinder? What is God's purpose in permitting such testings?

Scripture teaches us one reason is that the Lord is intent on conforming us to the image of Jesus Christ: "For whom he did foreknow, he also did predestinate to be conformed to the image of his Son, that he might be the firstborn among many brethren" (Ro 8:29). God is determined that we shall be brought to this point of perfection, no matter what the cost to Him, no matter what the cost to us. If we forget this all-important fact we are likely to misunderstand much of what happens to us in life and fail to recognize what God is trying to do when He allows trials to come our way.

One of the ways we may misunderstand Him is if we think that by allowing suffering to strike us, God does not care about us. When trials come it doesn't mean God has forgotten us. God does not forget His children: "...for he hath said, I will never leave thee, nor forsake thee" (He 13:5). In fact, there is an argument to be made that very often God may actually allow his children's trials to increase when they are in the process of drawing closer to Him. Knowing they are ready to go to the next step, spiritually speaking,

He may send them fresh challenges intended to produce greater maturity in their walk with Him.

Our understanding is finite. We cannot know all God is trying to accomplish in each of the trials He permits us to experience, but we do know that there is a definite purpose in everything He allows. At times, He may permit trials in order to purify us. On those "meat grinder" days, God may very well be "grinding up" the tough, sinewy texture of our fleshly selves. At other times, he may be strengthening us. Difficulties – if accepted with the right attitude – will often increase faith, trust, perseverance, gentleness, gratitude and any number of other fruits of the spirit. God may permit some of our trials in order to reach others through us. Sometimes people will not or cannot receive help from another unless they know that person understands from personal experience what they are going through. Another reason may be to chasten or correct us. If we are truly God's children, chastening will be an ongoing process: "For whom the Lord loveth he chasteneth, and scourgeth every son whom he receiveth. If ye endure chastening, God dealeth with you as with sons; for what son is he whom the father chasteneth not?" (He 12:6-7).

Whatever our difficulties may be, we ought to remember that at this point in time we have only a dim vision of the purposes of God. One day we will be able to look back on all the events of our lives – even the most painful – and realize God was able, through His love, to use them for our ultimate good, the good of others, and for His own glory.

OCTOBER 19 --

"Therefore encourage one another and build each other up, just as in fact you are doing." (I Th 5:11)

"What men need most in this world's struggle and strife is not usually direct help, but cheer.

A child was seen at a high window in a burning building. A brave fireman started up a ladder to try to rescue it. He had almost gained the window, when the terrible heat appeared too much for him. He seemed to stagger and was about to turn back, when someone in the throng below cried, 'Cheer him!' A loud cheer went up, and in a moment more he had the imperilled child in his arms, snatched from an awful death. Many men have fainted and succumbed in great struggles whom one word of cheer would have made strong to overcome.

We should never, then, lose an opportunity to say an inspiring word. We do not know how much it is needed or how great and far-reaching its consequences may be. One night long ago, during a terrible storm on the coast of England, a clergyman left his own cosy home, hurried away to the headland and lighted the beacon. Months afterwards he learned that the light had saved a great ship with its freight of human life. We do not know to what imperilled interests and hopes our one word or act of encouragement may carry rescue and safety. Nor do we know what destinies may be wrecked and lost by our failure to speak cheer."   – J. R. Miller

OCTOBER 20 --

"And immediately there fell from his eyes as it had been scales: and he received sight forthwith, and arose, and was baptized." (Ac 9:18)

When the Light of God's presence invades our souls, things that have been hidden from us are revealed. We begin to see the truth about God's true identity, about others, about circumstances, and about ourselves. Our spiritual blindness begins to lift.

Paul, who once thought of himself as an enlightened man, lived in spiritual darkness before he came to know Christ. Pride had blinded him. Before he met Christ he thought he was justified in uttering "threatenings and slaughter" against the disciples of the Lord (Acts 9:1). Then Christ came and shined the Light of His Presence into Paul's life. Paul's encounter with Christ took place on the road to Damascus. The brightness of Christ's presence appeared to him in the form of a light from heaven. When this Light pierced Paul's soul, he fell to the ground, blinded. There, in utter darkness and confusion, he got his first lesson about the contents of his own soul. He was forced to look at himself, and what he saw was darkness. He was forced to look to God and what he discovered was that Christ, the Crucified One, was in fact the Savior of the world. At this point, Paul was ready to have his life transformed.

God touched Paul's heart with the Light of His Presence and Paul believed on Him as Lord. Then He touched Paul's body with His healing power and Paul received healing in his eyes. After this experience, Paul's life would never again be the same.

Never again would he disdain the Lord's disciples. Instead, he became one of them. Never again would he urge beatings upon those who followed Christ. Instead, he endured them, and counted it a privilege to do so. His turn-around was the result of having a personal encounter with the Light of Christ. God desires to shine this same Light into the life of every one of His children. When we accept Him as Lord and walk with Him one day at a time, we will see more and more of our defects and shortcomings revealed by the Light of His Presence.

Dear One, if God is revealing more of your defects, shortcomings and sin, don't despair. This is part of His perfecting process. Like Paul, you and I must face many unpleasant truths about ourselves, but, like Paul, God will deliver us from our failures and sin, and heal us of our infirmities, until, one day, there will be no more darkness left within us. There will only be Light.

"That ye might walk worthy of the Lord unto all pleasing, being fruitful in every good work, and increasing in the knowledge of God; Strengthened with all might, according to his glorious power, unto all patience and longsuffering with joyfulness;" (Co 1:10-11)

"Yes, we need to be strengthened with all God's might, according to the measure of His glorious power, if we are to wait on God in all patience. It is God revealing Himself in us as our life and strength that will enable us, with perfect patience, to leave all in His hands. If any are inclined to despond because they do not have such patience, let them be of good courage. It is in the course of our feeble and very imperfect waiting that God Himself, by His hidden power, strengthens us and works out in the patience of the saints, the patience of Christ Himself.

Listen to the voice of one who was deeply tried: 'I waited patiently for the Lord; and He inclined unto me, and heard my cry' (Ps 40:1). Hear what he passed through: 'He brought me up also out of an horrible pit, out of the miry clay, and set my feet upon a rock, and established my goings. And He hath put a new song in my mouth, even praise unto our God' (Ps 40:2-3).

Patient waiting upon God brings a rich reward; the deliverance is sure. God Himself will put a new song into your mouth. O dear soul, do not be impatient, whether it is in the exercise of prayer and worship that you find it difficult to wait, in the delay of definite requests, or in the fulfillment of your heart's desire for the revelation of God Himself in a deeper spiritual life. Fear not, but rest in the Lord, and wait patiently for Him. And if you sometimes feel as if patience is not your gift, then remember it is God's gift, and take this prayer as your own: 'And the Lord direct your hearts into the love of God, and into the patient waiting for Christ' (II Th 3:5)."

– Andrew Murray

"He that hath an ear, let him hear what the Spirit saith unto the churches; to him that overcometh will I give to eat of the hidden manna, and will give him a white stone, and in the stone a new name written, which no man knoweth saving he that receiveth it." (Re 2:17)

"In ancient times they used to decide cases by white and black stones. The judges (for they were rather judges than jury) did not give their verdict upon the prisoner by oral testimony, 'guilty' or 'not guilty,' as in our country, but by dropping into an urn a white stone to express their opinion that the prisoner was innocent, or a black stone to declare their judgment that the prisoner was guilty.

The Lord has made use of this figure. He says, 'To him who overcomes I will give a white stone;' that is, I will give into his conscience a sentence of acquittal. As the white stone was dropped into the urn, so peace and pardon are dropped into the sinner's soul; and just as the judge, when he deposited the white stone in the urn, thereby declared the prisoner's innocence; so when the Lord is pleased to speak peace to the soul, he drops into the heart a white stone, to proclaim him discharged from the law's accusations, and a recipient of the benefits of Christ's love and blood.

'And on the stone a new name written.' What is this new name? Is it not a new heart, a new nature – Christ in the soul the hope of glory? This is the 'new name which no man knows except he that receives it.' New thoughts of Jesus, new openings up of Scripture, new meltings of the heart, new softenings of the spirit, everything made new by him who renews us 'in the renewing of our mind.' No man knows these things but he who receives them. It is all between the Lord and the soul, it is all between a pardoning God and a pardoned sinner; it is all mercy, all grace, all love, from first to last. Grace began, grace carries on, and grace finishes it; grace must have all the glory, and grace must crown the work with eternal victory."

--Joseph Philpot

OCTOBER 23 ---

"Then saith he to the disciple, Behold thy mother: And from that hour that disciple took her unto his own home." (Jo 19:27)

"What a rich reward John received for venturing near his Master's cross! To him the precious charge of the blessed Mary was confided; to him the tender words, 'Behold your mother,' were addressed. We do not hear that Jesus spoke to any of his disciples while hanging upon his cross, except to John. How great a proof the Lord gave him of his love when he entrusted his mother to his care, and even authorized him to regard her as his own. He still gives similar proofs of his love. Those who desire to serve him shall not be disappointed. Some service suited to his powers shall be assigned to each. To one the charge of an orphan family may be committed. To another a post in a missionary field may be assigned. But no office is more honorable than the care of the aged and destitute saints. It is a distinguished favor to be permitted to watch over their declining years, and to close their failing eyes.

What holy communion John must have held with his Lord's mother during the rest of her life. How many incidents concerning her blessed Son, that are not recorded in the Scriptures, must have been treasured up in her memory. She had watched beside him while he slept in the manger; had held him in her arms when traveling into Egypt; had guided his steps when a child in Nazareth. Yet she had never seen him commit a single sin; had never beheld his infant face inflamed with passion nor heard his lisping tongue utter deceit.

If parents love so fondly their sinful offspring, what must have been the affection of Mary for her sinless Son! We may also feel certain that Jesus loved his mother better than any other Son ever loved a parent. Though enduring the acute agonies of the cross, he thought of her desolate state. Did he not prove the infinite compassion of his heart by remembering her at such a moment? He would not leave her in this world without a home; he knew where she would be most tenderly loved, and most carefully watched over, and most highly honored; and therefore he consigned her to the care of the gentle and affectionate apostle John.

The Lord Jesus has taught children by his own example never to forget the kindness they received in their helpless infancy. When they are grown up they should use every exertion to provide for their parents a comfortable home. It is melancholy to see an aged father driven from his house to seek an asylum among strangers, while his children are enjoying many of the comforts of life.

But are there any who believe in the Lord Jesus Christ, and who yet fear that they will be forsaken in their sickness or old age? Let them remember that their Savior once said, 'He who shall do the will of my Father which is in heaven, the same is my brother, and sister, and mother.' If he provided for the support of his earthly mother's declining years, will he forsake his spiritual mothers, and brothers, and sisters? No, he will provide for their needs until their last breath...by some means or other the promise is always fulfilled: 'My God shall supply all your need according to his riches in glory by Christ Jesus.'"   -- F. L. Mortimer

OCTOBER 24 ---

"Oh that men would praise the Lord for his goodness, and for his wonderful works to the children of men!" (Ps 107:8)

Frances Jane "Fanny" Crosby (1820-1915) was a prolific American hymn writer and poetess who is probably best remembered for writing the lyrics to "Blessed Assurance." Ms. Crosby's father died while she was still an infant, and that same year she lost her sight when an inflammation of her eyes was misdiagnosed and the prescribed treatment caused her to go blind. She never held the mistake against the man who treated her condition: "I have not for a moment, in more than eighty-five years, felt a spark of resentment against him," she once said, "for I have always believed that the good Lord, in His infinite mercy, by this means consecrated me to the work that I am still permitted to do. When I remember how I have been blessed, how can I repine?"

Supported and encouraged by her mother and grandmother, Fanny became a curious, happy child who resolved that her blindness would not prevent her from living a full life or being useful in the world. She once wrote: "Darkness may throw a shadow over my outer vision, but there is no cloud that can keep the sunlight of hope from a trustful soul. One of the earliest resolves that I formed in my young and joyous heart was to leave all care to yesterday, and to believe that tomorrow would bring its own peculiar joy."

The great desire of her heart was to be able to learn, like other children. At the age of eleven Fanny asked God to open the way for her to go to school, and though there was no immediate response she was certain her prayer would be answered. Three years later, at the age of fourteen, her mother received a note from a friend informing her of the existence of the New York Institution for the Blind.

"I clapped my hands, and exclaimed, 'Oh, thank God! He has answered my prayer, just as I knew He would.' That was the happiest day of my life. The dark intellectual maze in which I had been living seemed to yield to hope and the promise of the light that was about to dawn. I did not crave bodily vision, it was mental enlightenment I sought."

Fanny Crosby attended the school for eight years. She excelled at English history, philosophy and science but her favorite subject was music. She learned to play the organ, guitar and piano, and by the time she graduated she had already had two books of poetry published. After graduation she was asked to stay on at the Institution as a teacher. Over the next fifteen years she taught English grammar, rhetoric and Roman and American history. This was the great developing period in her life, paving the way for the more than 8,000 hymns and poems she would write during her lifetime. While teaching at the Institution she met two Presidents -- Van Buren and Tyler – and was invited to meet many other distinguished American leaders, including Henry Clay, William H. Seward and General Winfield Scott.

She left the Institution in 1858, to continue her writing career and marry the love of her life, Alexander Van Alstyne, who was also blind and whom she had known as pupil and teacher in the Institution. After their marriage it was his wish that her literary name, Fanny J. Crosby, should still be used, as it had become known to the public through her poems. She said of him, "He was a firm, trustful Christian, a man of kindly deeds and cheering words."

Ms. Crosby always believed God had a special purpose for her life. When a pastor remarked to her that the loss of her sight was a great tragedy, she replied, "Do you know that if at birth I had been able to make one petition, it would have been that I should be born blind?" "Why?" asked the surprised clergyman. "Because when I get to heaven, the first face that shall ever gladden my sight will be that of my Savior."

Blessed assurance, Jesus is mine,
O what a foretaste of glory divine.
Heir of salvation, purchase of God,
Born of His Spirit, washed in His blood.

This is my story, this is my song,
Praising my Savior, all the day long,
This is my story, this is my song,
Praising my Savior, all the day long."
                                    -- Fanny Crosby

OCTOBER 25 --

"One shall say, I am the Lord's..." (Is 44:5)

"There is nothing more distressing in our day than the lack of growth among the children of God. They do not seem to be pressing forward or to be running a race. When I compare this year with last year, where is the difference? The same weakness and coldness persists. I fear that there is great laziness in divine things.

How different is the description of saints in the New Testament when the Spirit was poured out! They were like a willow that grows day and night and never ceases shooting out new branches. Cut it down and it springs up again. So would you, dear Christian, spring up if there were a flood of the Spirit in our day. Then you would care less about material success than prayer and praise. You would experience more change in your heart, victory over the world, the devil, and the flesh. Even in affliction you would grow in submission, humility, and meekness.

There is no greater joy than for a believing soul to give himself all to God. This has always been the way in times of refreshing. It was so at Pentecost. First they gave their own selves unto the Lord. It was so with Jonathan Edwards and all the holy men of old.

'I have this day been before God,' wrote Edwards, 'and have given myself – all that I am and have – to God, so that I am in no respect my own. I can claim no right to myself, in this understanding, this will, these affections. Neither have I right to this body, or any of its members: no right to this tongue, these hands, these feet, these eyes, these ears. I have given myself clean away.'

Oh, that you would know the joy of giving yourself away. You cannot keep yourself. This day, try and give all to Him. Lie in His hand. Little children, write on your hand: 'I am the Lord's.'"

                                    --Robert Murray McCheyne

"I can of mine own self do nothing: as I hear, I judge: and my judgment is just; because I seek not mine own will, but the will of the Father which hath sent me." (Jo 5:30)

"This was the secret which Jesus not only practiced, but taught. In one form or another, He was constantly insisting on a surrendered will as the key to perfect knowledge. 'If any man will do His will, he shall know of the doctrine, whether it be of God, or whether I speak of myself' (John 7:17).

There is all the difference between a will which is extinguished and one which is surrendered. God does not demand that our wills should be crushed. He only asks that they should say 'Yes' to Him.

Many a time, as the steamer has neared the wharf, I have watched the young boy there take his place at the vessel's stern, with his eye and ear fixed on the captain, waiting to shout out to the engineers below each word he hears his captain speak; and often have I longed that my will should repeat as accurately and as promptly the words and will of God, that all the lower nature might obey.

It is for the lack of this subordination that we so often miss the guidance we seek. There is a secret controversy between our will and God's. And we shall never be right till we have let Him take, and break, and make us.

Oh, do seek for that. If you cannot give, let Him take. If you are not willing, confess that you are willing to be made willing. Hand yourself over to Him to work in you, to will and to do of His own good pleasure. We must be as plastic clay, ready to take any shape that the great Potter may choose, so shall we be able to detect His guidance." – F. B. Meyer

"Likewise the Spirit also helpeth our infirmities: for we know not what we should pray for as we ought: but the Spirit itself maketh intercession for us with groanings which cannot be uttered." (Ro 8:26)

Laurie leaned back in her chair and took a sip of coffee. Her life of faith had started after she asked God to help her with an addiction to alcohol. He had healed her of her compulsion, but life had not been easy. She often struggled with wanting to do things her own way. Now, seventeen years into her recovery, she commented on the often circuitous and baffling pathway she had traveled in her walk with God.

"I'm grateful," she said, "that God has often neglected to give me what I have prayed for. How often I have asked God for things, only to find out later that if He had said 'yes,' I would have gone down a road that could very well have led to destruction. Today I can see how little I knew and how wise

God has been. Today I ask much more for God's will and much less for my own will, because it's safer to leave things up to Him. He knows what I need much better than I do."

When we first begin our journey of faith, we often start out by attempting to get God to give us our way. Later, we begin to recognize there is a great deal we don't know about the spiritual life and that His way, though sometimes at variance with the way we would choose, is always the best. Our true happiness lies in surrendering everything to God, and in asking Him to make all the decisions about where we go, what we will do and how we are to serve Him and glorify His name.

How often did I go to God and boldly ask that He
Would give the things I asked for to prove His love for me.
In trials I'd grow impatient, I'd struggle hard to find
A way to get the Lord to act and ease my troubled mind.

Year after year I struggled with wanting my own way,
Instead of seeking strength to know God's mind, and to obey.
But mercifully the Lord implored my heart to trust in Him,
To see beyond the problems that so much joy had dimmed.

He led me toward the Summit, just one step at a time,
He gave me hope whenever I grew weary from the climb.
He taught me that by leaning on His arm I would not fall,
That if I'd hold onto His hand, He'd every problem solve.

At last, the Summit looms ahead, so lovely words can't tell,
I hear those at the top call out, "Take heart, for all is well!"

OCTOBER 28 ---

"In the multitude of my thoughts within me thy comforts delight my soul." (Ps 94:19)

"It may seem impossible, when things look all wrong, to believe that God is really caring for us as a mother cares for her children; and, although we know perfectly well that He says He does care for us in just this tender and loving way, yet we say, 'Oh, if I could only believe that, of course I should be comforted.' Now here is just where our wills must come in. We must believe it. We must say to ourselves, 'God says it, and it is true, and I am going to believe it, no matter how it looks.' And then we must never suffer ourselves to doubt or question it again.

I do not hesitate to say that whoever will adopt this plan will come, sooner or later, into a state of abounding comfort.

The psalmist says, 'In the multitude of my thoughts within me thy comforts delight my soul.' But I am afraid that among the multitude of our thoughts within us there are far too often many more thoughts of our own discomforts than of God's comforts. We must think of His comforts if we are to be comforted by them. It might be a good exercise of soul for some of us to analyze our thoughts for a few days and see how many thoughts we actually do give to God's comforts, compared with the number we give to our own discomforts. I think the result would amaze us.

One word I must add in conclusion. If any of my readers are preachers of the Gospel of our Lord Jesus Christ, I would like to ask them what they are commissioned to preach.

The true commission in my opinion is to be found in Isaiah 40:1-2: 'Comfort ye, comfort ye my people, saith your God. Speak ye comfortably to Jerusalem, and cry unto her, that her warfare is accomplished, that her iniquity is pardoned; for she hath received of the Lord's hand double for all her sins.'

'Comfort ye my people' is the divine command; do not scold them. If it is the Gospel you feel called to preach, then see to it that you do really preach Christ's Gospel and not man's. Christ comforts, man scolds. Christ's Gospel is always good news, and never bad news. Man's gospel is generally a mixture of a little good news and a great deal of bad news; and even where it tries to be good news, it is so hampered with 'ifs' and 'buts,' and with all sorts of man-made conditions, that it utterly fails to bring any lasting joy or comfort.

The only Gospel that, to my thinking, can rightly be called the Gospel is that one proclaimed by the angel to the frightened shepherds who were in the field keeping watch over their flocks by night: 'Fear not,' said the angel, 'for behold I bring you good tidings of great joy, which shall be to all people. For unto you is born this day in the city of David, a Saviour which is Christ the Lord.'

Never were more comfortable words preached to any congregation. And if only all the preachers in all the pulpits would speak the same comfortable words to the people; and if all the congregations who hear these words would believe them, and would take the comfort from them, there would be no more uncomfortable Christians left anywhere. And over the whole land would be fulfilled the apostle's prayer for the Thessalonians: 'Now our Lord Jesus Christ himself, and God, even our Father, which hath loved us and hath given us everlasting consolation and good hope through grace, comfort your hearts, and stablish you in every good word and work' (II Th 2:16-17)."   – Hannah Whitall Smith

"Thou wilt shew me the path of life: in thy presence is fulness of joy; at thy right hand there are pleasures for evermore." (Ps 16:11)

The fight against sin and shortcomings goes on day by day. We constantly struggle to refrain from allowing our irritations, moodiness, foibles and failings to get the better of us. Sometimes we wonder, "Am I ever going to make real progress at becoming the kind of person God has designed me to be?"

God's answer is a resounding "Yes."

"Seek," He says; "Knock;" "Follow me." Even as we struggle with temptations and failures He tells us to cultivate the habit of turning to Him for help; I must actually go beyond this point; I must claim the help He has assured me is mine, by faith, even if I can't sense that it's mine. Over and over, I must remember to "act as if" I have His help and walk through my struggles in the knowledge that He is with me, strengthening me, guiding me, and, yes, changing me into the person I will one day become. Meanwhile, I'm to walk in whatever knowledge I have at the moment and put into action the tools I have already been given.

Am I weak in perseverance? Then let me not be surprised if God gives me all kinds of circumstances that require me to persevere. And let me apply whatever perseverance I have to these situations. In the process of doing so I will be given more.

Am I lacking in patience? Then let me recognize it is God's hand at work when problems arise like a flood. Let me apply the tiny measure of patience I have to those things that are annoying me. Somehow, some way, God will enlarge my supply of it, but only if I'm willing to do as He says: seek, knock, follow; not later, but now, when the battle is raging.

I am always called to practice the presence of God. I will get the victory, over sin and shortcomings and self, because God never fails to bless our faith when we will apply it. His promise to us is: "I will never leave thee, nor forsake thee" (He 13:5). God is able to deliver. God shall deliver!

Morning by morning, waken me, my Father,
Let Thy voice be the first my soul to greet,
Bidding my spirit rise from earthly slumber,
And sit a learner at Thy sacred feet.

Teach me to do Thy will, Thy pattern show me;
Reveal Thy purpose for my life each day;
Then for Thy service with fresh oil anoint me,
And with Thy Presence hallow all my way.
                                        --Freda Hanbury Allen

"Arise, shine; for thy light is come, and the glory of the Lord is risen upon thee." (Is 60:1)

"The world is full of resurrections. Every night that folds us up in darkness, is a death; and those of you that have been out early, and have seen the first of the dawn, will know this: the day rises out of the night like a being that has burst its tomb and escaped into life. But the day is yet more of a resurrection to you.

Think of your own condition through the night and in the morning. You die, as it were, every night. The death of darkness comes down over the earth; but a deeper death, the death of sleep, descends on you. A power overshadows you; your eyelids close, you cannot keep them open if you would; your limbs lie motionless; the day is gone; your whole life is gone; you have forgotten everything; an evil man might come and do with your goods as he pleased; you are helpless.

But the God of the resurrection is awake all the time, watching His sleeping men and women, even as a mother who watches over her sleeping babes, only with eyes that are larger and more full of love than hers. Then, you know not how, all at once you know that you are what you are; that there is a world that wants you, outside of you; and a God that wants you, Who is inside of you; you rise from the death of sleep, not by your own power, for you knew nothing about it; God put His hand over your eyes, and you were dead. He lifted His hand and breathed light on you, and you rose from the dead, thanked the God who raised you up, and went forth to do your work. From darkness to light, from blindness to seeing; from knowing nothing to looking abroad on the mighty world; from helpless submission to willing obedience -- is not this a resurrection indeed?"

– George MacDonald

"For thou hast delivered my soul from death, mine eyes from tears, [and] my feet from falling. I will walk before the Lord in the land of the living." (Ps 116:8-9)

There are many ways we can be down and out. We can be down and out emotionally, physically, morally or spiritually. Brokenness can take many forms.

When we go through a period of being down and out, we usually feel it is the worst thing that could happen to us, but being down and out can also be the point at which we begin to gain a new perspective on life. It can be the place where we take our first steps toward making necessary changes in our lives, where we finally make the decision to leave behind what is unhealthy and head in a new direction. When we are down and out, we are much more likely to reach out to God for the help we need, instead of staying under the illusion that we can handle life all on our own. Down-and-Out is often the place we must go to before we can begin to head toward Up-and-Over. It is also the place where many of us discover the grace of God.

God is the only answer for the person who is down and out. He is the only One who can provide a remedy for our moral bankruptcy, transform our hopeless situations, strengthen us to face our challenges and bind up our deep emotional wounds. He is the only One who is able to meet us right where we are, and who knows exactly what must be done to straighten things out. Being down and out is a painful thing, but many who have been there can testify that being down and out was the place they had to get to in order to experience the reality of God's love.

Lord, help me to turn over to You today all the areas of my life where I feel down-and-out. Please help me to walk in faith today, trusting that You will lift me up and over, and show me what it is You want me to do.

NOVEMBER 1 --

"Sanctify yourselves therefore, and be ye holy: for I am the Lord your God." (Le 20:7)

"The world judges religion not by what the Bible says, but by how Christians live. Christians are the Bible which sinners read. They are the epistles to be read of all men: 'By their fruits ye shall know them.' The emphasis, then, is to be placed upon holiness of life. But unfortunately, in the present-day Church, emphasis has been placed elsewhere. In selecting Church workers the quality of holiness is not considered. Fitness for praying is not taken into account. It was otherwise in God's movements and plans. He looked for holy men, those who were noted for their praying habits. Prayer leaders are scarce. Prayer conduct is not counted as the highest qualification for offices in the Church.

We cannot wonder that so little is accomplished in the work which God has in mind. The fact is that it is surprising so much has been accomplished with such feeble, defective agents. 'Holiness to the Lord' needs again to be written on the banners of the Church. Once more it needs to be sounded out in the ears of modern Christians. 'Follow peace with all men, and holiness, without which no man shall see the Lord.'

Let it be reiterated that this is the Divine standard of religion. Nothing short of this will satisfy the Divine requirement. What danger there is at this point. How near one can come to being right and yet be wrong. Many men may come near to the goal but still miss it: 'Many will say unto me, Lord, Lord, in that day,' says Jesus Christ, but then He says, 'I never knew you; depart from me, ye that work iniquity.'

Men can do many good things and yet not be holy in heart and righteous in conduct. They can do many good things and lack that spiritual quality of heart called holiness. How great the need of hearing the words of Paul, guarding us against self-deception in the great work of personal salvation: 'Be not deceived; God is not mocked: for whatsoever a man soweth, that shall he also reap.'"   – E. M. Bounds

NOVEMBER 2 --

"Finally, be ye all of one mind, having compassion one of another, love as brethren, be pitiful, be courteous." (I Pe 3:8)

"Most religions are meant to be straight lines, connecting two points: God and man. If man can be right with God, if he can please and pacify Him, all will be well.

But Christianity has three points: God and man and his brother, with two lines that make a right angle. Each one of us is at the point of the angle, looking up to God and out to our brother. What God sends down the perpendicular line we must pass along on the horizontal. If one hand goes up to God, the other must go out to our brother.

That was the way Jesus stood -- the Son of God and the Brother of men. What God gave him, he gave us. 'All things that I have heard of my Father I have made known unto you.' So He expects us to do the same. 'As my Father hath sent me, even so send I you.' Let us live, then, as our Master lived, giving our hearts to God and our hands to men. Even when I am alone in prayer, Jesus bids me say, 'Our Father,' remembering my brother.

If God sends me riches, I must bless my brothers; if poverty, I must set an example of rich faith. If I am tempted, I must look both ways, and consider my brother as well as my God. If I only look to God, I may decide to spend more money on myself and drink wine and ride my bicycle on Sunday afternoons, for in themselves these things may not be sinful. But when I look at my brothers, some poor, some weak, some worldly, I must hesitate. The law of liberty would permit me if I only looked up; but not the law of love as I look out.

Let us test our lives by this tri-square and look both ways, doing only that which is both filial and fraternal. Then men who see our good works will look to see where the light comes from that blesses them, and through us they will learn to glorify God."   – Maltbie Davenport Babcock

NOVEMBER 3 --

"And the Father himself, which hath sent me, hath borne witness of me. Ye have neither heard his voice at any time, nor seen his shape. And ye have not his word abiding in you: for whom he hath sent, him ye believe not." (Jo 5:37-38)

"If the Lord were to appear this day as He once did in Palestine, He would not come in the halo of the painters. Neither would He probably come as a carpenter, or mason, or gardener. He would more likely come in such a form as would relate to our present [society] in the way as the form that He came in bore to the motley Judea, Samaria and Galilee. If He came in this way, in a form unlooked for, who would they be that would recognize and receive Him?

The idea involves no absurdity. He is not far from us at any moment. He might at any moment appear. Who, I ask, would be the first to receive him? Now, as then, it would of course be the childlike in heart, the truest, the least selfish. They would not be the highest in the estimation of any church. They might not even be those that knew the most about the former visit of the Master, that had pondered every word of the Greek Testament. They would certainly, if any, be those who were like the Master; those, namely, that did the will of their Father and Christ's Father, that built their houses on the rock by hearing and doing His sayings. But are there any today who are enough like Him to know Him at once by the sound of His voice, by the look of His face? There are multitudes who would at once be taken by a false Christ, fashioned after their fancy, and would at once reject the Lord as a poor impostor. One thing is certain: they who first recognized Him would be those that most loved righteousness and hated iniquity."

--George MacDonald

NOVEMBER 4 --

"...to be full and to be hungry, both to abound and to suffer need. I can do all things through Christ which strengtheneth me." (Ph 4:12-13)

"We must imitate Jesus -- live as He lived, think as He thought -- and be conformed to his image, which is the seal of our sanctification. What a contrast! Nothingness strives to be something, and the Omnipotent becomes nothing! I will be nothing with You, my Lord. I offer You the pride and vanity which have possessed me until now. Help me. Remove from me the occasions of my stumbling; turn away my eyes from beholding vanity; let me behold nothing but You and myself in Your presence, that I may understand what I am and what You are.

Jesus Christ was born in a stable; he was obliged to fly into Egypt; thirty years of his life were spent in a workshop; he suffered hunger, thirst, and weariness; he was despised; he taught the doctrines of Heaven, and no one would listen. The great and the wise persecuted and took him, subjected him to frightful torments, treated him as a slave and put him to death between two malefactors, having preferred to give liberty to a robber, rather than to suffer him to escape. Such was the life which our Lord chose; while we are horrified at any kind of humiliation, and cannot bear the slightest appearance of contempt. Let us compare our lives with that of Jesus Christ, reflecting that he was the Master and that we are the servants; that He was all-powerful, and that we are but weakness; that he was abased and that we are exalted....

Let us not imagine that we can do this by our own efforts; everything that is within is opposed to it; but we may rejoice in the presence of God. Jesus has chosen to be made partaker of all our weaknesses; He is a compassionate high-priest who has voluntarily submitted to be tempted in all points like as we are; let us, then, have all our strength in Him, who became weak that He might strengthen us; let us enrich ourselves out of his poverty, confidently exclaiming, 'I can do all things through Christ which strengtheneth me.'"   – Francois Fenelon

NOVEMBER 5 --

"And be ye kind one to another, tenderhearted, forgiving one another, even as God for Christ's sake hath forgiven you." (Ep 4:32)

Much has been written about how important it is for believers to pursue the virtues of holiness and obedience, and certainly, we must strive on a daily basis to grow in these areas. But some of us have come to realize we can get carried away in our quest for holiness. We're the ones who struggle with the problem of "scrupulosity."

Scrupulosity is the trait of being overly concerned about whether or not we're getting it right where God is concerned. One encyclopedia describes scrupulosity as being "a psychological disorder." People can become so obsessed with living up to their moral or religious beliefs that they end up feeling they can never be good enough to "earn" God's love. Suffering from scrupulosity can be like having a noose around your neck. No matter what you do, you always sense that God wants you to be better than you are, and, since you always fall short, you figure He's never really happy with you.

It's a very good thing to strive to be obedient to God's word and will. But it isn't a good thing to be overly scrupulous. If we can't let ourselves fail or be human, we are more than likely still suffering from spiritual immaturity. It might also be a sign that we are still full of spiritual pride. Why else would we become upset with ourselves when we fail to measure up to our excessively high expectations?

A man who was working on his tendency to be overly scrupulous once said, "If someone were to treat a youngster the way I sometimes treat myself, that person would probably be arrested for child abuse. I need to remember that I'm not just supposed to be kind and patient with my neighbor; I'm also supposed to be kind and patient with myself."

Brother Lawrence told the Abbe of Beaufort how he avoided the problem of being overly scrupulous: "When I fail in my duty, I readily acknowledge it [to God], saying, 'I am used to doing so. I shall never do otherwise if I am left to myself.' If I have not failed in my duty, I give God thanks and acknowledge my success has come from Him."

NOVEMBER 6 --

"O bless our God, ye people, and make the voice of his praise to be heard: Which holdeth our soul in life, and suffereth not our feet to be moved. For thou, O God, hast proved us: thou hast tried us, as silver is tried." (Ps 66:8-10)

Some of you, even at this very hour, may be facing tests and trials that have plunged you into a season of deep suffering. You may have encountered financial troubles, emotional upheaval or times of painful loss or disappointment. When afflictions surround us it is so important that we not rely upon our own understanding. It is likely to deceive us and rob us of our faith in God. Our minds are not fit to judge our circumstances, especially when we are being assailed on all sides by fears and worries which, if able to gain a foothold, will dishearten and discourage us. Instead, we must remember what God has told us about our trials: He will not suffer our feet to be moved.

"Sure," you may respond, "easy for you to say. You're not facing what I'm facing. From where I sit I'm not even sure God is hearing my prayers."

Yes, Dear One, He hears. And yes, He will bring you through. But it may be that in the midst of your trial, God wants you to learn more about two important aspects of the life of faith.

First, He may want you to learn that when we suffer it does not mean that God has forgotten or abandoned us. To the contrary, God often permits trials to come into the lives of those who are especially close to His heart. Such trials are part of His perfect, although often mysterious, plan to take us up into the higher elevations of faith. "For thou, O God, hast proved us: thou hast tried us, as silver is tried." Like the silversmith who knows exactly how much heat to apply to remove the dross from the precious metal, God knows exactly how intense our difficulties must be. Trials are often the means He uses to remove the dross from our characters and to impart to them more of the precious traits we yearn to possess -- traits like love, understanding, empathy and gentleness. He watches over us carefully, as a smith watches over his fire. He knows when it is time to remove our trials and knows the blessings He wants to give us once we are on the other side of them: "For I know the thoughts that I think toward you, saith the Lord, thoughts of peace, and not of evil, to give you an expected end" (Je 29:11).

Let us remember that God is fashioning us, not for a few months or a few years or a few decades, but for eternity. The lessons we learn here are forever-lessons. They are important, and sometimes they hurt. Sometimes they hurt a great deal. But they are lessons that will eventually pass away, along with our suffering. God's plan may include trials and chastenings that are very painful for a time, but in the midst of them He will "holdeth our soul in life," that is, He will support us as we pass through our difficulties. He will sustain us with His very own life during these times. He will not forsake us if we flinch at the pain. Instead, He will help us. He will be patient with us. He will lead us and teach us to lean on Him when our strength fails. Our part in the process will be to recognize it is His strength and wisdom we need.

Secondly, God may want you to recognize that He alone is the One who can bring you through. Trials often teach us, as other things cannot, just how powerless we are. If we have been under the impression that we can handle life all on our own, we may encounter trials in order to dispel this illusion. It is God who has the resources we need -- not ourselves. As we take our hands off of the driver's wheel and allow God to be more and more in control of our lives, including our problems, we will discover He is the One who can teach us how to respond to our trials. He is the One who knows when they should be removed. If we will put our faith and trust in Him, He will be faithful to guide us. God will never desert His own.

And so, our course of action is clear. Trust is the answer in our times of trial. We can trust that our sufferings do not mean God has forgotten us, and we can trust that He will be our Deliverer, even if our challenges seem at present to be too big to handle. Nothing is impossible for God to overcome. "O bless our God, ye people, and make the voice of his praise to be heard."

NOVEMBER 7 --

"Beginning to sink, he cried, saying, Lord, save me." (Ma 14:30)

"Sinking times are praying times with the Lord's servants. Peter neglected prayer at the start of his venturous walk, but when he began to sink his danger made him a supplicant, and his cry, though late, was not too late. In our hours of bodily pain and mental anguish, we find ourselves as naturally driven to prayer as the wreck is driven upon the shore by the waves. The fox flees to its hole for protection; the bird flies to the wood for shelter. Even so, the tried believer runs to the mercy seat for safety. Heaven's great harbor of refuge is prayer; thousands of weather-beaten vessels have found a haven there, and the moment a storm comes on, it is wise for us to make for it with all haste.

Short prayers are long enough. There were but three words in the petition which Peter gasped out, but they were sufficient for his purpose. Not length but strength is desirable. A sense of need is a mighty teacher of brevity. If our prayers had less of the tail feathers of pride and more wing they would be all the better. Verbiage is to devotion as chaff to the wheat.

Precious things lie in small packages, and all that is real prayer in many a long address might have been uttered in a petition as short as that of Peter's.

Our extremities are the Lord's opportunities. As soon as a sense of danger forces an anxious cry from us, the ear of Jesus hears, and with him ear and heart go together, and His hand does not linger. At the last moment we appeal to our Master, but his swift hand makes up for our delays by an instant and effective action. Are we nearly engulfed by the waters of affliction? Let us then lift up our souls to our Saviour, and we may rest assured that he will not suffer us to perish. When we can do nothing, Jesus can do all things; let us enlist his powerful aid, and all will be well."

-- C. H. Spurgeon

NOVEMBER 8 --

"Blessed are the poor in spirit: for theirs is the kingdom of heaven." (Ma 5:3)

"Cultivate above all spiritual conditions – most prayerfully, earnestly and fervently – poverty of spirit. Do not rest until you have it. This is the legitimate fruit and the only safe evidence of our union to Christ and the indwelling of the Spirit in our hearts.

Nothing can suffice for it. Great talent, versatile gifts, profound speaking, glorious eloquence and even extensive usefulness are wretched substitutes for poverty of spirit. They may dazzle the eye and please the ear, and awake the applause of man, but, dissociated from humility of mind, God sees no glory in them.

To whom will He look? To the man who 'is poor and of a contrite spirit, and trembles at my Word' (Is 66:2). We may think highly of gifts, but let us learn their comparative value and true place from the words of our Lord, spoken in reference to John: 'Verily I say unto you, among them which are born of women, there is not a greater prophet than John the Baptist: but he that is least in the kingdom of God is greater than he.' Behold the true position which Christ assigns to distinction of office, of place, and of gifts: it is subordinate to lowliness of spirit. This is their proper rank. And he who elevates them above profound self-abasement and lowliness of spirit sins against God." – Octavius Winslow

NOVEMBER 9 --

"But straightway Jesus spake unto them saying, Be of good cheer, it is I, be not afraid." (Ma 14:27)

The Presence of Christ: Lesson I
"They were longing for the presence of Christ, and Christ came to them after midnight. He came walking on the water amid the waves; but they

didn't recognize Him, and they cried out in fear, 'It is a spirit!' (Ma 14:26) Their beloved Lord was coming near, and they knew Him not. They dreaded His approach. How often have I seen a believer dreading the approach of Christ, crying out for Him, longing for Him, and yet dreading His coming. And why? Because Christ came in a fashion that they did not expect.

Perhaps some have been saying, 'I fear I never can have the abiding presence of Christ.' You have heard about abiding in the presence of God and in His fellowship, and you have been afraid of it. You have said, 'It is too high and too difficult.' You have dreaded the very teaching that was going to help you. Jesus came to you in the teaching, and you didn't recognize Him.

Or, perhaps, He came in a way that you dreaded His presence. Perhaps God has been speaking to you about some sin. There is that sin of temper, or that sin of unlovingness, or that sin of unforgiveness, or that sin of worldliness, that love of man's honor, that fear of man's opinion, or that pride and self confidence. God has been speaking to you about it, and yet you have been frightened. That was Jesus wanting to draw you near, but you were afraid. You don't see how you can give up all that. You are not ready to say, 'At any sacrifice I am going to have that taken out of me, and I will give it up,' and while God and Christ were coming near to bless you, you were afraid of Him.

Perhaps at other times Christ has come to you with affliction. You have said, 'If I want to be entirely holy, I know I shall have to be afflicted, and I am afraid of affliction.' You have dreaded the thought, 'Christ may come to me in affliction.' The presence of Christ dreaded! Oh, beloved, I want to tell you it is all misconception. The disciples had no reason to dread that 'spirit' coming there, for it was Christ Himself. When God's Word comes close and touches your heart, remember that it is Christ out of whose mouth goes the two-edged sword; Christ in His loves comes to cut away the sin, that He may fill your heart with God's love. Beware of dreading the presence of Christ."

--Andrew Murray

NOVEMBER 10 --

"And he said, Come. And when Peter was come down out of the ship, he walked on the water, to go to Jesus." (Ma 14:29)

The Presence of Christ: Lesson II

"Peter's heart was right with Christ, and he wanted to claim His presence. He said, 'Lord, if it be Thou, bid me come unto Thee on the water' (Ma 14:28). Yes, Peter could not rest. He wanted to be as near to Christ as possible. He saw Christ walking on the water and remembered how Christ had said, 'Follow Me.' He remembered how Christ, with the miraculous draught of fishes, had proved that He was Master of the sea and the waters.

Peter also remembered how Christ had stilled the storm. Without argument or reflection, all at once he said, 'My Lord is manifesting Himself in a new way. There is my Lord exercising a new super-natural power. I can go to my Lord. He is able to make me walk where He walks.' He wanted to walk like Christ and near Christ. He didn't say, 'Lord, let me walk around the sea,' but rather, 'Lord, let me come to You.'

Friends, wouldn't you like to have the presence of Christ in this way? Not that Christ should come down to a worldly level, which is what many Christians would like. They want to continue their sinful, worldly walk; they want to continue in their old life; and they want Christ to come to them with His comfort, His presence, and His love. However, that cannot be. If I am to have the presence of Christ, I must walk as He walked. His walk was a supernatural one. He walked in the love and power of God.

Most people walk according to the circumstances in which they are. Most say, 'I am depending upon circumstances for my religion.' Hundreds of times, you hear people say, 'My circumstances prevent my enjoying unbroken fellowship with Jesus.' What were the circumstances that were around Christ? The wind and the waves -- and Christ walked triumphant over circumstances. Peter said, 'Like my Lord, I can triumph over all circumstances. Anything around me is nothing if I have Jesus.' He longed for the presence of Christ. May God work in us so that as we look at the life of Christ upon earth, as we look how Christ walked and conquered the waves, every one of us could say, 'I want to walk like Jesus.' If that is your heart's desire, you can expect the presence of Jesus. But as long as you want to walk on a lower level than Christ, as long as you want to have a little of the world and of self-will, do not expect to have the presence of Christ."

-- Andrew Murray

NOVEMBER 11 --

"And now also the axe is laid unto the root of the trees: therefore every tree which bringeth not forth good fruit is hewn down, and cast into the fire." (Ma 3:10)

"The picture is very suggestive. The axe lying at the tree's root, or raised in the woodman's hand to strike, shows that judgment impends, hangs ready to fall. Any moment the tree may be cut down. The axe lying at the tree's root unused tells of patience in the husbandman; he is waiting to see if the fruitless tree will yet bear fruit, The axe leaning quietly against the tree is very suggestive. The meaning is very plain. God waits long for impenitent sinners to return to him; he is slow to punish or to cut off the day of opportunity; he desires all to repent and be saved. Yet we must not trifle with the Divine patience and forbearance. We must remember that while the axe is not lifted to strike, still there is not a moment when it is not lying close, ready to be used; when the summons may not come, 'Hasten to judgment.'

The axe of death really lies all the while at the root of every life. There is not a moment when it is not true that there is but a step between us and death.

The lying of the axe at the root suggests that its use is not pruning but cutting down. God has two axes. One he uses in pruning his trees, removing the fruitless branches, and cleansing the fruitful branches that they may bring forth more fruit. The work of this axe is not judgment or destruction, but mercy and blessing. It is the good, the fruitful tree that feels its keen edge. Then God has another axe which he uses only in judgment, in cutting down those trees which after all his culture of them bring forth no fruit. Life is all very critical. There is not a moment in any day on which may not turn all the destinies of eternity. It certainly is an infinitely perilous thing for an immortal soul to rest an hour with the axe of judgment waiting to strike the blow that will end forever the day of mercy."   —J. R. Miller

NOVEMBER 12 --

"There remaineth therefore a rest to the people of God." (He 4:9)

"Beloved, have we entered into this rest?

'For he that is entered into his rest, he also has ceased from his own works as God did from His.' That is, he has learned at last the lesson that without Christ or apart from Him he can do nothing, but that he can do all things through Christ strengthening him; and therefore he has laid aside all self-effort, and has abandoned himself to God that He may work in him both to will and to do of His good pleasure. This and this only is the rest that remains for the people of God.

Scientific men are seeking to resolve all forces in nature into one primal force. Unity of origin is the present cry of science. Light, heat, sound are all said to be the products of one force differently applied, and that force is motion. All things, say the scientists, can be resolved back to this. Whether they are right or wrong I cannot say; but the Bible reveals to us one grand primal force which is behind motion itself, and that is God-force. God is at the source of everything, God is the origin of everything, God is the explanation of everything. Without Him was not anything made that was made, and without Him is not anything done that is done.

Surely, then, it is not the announcement of any mystery, but the simple statement of a simple fact, when our Lord says, 'Without me ye can do nothing.'

Even of Himself He said, 'I can of mine own self do nothing,' and He meant that He and His Father were so one that any independent action was impossible. Surely it is to reveal a glorious truth that Christ says we can do nothing without Him; for it means that He has made us so one with Himself that independent action is as impossible with us towards Him, as it was with Him towards His Father....

Let us believe, then, that without Him we can literally do nothing. We must believe it, for it is true. But let us recognize its truth, and act on it from this time forward. Let us make a hearty renunciation of all living apart from Christ, and let us begin from this moment to acknowledge Him in all our ways, and do everything, whatsoever we do, as service to Him and for His glory, depending upon Him alone for wisdom, and strength, and sweetness, and patience, and everything else that is necessary for the right accomplishing of all our living."   – Hannah Whitall Smith

NOVEMBER 13 --

"(For after all these things do the Gentiles seek:) for your heavenly Father knoweth that ye have need of all these things." (Ma 6:32)

"Though spoken originally by Jesus regarding temporal things, this may be taken as a motto for the child of God amid all the changing vicissitudes of his changing history. How it should lull all misgivings, silence all murmurings and lead us to unquestioning submissiveness; 'My Heavenly Father knows that I have need of all these things.'

Where can a child be safer or better than in a father's hand? Where can the believer be better than in the hands of his God? We are poor judges of what is best. We are under safe guidance with infallible wisdom. If we are tempted, in a moment of rash presumption, to say, 'All these things are against me,' let this word correct us. God's unerring wisdom and Fatherly love have pronounced it to be needful.

My soul, is there anything that is disturbing your peace? Are circumstances dark; are your crosses heavy? Are your spiritual props removed, your creature comforts curtailed? It was He who increased your burden. Why? 'It was needed.' Perhaps it was supplanting Himself. He had to remove it. It was He who crossed your worldly schemes, marred your cherished hopes. Why? 'It was needed.' Perhaps there was a lurking thorn in the coveted path. There was some higher spiritual blessing in communion with God. 'He prevented you with the blessings of His goodness.'

Seek to cherish a spirit of more childlike confidence in your Heavenly Father's will. You are not left alone to buffet the storms of life. A gracious pillar-cloud is before you. Follow it through sunshine and storm. He may lead you about, but He will not lead you wrong. Unutterable tenderness is the characteristic of all His dealings."   --John MacDuff

NOVEMBER 14 --

"O give thanks unto the Lord; for he is good: for his mercy endureth for ever." (Ps 118:29)

"When, with human weakness, we are afraid, faith, which sees good in all things and knows that all is for the best, remains full of a confident courage. As we know that God's activities include everything, direct everything and do everything (apart from what is sinful), the duty of faith is to adore, love and receive with joy all those activities. Full of joy and confidence, we must ignore the deception of appearances and so enjoy the triumph of faith. In this way, I assure you, you will honor God and treat him as God.

To live by faith is to live joyfully, to live with assurance, untroubled by doubts and with complete confidence in all we have to do and suffer at each moment by the will of God. We must realize that it is in order to stimulate and sustain this faith that God allows the soul to be buffeted and swept away by the raging torrent of so much distress, so many troubles, so much embarrassment and weakness, and so many setbacks. For it is essential to have faith to find God behind all this. The divine life is neither seen nor felt, but there is never a moment when it is not acting in an unknown but very sure manner."   – Jean-Pierre de Caussade

NOVEMBER 15 --

"And I will betroth thee unto me for ever; yea, I will betroth thee unto me in righteousness, and in judgment, and in lovingkindness, and in mercies." (Ho 2:19)

"Jesus Christ is the Eternal Word. He, and He alone, is the source of new life to you. For you to have new life, He must be communicated to you. He can speak. He can communicate. He can impart new life. And when He desires to speak to you, He demands the most intense attention to His voice.

Now you can see why the Scripture so frequently urges you to listen, to be attentive to the voice of God. 'Harken unto me, my people; and give ear unto me, O my nation: for a law shall proceed from me, and I will make my judgment to rest for a light of the people.' (Is 51:4)

Here is how to begin to acquire this habit of [attending to God]. First of all, forget yourself. That is, lay aside all self-interest. Secondly, listen attentively to God. These two simple actions will gradually begin to produce in you a love of that beauty which is the Lord Jesus! This beauty is inwrought in you by Him. One other thing. Try to find a quiet place. Outward silence develops inward silence; and outward silence improves inward silence as it begins to take root in your life. It is impossible for you to really become inward, that is, to live in your inmost being where Christ lives, without loving silence and retirement...

You are to be completely occupied, inwardly, with God. Of course, this is impossible if, at the same time, you are outwardly busied with a thousand trifles....

Be ready to turn within, again and again, no matter how often you are drawn away. Be ready to repeat this turning just as often as distractions occur. It is not enough to be turned inwardly to your Lord an hour or two each day. There is little value in being turned within to the Lord unless the end result is an anointing and a spirit of prayer which continues with you during the whole day."   – Jeanne Guyon

NOVEMBER 16 --

"This then is the message which we have heard of him, and declare unto you, that God is light, and in him is no darkness at all." (I Jo 1:5)

"All fear of the light, all dread lest there should be something dangerous in it, comes out of the darkness that is still in those of us who do not love the truth with all our hearts. This darkness will vanish as we are more and more interpenetrated with the light.

In a word, there is no way of thought or action which we count admirable in man, in which God is not altogether adorable. There is no loveliness, nothing that makes man dear to his brother man, that is not in God, only it is infinitely better in God. He is God our savior. Jesus is our savior because God is our savior. He is the God of comfort and consolation. He will soothe and satisfy His children better than any mother her infant.

The only thing He will not give them is permission to stay in the dark. If a child cries, 'I want the darkness,' and complains that God will not give it, God still will not give it. He gives what His child needs, often by refusing what he asks. If His child says, 'I will not be good; I prefer to die; let me die!' God's dealing with that child will be as if He said, 'No, I maintain the right not to give you your own will but instead to give you My will, which is your one true good. You shall not die; you shall live to thank me that I would not hear your prayer.'

There are good things God must delay giving until His child has a pocket to hold them in – until He gets his child to make that pocket. He must first make him fit to receive it and to have it. There is no part of our nature that shall not be satisfied, and that not by lessening it, but by enlarging it to embrace all God has for us.

Come to God, then, my brother, my sister, with all your desires and instincts, all your lofty ideals, all your longing for purity and unselfishness, all your yearning to love and be true, all your aspirations after self-forgetfulness and child-life in the breath of the Father; come to Him with all your weaknesses, all your shames, all your futilities; with all your helplessness over your own thoughts; with all your failure, yes, with the sick sense of having missed the tide of true affairs; come to Him with all your doubts, fears, dishonesties, meannesses, paltrinesses, misjudgments, wearinesses, disappointments, and stalenesses: be sure He will take you into

His care, into the liberty of His limitless heart! For He is light, and in Him is no darkness at all."   --George MacDonald

NOVEMBER 17 --

"Cast thy burden upon the Lord, and he shall sustain thee: he shall never suffer the righteous to be moved." (Ps 55:22)

We all know how pointless it is to worry, yet almost all of us do; and when we do, we probably also suffer from feelings of guilt, since we know as believers we are not supposed to allow ourselves to indulge in such a worthless pastime. Worry, among other things, is a sign of spiritual immaturity.

What exactly is worry? For one thing, it is yielding to fear. It can result from trying to carry tomorrow's load today, which goes against the Bible's instruction to concentrate only on the day before us. Sometimes worry is fretting over past mistakes, which the Bible also cautions against. It can arise from self-centeredness, or the desire to manage things that God has not given us to manage. Whatever the root of our worry, we know we shouldn't do it, but we still do. How do we stop worrying when we are so naturally prone to do it? S.D. Gordon gives us three simple rules to head off worry. The question before us is simple: are we willing to put them into practice?

"The first rule is this: [Be] anxious for nothing...Deliberately refuse to think about annoying things. Set yourself against being disturbed by disturbing things. Say to yourself, it is useless, it has bad results, it is sinful, it is reproaching my Master. I won't. That is the first simple rule....

The second rule helps to carry out the first. It is: [Be] thankful for anything. Thanksgiving and praise are always associated with singing. When you feel worry coming on — it is a mood that attacks you — when it comes, sing something, especially something with Jesus' name in it. These temptations to worry are from the Evil One. He can come in only through an open door. Remember that. Yet doors can seem plentiful. Even when we resolutely keep every door of evil shut, the enemy may open doors upon us. Singing something with Jesus' name in it will send him or any of his brood off quickly. They hate the Name of their Conqueror. They get away from the sound of it as fast as they can....

The third is: [Be] prayerful about everything. There are some unusually fine bits from the old Book to help here. Referring to the discipline which God's love makes Him use, David says: 'For His anger is but for a moment. His favor is for a lifetime. Weeping may come in to lodge at eventide, but joy cometh in the morning.' (Ps 30:5)... Again, David says, 'Cast thy burden upon the Lord, and He shall sustain thee' (Ps 55:22). The margin explains that the thing that weighs as a burden is something God has given us. He has sent it or allowed it to come. He has strong purposes in all He does.

Here the promise is not that the burden will be removed, but that He will take you and your burden into His arms and carry both of them. Many a man has praised God for the burden that made him know the tender touch of strong arms...

Probably Peter knew a good bit about this subject. His temperament was of the impulsive sort that knows quick squalls at sea. But he had learned how to ride through them undisturbed to the calmer waters. He says, 'Casting all your anxiety upon Him because He careth for you' (I Pe 5:7). The force of the French version is said to be 'unloading your anxiety upon Him.' Back the cart up, tilt it over, let down the tail-gate, let it all slip out over upon Him. The literal reading of that last half is, 'He has you on His heart.'"

– S. D. Gordon

Abiding by these three rules is to actively live in the Master's presence. If we will become willing to put them into practice on a daily basis, we will find God's power is able to make us anxious for nothing, thankful for anything, prayerful about everything.

NOVEMBER 18 --

"Blessed is the people that know the joyful sound: they shall walk, O Lord, in the light of thy countenance. In thy name shall they rejoice all the day: and in thy righteousness shall they be exalted." (Ps 89:15-16)

"The joy of the Lord is the strength of his people. Unbelief makes our hands hang down, our knees feeble, dispirits us and discourages others, and though it may give us a veneer of humility, it is in truth the very essence of pride.

The Lord promotes the desires of our hearts and answers our daily prayers by exercising us inwardly and outwardly. Would you have assurance? True assurance is to be obtained no other way. Young Christians are often greatly comforted with the Lord's love and presence, and may be spared for a season from having to encounter doubts and fears. But this is not assurance. As soon as the Lord hides his face they are likely to be troubled and ready to question the very foundation of hope. Assurance grows by repeated conflict, by our repeated experimental proof of the Lord's power and goodness to save. When we have been brought very low and helped, sorely wounded and healed, cast down and raised again, have given up all hope, and been suddenly snatched from danger and placed in safety -- and when these things have been repeated to us and in us a thousand times over -- we begin to learn to trust simply in the Word and power of God, beyond all appearances. This trust, when habitual and strong, bears the name of assurance.

You have good reason to suppose that the love of the best Christians for an unseen Saviour is far short of what it ought to be. If your heart is like mine, and you examine your love of Christ by the warmth and frequency of your emotions towards him, you will often be in sad suspense as to whether or not you love him at all. The best way to judge, which he has given us for that purpose, is to inquire if his Word and will have a prevailing, governing influence upon our lives and temper. If we love him, we try to keep his commandments, and it holds the other way. If we have a desire to please him, we undoubtedly love him. Obedience is the best test, and when, amidst all our imperfections, we can walk before Him in humble obedience, this is a mercy for which we ought to be greatly thankful. He that has brought us to be able to will, shall likewise enable us to do, according to his good pleasure. I do not doubt that the Lord, whom you love, and on whom you depend, will lead you in a sure way, and establish and strengthen and settle you in his love and grace."   – John Newton

"For it is God which worketh in you both to will and to do of [his] good pleasure." (Ph 2:13)

NOVEMBER 19 ---

"And he said unto them, Go ye into all the world, and preach the gospel to every creature." (Mark 16:15)

"Reader, what shall our occupation be as disciples of the Lord Jesus, while we watch and wait for His return? It is not enough that we have a personal experience of repentance, faith, forgiveness, adoption and sanctification; it is not enough that we study the Word to search out the deep things of God and prophecy. We must join heart and hand in the great practical work of evangelizing the world, for this is our Lord's command: 'Go ye into all the world, and preach the Gospel to every creature;' and He has said, 'This Gospel of the Kingdom shall be preached in all the world, for a witness to all nations, and then shall the end come' (Ma 24:14). While the Church remains on earth, she is certainly the agent to accomplish this purpose, because Jesus said: 'ye shall receive power, after that the Holy Ghost is come upon you: and ye shall be witnesses unto me both in Jerusalem, and in all Judea, and in Samaria, and unto the uttermost part of the earth' (Ac 1:8).
Let us engage, with all our might, in this world-wide mission work. Let us give of our means, our prayers and our words of encouragement to those who go to preach in distant lands and, if possible, let us go ourselves, thereby ensuring ourselves of His fellowship Who said, 'and I am with you always.' Thus shall we best please the Master. Thus we shall hasten the day of God.

'Watch therefore; for ye know not what hour your Lord doth come' (Matthew 24:42).

I must work the works of Him that sent me, while it is day: the night cometh, when no man can work' (Jo 9:4).

'Watch ye therefore: for ye know not when the master of the house cometh, at even, or at midnight, or at the cockcrowing, or in the morning: Lest coming suddenly he find you sleeping. And what I say unto you I say unto all, Watch' (Mark 13:35-37).

'Behold, I come as a thief. Blessed [is] he that watcheth...' (Re 16:15).

'Remember therefore how thou hast received and heard, and hold fast, and repent. If therefore thou shalt not watch, I will come on thee as a thief, and thou shalt not know what hour I will come upon thee' (Re 3:3).

'Behold, I come quickly: blessed [is] he that keepeth the sayings of the prophecy of this book' (Re 22:7).

'He which testifieth these things saith, Surely I come quickly. Amen. Even so, come, Lord Jesus' (Re 22:20).

--Adapted from *Jesus Is Coming* by William Blackstone

NOVEMBER 20 ---

"And one of them, when he saw that he was healed, turned back, and with a loud voice glorified God, And fell down on his face at his feet, giving him thanks: and he was a Samaritan. And Jesus answering said, Were there not ten cleansed? But where are the nine? There are not found that returned to give glory to God, save this stranger." (Lu 17:15-18)

Gratitude is a beautiful thing. It is one of the signs of a mature believer, for the person who lives close to God will be grateful during the rough times as well as when life is going his way. Gratitude is one way we can be a blessing to those around us. Gratitude tends to encourage others – it helps them feel grateful for their own blessings – while a lack of gratitude tends to dishearten those who are exposed to it. Gratitude is an attitude that can prepare us for greater things. The ungrateful person may not yet be spiritually ready to go to the next step with God, but someone who is grateful is often the one He knows He can trust with even greater blessings and responsibilities.

When the ten lepers cried out to Jesus to heal them, He told them to go and show themselves to the priests. They responded by doing as He said, and, as they went, they were healed. Only one, however, returned to Jesus to give Him thanks and praise. He happened to be a Samaritan, a "stranger," as the Lord called him. The other nine apparently went their way, never bothering to thank the Lord for what He had done.

Things are much the same today. It is often the one who has not been living in close proximity to the Lord, the one who is a societal outcast or a "stranger," who is most thankful and joyful when God blesses him with transformation or healing. In contrast, those who are more "familiar" with the Lord often fail to express their gratitude for His blessings or give all the glory to the Lord they claim to know so well. Which kind of believer are we? What can we thank God for today? Let us thank Him now, this minute, for the wonderful things He has done for us in the past and for what He is doing in our lives today.

NOVEMBER 21 --

"According to your faith be it unto you." (Ma 9:29).

Sometimes the walk of faith takes us out on a limb. We may resist it. We may do all in our power to avoid it. But it will happen anyway. Circumstances will force the issue and we will wake up one day to find ourselves out on a limb, with a decision to make. We will have to choose whether we want to go back the way we have come -- and thereby return to our former circumstances – or risk everything and jump off the limb, trusting that God will catch us and take care of us. These are the only two choices we have. Either we make the leap of faith or give in to our fear of the future and its uncertainty and therefore fail to make further progress in our life of faith.

Everything in our human nature will urge us to go back the way we came. Even when life becomes unbearable, we are prone to prefer the familiar to that which is unknown. Yet, it is the unknown we have to enter if we are to find what God has in store for us.

Abraham was confronted with this choice when God came to him and said: "Get thee out of thy country, and from thy kindred, and from thy father's house, unto a land that I will shew thee (Ge 12:1)." Though God promised Abraham that He would bless him, He gave him no specifics about His plan of blessing or where He would lead his servant. All God said was "Go," and Abraham had to make a choice: would he refuse, or would he follow God's directions solely by faith.

We may not be tested to the extent that Abraham was, by being told to leave everything we have known and head out upon a journey without even knowing where we are headed, but we may still be asked to take a risk that challenges all our tendencies to want to feel safe, secure and in control of our circumstances. Our test of faith may be in the form of a financial crisis, a family problem, a relationship issue, a career change, the surrender of our own will or even our plans for serving God. Anything may be asked of us, that God may reveal to us what our real priorities are and whether or not we are willing to put Him first.

"Now wait a minute," you may say, "this is all fine, but I can't just go out and behave like a crazy person. I have responsibilities. I have commitments. I can't act against all common sense and look like a fool."

It is true that we are not to act on whims or pursue courses of action without using our common sense. To the contrary, God has given us our common sense and He expects us to use it. But there are times when God asks us to put His plans ahead of our plans and to do what He asks whether we understand it or not.

The Apostle Peter didn't worry about how he would look when he encountered the lame man begging for help in the temple courtyard. Instead, he was willing to do what he sensed God wanted him to do. "Silver and gold have I none," he said, "but such as I have give I thee: In the name of Jesus Christ of Nazareth rise up and walk" (Ac 3:6). Immediately, the man's ankles and feet were healed and he entered the temple walking and leaping and praising God.

Our tendency, even as believers, is to want to see before we will believe. As we progress on our journey with the Lord, He may take us to places where we have to believe before we will see. These occasions are great blessings from God. They test us, stretch our faith, open the door to greater personal blessing and enable us to be more fruitful in the service of God.

"All I have seen," wrote Ralph Waldo Emerson, "teaches me to trust the Creator for all I have not seen." Or, as Matthew wrote: "According to your faith will it be done to you" (Ma 9:29).

NOVEMBER 22 --

"Sanctify them through thy truth: thy word is truth." (Jo 17:17)

"Many people may ask, 'How can I know that sin is being mortified in me?' We reply, 'by a weakening of its power.'

When Christ subdues our iniquities, He does not eradicate them, but weakens the strength of their root. The principle of sin remains, but it is impaired.

See it in the case of Peter. Before he fell, his besetting sin was self-confidence: 'Although all shall be offended, yet will not I,' he said. Behold him after his recovery: taking the low place at the feet of Jesus, and at the feet of the disciples, too, meekly saying, 'Lord, You know all things; You know that I love You.'

No more self-vaunting, no more self-confidence. His sin was mortified through the Spirit, and he became a different man. Thus, the very outbreak of our sins may sometimes become the occasion of their deeper discovery and their eventual diminishment.

Nor let us overlook the power of the truth, by which the Spirit mortifies sin in us: 'Sanctify them through Your truth.' The truth as it is in Jesus, revealed more clearly to the mind, and impressed more deeply on the heart, transforms the soul and gives it a more divine and holy nature. Our acquaintance with the truth, with Him Who is essential truth, will, therefore, be the measure of how much the Spirit is able to mortify the sin in our hearts.

Is the Lord Jesus becoming increasingly precious to your soul? Are you growing in poverty of spirit, in a deeper knowledge of your vileness, weakness, and unworthiness? Is pride more abased, self more crucified, and God's glory more desired? Does the heart more quickly shrink from sin, is the conscience more sensitive to the touch of guilt, and do confession and cleansing become more frequent habits? Are you growing in love toward all the saints, to those who may not have adopted your entire creed but yet love and serve your Lord? If so, then you may be assured the Spirit is mortifying sin in you.

Let us look away from everything but Christ. Do not look within for sanctification; look up to Christ for it. He is as much our sanctification as He is our righteousness. Your evidences, your comfort, your hope, do not spring from your fruitfulness, your mortification, or anything within you; but solely and entirely from the Lord Jesus Christ. 'Looking unto Jesus,' by faith, is like removing the curtains and opening the windows of a conservatory to admit the sun, whose light and warmth will make the flowers grow. Pull back the veil that conceals the Sun of Righteousness, and let Him shine in upon your soul, and the mortification of all sin will follow, and the fruits of all holiness will abound."   – Octavius Winslow

NOVEMBER 23 --

"Because thine heart was tender, and thou hast humbled thyself before the Lord, when thou heardest what I spake against this place, and against the inhabitants thereof, that they should become a desolation and a curse, and hast rent thy clothes, and wept before me; I also have heard thee, saith the Lord." (II Ki 22:19)

"This tenderness of heart was a mark in Josiah, on which the Lord, so to speak, put his finger; it was a special token for good which God selected from all the rest, as a testimony in his favor.

The heart is always tender which God has touched with his finger; this tenderness being the fruit of the impression of the Lord's hand upon the conscience. You may know the difference between a natural conscience and a heart tender in God's fear by this trait: that the natural conscience is always superstitious and uncertain; as the Lord says, it 'strains out a gnat, and swallows a camel.' It is exceedingly observant of self-inflicted austerities, and very fearful of breaking through self-imposed rules. And while it will commit sin which a man who has the fear of God in his heart would not do for the world, it will stumble at unimportant trifles at which an enlightened soul would not feel the least scruple.

But here is the mark of a heart tender in God's fear: it moves as the Spirit works upon it. It is like the mariner's compass, which, having been once touched by the magnet, always turns toward the north. It may indeed oscillate and tremble backwards and forwards, but still it will return to the pole, and ultimately remain fixed at the point at which it was temporarily disturbed. So when the heart has been touched by the Spirit, and has been made tender in God's fear, it may for a time waver to the right hand or to the left, but it is always trembling and fluctuating until it points back towards God, as the only and eternal center of its happiness and holiness."

— Joseph Philpot

NOVEMBER 24 --

"Therefore is my spirit overwhelmed within me; my heart within me is desolate." (Ps 143:4)

The God who lovingly watches over every sparrow and numbers all the hairs on our heads does not fail to care deeply when His children go through times of suffering or depression. These times come to almost all of us and may often be caused by the physical, mental, emotional or spiritual struggles we are enduring.

Depression can be an especially difficult burden to bear. As Christians we may believe that we of all people should not allow ourselves to "give in" to depression. But depression happens, and at such times, when we actually need understanding and encouragement more than ever, we may find ourselves misunderstood and even subject to criticism or rejection by those closest to us.

Charles Spurgeon was a man who understood depression. He suffered from it at various times throughout his illustrious career as a preacher, author and evangelist. His responsibilities made heavy demands on him, both emotionally and physically, and he was not ashamed to talk about the stress of having to bear up, day after day, under the heavy strain.

Spurgeon once observed that the "flesh can bear only a certain number of wounds and no more, but the soul can bleed in ten thousand ways and die over and over again each hour. It is grievous to the good man to see the Lord whom he loves laying him in the sepulcher of despondency...yet if faith could but be allowed to speak she would remind the depressed saint that ...God never placed Joseph in a pit without drawing him up again to fill a throne."

Spurgeon's acquaintance with depression made him a sympathetic and much loved minister. His parishioners knew he was able to understand many of the trials they were facing because he had faced many of them himself. Many a humble worker or burdened mother could listen to Spurgeon's lessons from the pulpit and know he had true compassion for what they were going through. One of his great gifts to his congregation was his transparency. He was not too proud to admit to them when he "was feeling low."

It is the person who has been low who is able to understand how stressful and debilitating trials can be, and can give encouragement to the one who is suffering. It is the person who has been low who can minister to those who are struggling along that same path, who can give them hope that the tunnel which now looks so hopelessly dark will indeed come to an end and lead to a new and brighter day.

In II Corinthians 1, we are reminded that one reason our sufferings are not removed is so "we may be able to comfort them which are in any trouble, by the comfort wherewith we ourselves are comforted of God. For as the sufferings of Christ abound in us, so our consolation also aboundeth by Christ" (v. 4 - 5). If we have encountered a time of affliction or depression, we can be assured that the Lord will see us through: "And our hope of you is steadfast, knowing that as ye are partakers of the sufferings, so shall ye be also of the consolation" (v. 7).

> Set apart - a chosen vessel to the King of kings,
> Set apart - forever severed from all earthly things.
> Set apart - to bear the fragrance of His blessed name,
> And with Him to share the sufferings of a Cross of shame.
> Set apart - with Him to suffer o'er a world undone,
> And to stand in fiercest conflict 'till the fight be won.
> Set apart - an earthen vessel, empty, weak and small,
> Yet the treasure that it beareth: Christ the Lord of all.
> --Freda Hanbury Allen

NOVEMBER 25 --

"So likewise, whosoever he be of you that forsaketh not all that he hath, he cannot be my disciple." (Lu 14:33)

"Three times over in this chapter, our Lord says these solemn words: 'he cannot be My disciple.'

There are three conditions of discipleship. First, we must be prepared to put first things first; second, we must be willing to suffer daily crucifixion; third, we must be detached from all things, because we are attached to Christ. The conditions seem severe, but they must be fulfilled, if we would enter Christ's School.

Disciple stands for learner (Luke 14:26). Our Lord is prepared to teach us the mysteries of the Kingdom of God, but it is useless to enter His class unless we have resolved to do as He says. Put first things first. When our Lord uses the word hate, He clearly means that the love we are to have for Him is to be so much greater than that of our natural affections that they will appear as if they were hate. No one could have loved His Mother more than our Lord did. In His dying agony His special thought and care was for her, but on three different occasions He put her aside. We are sometimes called to put aside those who are nearest and dearest, if their demands conflict with the claims of Christ.

In each of us there is the self-principle, and for each of us there is a perpetual necessity to deny self. Some talk about bearing the cross in a glib fashion, but its true meaning is shame, suffering, and sorrow, which no one fully realizes but God, and which perhaps strikes deeper down into the roots of our being as we grow older. There is an opportunity in your life, in respect to some person or circumstance, for an ever-deepening appreciation of union with Christ in His death, and for which you must be daily prepared to surrender your way and will.

It may be necessary to surrender all we have for Christ, or it may be that He will ask us to hold all as a steward or trustee, for Himself and others. No one can lay down the rule for another. The main point to decide is this: 'Am I willing to do what Christ wants me to do; to yield my will for Him to shape it and my life so that He may work through them?' If so, all else will adjust itself."   – F. B. Meyer

NOVEMBER 26 --

"Come; for all things are now ready." (Lu 14:17)

Jesus told a parable about a great feast that was being planned by the master of the house. In this parable, the master represents the Lord.

The Master instructed his servant to go out and find all those who had been invited to the banquet and tell them the time of the feast was at hand. The servant did as he was told, but when he returned he had to tell his Master that many who had been invited would not come. One man made the excuse that he had to tend to business. Another said he needed to care for his livestock. A third said he had just gotten married and therefore could not attend.

Many today are being called by God to prepare themselves to come to His feast. "All things are now ready," said the Master of the house to his servant. If God were to say to you, "All things are now ready," would you drop everything you are doing and respond to His call?

In the parable, the Master grew angry when His servant informed him that the invited guests would not come, so He said to him, "Go out quickly into the streets and lanes of the city, and bring in hither the poor, and the maimed, and the halt, and the blind." His servant obeyed and many came, but there was room for more.

"Go out into the highways and hedges [pathways] and compel them to come in, that my house may be filled," said the Master; referring to those who had earlier refused to come, he added, "None of these men which were bidden shall taste of my supper" (Lu 14:24).

God is calling all of us to prepare ourselves to go to Him. He is calling those who are poor in spirit and those who have been crippled by sin. He is calling those who have been blinded by arrogance or false teachings and those who have spent their lives among "the highways and hedges" of the world, which are often located far from His presence. All of us are being called to ready ourselves for the feast, now, while we are able. God wants His house to be full, and it shall be full, but this parable makes it clear that many who have been invited and have chosen instead to put other things before God may not be permitted to attend the feast.

Shall we be among those who are present at God's banquet? Have we accepted God's invitation to come to Him, or have we been making excuses and allowing our day-to-day concerns to crowd God out of the place He should occupy in our lives.? Christ is calling to us today. Let us thank Him for His invitation and tell Him we are ready and willing to come.

NOVEMBER 27 --

"Although the fig tree shall not blossom, neither shall fruit be in the vines; the labour of the olive shall fail, and the fields shall yield no meat; the flock shall be cut off from the fold, and there shall be no herd in the stalls; Yet I will rejoice in the Lord, I will joy in the God of my salvation." (Hab 3:17-18)

"The lesson the Lord is trying to teach us all the time is the lesson of self-effacement. He commands us to look away from self and all self's experiences, to crucify self and count it dead, to cease to be interested in self, and to know nothing and be interested in nothing but God.

The reason for this is that God has destined us for a higher life than the self-life. That just as He has destined the caterpillar to become the butterfly, and therefore has appointed the caterpillar life to die in order that the butterfly life may take its place, so He has appointed our self-life to die in order that the divine life may become ours instead. The caterpillar effaces itself in its grub form that it may evolve or develop into its butterfly form. It dies that it may live. And just so must we....

The prayer which is answered today may seem to be unanswered tomorrow; the promises once so gloriously fulfilled may cease to be a reality to us; the spiritual blessing which was at one time such a joy may be utterly lost; and nothing of all we once trusted to and rested on may be left us but the longing memory of it all. But when all else is gone, God is still left. Nothing changes Him. He is the same yesterday, today, and forever, and in Him is no variableness, neither shadow of turning. And the soul that finds its joy in Him alone, can suffer no wavering.

It is grand to trust in the promises, but it is grander still to trust in the Promiser. The promises may be misunderstood or misapplied, and at the moment when we are leaning all our weight upon them, they may seem utterly to fail us. But no one has ever trusted in the Promiser and been confounded.

The God who is behind His promises and who is infinitely greater than His promises, can never fail us in any emergency, and the soul that is stayed on Him cannot know anything but perfect peace.

The little child does not always understand its mother's promises, but it knows its mother, and its childlike trust is founded not on her word, but upon herself. And just so it is with those of us who have learned the lesson of this 'Although' and 'Yet.' There may not be a prayer answered or a promise fulfilled to our own consciousness, but what of that? Behind the prayers and behind the promises, there is God, and He is enough. And to such a soul the simple words, 'God Is,' answer every question and solve every doubt." – Hannah Whitall Smith

NOVEMBER 28 ---

"For the good that I would I do not: but the evil which I would not, that I do." (Ro 7:19)

"Someone says: 'Oh, I have passed through so much trial and suffering, and there is so much of the self-life still remaining, and I dare not face the entire giving of it up, because I know it will cause so much trouble and agony.'

Alas, that God's children have such thoughts of Him, such cruel thoughts. I come to you with a message, fearful and anxious one. God does not ask you to give the perfect surrender in your strength, or by the power of your will; God is willing to work it in you. Do we not read: 'It is God that worketh in us, both to will and to do of his good pleasure?' And that is what we should seek for — to go on our faces before God, until our hearts learn to believe that the everlasting God Himself will come in to turn out what is wrong, to conquer what is evil, and to work what is well-pleasing in His blessed sight. God Himself will work it in you...

I want to encourage you, and I want you to cast away every fear. Come with that feeble desire. If there is the fear which says, 'Oh, my desire is not strong enough; I am not willing for everything that may come, and I do not feel bold enough to say I can conquer everything,' then I implore you, learn to know and trust your God now. Say: 'My God, I am willing that You should make me willing.' If there is anything holding you back, or any sacrifice you are afraid of making, come to God now and prove how gracious your God is. Do not be afraid that He will command from you what He will not bestow.

God comes and offers to work this absolute surrender in you. All these searchings and hungerings and longings that are in your heart, I tell you, they are the drawings of the divine magnet, Christ Jesus. He lived a life of absolute surrender. He has possession of you; He is living in your heart by His Holy Spirit. You have hindered and hindered Him terribly, but He desires to help you to get hold of Him entirely. And He comes and draws you now by His message and words. Will you not come and trust God to work in you that absolute surrender to Himself? Yes, blessed be God, He can do it, and He will do it." – Andrew Murray

God already knows we cannot fix ourselves. However, we must come to this realization, too. This is why we are sometimes relentlessly bombarded by difficulties and challenges; we must recognize that our natures cannot be improved. They must be scrapped altogether -- reckoned crucified with Christ – and replaced with His own perfect nature.

NOVEMBER 29 --

"And he hath made my mouth like a sharp sword; in the shadow of his hand hath he hid me, and made me a polished shaft; in his quiver hath he hid me." (Is 49:2)

"In the shadow of His hand hath He hid me." What a wonderful image this gives us of our Father's care and concern. We are held in the palm of His hand, as a gentle caretaker might hold a new-born kitten or just-hatched chick. We are cuddled there, with no need to fear. We are under the Lord's protection. Nothing that can harm us will be allowed to touch us.

Yes, troubles may come, but they will only be allowed to approach us with His permission, and they will only be of the kind that He will give us the strength to handle. Any arrow that would destroy us will be deflected by His powerful hand. Any attack that would sever His grace and mercy from our lives will be repulsed by His immeasurable strength. And when the way becomes hard, He will overshadow us with His other hand, to make sure the heat does not grow so hot as to make us faint; when the way grows steep, He will carry us, so that our weaknesses do not cause us to fall by the wayside. Our Father's hand is mighty beyond words to describe. He will never fail to hold us close and do for us what needs to be done.

Hidden in the hollow of His blessed hand,
Never foe can follow, never traitor stand.
Not a surge of worry, not a shade of care,
Not a blast of hurry, touch the spirit there.
--Frances Ridley Havergal

"...Be strong and of good courage, and do [it]: fear not, nor be dismayed: for the Lord God, [even] my God, [will be] with thee; he will not fail thee, nor forsake thee, until thou hast finished all the work for the service of the house of the Lord."
(I Ch 28:20)

Anyone who has ever gone hiking in the high country can tell you it can be a daunting experience to walk along the edge of a cliff. Someone who has great courage and stamina in the valley may find himself frightened and light-headed when he has to make his way along the very edge of a precipice. God, however, must sometimes lead us along such paths. They are often the only means of reaching the summit, and are frequently the places where He chooses to accomplish His work of transformation upon the soul.

"He has not made us for naught; He has brought us thus far, in order to bring us farther, in order to bring us on to the end. He will never leave us nor forsake us; so that we may boldly say, 'The Lord is my Helper; I will not fear what flesh can do unto me.' We 'may cast all our care upon Him who careth for us.' What is it to us how our future path lies, if it be but His path? What is it to us where it leads us, so that in the end it leads to Him? What is it to us what He puts upon us, so that He enables us to undergo it with a pure conscience, a true heart, not desiring anything of this world in comparison with Him? What is it to us what terror befalls us, if we have His hand to protect and strengthen us? 'But now thus saith the Lord that created thee, O Jacob, and He that formed thee, O Israel, Fear not; for I have redeemed thee, I have called thee by thy name; thou art Mine. When thou passest through the waters, I will be with thee; and through the rivers, they shall not overflow thee; when thou walkest through the fire, thou shalt not be burned; neither shall the flame kindle upon thee. For I am the Lord thy God, the Holy One of Israel, thy Saviour' (Is 41:8,14; 43:1-3)." – John Henry Newman

"Satan is continually trying to weaken our faith by fear. He is a great metaphysician and knows the paralyzing effect of fear, the great enemy of faith. If he can cause us to fear, he will stop us from trusting and hinder the very blessing we need. Job found the peril of fear and gives us the sorrowful testimony: 'For the thing which I greatly feared is come upon me, and that which I was afraid of is come unto me' (Job 3:25). Fear is born of Satan, and if we would only take time to think a moment we would see that everything Satan says is founded upon a falsehood. He is the father of lies. Even his fears are falsehoods and his terrors ought to serve as encouragements. When Satan tells you, therefore, that some ill is going to come, you may quietly look in his face and tell him he is a liar. Instead of ill, goodness and mercy shall follow you all the days of your life. And then turn to your blessed Lord and say, 'What time I am afraid, I will trust in thee' (Ps 56:3). Every fear is distrust, and trust is the remedy for fear." – A. B. Simpson

DECEMBER 1 --

"Gracious is the Lord, and righteous; yea, our God is merciful. The Lord preserveth the simple: I was brought low, and he helped me. Return unto thy rest, O my soul; for the Lord hath dealt bountifully with thee." (Ps 116:5-7)

Our thoughts and feelings often provide a clue as to what we need from God. For instance, if we've been feeling angry for a while, it may mean it's time for us to have a talk with God about what is really going on. Are we afraid of losing something we have? Are we worried we won't get something we need? If so, what is it? Why is it upsetting us so much? God wants to help us track down the answers to such questions. Maybe we need to take the time to talk things over with Him, or with someone we trust who can give us the opportunity to share how we really feel. God desires to reveal to us the source of our difficulties. He wants to help us respond to them in the way that is best.

Once we are able to get in touch with what our thoughts and feelings are really saying to us, we are in a much better position to hear from God as to how He wants us to handle them. Perhaps He wants to show us how to receive His provision in our times of need. Maybe He wants to teach us how to step aside and let Him handle the problem we're facing. Perhaps He wants to show us how to set healthy boundaries or be supportive of others without trying to do everything for them. Maybe it's time to trust Him more. Maybe it's time to let Him comfort us. Maybe it's time to take more action instead of feeling upset and just hoping the problem will go away.

Every challenge we encounter will be different. What worked last time may not work this time. Only God knows the best way to handle each situation. If we will go to Him when our thoughts and feelings are troubling us, and give Him the time He needs to speak into our hearts with His still, small voice, we can trust Him to do whatever is necessary to help us. He will move mountains in our behalf, if that's what the situation calls for. If, on the other hand, we continually rush ahead of Him and try to handle our challenges all on our own, we probably won't see Him do much for us. He seldom gives guidance unless He is asked.

If we will humbly share with God the truth about what we are thinking and feeling, He will give us the wisdom we need. He is merciful with those who are candid and honest with Him. His desire is to help His children handle the challenges in their lives.

Lord, please help me today to listen to your still, small voice. Help me discern what You are really saying to me in the midst of my thoughts and feelings, and show me how to receive the guidance and help I need.

DECEMBER 2 --

"Oh that I knew where I might find him! that I might come even to his seat!" (Job 23:3)

"In Job's uttermost extremity he cried after the Lord. The longing desire of an afflicted child of God is once more to see his Father's face. His first prayer is not, 'Oh, that I might be healed,' nor, 'Oh, that I might see my children restored from the jaws of the grave,' or, 'Oh, that my property would once more be brought from the hand of the spoiler,' but the first and uppermost cry is, 'that I knew where I might find Him, who is my God, that I might come even to his seat!'

God's children run home when the storm comes on. It is the heaven-born instinct of a soul to seek shelter from all its ills beneath the wings of God. A hypocrite, when afflicted by God, will often resent the hardship, and, like a slave, would run from the Master; but not the true heir of heaven. He seeks shelter in the heart of God.

Job's desire to commune with God was intensified by the failure of all other sources of consolation. The patriarch turned away from his sorry friends, and looked up to God on His throne. He bid farewell to earth-born hopes and cried, 'that I knew where I might find my God!' Nothing teaches us so much the preciousness of the Creator, as when we learn the emptiness of everything else besides. Turning away with bitter scorn from earth's hives, where we find no honey but instead many sharp stings, we rejoice in the One whose faithful word is sweeter than the honeycomb. In every trouble we should first seek to realize God's presence with us. Let us but discover His smile toward us and we can bear our daily cross with a willing heart for his dear sake."   --C. H. Spurgeon

DECEMBER 3 --

"Better it is to be of an humble spirit with the lowly, than to divide the spoil with the proud." (Pr 16:19)

"Two things are capable of producing humility. The first is a sight of the abyss of wretchedness from which the all-powerful hand of God has snatched us, and over which he still holds us, suspended in the air. The other is the presence of that God, who is all.

Our faults, even those most difficult to bear, will all be of service to us if we will make use of them for our humiliation, without relaxing our efforts to correct them.

It does no good to be discouraged; that is merely the result of a disappointed and despairing self-love. The true method of profiting by the humiliation our faults cause us is to behold them in all their deformity, without losing our hope in God, and without having any confidence in ourselves.

We must bear with ourselves without either flattery or discouragement. This goal is seldom attained, for we are prone to either expect great things of ourselves or wholly despair. We must hope nothing from self, but wait for everything from God. Utter despair of ourselves, which is a result of being convicted of our helplessness, and unbounded confidence in God, are the true foundations of spiritual progress.

It is a false humility which would acknowledge itself unworthy of the gifts of God but then refuse to expect that He will give them to us, for true humility consists in a deep view of our utter unworthiness while maintaining an absolute confidence in God's goodness, without the slightest doubt that He will do great things in us."   – Francois Fenelon

DECEMBER 4 --

"Fathers, provoke not your children to anger, lest they be discouraged." (Co 3:21)

"In the training and education of the young there is a great call for encouragement. Parents are too apt to criticize their children and find fault with them for the imperfect manner in which they do their work. In too many homes the prevalent temper is that of fault-finding and censure. Is it any wonder that the children sometimes grow discouraged and feel that there is no use in trying to do anything right? They never receive a word of commendation. Nothing that they do is approved. The defects and mistakes in their work are always pointed out, often impatiently, and no kindly notice is ever taken of any improvement or progress made. Their little plans and ambitions are laughed at. Their daydreams and childish fancies are ridiculed. No interest is taken in their studies. They are not merely left to struggle along without encouragement or appreciation, but every budding aspiration is met by the chilling frost of criticism.

If we adults had to make headway in life against such repressing influences as many children meet, we should soon faint by the way and give up in despair. There is a better way. 'A kiss from my mother,' said the great artist Benjamin West, 'made me a painter.' Had it not been for her approving love and the cheer and encouragement which she gave to him when he showed her his first rude effort, he would never have gone on. A frown, a rebuke, a cold, indifferent criticism or a look or word of ridicule would have so discouraged him that he would never have tried again. No doubt many a grand destiny has been blighted in early youth by discouragement, by disapproval or by a sneer; and, on the other hand, proper encouragement and appreciation woo out the modest and shrinking powers of genius and start men on grand careers. Wise parents and teachers understand this. They notice every improvement, every mark of progress, and speak approvingly of it. They commend whatever is well done. They never chide for faults or mistakes when the child has done its best. They point out the defects in such a way as not to give pain or to discourage, but rather to stimulate to new effort. They never laugh at a child's visions or fancies or ridicule its plans, but regard them as the earliest germs of a beautiful life which they must try to propagate. They do not ridicule a child's answers or rebuke its questions. They treat every manifestation of its young life as tenderly as the skillful gardener treats his most delicate plants and flowers. They seek to make it summer about the budding life, so as never to stunt any growth, but to warm and cheer and to call out every lovely possibility of strength and beauty." —J. R. Miller

DECEMBER 5 --

"...prepare to meet thy God, O Israel." (Am 4:12)

"The prophet Amos cries, 'Prepare to meet thy God!' Every man and woman reading this must some day meet God. The rich man must meet God. The beggar must meet God. The scholar must meet God. The illiterate man must meet God. The king must meet God. The emperor must meet God. Every one must meet God. The supreme question of life, then, is this: Are you ready to meet God? None of us can tell how soon it may be that we shall meet God.... Some of us may meet Him within the next twenty-four hours; more within the year; many more within five years; and within forty years almost every man and woman who reads this will have met God. Are you ready? If not, I implore you to get ready...

How can we meet God with joy and not with dismay? There is only one way. That way is the atoning blood of Jesus Christ. God is infinitely holy, and the best of us is but a sinner. The only ground upon which a sinner can meet the holy God is on the ground of the shed blood of Christ. Any of us, no matter how outcast or vile, can go boldly to the Holy of Holies on the ground of the shed blood, and the best man or woman that ever walked this earth can meet God on no other ground than the shed blood. There is only one adequate preparation for the sinner to meet God; that is the acceptance of Jesus Christ as our personal Saviour, who bore all our sins on the Cross of Calvary, and as our risen Saviour is able to set us free from the power of sin.

Men and women, are you ready to meet God? If it be the will of God, I am ready to go up into His presence and meet Him face to face tonight. Have you never sinned? Alas, I have. Sinned so deeply as none of you will ever know, thank God. But, thank God still more, when Jesus Christ was nailed to the Cross of Calvary all my sins were settled. I, like a sheep, had gone astray. I had turned to my own way, but God laid on Him my sin (Is 53:6) and I accepted the sacrifice God provided.

Are you ready to meet God? Let me sum it up. There is a God. God is great. God is holy. You and I must meet Him. There is only one adequate preparation: the acceptance of Christ as our Sin-bearer, our Saviour, and Deliverer from the power of sin. Will you accept Christ?"

--Reuben Archer Torrey

DECEMBER 6 ---

"Let us run with patience." (He 12:1)

"To run with patience is a very difficult thing. Running is apt to suggest the absence of patience, the eagerness to reach the goal. We commonly associate patience with lying down. We think of it as the angel that guards the couch of the invalid. And, indeed, for those who are invalids, patience is likely the prime virtue, the crown of spiritual ripeness. Yet, I do not think the invalid's patience is the hardest to achieve. There is a patience which I believe to be harder -- the patience that can run.

To lie down in the time of grief, to be quiet under the stroke of adverse fortune, implies a great strength. But I know of something that implies a strength greater still; it is the power to work under the stroke. To have a great weight at your heart and still to run, to have a big grief in your soul and still to work, to have a deep anguish in your spirit and still to perform the daily task -- it is a Christ-like thing! Many of us could nurse our grief without crying if we were allowed to nurse it. The hard thing is that most of us are called to exercise our patience, not in bed, but in the street. We are called to bury our sorrow in active service -- in the exchange, in the business office, in the workshop, in the hour of social interaction, in the contribution to another's joy. There is no burial of sorrow so difficult as that; it is the 'running with patience.'

This was Your patience, O Son of Man. It was at once a waiting and a running: a waiting for the goal, and a doing of the lesser work meantime. How seldom, when I see You bearing my little crosses, do I think that, all the time, a big cross was in Your own heart. I see You at Cana turning the water into wine lest a marriage feast should be clouded. I see You in the desert feeding a multitude with bread just to relieve a temporary need. And, all the time, You were bearing a mighty grief, unshared, unspoken. You were carrying my cross up the Dolorous Way, and easing my heart when Your own heart was breaking.

Make me partaker of Your marvelous patience. Give me the power, Your power, to run the race when the heart is heavy. I should like to have so much of Your Divine patience that I could run the common race of life and make no sign. I should like to have a smile for the weary though my own soul be sad, to have a cheer for the downcast though my own spirit be drooping. Men ask for a rainbow in the cloud; but I would ask more from You. I would be, in my cloud, a rainbow -- a minister to others' joy. My patience will be perfect when it can work in the vineyard."

– George Matheson

DECEMBER 7 --

"And I will bring the blind by a way that they knew not; I will lead them in paths that they have not known: I will make darkness light before them, and crooked things straight. These things will I do unto them, and not forsake them." (Is 42:16)

"What is the mind of man – of any man -- under affliction? Let him be tried with pain of body, poverty of circumstances, sickness in his family, guilt of conscience, bondage in his own soul, without any beam of divine light upon his path, and what is he? A murmuring, rebellious wretch, without a grain of resignation, without a particle of contentment or submission to the will of God.

But let the glory of the Lord be revealed; let him have a view by faith of a suffering Jesus; let some ray of light shine upon his path; let there be some breaking in of the exceeding weight of glory that is to be manifested at Christ's appearing, and where are all his crooked things now? All made straight. But how? By his crooked will being made to harmonize with the promise, the precepts, the footsteps and the example of the blessed Jesus. The crookedness is not taken out of the man but it is straightened within the man; the cross is not removed from the shoulder, but strength – that strength which is 'made perfect in weakness' – is given to bear it.

So it was with Christ himself in the garden and on the cross; so it is with the believing followers of the crucified One."   --Joseph Philpot

> There are briers besetting every path,
> That call for patient care;
> There is a cross in every lot,
> And an earnest need for prayer;
> But a lowly heart that leans on Thee
> Is happy anywhere.
> --Anna Waring

"Fear not, little flock; for it is your Father's good pleasure to give you the kingdom."
(Lu 12:32)

"The music of the Shepherd's voice again! Another comforting word, and how tender. His flock, a little flock, a feeble flock, a fearful flock, but a beloved flock, loved of the Father, enjoying His 'good pleasure,' and soon to be a glorified flock, safe in the fold, secure within the kingdom. How does He quiet their fears and misgivings? As they stand panting on the bleak mountainside, He points His crook upwards to the bright and shining gates of glory, and says, 'It is your Father's good pleasure to give you these.' What gentle words. What a blessed consummation. We can say to our gracious Savior, 'Your gentleness has made me great.'

That kingdom is the believer's by irreversible and inalienable right. It is as sure as everlasting love and almighty power can make it. Satan, the great foe of the kingdom, may be injecting foul misgivings, and doubts and fears as to your security; but he cannot divest you of your purchased immunities. He must first pluck the crown from the One upon the throne before he can weaken or impair this sure word of promise.

Believers, think of this: 'It is your Father's good pleasure.' The Good Shepherd, in leading you across the intervening mountains, shows you memorials of paternal grace all along the way. He may lead you about in your way there. He led the children of Israel out of Egypt to their promised kingdom. How? By a forty year wilderness of discipline and privations. But trust Him; don't dishonor Him with doubts and fears. Don't look back on your dark, stumbling paths, nor within to your fitful and vacillating heart; but forward to the land that is far off. How earnestly God desires your salvation. The Gospel seems like a palace full of opened windows. From each one He issues an invitation, declaring that He has no pleasure in our death — but rather that we would turn and live."   – John MacDuff

"And we know that all things work together for good to them that love God, to them who are the called according to his purpose." (Ro 8:28)

"For those who abandon themselves to it, God's love contains every good thing, and if you long for it with all your heart and soul it will be yours. All God asks for is love, and if you search for this kingdom where God alone rules, you can be quite sure you will find it. For if your heart is completely devoted to God, your heart itself is this treasure, this very kingdom which you desire so ardently. The moment we long for God and to obey his will, we enjoy him and all his gifts, and the fullness of our enjoyment exactly matches the extent of our desire for him. To love God is to want to love him in all sincerity, and it is because we love him that we want Him to be able to act both in us and through us. The activity of God is not related to any shrewdness shown by a simple and holy soul, but to its loving desires. Nor is God concerned about the plans of this soul, its ideas and the projects it has in mind, for it can easily be wrong about them all, but its uprightness and good intentions can never lead it astray. Once God sees these good intentions, he ignores everything else and regards as having been done what would have been done if the soul's good will were inspired by sounder reasons.

So good will need not fear anything. Should it fall, it stumbles under the protection of that Almighty Hand which never fails to guide and support it whenever it goes astray. This is the hand which directs it toward its goal if it turns aside, and sets it again on the right path if it leaves it. It helps the soul when it falls into error because of its false judgment and makes it realize how it should mistrust its natural instincts and abandon itself absolutely to the infallible guidance of God. All the mistakes to which even the best of souls are liable cannot harm the self-abandoned, and never does it find itself caught off its guard, for 'all things work together' for its good."

--Jean-Pierre de Caussade

DECEMBER 10 --

"And Jesus said unto the centurion, Go thy way; and as thou hast believed, so be it done unto thee. And his servant was healed in the selfsame hour." (Ma 8:13)

"The trust which our Lord taught as a condition of effectual prayer is not of the head but of the heart. It is the trust which 'does not doubt in his heart.' Such trust has the Divine assurance that it shall be honored with satisfying answers. The strong promise of our Lord brings faith down to the present to count on a present answer.

Do we believe, without a doubt? When we pray, do we believe, not that we shall receive the things for which we ask on a future day, but that we receive them, then and there? Such is the teaching of this inspiring Scripture. How we need to pray, 'Lord, increase our faith,' until doubt be gone, and implicit trust claims the promised blessings as its very own.

This is no easy condition. It is reached only after many a failure, after much praying, after many times of waiting, after much trial of faith. May our faith increase until we realize and receive all the fulness there is in that Name which guarantees to do so much.

Our Lord puts trust as the very foundation of praying. The background of prayer is trust. The whole of Christ's ministry and work was dependent on implicit trust in His Father. The center of trust is God. Mountains of difficulties and all other hindrances to prayer are moved out of the way by trust and its virile henchman, faith. When trust is perfect and without doubt, prayer is simply the outstretched hand, ready to receive. Trust perfected is prayer perfected. Trust looks to receive the thing asked for -- and gets it. Trust is not a belief that God can bless, that He will bless, but that He does bless, here and now. Trust always operates in the present tense. Hope looks toward the future. Trust looks to the present. Hope expects. Trust possesses. Trust receives what prayer acquires. So that what prayer needs, at all times, is abiding and abundant trust."   – E. M. Bounds

DECEMBER 11 --

"And he took the blind man by the hand, and led him out of the town; and when he had spit on his eyes, and put his hands upon him, he asked him if he saw ought. And he looked up, and said, I see men as trees, walking. After that he put his hands again upon his eyes, and made him look up: and he was restored, and saw every man clearly." (Mark 8:23-25)

"The first thing Christ did with the blind man at Bethsaida was to take him by the hand and lead him out of the town. He thus separated him from the crowd, giving him time to think. He taught him to walk hand in hand with Himself and to trust Him in the dark. So Jesus first leads us out alone with Himself, long before we look in His face or know that He is leading us.

Next, Jesus began the work of healing the blind man by a simple anointing, as a sign. He put His hands upon his eyes. The result was a partial healing. Sight was distorted and unsatisfactory. Thus would He teach us that sometimes our progress is partial, in successive stages. Many never even get beyond the first stage.

There is a third stage: perfect sight. It comes from one cause: looking to Jesus. 'I see men,' the man said the first time. And while he saw only men, he saw nothing clearly. Then the Lord told him to 'look up.' Then he saw clearly. That looking up, to Jesus, even through the dimness, made all things clear and whole."   – A. B. Simpson

DECEMBER 12 --

"I am the good shepherd: the good shepherd giveth his life for the sheep." (Jo 10:11)

"You have one hard lesson to learn; that is the evil of your own heart. You know something of it, but it is needful that you should know more, for the more we know ourselves, the more we shall prize and love Jesus and His salvation. I hope what you find in yourself by daily experience will humble you, but not discourage you; humble you it should, and I believe it does. Are you not amazed sometimes that you should have so much as a hope that, poor and needy as you are, the Lord thinks of you? Don't let what you feel discourage you; for if our Physician is almighty, our disease cannot be desperate; and if He casts none out that come to Him, why should you fear? Our sins are many, but His mercies are more. Our sins are great, but His righteousness is greater. We are weak, but He is power. Most of our complaints are because of unbelief, and the remainder of a legal spirit; and these evils are not removed in a day.

Wait on the Lord, and He will enable you to see more and more of the power and grace of our High Priest. The more you know Him, the better you will trust Him. The more you trust Him, the better you will love Him. The more you love Him, the better you will serve Him. This is God's way. You are not called to buy, but to beg; not to be strong in yourself, but in the grace that is in Christ Jesus. He is teaching you these things, and I trust He will teach you to the end. Remember the growth of a believer is not like a mushroom, but like an oak, which increases slowly indeed, but surely. Many suns, showers, and frosts pass upon it before it comes to perfection; and in winter, when it seems dead, it is gathering strength at the root. Be humble, watchful, and diligent; and endeavor to look through all and fix your eye upon Jesus, and all shall be well. I commend you to the care of the good Shepherd." --John Newton

DECEMBER 13 ---

"Pray ye therefore the Lord of the harvest, that he will send forth labourers into his harvest." (Ma 9:38)

"Sometimes worry is carrying a load that one should not carry at all. I knew a man who said that he got along very comfortably after he gave up running the universe. Some good earnest people are greatly concerned about the way things in the world are going. I'm obliged to confess to some pretty serious blunders there. It seemed to me that there was so much to be done, so many people needing help, so much of wrong and sin to fight that I must be ever pushing and never sleeping. I had to sleep of course; but all my burden, which meant the burden of the world's need as I saw it, was lugged faithfully to bed every night. There was a lot of pillow-planning. But I found that the wrinkles grew thick, and the physical strength gave out, and yet at the end of vigorous campaigning there seemed about as much left to do as ever.

Then one day my tired eyes lit upon that wondrous phrase, 'the Lord of the harvest.' It caught fire in my heart at once. 'Oh, there is a Lord of the harvest,' I said to myself. I had been forgetting that. He is a Lord, a masterful one. He has the whole campaign mapped out, and each one's part in helping is mapped out, too. And I let the responsibility of the campaign lie where it belonged. When nighttime came I went to bed to sleep. My pillow was this, 'There is a Lord of the harvest.'

I knew a mother, one of whose sons was not a Christian man, and not of good habits. She was a devoted, true Christian woman, bearing her part in life's service with fine faith and a keen, sweet spirit. The children were all Christians except this one, her first-born, the beginning of her strength. The thought of him troubled her a great deal. She prayed fervently, and the years went on without change. And her face showed the burden upon her fine spirit. We would talk together about her son, and pray together, but her brow remained clouded.

Then I saw a change. The lines of tension in her face relaxed. A new light came into her eye. There seemed to be a gentle, intangible peace about her. And I knew there was no change in him. So one day I ventured to ask about the change, and I shall always remember the gentle voice and the quiet strength with which she said, 'I have given him over to my Father. And I know He will not fail me. I am still praying, of course, as ever, and I am trusting for him.' She had been carrying a load she should not have been carrying. And now, while the mother-heart was still concerned as much as ever, the sense of assured victory brought the change in her spirit."

-- S. D. Gordon

DECEMBER 14 --

"I beseech you therefore, brethren, by the mercies of God, that ye present your bodies a living sacrifice, holy, acceptable unto God, which is your reasonable service." (Ro 12:1)

The great Christian author James McConkey once recounted how he came to give his entire life and will over to the care of God. Like many of us, he found that letting go of his self-will was the most difficult challenge he ever faced.

As a young man, McConkey had started an ice business along with a friend. Misfortune seemed to dog their every step. For two years running, floods came and destroyed the ice. Soon they found themselves in dire financial straits. In the third year it looked like they would finally have good fortune. The weather turned cold enough to form thousands of tons of ice and McConkey received a large order. It was during this time, however, that he also sensed God was calling him to go to a deeper place in his spiritual life.

"God showed me it was His will that I should commit my business to Him and absolutely trust Him with it," wrote McConkey. "As best I knew how, I had done so. I never dreamed what testing was coming."

One evening, just before McConkey and his partner planned to harvest their ice, a storm developed. By midnight rain was falling in torrents and by noon the next day another flood had swept through the area, enveloping the ice. The prospect of facing almost certain bankruptcy served to throw McConkey into what he called "a great spiritual crisis in my life."

"That might seem strange," he noted, "to come into a spiritual crisis over a seemingly trivial matter. But I have learned this: A matter may be seemingly trivial, but the crisis that turns upon a small matter may be a profound and far reaching one. By mid-afternoon that day I had come face to face with the tremendous fact that down deep in my heart was a spirit of rebellion against God. And that rebelliousness seemed to develop in a suggestion to my heart like this: 'You gave all to God and this is the way He rewards you. Your business will be swept away, and tomorrow you will come into a place of desperate financial distress.' And I found my heart growing bitter at the thought that God should take away my business when I only wanted it for legitimate purposes. Then another voice seemed to speak: 'My child, did you mean it when you said you would trust me? Can you not trust me in the dark as well as in the light?'"

Back and forth went the arguments within McConkey's spirit, with ever-increasing intensity. It was one of the most intense struggles of his entire life.

"At the end of two hours, by the grace of God, I was able to cry out, 'Take the business; take the ice; take everything; only give me the supreme blessing of an absolutely submitted will.' And then came peace. Then and there I discovered that the secret of anxious care was not in surroundings, but in the failure to allow life and will to be wholly given to Him amid all circumstances and surroundings.

That night I lay down to rest in perfect peace, with the rain pouring torrents upon my field of ice, and with every prospect that my business would lie wrecked the next morning. But it did not.

By midnight there came another sound, that of wind. By morning the bitterest blizzard of the year was upon us. By evening the mercury had fallen to the zero point. And in a few days we were harvesting the finest ice we ever had. God did not want my ice. But He did want my yielded will and my absolute trust in Him. When that was settled, He gave back the ice; He blessed the business; and He led me on and out, until He guided me from it entirely, into the place He had for me from the beginning, that of a teacher of His word. Do you believe, when you give your life to God, that He wants to wreck your life, rob your life, despoil your life? No, God will give you back your life, enriched and glorified, a life of trust in Jesus Christ."

DECEMBER 15 --

"Who comforteth us in all our tribulation, that we may be able to comfort them which are in any trouble, by the comfort wherewith we ourselves are comforted of God." (I Co 1:4)

Pastor Maltbie Babcock, responding to a friend who had just suffered the loss of a beloved child, penned these words of faith and encouragement:

"My heart goes out to you, twice over, for the sorrow that has come to you, and for the thought that I could perhaps be a help to you. This shows that you see already one reason why sorrow comes to us; you turn to me because you know I have tasted the same cup. Some day someone will come to you, and you will 'comfort with the comfort wherewith you yourself have been comforted.' Perfect sympathy cannot spring from the imagination. Only they who have suffered can truly sympathize.

I am sure you are saying, like the little child in the dark, 'Speak, Lord, for Thy servant heareth.' The worst of all losses is a 'lost sorrow,' for then everything is lost. Your little child is safe, and I believe your sorrow is safe, too, for you are your Father's child, and you want to please Him. I would not ask 'why' if I were you. 'How' is a better word; how can I glorify You, Lord? How well can I show those who know me how the Father can help His child? God's will is not to be borne, but to be done. Now you are to do His will under new, hard, distressing and depressing circumstances. If we were pagans, we might hide ourselves and our despair, but we are Christians who say 'Our Father,' and who hear our Savior's words, 'Because I live ye shall live also.' Heirs, then, of eternal life and love -- our own, ours forever, sleeping or waking, here or there -- with uplifted faces, brave hearts and faithful hands, we must do our work, help lift others' burdens, scatter kindnesses, following him who said, knowing it would lead to the Cross, 'Follow Me.'

I did not mean to write all this. I only meant to tell you how sorry I am for you. Enter the door of a brave and patient trust. 'Blessed are they who have not seen, and yet have believed.' This is the only world in which you can suffer, so do it perfectly, trustingly, unselfishly, seeking through your grief to be better fitted to serve in Christ's name and way those who need. Always think of me as your friend, and take any advantage of my friendship. What are we for, but to love and help one another?"   –Maltbie Babcock

Is your spirit saddened, pierced by thorns?
Are you wounded so deeply the pain can't be borne?
Does an ache unceasingly tear at your heart,
Do the clouds overhead refuse to depart?

Permit your Father to draw you near,
To hold you close and dry each tear,
Though all your hopes be bruised and torn,
God will not leave His child forlorn.

We flourish here for a little while,
Then encounter pain and trial,

They teach us what a gift is life,
Though we once thought it ours by right.

Our former hopes of victory
Wither like leaves upon a tree,
Suffering comes to take their place,
To guide us toward the door of grace.

For now, the darkness hides the Way,
The clouds obscure the light of Day,
But soon you'll feel His loving care,
It shall transform the Cross you bear.

DECEMBER 16

"That Christ may dwell in your hearts by faith; that ye, being rooted and grounded in love, May be able to comprehend with all saints what is the breadth, and length, and depth, and height; And to know the love of Christ, which passeth knowledge, that ye might be filled with all the fulness of God." (Ep 3:17-19)

When we make the choice to leave the world and enter into God's Kingdom, we embark upon a process that is much like being transplanted. In a spiritual sense, it is as if we took our "roots" out of the old, barren soil of the world and placed them into the rich, life-giving soil of God's eternal kingdom. In Colossians, the Apostle Paul explains this process by noting it is God "Who hath delivered us from the power of darkness, and hath translated us into the kingdom of his dear Son" (v. 13). The word "translated" in this instance means "to move from one position to another," or, to be "transplanted."

Once we have moved into the rich soil of God's Kingdom, our damaged roots can spread out, reach down and begin to drink in the life-giving substances they need, such as God's love, forgiveness, strength, tenderness, goodness, understanding and wisdom, just to name a few. This is a wonderful and miraculous process, but it does have a challenging side to it that shouldn't be overlooked -- indeed, anyone who has experienced this process can attest to the fact that it can be a traumatic one.

Being transplanted can put an organism into shock, especially if the change is drastic. If we have come to know the Lord after living for years in an unhealthy or negative environment, it can take quite a while for our "root system" to recover from all the upheaval that happens during the conversion process. It may take time for us to settle down into our new environment and begin to develop healthier patterns of living. We may need to reach out for support as we get acclimated to the Christian life. We may find it necessary to be patient with ourselves as we undergo many new experiences.

We may have to accept the fact that we aren't going to become perfect overnight, and we shouldn't expect others to get perfect, either. It may take time for God to reveal the new plans He has for us. We may discover our growth process takes longer than we had hoped.

If we're fairly new to the Christian life, or even if we're not -- but find ourselves going through emotional or spiritual changes -- we might remind ourselves that God is the One who should set the time frame for how quickly we change and grow. We can trust Him to bring us along at the pace that is best for us; to guide us, step by step, according to His perfect plan. Only God knows how much we can handle at one time, how quickly we are able to grow and how much time it will take our "root systems" to adapt to their new environment. If we will cling to Him, God will see to it that our roots receive everything they need to adjust to their new surroundings, grow in His grace and become strong enough to support the fruit He wants us to bear in the years ahead.

> Lord, my broken heart I yield,
> Place me in a fertile field,
> There, I'll lay my seed of pain,
> There, a new beginning gain.
>
> Clutching to Your fertile breast,
> Heartsick souls may find their rest,
> Experience the sun and rain,
> Hear the robin's sweet refrain,
> Drink of Love's eternal flow,
> Feel their roots begin to grow.

DECEMBER 17 --

"After this manner therefore pray ye: Our Father which art in heaven, Hallowed be thy name." (Ma 6:9)

There is a great need among many in today's world. It is such an essential need that if it is not met it can become the root of many emotional and spiritual problems. It isn't the need for food or clothing or money. It isn't the need for political reform or peace between nations. It is the basic, fundamental need to have a relationship with one's father.

Countless people today have no idea of what it is like to be able to trust and rely upon a loving father and, unfortunately, without some knowledge of what the love of a father is like, it can be difficult to understand the kind of fatherly love God offers to His children. Though there are exceptions, it is often true that our relationship to our father on earth will in some way affect the way we view and respond to God as our spiritual Father. If an earthly father hasn't taken the time to love and care for us, we may have a difficult time trusting that God really wants to be there for us as our heavenly Father.

What, on an emotional level, does Fatherhood mean to us? When we think of God, do we view Him as Someone who is loving, patient and tender-hearted, or do we see Him instead as demanding, angry or distant? Do we recognize, when He corrects us, that He is doing so because He cares for us, or do we feel it only means He is angry and wants to punish us? Those who have known the healthy love of an earthly father, who have received a father's counsel and care, have experienced one of life's greatest blessings. They will more than likely be able to comprehend the loving, fatherly relationship God seeks to have with them. But those who have never experienced a secure, caring relationship with an earthly father may find it hard to want another "fatherly" relationship in their lives.

When Jesus taught His disciples to pray the Lord's prayer, the word he used for Father was "Abba," which, being interpreted, means "Daddy." This is the image Jesus had of His Father. God was his beloved "Daddy," not just his "Father." This was the image Christ wanted his followers to have of God. In those days, referring to God as "Daddy" was unheard of. People spoke of God only with reverence, awe and fear. They didn't go around calling Him "Daddy." But that is the way Jesus referred to Him. He knew His Father as a loving, caring, nurturing parent and He wanted his disciples to learn to know their Father in exactly the same way.

For those who have been hurt or disappointed by their earthly fathers, there is a tremendous message of hope and comfort in the Lord's Prayer. It teaches us that God is a perfectly loving parent. He loves you beyond words and is not angry, critical or mean-spirited. He will not abandon you. He is kind. He wants what is best for you. He wants to heal wounds, not inflict them, and to help you learn about His perfect fatherly love. You can trust God not to betray you if you let Him into your life. He will not fail you. He desires to give you all the good things He has prepared for you, if you will not shut Him out because of what may have happened to you in the past. Allow Him to come close and teach you all about His Fatherly love.

DECEMBER 18 --

"And he dreamed, and behold a ladder set up on the earth, and the top of it reached to heaven: and behold the angels of God ascending and descending on it." (Ge 28:12)

"A ladder is a way for feet to climb; Christ is the way by which the worst sinners may go up out of their sins, into the purity and blessedness of heaven. Simple and plain as the figure of the ladder may be, it also has many striking and instructive suggestions.

The ladder's foot rested on the ground; our lives start on the earth, often times very low down, in the common dust. We do not begin our career as radiant angels but as fallen mortals. We are all alike in this; the holiest saints began as vile sinners. He who would go up a ladder must first put his foot on the lowest rung. We cannot start in the Christian life at the top, but must begin at the bottom and climb up. He who would become a great scholar must first hold in his hand and diligently master the beginner's spelling book. Likewise, he who would rise to Christlikeness, must begin with the simplest duties and obediences....

Every step of the heavenly way is uphill, and steep at that! Heaven always keeps above us, no matter how far we climb toward it. We never in this world get to a point where we may regard ourselves as having reached life's goal; as having attained the loftiest heights within our reach; there are always other rungs of the ladder to climb.

Mozart, just before his death, said, 'Now I begin to see what might be done in music.' That is all the saintliest man ever learns in this world about living. He just begins to see what might be done in living. It is a comfort to know that this really is the whole of our earthly mission -- just to learn how to live, and that the true living is to be beyond this world.

This wonderful vision of the ladder was radiant with angels; we are not alone in our difficult climb. We have the companionship and ministry of strong friends whom we have never seen. The going up and coming down of these celestial messengers reveals there is a never-interrupted communication going on between God and those who are climbing up the steep way. There is never a moment nor any experience in the life of a true Christian from which a message may not instantly be sent up to God, to which help may not instantly come. God is not off in heaven, at the top of that steep ladder, merely looking down upon us as we struggle upward in pain and tears. If we listen we can hear him speak to the sad, weary man who lies there at the foot of the stairway, saying 'Behold, I am with you always, and will keep you in all places where you go; I will never leave you nor ever forsake you.' Not only angel companionship, precious as that is, is promised to us, but divine companionship also, every step of the way, until we get home. It is never impossible, therefore, for anyone to mount the ladder to the summit. With God's strong, loving help, the weakest need never faint nor fail!"   – J. R. Miller

DECEMBER 19 --

"And Mary arose in those days, and went into the hill country with haste, into a city of Juda; And entered into the house of Zacharias, and saluted Elisabeth." (Lu 1:39-40)

"The angel had told Mary of the great power and glory of the Son she should have. He next told her of the holiness of his nature. His body was to be miraculously formed by the power of the Holy Spirit, though born of a human mother. Jesus had flesh and blood like ourselves (Hebrews 2:14;), and he was subject to all our bodily weaknesses; he needed food and sleep; he suffered pain; he shed tears and sweated drops of blood; but he was without sin (Heb. 4:15); he was 'holy, harmless, undefiled' (Heb. 7:26). Such was the child of whom Mary was to be the mother. Were such wonderful tidings ever delivered to any human creature, as were then spoken to Mary? Yet she believed.

What a prospect lay before her! Many would disbelieve her story, and treat her with contempt. Yet Mary was willing to bear the trial. She said, 'Be it unto me according to your word.' God often makes those suffer most deeply whom he designs to honor most highly. When God intends that people should do much good to souls (and this is one of the highest honors), he often permits suspicion to be cast upon their characters; but at length he clears their innocence.

Mary had heard from the angel of the mercy shown to Elisabeth; and she went immediately to see her. How interesting it is to hear what happened when these two holy women met. There was a great difference between their ages. Elisabeth was very old; it is probable Mary was very young. Yet she was far more honored than her aged relative. The old are often envious of the young, but the pious Elisabeth was ready to do honor to Mary. When she saw her, she spoke by the power of the Holy Spirit, and acknowledged her as the mother of the Lord. It must have comforted Mary to find that Elisabeth also believed in the things that were coming to pass. How she must have rejoiced to hear her say, 'Blessed is she who has believed.' These words do not apply to Mary alone; but to everyone that believes. What ought we to believe? All the promises of God.

He has promised to cast out none who come to him, but to give them everlasting life. If we believe this promise, we shall come to him. If we have come to him, how many precious promises belong to us. God has promised to hear our prayers, to make all things work together for our good, to deliver us out of every temptation, and to give us, even in this life, peace which passes all understanding. Those who trust in these promises find there is a performance of the things that were told them. It was a good answer that was once given by a poor woman to a minister who asked her, 'What is faith?' She replied, 'I am ignorant, I cannot answer well, but I think faith is taking God at his word.'"   – F. L. Mortimer

DECEMBER 20 --

"Many are the afflictions of the righteous; but the Lord delivereth him out of them all." (Psalm 34:19)

Has disappointment or anguish come across your path today? Has a flood of fear or heartache swept into your life? Are you being asked to climb a steep mountain of sorrow or failure? Then cling to a very simple truth that applies no matter how difficult or seemingly impassable the road you are now traveling. God is with you. He stands beside you. And even should the way out of your trial yet remain a mystery, it is no mystery to Him. God knows the way, and, if you will let Him, He will reveal it. He will show you the way by going before you and leading you where you need to go.

Does this appear too hopeful a promise? Does it seem impossible that the Lord is beside you at this moment, when wherever you look the road appears empty and dark and you cannot feel His presence? Dare to believe it, for it is true. Something else is also true: it is often when God seems entirely hidden from us that He is in fact in closest proximity. At just these times He is often holding us in His arms, carrying us forward, lifting us up into that place which is higher than we have ever been before. Sometimes God even empowers His chosen ones to walk without any visible means of support at all, enabling them to walk by faith alone.

Look today to this promise, Dear Friend. Look to it and cling to it and remember that God's promises are surer and more dependable than anything the eye can see or the ear can hear or the hand reach out and touch. Study His promise well: does it say He will deliver us out of a few of our afflictions? Does it say He will bring His hopeful children through a portion of their trials? No, indeed! Never! It says our Lord shall deliver us out of all of them! And that means all! He has already measured every step you will be asked to take, every minute you will need to endure, every heartache you will have to bear. Everything about your burden has been sifted through His love before it was ever allowed to enter your life. God has something holy and worthwhile in mind for you. It is greater, much greater, than you can know or understand at this moment, but one day you will know, and you will be able to praise Him yet again for His depth of love and goodness, and for His ability to transform even the hardest and most painful experiences into a source of eternal blessing.

DECEMBER 21 --

"...Lord, teach us to pray..." (Lu 11:1); "Trust in Him at all times; ye people, pour out your heart before Him: God is a refuge for us." (Ps 62:8)

"Ever since the days of St. Augustine, it has been a proverb that God has made the heart of man for Himself, and that the heart of man finds no true rest till it finds its rest in God. But long before the days of St. Augustine, the Psalmist had said the same thing. The heart of man, the Psalmist said, is such that it can pour itself out nowhere but before God. In His sovereignty, in His wisdom, and in His love, God has made the heart of man so that at its deepest it is absolutely solitary and alone. So much so that even though others may see us smile or hear us sigh, the reasons why we smile or why we sigh are fully known to God alone.

Now the whole profit of this fine text will lie in our particular application of it to ourselves. It initially rose out of David's experience, and it is offered to us for our experience also. That is the reason why those holy men of old wrote out, to all the world, their most secret experiences. They were moved to do so by the Holy Ghost in order that we might learn to follow them in their walk with God, and in their deepest spiritual life.

When we really study the lesson he has given us, we see how David came to be so tempted to bad passions and to evil thoughts of all kinds; to revenge and retaliation against his enemies, to doubt and despair of God's fatherly care. We also are often tempted in our adverse circumstances, in ways that, like David, we can tell to no one. No man, we say with David, cares for our souls. But then, that is just our opportunity. That is just the very moment for which God has been working and waiting in our case. Do not let us miss it. Only let us pour out all our loneliness and all our distress, and all our gloom, before God, as David did, and all will immediately be well. For either He will remove our trouble at once and altogether, or else He will do better; He will make His love and His peace fill our hearts so we may say with David, 'In God is my salvation and my glory; the rock of my strength, and my refuge is in God.'

And, as with all our trouble, so let us do with all our sins. For our sin is the mother of all our trouble: get rid of the mother, and you will soon get rid of her offspring. And the only way to get rid of sin, as well as of sorrow, is to pour it out before God. For one thing, you are often tormented and polluted, are you not, with sinful thoughts? Now, as soon as they enter, as soon as they arise, pour them out before God. Pour them out before they are well in. Cleanse your heart of all unclean thoughts, of all angry and revengeful thoughts; of all envious and jealous thoughts; of all malicious and murderous thoughts. Repudiate them. Deny them. At that moment pour out your heart before Him. He knows all that is in your heart in that moment of temptation and He waits to see what you will say to Him about your heart, and what you will do with it. He has told you a thousand times what you are to do at that moment. Do it. Do what David did. Do what God's tempted and tried people are doing every moment all around you. 'Trust in Him at all times: ye people, pour out your heart before Him: God is a refuge for us.'

We do not, properly speaking, pour out our hearts before God; we pour our hearts upon God. We do not pour out our hearts before His feet: we pour out our hearts upon His heart. We press through all His angels. We shut our eyes to all the blinding glory. We pass in through all His power, and all His majesty, and we are not content till we come to His heart, to God's very, very heart. What a thought! What a heart must God's heart be. What knowledge it must have. What pity it must hold. What compassion. What love. How deep it must be. How wide. How tender. What a mystery. What a universe we belong to. What creatures we are and what a Creator we have!

I must mention four reflections that have been much in my mind all through this meditation.

First, the greatness, the all but Divine greatness of the heart of man. I do not know that the highest and most rewarded archangel of them all has an honor and excellency of grace bestowed upon him anything like this -- to be able to exchange hearts, so to speak, with God: we pouring our heart upon God, and He pouring His heart out upon us. Second, the unspeakable happiness, even in this life, of the man who pours out his heart, at all times, upon God. Third, the awful folly of carrying about a heart and never pouring it out upon God, even when permitted and commanded so to do.

And, fourth, never for a day, never for an hour, forget this golden Scripture: 'Trust in Him at all times: ye people, pour out your heart before Him: God is a refuge for us.'"   – Alexander Whyte

DECEMBER 22 ---

"And he said, the things which are impossible with men are possible with God."
(Luke 18:27)

"The text contains two thoughts -- that in religion, in the question of salvation and of following Christ by a holy life, it is impossible for man to do it. And then, alongside that, is the thought that what is impossible with man, is possible with God.

The two thoughts mark the two great lessons that man has to learn in the Christian life. It often takes a long time to learn the first lesson: that in the Christian life man can do nothing, that salvation is impossible to man. And often a man learns that, and yet he does not learn the second lesson: what has been impossible to him is possible with God. Blessed is the man who learns both lessons. The learning of them mark stages in the Christian's life.

Lesson One: Man Cannot

The one stage is when a man is trying to do his utmost and fails, when a man tries to do better and fails again, when a man tries much more and always fails. And yet, very often he does not even then learn the lesson: With man it is impossible to serve God and Christ. Peter spent three years in Christ's school, and he never learned it is impossible until he had denied his Lord, went out, and wept bitterly. Then he learned it.

Just look for a moment at a man who is learning this lesson. At first, he fights against it. Then, he submits to it, but reluctantly and in despair. At last, he accepts it willingly and rejoices in it. At the beginning of the Christian life, the young convert has no conception of this truth. He has come to God; he has the joy of the Lord in his heart; he begins to run the race and fight the battle. He is sure he can conquer, for he is earnest and believes God will 'help' him. Yet, somehow, he soon fails where he did not expect it and sin gets the better of him. He is disappointed, but he thinks: 'I was not cautious enough. I did not make my resolutions strong enough.' And again he vows and prays, and yet he fails. He thinks: 'Am I not a redeemed man? Have I not the life of God within me?' And he thinks again: 'Yes, and I have Christ to help me. I can live the holy life.'

At a later period, he comes to another state of mind. He begins to see such a life is impossible, but he does not accept it. There are multitudes of Christians who come to this point: 'I cannot.' They then think that God never expected them to do what they cannot do. If you tell them that God does expect it, it is a mystery to them. A good many Christians are living a low life, a life of failure and of sin instead of rest and victory, because they began to say: 'I cannot, it is impossible.' And yet they do not understand it fully. So, under the impression, I cannot, they give way to despair. They will do their best, but they never expect to get on very far.

But God leads His children on to a third stage -- when a man comes to reckon that it is indeed impossible, and yet, at the same time says, 'I must do it, and I will do it;' when the renewed will begins to exercise its whole power, and, in intense longing and prayer, begins to cry to God, 'Lord, what is the meaning of this? How am I to be freed from the power of sin?'

Praise God for the divine teaching that makes us helpless. Accept that position, and maintain it before God: 'My heart's desire and delight, O God, is absolute surrender, but I cannot perform it. It is impossible for me to live that life. It is beyond me.' Fall down and learn that when you are utterly helpless, God will come to work in you not only to will, but also to do."

– Andrew Murray

DECEMBER 23 --

"And he said, the things which are impossible with men are possible with God."
(Luke 18:27)

"Lesson Two: God Can.

Now comes the second lesson: 'The things which are impossible with men are possible with God.'

Your Christian life is to be a continuous proof that God works impossibilities. Your Christian life is to be a series of impossibilities made possible and actual by God's almighty power. That is what the Christian needs. He has an almighty God that he worships, and he must learn to understand that he does not need a little of God's power, but needs the whole of God's omnipotence to keep him right and to live like a Christian.

The whole of Christianity is a work of God's omnipotence. Look at the birth of Christ Jesus. That was a miracle of divine power, and it was said to

Mary: 'With God nothing shall be impossible' (Luke 1:37). It was the omnipotence of God. Look at Christ's resurrection. We are taught that it was according to the exceeding greatness of His mighty power that God raised Christ from the dead.

Every tree must grow on the root from which it springs. An oak tree three hundred years old grows all the time on the one root from which it had its beginning. Christianity had its beginning in the omnipotence of God. In every soul, Christianity must have its continuance in that omnipotence. All the possibilities of the higher Christian life have their origin in a new understanding of Christ's power to work God's will in us. I want to call on you now to come and worship an almighty God. Have you learned to do it? Have you learned to deal so closely with an almighty God that you know omnipotence is working in you? In outward appearance there is often little sign of it. The apostle Paul said: 'I was with you in weakness and in fear and in much trembling, and ... my preaching was ... in demonstration of the Spirit and of power' (I Corinthians 2:3,4). From the human side there was feebleness; from the divine side there was divine omnipotence. And that is true of every godly life. If we would only learn that lesson better, and give a wholehearted, undivided surrender to it, we would learn what blessedness there is in dwelling every hour and every moment with an almighty God.

The cause of the weakness of your Christian life is that you want to work it out partly, and to let God help you. And that cannot be. You must come to be utterly helpless to let God work. He will work gloriously. It is this that we need if we are indeed to be workers for God.

Have you believed that Almighty God is able to reveal Christ in your heart, to let the Holy Spirit rule in you so that the self-life will not have power or dominion over you? Have you coupled the two together, and with tears of penitence and with deep humiliation and feebleness, cried out: 'O God, it is impossible to me; man cannot do it, but glory to Your name, it is possible with God!' Have you claimed deliverance? Do it now. Put yourself afresh in absolute surrender into the hands of a God of infinite love. As infinite as is His love is His power to do it."   – Andrew Murray

DECEMBER 24 --

"…great is the mystery of godliness: God was manifest in the flesh..." (I Ti 3:16)

"…the angel Gabriel was sent from God unto a city of Galilee, named Nazareth, to a virgin espoused to a man whose name was Joseph, of the house of David; and the virgin's name was Mary. And the angel came in unto her, and said, Hail, thou that art highly favoured, the Lord is with thee: blessed art thou among women. And when she saw him, she was troubled at his saying, and cast in her mind what manner of salutation this should be. And the angel said unto her, Fear not, Mary: for thou hast found favour with

God. And, behold, thou shalt conceive in thy womb, and bring forth a son, and shalt call his name JESUS. He shall be great, and shall be called the Son of the Highest: and the Lord God shall give unto him the throne of his father David: And he shall reign over the house of Jacob for ever; and of his kingdom there shall be no end. Then said Mary unto the angel, How shall this be, seeing I know not a man? And the angel answered and said unto her, The Holy Ghost shall come upon thee, and the power of the Highest shall overshadow thee: therefore also that holy thing which shall be born of thee shall be called the Son of God… And Mary said, Behold the handmaid of the Lord; be it unto me according to thy word. And the angel departed from her."– (Lu 1:26 - 35, 38)

"A mystery indeed it is, a great, a deep, an unfathomable mystery; for who can rightly understand how the divine Word, the eternal Son of God, was made flesh, and dwelt among us? 'Who shall declare his generation?' (Is 53:8); either that eternal generation whereby he is the only-begotten Son of God, or the generation of his sacred humanity in the womb of the Virgin, when the Holy Spirit came upon her, and the power of the Highest overshadowed her?

These are the things 'which the angels desire to look into;' which they cannot understand, but reverently adore. And well may we imitate their adoring admiration, not attempting to understand, but believe, love, and revere; for well has it been said, 'Where reason fails, with all her power – there faith believes, and love adores.'" – Joseph Philpot

DECEMBER 25 --

"And there were in the same country shepherds abiding in the field, keeping watch over their flock by night. And, lo, the angel of the Lord came upon them, and the glory of the Lord shone round about them: and they were sore afraid. And the angel said unto them, Fear not: for, behold, I bring you good tidings of great joy, which shall be to all people. For unto you is born this day in the city of David a Saviour, which is Christ the Lord. And this shall be a sign unto you; Ye shall find the babe wrapped in swaddling clothes, lying in a manger. And suddenly there was with the angel a multitude of the heavenly host praising God, and saying, Glory to God in the highest, and on earth peace, good will toward men. And it came to pass, as the angels were gone away from them into heaven, the shepherds said one to another, Let us now go even unto Bethlehem, and see this thing which is come to pass, which the Lord hath made known unto us. And they came with haste, and found Mary, and Joseph, and the babe lying in a manger." (Lu 2: 8-16)

When Mary was about to give birth to Jesus, she and Joseph traveled from Nazareth to Bethlehem to report for the census. In Mary's time a trip of that distance, about 90 miles, would have been an arduous one for someone in her condition. It probably took about seven to ten days to make the journey. In addition, it would have been the rainy season, which in Palestine begins in early November. The roads were probably muddy and the nights cold and damp. Luke tells us there was no "room for them in the inn." In those days, what were often referred to as "inns" were in fact large, roofless enclosures capable of accommodating the many caravans that often arrived in the city. In these enclosures the animals were placed in a central, open area and their owners were sheltered under porches that surrounded it. Even if Mary and Joseph could have found a place to stay in one of these crowded, noisy camps, it would have presented a most difficult situation for a woman in her condition. The out-of-the-way place they finally selected, though humble in the extreme, at least provided the couple with a measure of quiet and privacy.

So it was within a remote stable, surrounded by livestock, that the Lord Jesus slipped almost unnoticed into the world, a world which He had created, to lie in a manger nestled amidst the dust and clutter and hay. Today, Christ is still willing to be born into such lowly places. Whenever a repentant sinner reaches out to Him, Jesus comes and quietly slips into the manger of the believer's heart, and there begins anew the process of healing transformation that makes hopeless sinners into blessed children of the Living God.

What an unfathomable miracle, that the Son of God, the King of the Universe, was once willing to be born in a stable, and is still willing to be born in our hearts, so that we may be delivered from the power of sin.

Lord, I welcome You into the manger of my heart. May I, like Mary, magnify You with my soul and ponder the deep things of God.

"We see Jesus in the manger. We adore Him; we worship Him; we glorify Him. We stand overwhelmed before such love – a love stronger than death – a love so strong that it consented to die that we might live. We thank You for the sweetness of human love, but how could we ever have dared to think that such love was in the heart of God for us? We look on nature and see Your beauty and Your majesty, but we are afraid, for we have sinned. And then we learn that You have sent Your Son, to be bone of our bone, flesh of our flesh; and before such inconceivable love we can only worship and adore. We are so weary of our failures and our slow growth toward You. Cleanse us deeply from sin, strengthen our moral purposes."

--Maltbie Babcock

"As the words we speak reveal our character, so Jesus is the speech of the invisible God. He has uttered or declared God (Jo 14:9). The Psalmist said that the heavens declare the glory of God, and the firmament showeth His handiwork to the ends of the earth, but in the fairest panorama of the starry heavens or sunset clouds, there was never such a presentation of God in nature as we have in Jesus."   – F. B. Meyer

"Arise, shine; for thy light is come, and the glory of the Lord is risen upon thee." (Is 60:1)

> The kingdom of this world is become
> The Kingdom of our Lord and of His Christ;
> And He shall reign for ever and ever,
> Hallelujah! Hallelujah! Hallelujah!
> King of Kings, and Lord of Lords,
> King of Kings, and Lord of Lords,
> Hallelujah! Hallelujah! Hallelujah! Hallelujah! Hallelujah.
>   – From Handel's "Messiah"

DECEMBER 26 --

"For unto us a Child is born, unto us a son is given: and the government shall be upon His shoulder: and His name shall be called Wonderful, Counsellor, The mighty God, The everlasting Father, The Prince of Peace." (Is 9:6)

"Many are celebrating at this time our Lord's coming; let us turn our thoughts to the promise of His second coming. This is as sure as the first advent and derives a great measure of its certainty from it. He who came as a lowly man to serve will assuredly come to take the reward of His service. He who came to suffer will not be slow in coming to reign. This is our glorious hope, for we shall share His joy. Today we are in our concealment and humiliation, even as He was while here below; but when He comes it will be our manifestation, even as it will be His revelation. Dead saints shall live at His appearing. The slandered and despised shall shine forth as the sun in the kingdom of their Father. Then shall the saints appear as kings and priests, and the days of their mourning shall be ended. The long rest and inconceivable splendor of the millennial reign will be an abundant recompense for the ages of witnessing and warring. Oh, that the Lord would come! He is coming! He is on the road and traveling quickly. The sound of His approach should be as music to our hearts. Ring out, you bells of hope!"
                                                    --Charles Spurgeon

DECEMBER 27 --

"And the shepherds returned, glorifying and praising God for all the things that they had heard and seen, as it was told unto them." (Lu 2:20)

"In the circumstances of our Savior's birth, there was a great mixture of lowliness and glory. Jesus was laid in a feeding trough; yet angels announced his appearance. But to whom did angels announce it? Not to princes, but to shepherds; thus showing that God had chosen the poor of this world.

Through all our Savior's life, there was the same mixture of lowliness and glory. He lived with fishermen, yet was sometimes visited by angels; he had a sorrowful countenance, yet once it shone brighter than the sun; he was poorly clothed, yet, on one occasion, his clothing was whiter than any launderer on earth could whiten it; he was so weak that he could not bear his cross, yet so strong that he could raise the dead from their graves.

Christ's people are like their master—they are often poor and afflicted, yet there is a glory about them that makes them as the sons of God; for their minds are filled with nobler thoughts than those which occupy the kings of the earth. While princes are thinking of their sumptuous feasts, their high titles and glittering crowns, the children of God are meditating upon the wedding supper of the Lamb, the thrones of light and the God of glory. How astonished the poor shepherds were with the appearance of the angel, who turned the darkness into day. How much his message must also have surprised them. He told them that the Son of God was now come into the world, and was in the city of David. Was not this news hard to believe? But what the angel added made it harder still; for he said that this glorious baby was lying in a feeding trough. Immediately, however, God confirmed his words by causing a multitude of angels to appear in the heavens; not two or three witnesses, but, perhaps, two or three million.

These angels were not silent witnesses; they sang a song, whose very words are handed down to us. It is the only song sung by angels upon earth that we ever heard. In the book of Revelation some of their songs in heaven are recorded; such as, 'Worthy is the Lamb to receive honor, power, and glory;' and, 'You have created all things, for your pleasure they are and were created.' But here we read of a song to which poor shepherds listened. It is a short song, but contains much; for it explains the purpose for which the Savior was come into the world, and the reason he was sent. The purpose was to bring glory to God, and peace on earth. The reason he was sent was because God had good will towards men: 'Glory to God in the highest, and on earth peace, good will towards men.'

Has not Christ's coming brought glory to God? Since Christ came into the world, how many redeemed sinners have glorified God for the gift of his Son. But what are these praises compared to the songs of believers and angels throughout eternity? Never will they cease to praise the God of love for sending his only Son to die for wretched men. But we may ask, 'Is there peace on earth?' Not yet; but there will be. This earth shall be filled with the knowledge of the Lord, and then war shall cease; the swords shall be turned into ploughshares, and the spears into pruning-hooks (see Isaiah 2) because the Prince of Peace shall reign.

And are these God's gracious promises to men? Let us not doubt the Lord's good will towards us. It hurts a tender parent, if he perceives that his children doubt his good will towards them — he tries to convince them of it by numerous acts of kindness, and he is much disappointed if he cannot succeed in winning their confidence. Has not the Lord done enough to convince us of his good will? Ought we not always to say, 'If God spared not his own Son, but gave him up for us all, will he not with him freely give us all things.'" --F. L. Mortimer

DECEMBER 28 --

"That, according as it is written, He that glorieth, let him glory in the Lord." (I Co 1:31)

"I beseech you not to listen to self. Self-love whispers in one ear and the love of God in the other; the first is restless, bold, eager, and impetuous; the other is simple, peaceful, and speaks but a few words in a mild and gentle voice. The moment we attend to the voice of self crying in our ear we can no longer hear the modest tones of holy love. Each speaks only of its single object. Self-love entertains us with self, which, according to it, is never sufficiently well attended to; it talks of friendship, regard, esteem, and is in despair at everything but flattery. The love of God, on the other hand, desires that self should be forgotten, that it should be trodden under foot and broken as an idol, and that God should become the self of espoused souls and occupy them as others are occupied by self. Let the vain, complaining babbler, self-love, be silenced, that in the stillness of the heart we may listen to that other love that only speaks when addressed." – Francois Fenelon

"Vain is the man who puts his trust in men, in created things. Do not be ashamed to serve others for the love of Jesus Christ and to seem poor in this world. Do not be self-sufficient but place your trust in God. Do what lies in your power and God will aid your good will. Put no trust in your own learning, nor in the cunning of any man, but rather in the grace of God Who helps the humble and humbles the proud.

If you have wealth, do not glory in it, nor in friends because they are powerful, but in God Who gives all things and Who desires above all to give Himself. Do not boast of personal stature or of physical beauty, qualities which are marred and destroyed by a little sickness. Do not take pride in your talent or ability, lest you displease God, to Whom belong all the natural gifts that you have.

Do not think yourself better than others, lest, perhaps, you be accounted worse before God Who knows what is in man. Do not take pride in your good deeds, for God's judgments differ from those of men and what pleases them often displeases Him. If there is good in you, see more good in others, so that you may remain humble. It does no harm to esteem yourself less than anyone else, but it is very harmful to think yourself better than even one. The humble live in continuous peace, while in the hearts of the proud are envy and frequent anger." – Thomas a'Kempis

DECEMBER 29 ---

"...and be content with such things as ye have: for he hath said, I will never leave thee, nor forsake thee." (He 13:5)

"You are just where [God's] providence has, in its inscrutable but all-wise and righteous decision, placed you. It may be a position -- painful, irksome, trying -- but it is right. Oh yes, it is right! Only aim to glorify him in it. Wherever you are placed, God has a work for you to do, a purpose through you to be accomplished, in which he blends your happiness with his glory. And when you have learned the lessons of his love, he will transfer you to another and a wider sphere, for whose nobler duties and higher responsibilities the present is, perhaps, but disciplining and preparing you.

Oh yes, beloved reader, thank God that your times, your interests, your salvation, are all out of your hands, and out of the hands of all creatures, and supremely and safely in his. Go forward in the path of duty and of labor. Aim to resemble Christ more closely in your disposition, your spirit, your whole life. Soon will it be said: 'The Master is come, and calls for you.' He is coming. 'Prepare to meet your God.' Let your motto for this [coming] year be: 'Forward! Patient in endurance, submissive in suffering, content with God's allotment; zealous, prayerful, and watchful...'

Trust God implicitly for the future. No sorrow comes but shall open some spring of comfort; no necessity transpires but shall endear a father's care. In him meet all streams of grace for your hourly, momentary need. Let your constant prayer be: 'Hold me up, and I shall be safe.' Let your daily precept be, 'Casting all your cares upon him, for he cares for you.' And then leave God to fulfill, as most faithfully he will, his own gracious, precious promise: 'As your days, so shall your strength be.' Thus walking with God through this vale of tears, until you exchange sorrow for joy, suffering for ease, sin for purity, labor for rest, conflict for victory, and all earth's checkered, gloomy scenes for the changeless, cloudless happiness and glory of heaven.

Happy souls who fear the Lord,
Time is not too swift for you;
When your Savior gives the word,
Glad, you'll bid the world adieu.

312

Then he'll wipe away your tears,
Near himself appoint your place;
Swifter fly, you rolling years,
Lord, we long to see your face."
                    --Octavius Winslow

"For, lo, the winter is past, the rain is over and gone; The flowers appear on the earth; the time of the singing of birds is come, and the voice of the turtle[dove] is heard in our land;" (SS 2:11-12)

Sometimes life seems like it is only made up of winter days. The sun disappears behind the clouds. The air grows damp and cold. And all our attempts to find a place to warm ourselves seem to fail. We wonder if Spring will ever come.

But God has appointed the seasons, and we know that as surely as Winter must come, so must the Spring. It is destined to follow even the coldest and most bitter days. And because we know the time of Spring will come again, we also know that nothing is hopeless where God is concerned.

Perhaps this year has contained challenges and burdens you did not expect, and the answers to your prayers seem far away. Days can be difficult when we find ourselves in God's waiting room. But take heart, Dear One. God will not keep you waiting longer than is absolutely necessary. He can be counted on to arrive with the answers you need.

Perhaps you have endured a season of unexpected sorrow or loss. Something or someone has been taken away, and even the ordinary, day-to-day activities of life seem almost too hard to bear. Hang on, then, to the precious promise of God, who teaches us that even our deepest suffering is part of a glorious plan He will unfold to us one day: "And we know that all things work together for good to them that love God, to them who are the called according to his purpose" (Ro 8:28).

Nature has its winters. So does the human heart. But God promises to both the eventual arrival of another Spring. Until then, we can trust that God will hold us close as we await a renewed sense of His presence and the warmth it is sure to bring. Until then, we can know that He never keeps His children waiting for answers unless there is a good reason for them to wait.

"For, lo, the winter is past, the rain is over and gone; The flowers appear on the earth; the time of the singing of birds is come, and the voice of the turtle[dove] is heard in our land."

I long to see the hallowed earth
In new creation rise,
To find the germs of Eden hid
Where its fallen beauty lies,
To feel the spring tide of a soul
By one deep love set free,
Made meet to lay aside her dust
And be at home with Thee.

And then there shall be yet an end,
An end now full to bless,
How dear to those who watch for Thee
With human tenderness.
Then shall the saying come to pass
That makes our hope complete,
And, rising from the conquered grave,
Thy parted ones shall meet.

                              --Anna Waring

DECEMBER 31 --

"Let not your heart be troubled: ye believe in God, believe also in me. In my Father's house are many mansions: if it were not so, I would have told you. I go to prepare a place for you." (Jo 14:1-2)

What wonderful words the Lord bestowed upon His disciples just prior to His departure: "I go to prepare a place for you." Think upon them and marvel at their meaning. Our Lord loved His little flock so much He lifted a corner of the veil that exists between earth and eternity and let them have a fleeting glimpse of the glory that lay ahead: See? There it is, just beyond the curtain that separates the finite from the infinite, dwelling places that I Myself will prepare for you because I love you. And until the time comes when you shall be called home by our heavenly Father, I want you to be comforted and reassured: 'In my Father's house are many mansions... I go to prepare a place for you.'

Christ's words reveal to us that His intercessions on our behalf have been heard by the Father. And not only heard, but answered in the affirmative. For all who name Christ as their Lord, there need be no doubt, no fear, no trepidation as to their futures. A place has already been chosen for us. Even at this moment it is being prepared. Our destiny is to be citizens in the Kingdom of God's dear Son. Our Savior is a Loving Lord who waits with great longing for His flock to come home.

What bliss, to know that the blood and tears Christ shed on earth shall reap a harvest of joy for us throughout eternity. To know we have a place near Him, because He chose to go to Calvary in our place. What bliss to know there is a "mansion" waiting for us, and yet, we also know it shall be as nothing compared with the fact that we shall be with Christ Himself. To know Him! To hear Him! To see His Presence illuminate the City of God!

Let us praise the Lord this last day of the year. To think that He has thought of us, created us, saved us, and now waits with longing for the day when those in His flock shall come home. Let us surrender everything to such a loving Lord, and long for the time when we shall be with Him in the place He is preparing for us; the place where we belong: "Father, I will that they also, whom thou hast given me, be with me where I am; that they may behold my glory, which thou gavest me: for thou lovedst me before the foundation of the world."

And since his name we knew,
How gracious has he been:
What dangers has he led us through,
What mercies have we seen!

Now through another year,
Supported by his care,
We raise our Ebenezer here,
'The Lord has helped thus far.'

Our lot in future years
Unable to foresee,
He kindly, to prevent our fears,
Says, 'Leave it all to me.'

Yea, Lord, we wish to cast
Our cares upon thy breast,
Help us to praise thee for the past
And trust thee for the rest.
--John Newton

The Lord always stands ready to welcome one of his weary children into the Kingdom of His Dear Son. The thief on the cross said only nine words to Jesus: "Lord, remember me when thou comest into thy kingdom" (Lu 23:42), yet they were enough to prompt an assurance of salvation. Jesus' response was: "Verily I say unto thee, today shalt thou be with me in paradise" (Lu 23:43).

If you would like to make Jesus Christ the Lord of your life, a simple prayer, such as the one that follows, is all that is necessary:

"Lord, I confess I am a sinner. I ask You to forgive me of the things I have done wrong. I repent of them and ask You to come into my heart and cleanse me. I believe Jesus Christ is the Son of God and died in my place so my sins could be forgiven. I now surrender my life into Your hands and ask You to be my Lord."

The Bible says, 'For God so loved the world, that he gave his only begotten Son, that whosoever believeth in him should not perish, but have everlasting life" (Jo 3:16). If you have put your faith in Christ today, you have the assurance of God's Word that you are now a child of the King and that you shall live with Him throughout eternity.

> Come, ye thankful people, come,
> Raise the song of harvest home,
> All is safely gathered in,
> 'Ere the winter storms begin.
> God our Maker doth provide
> For our wants to be supplied,
> Come to God's own temple, come;
> Raise the song of harvest home.
>
> Even so, Lord, quickly come;
> Bring Thy final harvest home,
> Gather Thou Thy people in,
> Free from sorrow, free from sin;
> There, forever purified,
> In Thy garner to abide,
> Come, with all Thine angels come;
> Raise the glorious harvest home.
>   --Henry Alford

INDIVIDUAL AND GROUP STUDY GUIDES

The following study guides have been developed to assist you in delving more deeply into the Scriptures and meditations contained in *Songs From the Summit*. Both the Individual and Group Study Guides suggest keeping a journal as a means of recording thoughts and insights gleaned during your devotional time. Journaling can also help us keep track of the many ways God provides us with guidance in our day-to-day lives, and responds to our temporal and spiritual needs.

INDIVIDUAL STUDY GUIDE

1.   Before you begin reading the day's meditation, ask the Holy Spirit to direct your thinking and to prepare your heart to receive any insights and guidance He may provide.

2.   Read the day's message, without stopping, to absorb the general thoughts and ideas presented; then go back and read it again, more slowly, focusing on portions that may have special meaning for you.

3.   After you have read the message, you may wish to answer the following questions and record your thoughts: (a) Can you identify with any of the experiences or insights presented in the message? If so, what parts were most meaningful to you? (b) Did the message discuss any areas where you know God has already brought a measure of growth or healing into your life? If so, describe the growth or healing you have experienced. You might wish to stop at this point to offer Him thanks and praise for these blessings. (c) Do you sense as a result of this message that there is more growth, healing or transformation God wants to impart into your life? If so, in what areas? If you feel led to do so, you might pray over these areas and offer them to God to make whatever changes He deems necessary. Is there some action you feel you would like to take as a result of the insights in this message? If so, what is it?

GROUP STUDY GUIDE

To Group Leaders:
At the beginning of your group study, ask all participants to obtain a notebook in which they will record their thoughts and insights. They should plan to set aside a minimum of thirty minutes each day in order to read and journal on the message for that day. You may wish to ask them to select the message they found most meaningful during their (week/month) of study and be prepared to share their thoughts about this message with the group the next time it meets.

Study Guide for Group Members:

1.　Before you begin reading the day's meditation, ask the Holy Spirit to direct your thinking and to prepare your heart to receive any insights and guidance He may provide.

2.　Read the day's message, without stopping, to absorb the general thoughts and ideas presented; then go back and read it again, more slowly, focusing on portions that may have special meaning for you.

3.　After you have read the message, you may wish to answer the following questions and record your thoughts:　(a) Can you identify with any of the experiences or insights presented in the message?　If so, what parts were most meaningful to you?　(b) Did the message discuss any areas where you know God has already brought a measure of growth or healing into your life?　If so, describe the growth or healing you have experienced.　You might wish to stop at this point to offer Him thanks and praise for these blessings. (c) Do you sense as a result of this message that there is more growth, healing or transformation God wants to impart into your life?　If so, in what areas? If you feel led to do so, you might pray over these areas and offer them to God to make whatever changes He deems necessary.　Is there some action you feel you would like to take as a result of the insights in this message?　If so, what is it?